YEARS OF CRISIS

E 70
JAMES HITCHCOCK

YEARS OF CRISIS

Collected Essays, 1970–1983

IGNATIUS PRESS   SAN FRANCISCO

Copublished with Roman Catholic Books
P.O. Box 255, Harrison, N.Y. 10528

Cover by Nan Runde

With ecclesiastical approval
©1985 Ignatius Press, San Francisco
ISBN 0–89870–049–3 (HB)
ISBN 0–89870–069–8 (PB)
Library of Congress Catalogue Number 84–80758
Printed in the United States of America

CONTENTS

PREFACE

Every collection of previously published articles appears under an obligation to justify itself. Having been once published, and read, why should they be offered a second time? Are they really still relevant, even as much as fifteen years after they first appeared?

If such a claim can be made, its justification lies mainly in the subject matters themselves. Every piece included here treats an issue which is still alive, and still debated, years after its first appearance.

By now it is obvious that our culture is in a continuing state of crisis, and there will not soon be a return to a stable moral and social order. Thus the issues discussed here, some of them in essays written at the time when the issues themselves first began to attract public notice, will be with us for years to come.

Some of these offerings—on abortion in the election of 1976, for example, or on the 1980 White House Conference on Families—are by definition dated. They have been included because they seem to be particularly striking illustrations of general problems—case studies of larger patterns of social disintegration.

All the works included here seek to go beyond the ephemera of events to an understanding of the cultural forces which motivate those events. In a few cases, for example the essay entitled "The Dynamics of Popular Intellectual Change", an attempt is made at a theory of social change.

The subjects cluster rather obviously into several categories, reflecting the author's major preoccupations over a decade and a half—the "life issues", of which abortion is the harbinger and still the touchstone; the political-cultural upheaval generally talked about under the title of the New Left; educational change, mainly at the college level; the rise of a militant, antireligious secularism; the crisis of the family; and the secularization of religion itself.

Unhappily, the tone and thrust of most of these essays can be termed negative, in that they seek to identify pathologies and to make surgical incisions. That tone is dictated by the prevailing spirit of the culture, which is in a phase of disintegration. A secondary theme in a number of essays is that many of the wounds suffered by contemporary institutions and communities are self-inflicted, often through a process only dimly understood.

Historians are supposed to confine themselves to the study of the past. However, when one lives in "interesting times" (in the sense of the Chinese curse) ignoring what is happening all around requires a superhuman, and ultimately deforming, kind of self-denial.

In a sense the historian cannot claim any greater competence than anyone else in perceiving the direction of the future. However, historians may perhaps at least claim some sensitivity with regard to the dynamics of society and culture. Perhaps the single most serious absence in contemporary culture is precisely the lack, on the part of most people, of a sense of history. By this I mean not so much ignorance of the past (although there is a great deal of that) as the lack of all sense of being part of a historical process. Decisions are habitually made on the basis of their promised short-term effects, without regard for the way in which they can damage and even destroy viable human communities in the long run. Perhaps never in the history of the world have people been so thoroughly present-minded as they are now, despite a good deal of popular interest in the search for "roots".

Part of that truncated present-mindedness is a failure to comprehend the Eternal Present, within which history itself unfolds. The times are such that even the religious believer finds himself drawn irresistibly toward what is merely contemporary. Two essays—"Ever Ancient, Ever New" and "Eternity's Abiding Presence"—here serve as a kind of apologia for all the others.

James Hitchcock
October 7, 1983
Feast of the Holy Rosary

ACKNOWLEDGMENTS

For permission to reprint the essays included in this volume the author and publisher wish to express their gratitude to the following publications:

To America Press, Inc., for "Here Lies Community, R.I.P.", *America*, May 30, 1970, and "The Church and the Sexual Revolution", *America*, Sept. 23, 1972. Reprinted with permission of America Press, Inc., 106 W. 56th Street, New York, NY 10019. Copyright 1970 and 1972, all rights reserved.

To the American Jewish Committee for "The Intellectuals and the People", *Commentary*, March 1973.

To the Council on Religion and International Affairs for "Prophecy and Politics: Abortion in the Election of 1976", *Worldview*, March 1977, and "The Not So New Anti-Catholicism", *Worldview*, November 1978.

To Doubleday and Company For "Eternity's Abiding Presence", *Why Catholic?*, ed. John Delaney (Doubleday, 1979).

To Duke University School of Law for "Church, State, and Moral Values: The Limits of American Pluralism", *Law and Contemporary Problems*, Spring 1981. Copyright 1981, Duke University School of Law.

To Fordham University Press for "American Culture and the Problem of Divorce", *Thought*, March 1983. Reprinted by permission.

To Kappa Delta Pi for "The Catholic College in an Age of Irony", *Educational Forum*, November 1977.

To *National Review* for "Is Life a Spectator Sport?" *National Review*, Feb. 6, 1981, and "A Child of His Times", *National Review*, March 19, 1982. Copyright by National Review, Inc., 150 East 35th Street, New York, NY 10016. Reprinted with permission.

To the *New Oxford Review* for "Does Christianity Have a Future?" *New Oxford Review*, June 1980, July–Aug. 1980. Reprinted with permission of the *New Oxford Review*, 1069 Kains Avenue, Berkeley, CA 94706.

To *The Scholastic* for "The Catholic Curriculum: What to Teach", *The Scholastic*, March 1982.

To the Thomas More Association for "Ever Ancient, Ever New", *On the Run*, 1974, and "The Problem of Decadence in Catholicism", *The Critic*, April 1973.

To the United Chapters of Phi Beta Kappa for "The Dynamics of Popular Intellectual Change", *The American Scholar*, October 1976, and "Post-mortem on a Rebirth: The Catholic Intellectual Renaissance", *The American Scholar*, Spring 1980.

EVER ANCIENT, EVER NEW

Perhaps like most people in this age, I find myself living to a great extent off spiritual capital accumulated earlier, in a time which at least seemed more settled, certain, and tranquil, more conducive to inner spiritual development than the present. Although I sense that in some ways I have "grown in grace" in the past ten years, I have even more the sense of resting on an unseen and often only barely felt foundation which has its weak places but on the whole has proven remarkably strong and sustains me in situations I might not otherwise survive.

The familiar metaphor of the foundation in the spiritual life easily gives way to that of the replenishing stream, and in terms of this shift I am conscious also that my soul's life is continually irrigated from obscure subterranean sources, sometimes in bare trickles, occasionally in bracing gushes, over which I appear to have little control but which are the accumulation of waters from earlier and heavier rains.

In part this is probably true of everyone, in that the religious sense as developed in childhood and impressionable adolescence doubtlessly shapes adult perceptions. Insofar as I can analyze my own case, I think that a sensitivity to religious symbol and a sense of religious awe, stimulated in childhood, are the most important prerequisites for an adult religious life. Everything which comes later is in some sense a variation on this.

In part, also, it appears to be a function of the times, which, despite the recent revival of interest in religious disciplines and prayer, do not seem highly conducive to religious development. In all probability the foundations of this development have to be laid in times of relative tranquillity, although stress and turmoil can be, judging from the lives of the saints, occasions of growth. We do not, however, live in an age which is particularly sympathetic even to the idea of the spiritual life, and our age increasingly seems to impose, with iron-willed system, that greatest of all enemies of true spirituality—distraction, the constant filling of one's mind and one's daily life with quantities of information, ceaseless entertainment, repeated invitations to action and involvement, so as to make any concern with the inner life seem in fact a luxury. At the same time the unsuitability of the spirit of the age should not be exaggerated. John Donne, writing 350 years ago, might have been describing most of us:

> I throw myself down in my chamber, and I call in and invite God and his Angels thither, and when they are there I neglect God and his Angels, for the noise of a fly, for the rattling of a coach, for the whining of a door. I talk on, in the same posture of praying, eyes lifted up, knees bowed down, as though I prayed to

II

God. And, if God or his Angels should ask me when I thought last of God in that prayer, I cannot tell. Sometimes I find that I forgot what I was about, but when I began to forget I cannot tell. A memory of yesterday's pleasures, a fear of tomorrow's dangers, a straw under my knee, a noise in mine ear, a light in mine eye, an anything, a nothing, a fancy, a chimera in my brain troubles me in my prayer. So certainly is there nothing in spiritual things perfect in this world.

The perennial relevance of Donne's account, along with the fact that, as far as we can tell, he was a man of genuine prayer and deep devotion after all, helps explain my conviction that classical models of spirituality have not been superseded and that, if they are in temporary eclipse, this is due less to them and more to the immense psychological pressures brought against them in this age, pressures which paradoxically serve merely to reemphasize their importance.

A vital spirituality seems to depend first of all on the persistence of some kind of vision, one which may fade in and out but which is never wholly absent. With such a vision various formalized approaches to spirituality may be more or less helpful; without it they are useless. How such a vision comes about remains mysterious. For myself, I am highly conscious of what François Mauriac describes as a "sense of invisible reality" present from childhood on. For most believers such a vision is probably formed quite early, but the phenomenon of adult conversions is sufficiently familiar to demonstrate that it need not be.

This vision is, for me, ultimately ineffable. Phrases like "union with Christ", "the majesty of God", "the presence of mystery", "penetrating the veil of appearances", "the nearness of eternity", "the love of God", and many others resonate with the sense of invisible realities which I find ebbs and flows within me. What precisely such phrases mean, I cannot say. That they denote something more real than newspaper headlines or even the most acute insights of modern "secular" men, I am certain. The riveting power of sanctity, as a distinct and recognizable Christian category, seems to me more compelling than any merely human heroism. The most attractive saints — Catherine of Siena, Philip Neri, Vincent de Paul, Charles de Foucauld, and others — seem to reveal in their persons a profound dimension of reality not found in secular heroes no matter how courageous or devoted.

Religion seems to me primarily an esthetic thing, not in the sense that it is a self-fulfilling experience or a search for pleasure, but in the sense that it is, ideally, an almost unfree response to overwhelming beauty. It is, as Baron von Hügel succinctly stated, pure adoration. C. S. Lewis insisted that there is in Christianity some idea of God as the "Great Interferer", and no aspect of Christianity has been more a stumbling block to enlightened modern men. But God is first of all the Interferer not in a moral or physical sense but as an overpowering reality who cannot be ignored, who intrudes himself into self-contained human existence in the way that the ocean or a Beethoven symphony intrudes. Away from either, we may find their memories dimming, their power growing doubtful. In their proximity again, we realize that we have been living in a deliberately circumscribed and impoverished world. More and more I find music the purest expression of religion and the greatest stimulus to devotion. (The fact that I am largely devoid of technical and scholarly competence about music probably enhances this experience.)

The tension of "vertical" and "horizontal" in religion has exercised far too much influence over recent theological and ascetical discussion. The "correct" position is obvious enough—the true Christian must be both God-oriented and man-oriented. Those who are truly both are probably fairly well along the road to sainthood. I confess to the discouraging sense that such a balance is rare in actual people, that most serious Christians are tipped either one way or the other, although never, of course, completely. Those with a taste and a capacity for contemplation do seem able to shut out a good deal of the world, to prune away distractions and conflicting demands on their time and attention, while the social apostles often appear to have little interest in devotion and a strong propensity for losing themselves in worldly events. The exceptions are, mercifully, sufficiently numerous to indicate the possibility, but not so numerous as to permit complacency.

I find that I cannot be a "secular man" because the reality which is formulated in the doctrine of the Mystical Body of Christ in effect gives the believer special glasses, somewhat like those we wore for a brief while at "3–D" movies, which reveal new dimensions to the world and to human existence. On one level I am very concerned with the concrete texture of life and with its preservation, and few things seem clearer to me than that most of the forces of modern life, whether of the "right" or the "left", seek to destroy that texture. Yet in another sense I find myself believing, often, that this does not matter, that one's sexual, racial, national, professional, or familial identities are ultimately absorbed into the unity of Christ. I am at least a moderately "political" person, in that I care about society and human culture. Yet I also sometimes think public events are of small consequence, that victories and defeats, achievements and failures, are ultimately cancelled out by eternity.

It seems to me altogether appropriate that Christianity should be full of paradoxes which approach being contradictions, and it is one of the most distressing features of the contemporary Church that so much effort is being expended to resolve these paradoxes in a rational and "secular" way. We are in the world but not of it. What we do on earth matters greatly and matters not at all. God desires our prayers but has no need of them. He is all-just and all-merciful. Christ was fully God and fully man. It seems to me that nowhere has the inherently paradoxical nature of human existence been better recognized than in the fundamental Christian dogmas and in the basic, ingrained attitudes of traditional spirituality. ("Pray as though everything depends on God; work as though everything depends on you.")

One of the most profound "religious" experiences I have had (less common now that the Church has become so factionalized) is of Mass in a large city church at rush hour on a holy day: crowds of the most diverse people gather together to participate in a great transcendent act of worship which leaves our differences unaffected (we need not even greet each other or smile; we are in a hurry to get home in any case) while subsuming them into the eternal and the infinite. Many have come out of a sense of obligation, but they come reverently nonetheless. Our humanity is all too apparent, but briefly at least we are made aware of our divinity as well.

Paradoxically also, the pure beauty, the unbounded love, the perfect freedom which are the ends of our spiritual life seem attainable only through a measure of asceticism and self-denial, the acceptance of discipline, the adoption of a regimen. Great art is never either created or apprehended solely through spontaneity; training and discipline are required, and also experience. Prayer never seems more meaningless than when I have neglected it for a while, or more nourishing than when I have forced myself to practice it for a few days. The talk about introducing Catholics to an "adult spirituality" seems to me often to miss the point. It is precisely the mark of childhood to be fresh, spontaneous, and indiscriminate in enthusiasms, to care nothing for the future, to acquire and drop new loves daily, to rely on "the spirit blowing where it will". The adult learns to discern the real from the chimeric, to limit enthusiasms to what is digestible, above all to adopt methods and strategies which prolong pleasures and commitments, to live in a sense according to rules. The adult recognizes that the waning of first emotions does not betoken necessarily the waning of commitment.

It is perhaps the central genius of Catholicism that it has devised so many ways to prolong the effects of spontaneous insight long after the insight itself has become obscured. That is the principal point of dogma, of fixed liturgy, of behavioral rules, of guides to the spiritual life. Catholicism has been accused of being a religion of rote and of blind obedience. Where it fails to take inner root in its adherents, it does in fact become this. However, its aim is something different. Catholicism rather teaches that, if the sincere individual undertakes to live a certain way of life, to follow a certain designated path, he or she will come finally to the clear place in the forest or, to vary the metaphor, to the crown of the hill from which the Promised Land can be glimpsed in the distance. The discipline precedes the understanding and, once the understanding is attained, also sustains it.

What historical Catholicism in effect does is to seize upon deep spiritual insights, moments of overwhelming grace, and crystallize them. The most important of these crystallizations are in the liturgy, and the liturgy remains for me the culmination, in a very tangible and personal way, of the life of the spirit. I simultaneously approach liturgy in an "objective" way—as the actual celebration of a divine rite whose true meaning is mystical—and in a "subjective" way—I am perhaps overly sensitive to the way in which liturgy is celebrated. The recitation of the Divine Office by monks and nuns, the smoke of incense rising to heaven, the performance of prescribed rituals, all seem to me to have objective religious validity; it is good that they occur, apart from the personal state of those who do them. At the same time I recognize that the symbolic power of liturgy can be greatly enhanced and obscured by, among other things, the style of celebration. On the subjective side the reform of the liturgy has for me largely diminished this power, as I believe it has also for many other people.

In his autobiography, Thomas Merton records that, when he first thought of turning to religion as a young man, he began by going to the rather drab and uninspiring little Protestant church he had dropped out of years before. It was, he said, as though God wanted him to climb back up the way he fell. Like many people, I gave up a good many of the traditional devotions after the Second Vatican Council, not in order to become "secular" but in order to discover a "higher" kind of spirituality. Gradually I have been recognizing the barely concealed pride in that action, which perhaps as much as anything else has prevented the flowering of that hoped-for higher life. I have come to realize, as Pascal and others have often pointed out, that simple things like kneeling to pray, using holy water, or reciting the great traditional prayers, do make a difference. Perhaps, having been away from them for a time, I come to them refreshed and with a clearer view. In any case I recommend to anyone seeking the renewal of his spiritual life that he begin with a fixed and even arbitrary regime—a certain time set aside, certain prayers to be said, certain books to be read, kneeling, making the sign of the cross, et cetera.

In saying that I often have the feeling of living off previously gained spiritual capital, I mean also that I now realize the importance of ingrained images, words, sentences, gestures which have been deeply rooted in the subconscious over a period of time and which come to the surface unexpectedly. Phrases from the traditional liturgy, sometimes in Latin, sentences from Scripture (usually in the Douay-Reims version we heard for so long), recollections of particular works of religious art, come into the mind unbidden and, for someone still in the foothills of the spiritual life, help to make possible the fulfillment of Christ's injunction to "pray always". The secularity and spiritual dryness of many contemporary Catholics is doubtlessly related to the fact that so many powerful images from the past—verbal and iconographic—have been allowed to fade. I do not think the newer images will prove nearly so powerful; in part they are designed not to be.

Although my sense of the meaning of religion is that it is ultimately a response to great beauty, the "negative" side of faith has always seemed important to me also. The final glory is precious only because we have first fallen to the valley of tears. Concepts like "sin" and "repentance" seem to me much closer to true human reality than talk about "growth", "fulfillment", or "potential". Although I cannot follow him all the way, Martin Luther has been one of the strongest theological influences on me in his determination that man shall first confront his own sinfulness in all its depth before he shall enjoy the comforts of salvation. The seemingly exaggerated importance which St. Augustine gives to his theft of a few pears also seems real to me in that the moral universe I perceive is one in which small deeds, even small thoughts, can have immense personal consequences. I have always been attracted to the rather astringent, sin-conscious Gallic piety represented in recent times by Mauriac, Bernanos, and Claudel and correspondingly put off by the cheerfulness of a certain English attitude expressed by people like Chesterton and C. S. Lewis. To say that one senses in himself the capacity for every kind of sin is both self-dramatizing and probably untrue, but some approximation of this seems to me necessary for full spiritual development.

Like most Catholics, I go to confession less often than I used to, although I am not sure why. The idea of it still appeals to me. Probably the greatest problem with it, so far as I am concerned, is the discrepancy between what it promises to be and what it is, subjectively speaking—so often it turns out purely routine and perfunctory. Still, the forgiveness is pronounced and the grace imparted. At the least it is a reminder that we are constantly under God's judgment. A seminarian once said to me, "I'm a Christian to help prevent me from being myself", and that seems to me exactly right. Nothing in the "new church" seems to me more ill-conceived than the apparent general optimism about human nature which is now so pervasive. My vision of evil is of pure and unbridled egotism, and we live in an age which appears systematically to encourage this.

Most of the time I experience no particular fear of hell or desire for heaven, which is more a sign of worldliness than of advanced spirituality. I also find that my worldly desires seem to be fewer and my ability to endure disappointments greater, which are more likely to be evidences of aging than of purification. I think, however, that I am beginning to see the truth in the assertion that Christianity does not promise happiness as the world understands it, that happiness in this sense is ultimately irrelevant. In retrospect my greatest human disappointments seem to me in some ways providential, and I am sometimes surprised at the ease and subtlety with which God has seemingly guided me in ways I did not intend to go and given me tasks I did not intend to undertake.

AMERICAN CULTURE AND
THE PROBLEM OF DIVORCE

Any consideration of divorce in contemporary America cannot overlook the central irony of the situation—that the divorce rate continues to increase even as married couples have access to resources unequalled at any time in human history. The very openness of society is one such resource. Merely from living amidst their own relatives and neighbors, engaged couples probably learn more about marriage than formerly, when relationships were more formal and therefore less open to view. Parents are likely to speak to their children about marriage more frankly than their own parents spoke to them. Television increases this familiarity, since it no longer portrays idealized, essentially untroubled marital relationships (Ozzie and Harriet) but puts married people on the screen warts and all (Rhoda, the Jeffersons). There is little excuse today for a person to enter into marriage naive and starry-eyed. Moreover, there are formal courses on marriage and family life taught in the schools as part of the regular curriculum. These include not only factual courses about sexuality but those which cover the entire range of things deemed necessary for a good marriage—basic psychology, differences between the sexes, economics, and housekeeping.

The contemporary approach to sexuality in particular represents a remarkable change from the past. If sexual dysfunction was a principal cause of problems in marriage, then those who marry today are maximally protected against it—they have much more formal instruction, more actual experience, and greater access to professional advice than their ancestors would have thought either possible or proper. Organized religion makes its own contribution to this preparation. Not only do many churches offer engaged couples instruction which in many ways duplicates that already available elsewhere, including advice about sexuality and housekeeping, they also seek to instill in them a highly personalistic and in some ways even mystical understanding of marriage. Although in the Catholic Church, to take one example, the theology of marriage seems to have undergone certain changes in the past quarter century, it is also true that, for those couples who are paying attention, the Church seeks to introduce them to a far more sophisticated understanding of matrimony than was taught in the past.

An indeterminate but apparently rather large number of couples now choose to live together before marriage, enjoying, as it were, the opportunity for testing their relationship in a laboratory setting. Many people now marry only after they have had the opportunity to test whether they can live together happily. Once married, these couples find that the resources at their command have not diminished. If money is another major cause of marital tension, today's married couples are likely to be far better off than their parents were at the same age. Not uncommonly, both spouses have full-time jobs. Credit is easy. Houses and cars, which earlier generations had as distant goals, are usually obtained by the time of the wedding itself. Most middle-class couples find that, although they may need to pinch pennies from time to time, there is usually enough money for annual vacations, dinners in good restaurants, shows, and athletic events. Scarcely anyone today is confined to home merely because of financial embarrassment. Large families can be a cause of strain on parents, and most of today's parents have chosen to have only a few children, and to have them only under optimal conditions—exactly when they want them and only after they have planned carefully for them. Their children are by far the healthiest in the history of the world, most of them causing their parents little anxiety in this regard.

The concept of parenthood has also changed. Increasing numbers of parents share with one another the responsibilities of caring for children so that the mother need not feel weighed down. Baby-sitting services are available to almost everybody. Within the home, television, electronic games, and other kinds of recreation are constantly available. Relatively inexpensive telephone calls make it possible to remain in contact with relatives and friends in other cities and thus to feel less isolated. Married couples now generally practice the kind of "togetherness" ritualistically extolled in the slogans of the 1950s. There is no longer a rigid division between male and female activities, so that husbands and wives can do most things together, exploring new facets of their relationship and broadening their common interests.

If the marriage should begin to falter, unprecedented resources are available. It is now socially acceptable to talk freely about marital problems, so that friends and relatives are more sympathetic and helpful than in the past. There is also a vast array of professional services available—married couples can get expert advice (often free or at nominal cost) on everything from balancing their checkbooks to improving their sexual performances. Personality conflicts can be talked through endlessly in the presence of trained counsellors who seek to help the couple identify the precise root of their problem and who make suggestions for overcoming it. Beyond this, there is even a large industry dedicated simply to making people better people. An endless series of workshops, retreats, and therapy programs exist to help people find "self-fulfillment", "discover who they are", "actualize their potential", et cetera. As part of this industry there is also an endless flow of books, magazines, television programs, and tapes. Yet one overwhelming irony emerges from all this—this generation of married people, better prepared and more thoroughly supported than any generation in the history of the world, is also the generation which is getting divorced in larger numbers than any generation in the history of the world. All the resources put into the effort to enrich and strengthen the marriage bond seem almost to have had the opposite effect.

It is useful to divide divorces into two broad categories, those attributable primarily to what might be called "hard" causes—alcoholism and drug use, personal violence, desertion, infidelity, or mental illness—and those attributable to intangible and elusive discontents. The literature of divorce, documentary and fictional, as well as personal experience with the modern middle class, suggest that divorces for "soft" reasons are now becoming more common, that is, divorces not for any specific and definable cause but from a vague sense that, as it is variously put, the marriage "wasn't working out any more", "we weren't growing together", "I felt unfulfilled". Divorces are now much easier to get than formerly, and attitudes toward marriage have themselves undergone a revolutionary change.

In one sense the wonder is not that divorces have become common but that they are not even more common, because there is little doubt that prevailing cultural winds strongly militate against marriage. This, of course, is reflected in the large number of people choosing to live together without benefit of marriage, as well as the probably even larger number who are satisfied to have a series of passing romantic encounters. When living together out of wedlock first became respectable, in the late 1960s, some pains were taken to insist that such an arrangement differed from marriage only in the absence of a "piece of paper". Unwedded cohabitation was even invested with a kind of moral superiority; the participants, allegedly, could make a deep and lasting commitment to one another without the "security blanket" of a legally binding agreement. It is doubtful, however, that very many people ever seriously believed this claim, for it has always been obvious that the main reason for not entering into a legally binding commitment is to be able to abandon such arrangements with the least amount of trouble. Cohabitation replaced marriage in some circles since temporary relationships were to be preferred to permanent ones, established by the pattern of "serial monogamy" notable among society's avant-garde for many years.

This pattern can perhaps be explained simply by the low tolerance of boredom seemingly bred into people by the conditions of modern life. Those who change houses and jobs frequently, who constantly expect fresh stimuli from life, are likely to find a lifetime with one spouse unendurably constricting. Some respected authorities seem to say that all married couples ought to divorce at some point, that failure to do so is prima facie evidence of personal stagnation. There is another subtle irony here. Modern culture promises to teach people how to explore "inter-personal relationships" more deeply than ever before. Each such relationship is now held out as, ideally, an adventure. The depths of human personality are thought to be such that one could spend a lifetime plumbing both one's own psyche and that of another without exhausting their possibilities. All this supposedly opposes even the recent past, when people were content to live on a superficial psychological level. Yet in practice human relationships, despite all the resources invested in improving them, seem to exhaust themselves remarkably fast. The divorce statistics, and the rationales offered by sophisticated people to explain those statistics, help to bear this out. Divorce in modern America, as well as virtually all other forms of personal behavior, cannot be understood apart from what can be broadly termed the "therapeutic culture"[1] — a culture which systematically encourages people to expect from life a sense of total personal well being, achieved at little cost and based upon the systematic rejection of all "impositions" on the self by society. It is a culture which at least potentially treats every person as a patient — not as emotionally sick but as emotionally impoverished and, with proper help, capable of achieving complete emotional fulfillment.

Much has been said about the "me decade" of the 1970s, supposedly a departure from the politically oriented altruism of the 1960s. In fact there was a direct continuity between the two decades: the essence of 1960s culture was the radical assertion of selfhood in the face of a "repressive" society, not a truly empathetic concern for others. The 1970s differed from the 1960s only in their more explicit concentration on self-gratification, a concentration so far not materially altered in the early 1980s despite a supposed "swing to the right". (Politically and economically, such a "swing" is perfectly compatible with egocentrism, as in the philosophy of libertarianism.)[2]

The roots of this attitude probably date back to the end of World War II, and its chief cause has been the prolonged prosperity Americans experienced after about 1945. Put simply, during the period from 1945 to 1965, Americans came to expect that all their desires would be satisfied. Each year they found themselves better off than they were the year before. For a time this pattern coexisted quite comfortably with a remarkable degree of social stability. In the 1950s the divorce rate actually declined for a time. For the first two decades after 1945, burgeoning prosperity mainly supported and strengthened family commitments. It enabled people to find suitable housing, beget more children, and enjoy enough leisure to engage in family activities. By the middle 1960s, however, the balance had begun to tip sharply, as the effects of prosperity began to make people more frankly individualistic. The pattern first manifested itself among the children of affluence, who in the 1960s were estranged from their parents to an unprecedented degree. (The "generation gap" was one of the most analyzed phenomena of the decade.) In the next decade the estrangement caused by radical individualism was felt most keenly between spouses rather than between parents and children.

[1] See Philip Rieff, *The Triumph of the Therapeutic* (New York, 1964).
[2] For a discussion of this see Hitchcock, *The New Enthusiasts* (Chicago, 1982), chaps. 3 and 4.

So long as the sense of self-gratification remained on the material level, it caused strains in personal relationships but was rarely fatal. However, once a certain level of material prosperity could be taken for granted, the search for self-fulfillment began to involve less tangible things as well. Gradually it came to include the desire of individuals to place themselves in whatever emotional state seemed attractive, no matter what social barriers stood in the way. The radical young of the 1960s had led the way, defining every kind of social relationship—parent and child, pupil and teacher, citizen and government—as oppressive and destructive of human freedom. Inevitably the marital relationship was bound to be experienced in the same way. Little had changed with respect to marriage; if anything, the conditions of its existence had improved greatly since World War II. What had changed were people's expectations. Hence arose the irony whereby the relentlessly growing phenomenon of divorce has been accompanied by a massive industry endeavoring to help people live more successfully within marriage. Despite its rapid growth, and despite the sincerity and intensity with which it has been pursued, it cannot run fast enough to keep up with people's expectations. Arguably, in fact, it makes conditions worse by reinforcing and legitimizing expectations which in the nature of human relationships few people are likely to fulfill.

There are many possible explanations of this mystery, among them the question whether it is possible, in a formal educational setting, to teach people how to live. Beyond that is a tendency, perhaps typically American, to see all failure as technical failure, hence the solution to all failure as the ability to make technical adjustments. The popularity of the term "marital breakdown" is an obvious indication of this. Like other contemporary neologisms, this term aims to evacuate all moral implications from the fact of divorce. The prevailing currents of popular psychology (flowing deep within the churches, among other places) hold that it is wrong and destructive to make, or even to imply, moral judgments about human actions. Instead of condemnation, the argument runs, people should be enabled to understand their problems and then "cope" with them, with moral judgment treated as at best an unproductive luxury, at worst a grim survival of a barbarian past. However laudable such an attitude may be from the standpoint of sparing people's feelings, it is itself destructive insofar as it encourages people to think that what happens to them is beyond their control, that they are simply part of a process to which they must adjust, and that their salvation (if a traditional theological term may be used) will come as a result of advances in what might be called the technology of human relationships. (The "human potential" industry is constantly offering new techniques guaranteed more effective than the old ones in teaching people how to "relate".)

If the term "breakdown", as applied to a marriage, is a mechanistic metaphor, the term "death" is only a limited improvement, for although it recognizes that marriage is a living thing, it also implies something both inevitable and essentially beyond anyone's control. (The term "growth", similarly invoked in matrimonial situations, obviously tends to the same point—although growth can be a freely willed process, it can also be regarded as merely another of nature's marvels, which mysteriously occurs in some cases and not in others.) What many people now seek from marriage is nothing less than an approximation of perfect happiness, as they understand happiness. They seek an almost mystical union with another person which at the same time does not require even the smallest surrender of themselves. They are products of a culture which for years has encouraged people to think that all things are possible and that what one desires can be had at little cost, which above all does not acknowledge that certain things in life (for example, a faithful marital relationship) can usually be bought only at the expense of certain others (constantly new stimulation). This is not a spontaneously achieved attitude. It is relentlessly inculcated into people by the principal agencies of their culture—the mass media, peers, sometimes the schools and the churches.

The more stable period before 1960 helped prepare the way for this by its overromanticization of marriage. It is appalling to notice, for example, how films of the post-war period presented marriage as the denouement of every situation, the resolution of every difficulty, all problems subsumed into the final kiss. A generation of young people were propagandized to the belief that marriage constituted a permanent plateau of untroubled happiness. One of the serious flaws in the philosophy of "self-fulfillment" is the absence of any even approximately precise idea of what such fulfillment might be like. In practice it seems often to involve nothing less than a rejection of the entire human condition, a demand to be liberated from all natural limitations.

Since marriage is by far the most intense of human relationships, it is a crucial test of the proclaimed humanism and personalism of modern man, a test many people now fail. Ironically, the expectation of full and complete human fulfillment, based on a supposedly high regard for human dignity, leads almost inevitably to a repudiation of that relationship. It is also a crucial test of the responsible use of freedom, also frequently failed, in that prevalent notions of freedom seem to prevent people from making the necessary concessions to the freedom of others which would render such relationships possible. As Joseph Epstein, the author of perhaps the most penetrating study of divorce, has written,

> Patriarchy is dead, replaced not by matriarchy, the rule of women, but by a variety of psychic Marxism in marriage, which holds that to each is accorded his own emotional needs—provided, of course, that these needs do not conflict with the emotional needs of the marriage partner. If the emotional needs do

conflict — which they cannot help but do, in many cases frequently and irreconcilably — well, that is what divorce courts are for. . . .

What the loss of a sense of community involves is the loss of the ability to imagine that one's actions have any consequence outside one's own life; the accompanying inability to imagine anything more important than one's own happiness.[3]

Most modern people would probably admit that self-sacrifice does have a legitimate place in love and marriage. However, this is affirmed merely as an abstract reality, one which in practice is systematically evaded by people whose tolerance for the idea is quite low. Traditionally love has been thought of as self-fulfilling through self-giving; contemporary culture seeks to reverse this process, often with the effect of achieving neither. Here lies another of the central ironies of modern culture. For, as people assert their freedom with increasing tenacity, and as they refuse to accept conditions they see as imposed on them by society, they simultaneously refuse to take full personal responsibility for what happens in their lives, including marriage. Indeed, the principal aim of much of modern culture is to "free" people from their own freedom, that is, to divest them of any sense of personal responsibility for their actions. Instead they are encouraged to think of their lives as shaped by forces over which they have little control and to which they should prudently surrender.

In terms of what were previously described as "hard" and "soft" reasons for divorce, it is worth noting that the latter also influence the former. If, as is claimed, unemployment and other economic troubles tend to have deleterious effects on marriage, it is surely worth recalling that the classical idea of marriage holds that adversity should if anything strengthen the couple's loyalty to one another. Ill health and financial reversal often seem now merely to expose the already fragile nature of the commitment, which was sustainable only on a basis of concurrent self-satisfaction. Even where pathologies like alcoholism and mental illness exist, the history of marriage provides numerous instances of healthy spouses who, through genuine fidelity and deep caring, have helped their troubled spouses recover. Now popular wisdom seems to hold that a spouse caught in such a situation has no particular obligation to his or her partner, since one's own happiness is the highest good. (When Henry Fonda died, obituaries recalled that one of his wives had been institutionalized for insanity. Eventually she was released, ostensibly cured. He then told her that he wished to marry another woman, whereupon she killed herself. No one who recalled this story seemed to draw any particular moral lesson from it. It was treated as merely another of those tragedies which modern man seems fated to experience.)

[3] *Divorce in America* (New York, 1974), pp. 88, 94–95.

On one level modern culture has taught people to be articulate in ways they never were before, and this is particularly true in terms of popular psychology, where there is available a vocabulary sufficient for rationalizing practically any human action. Where marriage is concerned, it is remarkable, for example, how the simple fact of infidelity—both in the narrow sense of adultery and the broader sense of broken commitments—is so often ignored. Common sense and daily experience argue that many marriages break up mainly because one or both partners simply want to be married to someone else (and to someone else's spouse). They do not feel bound to any commitment they may have made to their own spouses. Often the innocent party in such an affair is devastated by the discovery of the infidelity, which is the crassest kind of callous betrayal. Yet such occurrences are rarely discussed in frank terms but are papered over by the kind of rhetoric which, as noted, seems to treat marriage as a mechanism which from time to time gives way under impersonal pressures for which human beings have no ultimate responsibility. In a society which seems obsessed with considerations of justice, justice is rarely accorded to the victims of unfaithful spouses, even in so elementary a way as by acknowledging the moral wrong of the infidelity.

The removal of the social stigma from divorce involves more than merely a laudable resolve not to inflict unnecessary pain on people who have already suffered a great deal. Taken far enough, it involves a refusal to make any moral judgment about a relationship which involves the full range of human moral actions in a way few other relationships do. If society refuses to decide whether certain people have been bad husbands or wives, in effect it refuses to admit human responsibility for the successful maintenance of marriages. The point is not that divorced people should be ostracized but that divorce should not be treated as merely one more unavoidable social malfunction.

The revolutionary change of attitudes is nowhere more dramatic than in the Catholic Church, which still officially disallows divorce and remarriage but increasingly finds it possible to annul marriages which previously were considered binding. The merits of the "new norms" for annulments are not at issue here. What is at issue are the attitudes expressed by the clerical leaders of what can be called the Catholic revisionist movement, who seem able to confront divorce with remarkable insouciance. One priest blandly asks, for example, ". . . how can we talk about the indissolubility of marriage in a world where everything dissolves? The only constant is change." He goes on to ridicule what he calls the "finger-in-the-dike" approach to marriage, whereby the Church upholds an ideal which is no longer widely accepted: "I think we Roman Catholics should take our fingers out of the dike and learn to swim in this new human era."[4] In another context he has argued that it is a

---

[4] James J. Young, C.S.P., "Misimpressions about Marriage", *Commonweal* (Nov. 22, 1974), 187–88.

sign of hope that so many divorced people get remarried, since it shows their commitment to the institution,[5] a logic whereby it could be argued that, the more divorces, the better, since each divorce provides the divorcee with the opportunity to marry yet again. The point, once again, is not that Church officials should seek to ostracize divorced people but that misplaced understanding of "compassion" has brought about a situation in which even religious authorities find it impossible to support the ideal marital fidelity. Their moral energies are mainly directed at easing the Church's acceptance of the divorced, not in attempting to persuade people that commitments are meant to be honored. (As G. K. Chesterton observed, "I take it . . . that advocates of divorce do not mean that marriage is to remain an ideal only in the sense of being almost impossible. They do not mean that a faithful husband is only to be admired as a fanatic.")[6]

Part of the distortion of personality which has occurred in recent times is the assumption that all human decisions are made as a result of mature, deliberate, conscientious communing with the self and such a decision manifests that self's responsible and courageous freedom. (One Catholic theologian somehow links the growing divorce rate with the increasing "maturity" of today's youth.)[7] In fact, however, most people make decisions in accordance with the signals they receive from their culture. In earlier times those signals were overwhelmingly unfavorable to divorce. Today the reverse is more nearly the case, and it is not surprising that people do not work harder to overcome their marital difficulties when many even of their religious leaders seem to be telling them that the effort is misplaced. From an excessive harshness by which divorcees were made to feel rejected and despised, the social pendulum has swung to an easy acceptance in which few moral leaders bother to uphold marital permanence even as an ideal. (It is noteworthy that the logic of the present situation seems to dictate not only the permissibility of divorce but almost its desirability, since it can be assumed that few people find with one partner the total fulfillment they seek, and to remain faithful to that partner is thus to settle for a needlessly stunted existence.)

It is extraordinary how few leaders of society, including religious leaders, bother to defend the binding nature of marital vows, except in the most formal and perfunctory way. Contemporary Americans have seemingly settled for a view of life in which no obligation can be binding which interferes with the individual's own quest for fulfillment. (Thus for some years the media have been dealing very sympathetically with parents, usually mothers, who

---

[5] Young, "Stabilizing Marriage by Permitting Divorce", *National Catholic Reporter* (Feb. 1, 1974), 12.

[6] *The Superstition of Divorce* (New York, 1920), p. 134.

[7] Bernard Haering, C.SS.R., in *Divorce and Remarriage in the Catholic Church*, ed. Lawrence Wrenn (New York, 1973), p. 22. For similar remarks see Msgr. Stephen J. Kelleher, *Divorce and Remarriage for Catholics?* (Garden City, N.Y., 1973), p. 96.

in effect abandon their children in order to "find themselves".) Among both religious leaders and secular professionals, the new conventional wisdom about marriage is that its problems will mainly be solved by the great liberal panacea of more and better education. For example, priests who do not find it possible to accept the permanency of marriage with any conviction are enthusiastic about new requirements that candidates for matrimony take lengthy courses of instruction and refrain from making hasty commitments.

As argued previously, such requirements are at best likely to have a modest effect, since the problem for most people is not a faulty understanding of marriage and its responsibilities, nor even necessarily that they have chosen the "wrong" partner, but unwillingness to make the kind of commitment which marriage requires. Psychotherapy has triumphed even in the churches in its insistence that it does no good to approach human problems in terms of moral exhortations to do better. Yet it seems precisely the right kind of will which is today lacking in so many human relationships, and if moralizing is deemed ineffective, no other remedies for faulty wills have yet been discovered. (Even if moral exhortations do not significantly affect particular individuals, their expression at least signals that a culture is serious about certain subjects. Their absence is likely to be interpreted in the contrary sense.)

Like all social pathologies, divorce is self-reinforcing. Today there is scarcely a family in the United States which does not have some experience of it—if not in the immediate family, then among aunts and uncles, cousins, or in-laws. As a result, it has become in a sense a taboo subject—no one can afford to be in the position of seeming to disapprove of it, even in an abstract way, lest this be felt as a moral condemnation of particular individuals. There is a virtual conspiracy to treat divorce almost as a normal occurrence, lest anyone be offended by signs that it is not. Once again the clergy play a central role—many of them have proven unable, in practice, to separate a stance of compassion and concern toward the divorced from a stance of moral approval of the act itself. The latter stance is often deemed the quickest way to achieve the former. (There are no people in America today more heroic or lonely than divorced Catholics trying to live in accordance with the Church's teaching in the face of priests who in effect tell them they are being foolishly scrupulous.) As part of this conspiracy, it has been necessary to underestimate the effects of divorce on the fabric of society itself. Until a mere decade ago, conventional wisdom in the social sciences and the "helping professions" attributed all kinds of social pathologies to the effects of "broken homes". Suddenly, as if on cue, the same professions began producing studies purporting to show that having two parents is not necessarily more beneficial than having one and that children do not suffer unduly from the trauma of divorce. Once again, both common sense and available evidence suggest that this is not true. Like the fervent hope that better education will strengthen people's commitments to one another, new beliefs about the effects of divorce mainly reflect the common American hope that things can be bought without cost, that one is never required to make difficult choices in life.

The emphasis on better preparation for marriage has had the virtue of focusing attention on what might be called the objective criteria for marrying—communality of interests, realistic assessment of financial capabilities, et cetera. But it is arguable that the gravest deficiency in choosing a partner is still for most people insufficient attention to their objective suitability for one another. The culture encourages an approach to marriage which stresses primarily its personal emotional satisfactions. Rarely is it even suggested to young people that they consider marriage in terms of their objective complementarity to one another. This is puzzling. The rise of militant feminism has obviously placed great strain on many marriages and has undoubtedly contributed to many divorces. However, in self-consciously advanced circles virtually everyone is a feminist. When the wife makes that commitment, her husband usually makes it too, and it is common to hear testimony from such people about how their shared feminist perspective has actually strengthened their bond. (The husband does half the housework and takes responsibility for the children as the wife pursues a career.) Yet no one is surprised when such marriages break up, as they seem to with some regularity. Indeed, it seems to be precisely among people who have a shared social and political ideology that fragility of personal relationships is most obvious, possibly because these very ideologies tend to undermine the sense of commitment which is essential for marriage. The same development which leads the couple to embrace militant feminism also deprives them of any real basis for treating marriage as sacred. (Conversely, there is considerable evidence that a deeply shared religious commitment does support marital stability.)

The moral and social crisis reflected in divorce statistics is obviously not a passing thing, nor is it likely to be resolved by any of the quasi-technical solutions which proclaimed "experts" now favor. In times past marriage was primarily thought of as a network of rights and responsibilities, to which the partners committed themselves. For at least two centuries it has been understood in increasingly personalistic terms, to the point where its meaning today is commonly expressed only in those terms. It seems appropriate to ask whether the crisis of marriage, which is merely one manifestation of a deeper crisis of families, does not show personalism at the end of its rope, turned back upon itself and in danger of devouring the very values which it is supposed to promote. What may be required to save both the institution of marriage and civilization is a revolution in attitudes at least as radical as that which ushered in the modern era of marriage.

THE CATHOLIC CURRICULUM

The history of religiously affiliated higher education in the United States does not provide much hope for the survival of Catholic colleges and universities into the next millennium. The vast majority of private institutions in America were originally founded under religious auspices for the purpose of providing religious and moral education for their students. Most of the older ones (those founded before the Civil War) were designed primarily to educate clergy. Yet in the vast majority of cases this religious character has eroded over the years to the point where it is at best nominal, and often nonexistent.

One reason for the great proliferation of private colleges in America has been precisely this secularization process. As older religious colleges were perceived as no longer serving the purpose for which they were founded, new ones were started. In time these also became secularized, or were perceived as such, and still newer ones were begun. In modern times only two kinds of religiously affiliated institutions exist in any meaningful numbers — Roman Catholic and Evangelical Protestant.

On the whole Catholic colleges are somewhat older than the Evangelical institutions, and thus they face the prospect of secularization more acutely. The reasons for this are complex and difficult to summarize. Besides factors distinctive to the American experience, the turbulent life of the Catholic Church since about 1960 has obviously had its effect. The key to the character of most Catholic colleges has been the religious communities which operate them. Few communities have escaped racking crises of self-identity in the past twenty years. Many have agonized over whether they should even be involved in higher education, and a number of Catholic colleges have been closed.

But from all the mass of conferences, committee reports, position papers, convention speeches, et cetera, which have dealt with Catholic education, no consensus has emerged as to what a Catholic institution might or should look like in practice. The reasons for this uncertainty are partly educational, but even more religious. It is not really possible to define what a Catholic university might be like without a fairly clear idea of what Catholicism is. Disagreements over educational policy and practice are, more often than not, disguised disagreements over belief.

The pressures for the secularization of religious colleges are multiple, and to a large extent they are unconscious — only in a relatively few cases have Catholic colleges made a deliberate decision to secularize. Two factors in particular might be pointed to as crucial.

One is professionalization, which has affected all of American life, and especially American higher education, quite profoundly since World War II.

Professionalization is a complex process, but, whatever else it means, it means a situation in which the criteria for what constitutes good education are set outside the institution itself, generally by professional associations of physicians, lawyers, historians, philosophers, et cetera. Although in a time of shrinking enrollments colleges like to talk about how they are distinctive, professionalization tends to work against distinctiveness. It posits uniform standards for all institutions. Thus, all other things being equal, it gives the advantage to the institution with the most money, since meeting professional criteria is usually the function of money, expressed in such factors as the scholarly reputation of the faculty, the size of the library, the quality of the scientific equipment.

To a lesser extent student expectations have also influenced the process. As Catholics "arrived" in American life by around 1960, young Catholics became increasingly conscious of the remaining gaps which separated them from the mainstream of their culture, and especially of factors in their background which might retard full acceptance into that mainstream. Some decided that Catholic education itself was a handicap. Others, perhaps more often than not imbibing an attitude first held by faculty members, decided that Catholic education still had a future, but only to the degree that its distinctiveness was minimized. The goal, often not stated, was to transform the Catholic colleges so as to make them as much as possible like private colleges which had already undergone the secularization process.

Catholic institutions in the United States have never been able to find the proper balance between commitment and openness. Prior to the 1960s there was much of the former but little of the latter, as indicated, for example, by a reluctance to hire faculty from outside the Catholic tradition. Since 1965 there has been no end of openness, with few institutions willing to tackle the difficult (and highly sensitive) issue of maintaining identity.

Obviously any education worthy of the name has to open students' minds, enable them to relate to a complex and variegated world. However, an education which merely does that ill equips the student to live in such a world, because it gives him little basis on which to discriminate, judge, choose, or evaluate. Leaving the dogmatic claims of religion aside, liberal education itself cannot be the now standard smorgasbord of courses, nor can it be merely a smorgasbord of opinions, all of them more or less equal to one another. Prior to the 1960s even the secular universities believed they possessed a core of common wisdom, derived from the entire Western cultural tradition, which could serve as the basis of all education. Now, despite widespread desires to recover such a core, as expressed, in particular, in curricular requirements, there is no agreement as to what it should be. Catholic institutions ought to be in an advantageous position in trying to recover such a core, both because of the true claims of the faith itself and because the Catholic tradition can serve, at a minimum, as a principle of organization, a center of intellectual focus.

The ideal of "objectivity" in scholarship—a kind of passionless, detached scrutiny—no longer holds sway. Its existence is difficult to justify in theory, and in practice scholars do tend to have commitments which they may or may not recognize, or else they study subjects in which they invest nothing of themselves, the results of which are likely to be desiccated and irrelevant.

What students have a right to expect from faculty is not objectivity but honesty. A professor may have a strongly held position of his own, which he defends in his teaching. Indeed it is usually desirable that he have such a position, for in this way alone can education truly become "relevant". However, the committed scholar, all the more because of his commitment, has an obligation to treat other positions as honestly as he can. He must not omit, distort, or caricature. He must be ready at all times to engage in genuine dialogue with others, which in no way implies compromising his own commitment.

For years Catholic educators have been nervous about the charge that they engage in indoctrination, not education, and that religious orthodoxy is incompatible with free inquiry. This nervousness is merely a reflection of the persistent inferiority complex of many American Catholics, despite their having supposedly "come of age". Among other things, it blinds them to some of the realities of American higher education.

Despite the official rhetoric about total openness and freedom of expression, working orthodoxies operate in even the most prestigious secular universities. For years logical and linguistic analysis has dominated most philosophy departments, and few proponents of other theories are even given a fair hearing, much less offered teaching positions. In the social sciences one or another form of behaviorism is also dominant in the great majority of institutions. In every academic discipline there exist orthodoxies which are enforced in terms of hiring, tenure, and publication. (Recently at Yale University a senior professor of political science stated publicly that "there are two kinds of political theorists we don't want in this department—Leninists and Straussians", this in connection with the denial of tenure to a Straussian.)

The ideal of total openness is also compromised by a brute physical fact—it is simply impossible to teach "everything". Colleges and universities are constantly engaged in the process of deciding (sometimes for philosophical reasons, sometimes for economic reasons) that certain things will or will not be taught. Professors in the classroom cannot possibly present the totality of their subjects. They continually make decisions as to what to include and what to omit.

While Catholic institutions are frequently under suspicion for imposing religion on their students, little notice is taken of the odd anomaly whereby many institutions of higher learning (especially those under state sponsorship) do not even have departments of religious studies.

Religion has been the most deeply rooted phenomenon in human history, but there are colleges and universities which seemingly believe that it is sufficient if their students learn about it in snatches and fragments, in history, literature, or art classes. Not uncommonly, this omission is not mere obtuseness; it reflects the antireligious sentiments of faculty themselves. Leaving aside its dogmatic claims, the study of Christianity, and especially of Catholicism, provides a key for the widest and most comprehensive approach to the study of Western civilization.

At a minimum Catholic colleges and universities ought to be able to assume a high degree of interest in religion on the part of their students. Furthermore, they have a right to assume that being a Catholic implies a certain view of the world and that one of the major purposes of Catholic higher education is to explore that world view systematically and in depth. Those who find the Catholic world view unacceptable or repugnant will presumably not choose to attend Catholic institutions. Trying to accommodate them is destructive to the whole process of Catholic education.

Catholic education does not necessarily presume belief—it ought to be possible to educate students in the Catholic tradition merely by showing that it is coherent and plausible. But plausibility is important. It should also be the purpose of Catholic education, assuming the presence of committed teachers, to show at least the formidability of that tradition, that it must be taken seriously and respected even if finally rejected. In the real order it is likely that a high percentage of faculty and students in a Catholic institution will be believers.

Catholicism impinges on the educational process most comprehensively and most obviously with regard to ethics, a subject from which no other subject in the curriculum is entirely divorced, except perhaps pure mathematics. Almost every other discipline has practical applications which require moral judgments on the part of its practitioners. Thus future physicians, lawyers, accountants, physicists, and computer specialists must have a solid grounding in morality, taught both as philosophy and as theology. A Catholic institution can never content itself with simply training its students in technical skills.

However, the relevance of religion and morality to professional training is not exhausted by ethics in the narrowest sense. One of the most poignant signs of the inadequacies of present Catholic education is the way in which this relationship is now often discharged by a single course in ethics (sometimes not even by that). All education is personal as well as theoretical. Especially in professional education students learn what it means to be responsible practitioners of a discipline by seeing others who are already such practitioners. Catholic professional schools will, therefore, confront their students with professors who are living examples of competent, responsible professionalism wedded to religious and moral commitment.

Although ethics is the obvious rubric under which the moral and religious dimensions of professional education are discussed, it is important to recognize that the questions involved here are really metaphysical—what does it mean to be human? what can legitimately be done to and for human beings? what is a just society? If professional ethical training is approached primarily as a specialized set of rules imposed in particular cases, it will seem to many students rather arbitrary. In every profession now the important ethical questions transcend the limits of the profession itself.

Catholic schools are in an advantageous position in this regard because Catholic ethical theory grows out of a whole nexus of thought and belief, as well as a long and deep tradition, in which these basic questions have been endlessly debated and explored. In the end professional ethics is unpersuasive divorced from a wider view of human nature and human society, which the Catholic tradition is almost uniquely equipped to impart. For this reason students enrolled in a Catholic professional school who lack the background of Catholic education may find it difficult to relate to a course in professional ethics as such. For the same reason, the education which a Catholic university gives to preprofessional students may be even more important than that which it gives in the professional schools themselves.

In professional ethics as elsewhere, the most destructive temptation for the Catholic colleges is likely to be excessive professionalization. Usually this takes the form of an approach to professional ethics which simply seeks to justify whatever it is that professionals do. (This is most obvious with regard to medicine, but can apply to other areas, such as business.)

The natural sciences and applied mathematics are perhaps the farthest removed from any readily definable relationship with Catholic doctrine, except as they too have their ethical dimensions (e.g., the uses of nuclear power). However, in all disciplines a Catholic school should boast of faculty who are highly conscious of the ultimate significance of divine creation. While this may not influence the specific way in which a professor teaches physics or chemistry, it means that he is ready to discuss with students, and with other faculty members, the possible religious implications of scientific theories (as in the work of Stanley Jaki). Perhaps not a great deal of time will be spent on this in the classroom, but an occasional lecture, even an occasional passing remark, can be a great stimulus to student thinking and toward students' being able to integrate their educations into some kind of totality.

If the social sciences are commonly taught in a "value-free", behavioristic way in American colleges and universities, there is no excuse for this in an institution calling itself Catholic. As with other disciplines, students should naturally be taught the requisite professional methods. But a genuinely Catholic education must go far beyond that.

The key issues are again metaphysical—who is man? what is a just society?

The social sciences cannot be pursued properly if they are pursued only in their own terms. This requires, once again, faculty who are sensitive to the entire Catholic tradition, willing to explore relationships between their disciplines and the widest possible context of belief and thought.

At a minimum Catholic departments of social sciences should manifest a particular interest in the classical traditions in their own disciplines — political theory, classical social, and economic thought. This is not because the masters of the past are automatically conceded supremacy but because it is in these classical traditions that the fundamental questions are discussed. Their study thus serves to give the student a point of contact between a specialized modern discipline and the kind of religious and philosophical considerations which ought to inform it.

As with professional ethics, the study of the social sciences in Catholic schools must negotiate a balance between absolute principles (as to what constitutes man or what constitutes a just society) and sometimes untidy realities. (In economics students would study not only Catholic teaching concerning a just economic order but also the way in which the modern economy functions in practice. Every effort should be made to bring about some kind of meeting point, so that the demands of one do not do violence to the legitimate claims of the other.)

In the humanities it can be naturally assumed that faculty and students have a greater than average interest in religious themes, as developed in art, music, and literature. There will be an immediate recognition process, whereby symbols, allusions, and language have a significance which they may not have for nonbelievers. Humanities departments in Catholic schools will emphasize the pervasive influence of religion on the whole of Western culture.

But humanities properly taught are not merely academic exercises. They are studied precisely to illumine the human situation. Thus, in a Catholic school, it is assumed that what might be called religious dilemmas and religious experiences are real to faculty and students. Poems and novels on religious themes will be studied because they are found to have an urgency and a personal relevance which they may not have for others. Through them the individual seeks to explore and ultimately resolve the dilemmas posed by a lived faith. What may be absent from one's own life can be experienced imaginatively, and one of the purposes of religious art is to enable people precisely to experience their faith in a more intense way than they might ordinarily do.

History partakes of the character of both the social sciences and the humanities, and what has been said about both can be said about it. Given the profound influence of Christianity on Western civilization (including America), it does no violence to the integrity of the historian to devote a great deal of attention to religious history, especially the interrelationship between religion and culture, perhaps most extensively explored in the works of Christopher Dawson. In Catholic schools students and faculty will be people for whom religious subjects have an immediate meaning, and toward which they find themselves drawn by curiosity, if nothing more.

More ambitiously (in practice seldom achieved), it ought to be the task of the Catholic historian to contribute to an understanding of the relationship between time and eternity, to identify those points at which the historians' skills become inadequate to a full illumination of man's place in the world, those points in time which offer glimpses of eternity.

The study of philosophy was for many years the center of the Catholic college curriculum, mainly in terms of a single philosophical system—Thomism—which was deemed an adequate foundation for all other knowledge. The decline of Thomism since about 1965 has left most Catholic colleges precisely as philosophical smorgasbords. Since philosophy must be the integrating discipline beneath all others, students are thus left, in terms of the integration of their own educations, largely to the personal predilections of the teachers under whom they happen to study.

As in other disciplines, philosophers in Catholic schools will find the direction of their thought, and the form which it takes, deeply affected by the fact of belief and by the cultural tradition of Christianity. For them certain questions will have special meaning which they may not have for nonbelievers.

The place of theology in a Catholic college or university hardly needs emphasis. However, as the experience of the past twenty years has shown, it is by no means certain what Catholic theology is.

A liberal education requires that students be exposed to other religious traditions besides their own. Catholics must know something about Protestantism, Christians about non-Christian religions. However, such knowledge cannot be a substitute for knowledge of Catholicism itself. If students graduate from a Catholic college knowing little about Catholic theology, there has been a failure not only from the standpoint of faith but in terms of liberal education itself.

Part of the function of theology within the framework of Catholic liberal education is to deepen students' understanding of their faith. There is a presupposition of faith, not necessarily in the sense of personal belief but in the sense that the existence of the Catholic tradition is taken for granted and respected. It is assumed that an exploration of that tradition is valid and indeed essential.

The primary purpose of Catholic theology should be to explore and illumine the traditions of the Church itself. The theologian should also bring that tradition into relationship with the contemporary world in all its fullness. However, within the total context of the curriculum, theology's principal task is to illumine the tradition. Much of the work of relating it to the modern world will be done, ideally, elsewhere than in the theology department, by scholars in other disciplines who are committed and learned in their faith.

In all disciplines, professional or liberal arts, Catholic scholars ought to be distinguished by their sensitivity to certain questions, their curiosity about certain realities which might elude the nonbeliever. For example, a Catholic psychologist might be drawn to explore the moral implications of humanistic psychology, as Paul Vitz does in his book *Psychology as Religion*. A Catholic sociologist is likely to have special concern for the family as the foundation of society and to be sensitive to those things which strengthen or weaken it. A Catholic student of art or literature will be attuned to the metaphysical implications of various artistic visions.

As noted, no college or university can do everything. This may mean, in the practical order, that a Catholic institution will choose to strengthen certain departments at the expense of others or that certain programs will not be started because they seem relatively remote from the institution's major commitment. Students' schedules are also finite, and it may be that in the course of four years a student will learn less about certain things in order to learn more about the things which have a discernible relationship to the Catholic tradition. There is no embarrassment in this so long as it is recognized that such negotiations go on in all institutions and are a necessary part of every education. The key question is whether the Catholic tradition does provide a valid focal point for education. If the answer is no, then there is no excuse for Catholic colleges. If the answer is yes, then it is necessary that such schools have purpose, direction, self-consciousness, all those things which make meaningful intellectual community possible.

At present very few institutions exist which answer to this prescription. Even under the best of circumstances, given the process of drift and disintegration over the past twenty years, it is difficult to see how such institutions can recover their Catholicism fully. As a new wave of "neo-Catholic" colleges are founded, it remains to be seen whether those institutions which have historically borne the Catholic name possess either the ability or the will to save themselves.

A CHILD OF HIS TIMES

Larry, aged forty, has just returned to his hometown in the Midwest after several years in California. He is living with his two children, both in grammar school, on a farm on the outskirts of a metropolitan area.

Larry is divorced, and his ex-wife legally has custody of the children. However, at the end of one visit he simply failed to send them back. She is married and living in another state, and she has not made an issue of the matter. Larry has a middle-level management position with a company in the city and sleeps in town several nights a week, at which time the children are on their own. He justifies keeping the children from their mother on the grounds that "she won't give them the kind of attention I do."

There is more than crude rationalization in this seeming contradiction, however, for Larry is convinced that the usual criteria of good parenting not only do not apply in his case but, in fact, are generally pernicious. To have his children raised in a conventional suburban setting would be to corrupt them and handicap them for life. His own frequent absences are mild disadvantages by comparison and have the benefit of freeing the children psychologically from dependence on a parent. The traditional family, in Larry's view, is the source of most of the world's problems, since it imparts attitudes of closed-mindedness and possessiveness toward both goods and people. The worst expression of these attitudes is traditional sexual morality, which Larry regards as the root of most other evils.

When Larry and Rita's marriage broke up their friends were surprised, but not for the usual reasons. Infidelities on both sides had been so common for years that there seemed little reason for them to divorce. What insult, people wondered, could still give offense to either? Why bother with the complications of a legal divorce? The reasons for the divorce are still not clear to outsiders.

Larry and Rita were both raised in fairly strict Catholic families and attended religious schools at every level. Rita's piety was conventional and unreflective; it was, apparently, shed with little trauma. Larry tended to go through alternating periods of rebellious skepticism and intense belief before giving religion up permanently shortly after he got married.

Until women's liberation penetrated the rather provincial circle in which he moved, Larry was a classic male chauvinist. In college he used to say that he would never marry a girl unless he was convinced that, if he told her they were moving out of town the next day, she would start packing without even asking why. Rita appeared to be such a girl, someone who was psychically and perhaps even physically deenergized, passively willing to have someone tell her what to think, say, even wear. Although her entire set of conscious values must have been affronted, she complied with Larry's request, first, that she pose for hundreds of nude photographs; second, that she permit these to be shown around (once at Larry's high-school reunion); and, finally, that she participate in various kinds of sexual activities with a widening circle of friends and acquaintances. While married, Rita gave practically no overt indication that she disliked any of this. Afterward Larry was indignant that she complained of coercion.

Today Larry buys the whole ideology of women's liberation almost without reservation, and he can chuckle over the fact that Rita went to her first "consciousness-raising" sessions on his orders. At that point, he still wanted a wife who was subservient to him, but one who could also entertain the daring ideas that seemed to make life more interesting. Since his divorce Larry has preferred much younger women who combine sexual liberation with an independent attitude. For a time he lived with a girl of admitted lesbian tastes, and he took it as a compliment that she found him satisfying. But she moved out after a few months, and he now recognizes that marriage is for him psychologically impossible, even if it were theoretically desirable. Among other things, he no longer finds his sexual appetites very urgent.

As sex starts to recede as a major obsession, private property, always a close second, seems to move up. Larry has no theoretical case against private property, merely a visceral antagonism toward it. He has not read enough to be even an elementary Marxist, and he is in any case casually contemptuous of both politicians and intellectuals. He has, however, roughly divided the world into two classes: those who possess too much property and those who possess too little; and he sees much of life as a continuing combat between the two.

Membership in the deprived group is not based on measurable criteria. At certain periods of his life Larry has probably had an annual income approaching $50,000, yet he has never ceased thinking of himself as a member of the class of people being "ripped off" by the wealthy. He regards virtually all violent crime as economically motivated and dismisses as irrelevant the fact that many street criminals are better off than their victims. Being oppressed is a state of mind, he insists, and if a man believes himself to be oppressed no one can legitimately tell him he is not.

Larry and a friend once devised a rather simple but almost foolproof scheme for cashing bad checks in supermarkets, using several bank accounts newly opened under aliases. The ease of it delighted him more than the money. Twice his power lawnmower was stolen from his garage. Each time he found it ridiculously easy to carry a replacement out of a store. While he would not claim that the store "owed" him a replacement, at some level of his being he seems to believe that. In any case the store is seen as an obscenely rich institution which deserves to be victimized.

At the same time Larry is anything but greedy. At several points in his life he has given up well-paying jobs he found unsatisfying. Once he invested a substantial sum of money in a small business, and although he strongly suspected the manager was cheating him, he did nothing about it. Eventually he moved away without even claiming his investment.

Since Larry's level of reflection falls short of the philosophical, he cannot be said exactly to be proving a point in his assaults on retail establishments. Rather he has a deeply rooted visceral need to punish them in some way, based on an image of a world divided between "us" and "them" in which "them" is the impersonal corporation. People constantly point out to him that shoplifting losses are passed on to the customers, so that it is Larry's neighbors who are being robbed by his actions. He dismisses this, however, as corporate propaganda. Larry can be generous in his dealings with individuals, and even forgetful of personal injuries. But it is of the essence of his working creed that he acknowledge no such thing as social obligation. To entertain the possibility that by shoplifting he is robbing ordinary people would be to recognize such an obligation, to posit a web of relationships he has spent most of his adult life denying. In traditional religious terms, he is capable of occasional acts of charity while virtually denying the reality of justice, except as it applies to individuals who feel aggrieved by "the system".

During the 1960s he held conventional left-liberal opinions, although he was never an activist. Since the government, especially in such incarnations as the army and the police, was self-evidently an institution that existed to oppress individuals, he found it easy to adopt practically the whole New Left outlook. He remained outside the movement per se because he saw political action as boring and pointless, the activists themselves as naive and ridiculously self-important.

In the end, Larry was one of those people for whom the New Left was merely an unsatisfying rehearsal for the counterculture. To assert one's defiance of the draft, or to support the claims of aggrieved social groups, failed to get at the heart of the problem, which was the need for a systematic rejection of all forms of restraint on the self. After the outer layers had been peeled away, it was institutions with spiritual claims on people—churches, marriage, and the family, finally morality itself—that were found to be the most oppressive.

As a fairly typical product of the 1950s, Larry had been part of the beer-drinking culture, which was initially hostile to drug-users. Before long, however, he discovered that drugs could indeed be pleasurable, and the fact that they were forbidden by law greatly enhanced their attractiveness. Using drugs was both an act of defiance of social conventions and an important step along the road to total sensual fulfillment. In Larry's mind, the greatest evil (closely linked with, and ultimately more serious than, private property) came to be the denial to anyone of the right to follow his sensual instincts. He regarded narcotics officers, for example, as self-evidently evil people, a particular case of police in general.

Seemingly devoid of self-destructive impulses, Larry always used drugs moderately. Today, however, he can refer casually to the deterioration of his memory as a direct result of his indulgence. He has seen people ruined by drugs, as he has seen numerous marriages ruined by the kind of sexual adventurism he has promoted. To some extent he seems to regard these breakdowns almost benignly, as if they represented creative personal choices; in any case, in his view they have desirable social results in further undermining established social conventions. Insofar as he acknowledges the undeniably bad effects of sensual self-indulgence, he seems to believe that the good effects are worth the price.

Until women's liberation forced him to adopt a different style, Larry was incorrigibly "macho". He once threw a homosexual hitchhiker into the street, an act which he boasted about for some time afterward. His sexual instincts are still uniformly heterosexual. But he admits it is important in his world to remain "open to all experiences". He also recognizes the ideological importance of the "gay rights" movement as an assault on traditional moral and social values, and thus he supports it.

As we have noted, Larry was never really political, although he held most of the fashionable New Left opinions ten years ago. However, at one point in his life he was motivated at least in part by a kind of moral idealism. He left a well-paid executive job to teach in a ghetto school, and for a time he lived in a largely black neighborhood, his instincts making it easy for him to identify with an underclass resentful of an oppressive Establishment.

He left his ghetto school without warning in the middle of the semester, after a quarrel with the principal, and, since he habitually used false addresses to avoid bill collectors, the school was unable to contact him. For days the principal was not even sure if Larry was coming back.

This break apparently marked the beginning of his disillusionment with even the semblance of idealistic politics. His hatred of "the Establishment" receded not at all. However, his antiestablishmentarianism now expanded paradoxically to include almost everyone who claimed to be on the side of the oppressed. In particular it included black "militants" of all kinds, whom he came to regard as self-seeking hypocrites.

Now Larry spices his conversation with overtly racist remarks, partly to shock his liberal friends who can no longer be shocked by his ideas about sex, but in the main probably out of sincerity. He regards all strategies for racial integration as further examples of dictatorial repressiveness on the part of the Establishment and openly proclaims that he has chosen to live on a farm so his children will not have to attend school with blacks. Even if he were not personally hostile to blacks, of course, he would still have to reject without compromise the notion that white people have any kind of moral obligation toward them. Such a concept of human relations is utterly outside his powers of imagination. The very idea of "obligation" is translated into "imposition".

Since his antipolice and antimilitary attitudes were already fairly well formed before the New Left gave them intellectual respectability, they remain almost entirely unchanged, if somewhat less fanatical. Larry presents the paradox of the pacifist who does not believe in the sanctity of human life. For him pacifism, while an absolute, is not arrived at positively; it is dictated by a series of negative imperatives: there is nothing in the world worth fighting for; society cannot make demands of this kind upon its members; wars serve only the interests of the Establishment; war implies some illusory transcendent moral or social purpose in life. It is precisely because of his profound *indifference* to the fate of others that Larry finds the idea of war unthinkable.

Larry does admit to a lingering, essentially atavistic sense that human life is somehow sacred. He has never been a physically violent person, and he tells his children it is best to avoid fistfights whenever possible. (Over the years he has sometimes preferred theft or vandalism as means of revenge against those who have offended him.) However, when asked directly if he thinks human life embodies a kind of moral absolute, he first temporizes and then says no. There seem to be two key considerations for him. One is his need to keep all "options" open, not to close off any possibilities of conduct, especially when established opinion has declared them forbidden. The other is the fact that one of the few things that call forth his unreserved respect is some act of daring iconoclasm. He has a sneaking, or not so sneaking, admiration for the individual who resorts to direct and violent deeds to get what he wants or to thwart a perceived oppressor. Killing is, after all, the ultimate act of self-assertion, the ultimate rejection of established values, the ultimate catharsis of personal frustrations.

Another of Larry's very small but serviceable stock of negative absolutes is the imperative never to pass moral judgment on any kind of human behavior, especially that which runs counter to social respectability. The undeniable fact that innocent people are slain every day must be brushed aside, apparently on the understanding that killers wouldn't kill unless their impulse was very strong.

The very word "moral" grates on Larry's ears, irredeemably tied as it is to notions of social respectability and establishmentarian repression. Those who claim to know the difference between right and wrong seem to him to be trying to proclaim themselves better than others. Morality is simply a ploy to gain certain kinds of social control. Larry is genuinely tolerant even of "straight" people, so long as they give no hint of thinking their way of life rests on anything other than personal preference.

Systematically open to every new idea, Larry in the late 1970s came upon the philosophy of "mellow". By nature combative and obsessedly vigilant against violations of his rights, he now smiles tolerantly even at deliberate insults, remains relatively calm even in the midst of passionate argument, and shows no disposition to get revenge for palpable injuries like the loss of his money in the business venture.

The philosophy of "mellow" has come to serve a practically indispensable function in Larry's life, in a way rather reminiscent of Hobbesian political philosophy. At bottom, Larry seems to view life as the warfare of innumerable self-interests, some of them using hypocritical idealism as a cloak. There is thus no moral basis for imposing either self-control or restraints on others. The logical result would seem to be precisely the self-destructive predatoriness which Hobbes foresaw (for example, when asked what would happen if everyone acted as he does with regard to property, Larry cheerfully admits that the results might be chaotic). "Mellow" allows for a respite from this strife which is wholly amoral and has the additional advantage of being fashionable. The point of being mellow, in Larry's case, is that getting upset at what others do is simply allowing others to impose yet another mode of control.

Although Larry is a college graduate, his degree was in business, and insofar as he has attempted to form a view of the world which is at all philosophical he is essentially an autodidact. Through all his years of schooling (he even put in a bit of time in graduate school) he has managed to retain the pugnacious suspiciousness toward learning which is characteristic of self-conscious graduates of the school of hard knocks. He takes no idea seriously unless he has somehow discovered it for himself, and he remains convinced that most people who claim to know anything about the world are self-important frauds. He enjoys classical music as a sensuous experience. However, almost all other aspects of high culture remain closed to him. He is continually revolving ideas which philosophers and novelists have probed for centuries, but he remains both oblivious to this history and wholly incurious.

In the odd way characteristic of many autodidacts, he is simultaneously densely resistant to outside influences and highly impressionable. Friends sometimes discover, after hours of intense discussion, that he has understood their arguments hardly at all, since his own categories of understanding are so ironclad that they cannot easily admit new data. On the other hand, these same friends are also startled when they learn that a chance remark of theirs, dropped years before, has been part of Larry's mental furniture ever since, because at some moment in time it was the precise tool needed to articulate an obscurely felt instinct.

Larry reads relatively little. For a time, what used to be called men's magazines constituted his chief literary diet, and he absorbed Hugh Hefner's "playboy philosophy" almost as if it were written for him personally (although, characteristically, he also regarded Hefner as pompous and long-winded). His great intellectual discovery in the mid-1960s was the "human potential" movement, and for a time he devoured writers like Thomas Harris (*I'm OK, You're OK*) and Eric Berne (*Games People Play*).

It is doubtful, however, that Larry is open to a genuinely new idea. What these writers did for him was mainly to articulate a way of looking at the world which corresponded to his inveterate feelings and at the same time to give those feelings a certain respectability. Regardless of what the authors may have intended, what Larry took from them was the lesson that self-assertiveness is the essence of life, that all moral claims are impositions by others, and that personal feelings and desires largely define acceptable and unacceptable behavior. For most of his life Larry had been taught about duty and restraint, concepts at which he was usually inclined to thumb his nose. Suddenly it dawned on him that the most "advanced" thinkers in his culture were doing exactly the same thing.

In essence, what the cultural revolution of the past twenty years has done for Larry is to legitimize *ressentiment*, to make it unnecessary to discriminate between a genuine thirst for freedom and justice, on the one hand, and envy and willful indifference, on the other.

Ostensibly Larry is hopeful about the long-range future of society, and he has spun out a rather complex if hardly original theory whereby, if children are raised in a wholly permissive environment, they will not develop those neuroses — possessiveness, insecurity, craving for order — which are the root of all the world's problems. Although he found the book excessively abstract and naive, fundamentally he agrees with Charles Reich's *The Greening of America*, especially its dismissal of political action as a means of social change, with psychological transformation taking its place. In an odd way, despite his contempt for the marketplace, Larry espouses a psychic theory parallel to Adam Smith's economic laws: If each person consistently follows his or her pleasure-seeking instincts, the ultimate result cannot help but be beneficial to all.

At the same time, however, one quickly senses a kind of restless nihilism at the root of Larry's ideologies. His life follows a pattern in which sooner or later every apparently positive element — marriage, career, business — is destroyed. What seems to be involved is nothing so simple as a self-destructive impulse. It is rather an extreme case of the kind of narcissistic solipsism which has been identified as the besetting psychic disorder of the age. On one level, he cannot believe that anything outside himself is real. On another level, insofar as he acknowledges external reality, he finds it threatening and oppressive. The only world in which he is comfortable is one entirely of his own making, one in which everything external is transformed to his liking.

Larry's "idealistic" phase of life, roughly coinciding with the earlier, idealistic phase of the New Left, was lived in service to a nihilistic purpose not understood at the time even by Larry. Conventional morality, and the institutions which embodied that morality, could be attacked and ultimately destroyed in the name of a higher morality. But once socially reinforced values had been discredited, what remained for people like Larry was not a higher morality but no morality at all, a cynicism so deep that it did not even need to express itself in the cynic's usual mocking sallies. The urge to negate, to discredit, to destroy whatever is established is now purely reflexive; it goes into operation with scarcely any conscious advertence. Thus, Larry can admit without embarrassment that the prospect of an America annihilated by some enemy is not altogether unpleasing to him. He cannot conceive that anyone could be so attached to the existing conditions of life as to be willing to defend them to the death.

In fairness to Hugh Hefner, it might be said that Larry is perhaps not exactly the product the "playboy philosophy" was intended to spawn. Yet he is a product which could have been easily predicted. If the disease of solipsism is not the creation of the "self-fulfillment" prophets of the past two decades, they nonetheless have functioned rather like physicians prescribing sugar to diabetics. Rarely in history has there been so obvious a case of the cure being worse than the disease or, more accurately, a cause of the disease. Larry is the result, not of the honorable tradition of liberalism itself, but of what Leopold Tyrmand has called liberal culture, that is, the final debasement of liberalism into the indiscriminate huckstering of whatever calls itself by the name of freedom.

How typical is Larry? Obviously he is an unusually well-developed "ideal type", met with in pure form somewhat rarely. But he is representative of a type which attracts open or covert admiration from many other people, some of them in influential social positions, who for various reasons fall short of living that way themselves, rather as a devout Catholic might admire monks without intending to become one.

Larry is part of the living evidence of the permanent victories which the counterculture has won in America, victories so thoroughly ratified that to the unobservant they might pass unnoticed. It is important to recognize, however, that what engages his energies is not simply a continuation of the social and cultural battles of the decade past. The very notion of a battle in that sense is already foreign to Larry's evolved temperament. The question he contemplates is not whether human society should be transformed, and how, but whether it should exist at all. For many persons of Larry's generation, this remains an open question.

GUILT AND THE MORAL REVOLUTION

The *Police Gazette*, probably America's most popular "men's magazine" of the late nineteenth century, was fond of comments like, "They drink the way clergymen drink—on the sly." Clergy were almost never mentioned in the journal except as self-righteous hypocrites, secretly addicted to the vices which they publicly condemned.

Such a conceit is surely one of the most rooted and even primitive of human instincts—to shout "You're one too" at anyone whose social task it is to announce moral judgments. In fact it was probably a minority of American clergy who condemned drink totally even in 1895, and it was certainly a tiny minority who were secret tipplers or adulterers. But it was a necessary part of the *Police Gazette's* view of the world to imply that any moral censure directed at itself or its readers was poisoned at the source.

In the second half of the twentieth century the closest approximation of the *Police Gazette* in America has been Hugh Hefner's *Playboy*. The *Gazette* seems for the most part to have been read in saloons and barber shops. *Playboy* was for a long time sold under the counter and kept hidden in the bottom of drawers at home. But unlike the *Gazette*, *Playboy* finally achieved respectability. In 1980 Hefner was the guest of honor at a testimonial fête whose host was the senior senator from Illinois, Charles Percy.

The revolution which made *Playboy* respectable was to a great extent a self-propelled revolution. It was Hefner who pulled the strings that turned him and his empire from pariahs into comfortable fixtures of the establishment. Many means were used to that end, including the lavish distribution of money to persuade respectable people to write for the magazine. Part of the means was also Hefner's tedious, seemingly interminable "playboy philosophy", spun out through issue after issue during the 1960s.

Almost no one ever made a serious study of Hefner's turgid prose, and it is doubtful if very many people even read it carefully. But the playboy philosophy was so repetitive that it was not necessary to read it regularly in order to understand it. Occasional samples were sure to yield a microcosm of the whole.

Those who took such samples were treated to something rather similar to the *Police Gazette's* jibes at the clergy. But whereas the *Gazette* had merely dealt a few glancing blows, *Playboy* aimed at nothing less than the total discrediting of those who held to traditional sexual morality. Even Hefner's audience would probably have been sceptical of the claim that all moralists secretly practice the vices they condemn, although he implied as much from time to time. His guns were trained higher, and his bold claim was that traditional

44

moralists, whether or not they practice what they preach, are rigid, insecure, unloving, and destructive.

The *Police Gazette* was content to claim that its readers were no worse than the common run of humanity and that those who claimed to be better were the same under the skin. *Playboy* went a step farther—those who fall under the censure of moralists are themselves superior to those who condemn them. In Hefner's world vice came to be virtue and virtue vice, and the "immoralists" were revealed as those whose morality, essentially that of "openness" and "tolerance", is actually superior.

Both Hefner and Richard K. Fox, the publisher of the *Police Gazette*, exploited one of the most basic of human impulses—that of denying one's own moral culpability by calling attention to that of others, particularly one's accusers. (It is the instinctive weapon of children caught in some transgression.) To a degree it touches a sensitive moral point—when we contemplate our own sins, who can condemn others?

But it also misses the point. Good preachers have always spoken in the first person in condemning sin, and it is finally irrelevant whether moralists themselves have clean hands. The purpose of the Fox–Hefner strategy is not to deepen public awareness of sin by revealing more of it, but to deny all sin by implying that virtue itself is not real. The moralist is subjected to scrutiny not as a flawed individual but precisely as a representative of the moral order. What is held up to ridicule is not the man but the morality which he represents.

Friedrich Nietzsche discovered what he called *"ressentiment"* at the root of Christian morality. Put simply, it is the revenge of life's losers against those whom they see placed over them.[1] Thus, according to Nietzsche, Christianity gave birth to a "slave morality" in which humility was honored instead of manly pride, meekness over a warrior's boldness, poverty instead of wealth. The lowly Christians avenged themselves on their Roman persecutors finally by erecting a moral structure which, in the name of a higher idealism, destroyed all that the Romans valued.

The phenomenologist philosopher Max Scheler (1874–1928), was fascinated with Nietzsche's concept but also determined to acquit Christianity of the charge. Scheler, while admitting that it is often hard to distinguish genuine Christian love from some form of *ressentiment*, nevertheless insisted that such love is real and has nothing in common with its counterfeits. It is pure and transforming.[2]

[1] See particularly *The Genealogy of Morals*, published along with *The Birth of Tragedy*, trans. Francis Golffing (Garden City, N.Y.: Doubleday, 1956).
[2] *Ressentiment*, trans. William W. Holdheim, with an introduction by Lewis Coser (New York: Schocken Books, 1972). The original German edition was published in 1912, expanded in 1915.

Defined succinctly, Scheler's version of *ressentiment* is the desire to smash pedestals. More fully, he described it as feelings of envy, malice, and resentment directed by the weak and impotent against those who appear nobler, and certainly more privileged, than themselves. It was essential to Scheler's definition that this be largely unconscious. He believed that those who engage in overt acts of hostility—criminals, for example, or a militant proletariat—are less likely to experience *ressentiment*. It is in the nature of the latter to disguise itself. It often erects ambitious and ostensibly idealistic moralities whose real purpose is to get revenge on enemies.

The enemies, however, are not such in the ordinary sense. *Ressentiment* is not directed at those who have perpetrated some specific and undeniable injury or injustice. Properly speaking, *ressentiment* does not even apply to classes of people who might be thought of as oppressors in a Marxist sense. Finally, for Scheler, certain people inspire *ressentiment* simply because of who they are. It is their very existence which is hated, not anything they have done.

Scheler's analysis is most easily seen in a quasi-political context. In traditional aristocratic societies, for example, conscious thought concedes to the aristocracy their right to a superior position. Unconsciously, however, *ressentiment* builds up, expressing itself, perhaps, in a popular fascination with the misfortunes of the privileged. However, Scheler saw it as expressing itself in certain essentially nonpolitical ways also, for example, the stereotyped prudish censoriousness of the spinster as deriving from her resentment of those who have found in life the happiness which has eluded her.

Social distinctions imply distinctions of worth and thereby invite *ressentiment*. However, the levelling process proves to be endless, because societies which have gone far in the direction of abolishing social distinctions cannot do so perfectly. Some people simply remain more attractive, more creative, more energetic, more talented, more likable than others. Scheler suspected that *ressentiment* would be minimized in modern democratic societies and would be most evident in those societies in which an official ideology of equality is at variance with the continued reality of social class, as in England. However, in this and in other ways Scheler failed to grasp all the implications of the phenomenon he was describing. For even those societies which have gone far in the abolition of social distinctions merely invite ever more microscopic scrutiny of their structures. The New Left of the 1960s was extremely adept at uncovering remnants of "hypocrisy" among its older liberal allies.

However, Scheler was quite perceptive in noticing that political and class distinctions are finally not at the heart of *ressentiment*. Morality is. It is the claim of some, whether implicit or explicit, conscious or unconscious, to represent an authoritative truth which inspires the bitterest hostility. It might even be argued that all social and political claims imply moral claims and that this is why they are ultimately hated, with political or economic griev-ances put forth primarily as rationalizations for much deeper resentments.

Ressentiment issues in moral nihilism for two reasons. On a superficial level it manifests the *Police Gazette* mentality—those who claim to speak with moral authority must be put in their place; hence morality itself must be discredited. However, if a way could be found to convey moral judgments in some wholly impersonal fashion, the problem would not be obviated. For *ressentiment* is ultimately directed at the fact of morality itself, an authority outside the self by which the self is judged and, virtually always, found want-ing. This sense of being under judgment, of always falling short of what one ought to be, can be neurotic and crippling. However, it is also the greatest force for moral improvement within human affairs. The alternative is a self-satisfaction which gradually turns into moral insensitivity and cynicism.

Scheler identified the religious apostate as perhaps the purest example of *ressentiment*—the individual who has rejected a creed once held and has done so with passion and even hatred. The apostate spends the whole of his life at war with his former beliefs, which obviously have a hold over him that re-mains constantly threatening.

It is in religious apostasy that the real nature of *ressentiment* is also un-covered. For on a conscious and rational level the apostate declares his former beliefs to be false and pernicious. However, if this were the whole of the story such beliefs would simply be thrust out of mind and never recalled. The bit-terness of the apostate, his obsession with his rejected faith, is due precisely to his rooted suspicion that his former beliefs are indeed true. He continues to hate his old creed, and often the hatred increases with the years, because it continues to stand in judgment over him. It is because he cannot help suspect-ing that the creed is indeed true that he hates it with such fury. As Scheler put it, *ressentiment* falsifies values, but the falsification proves to be transparent, and through the false values the outlines of the true ones can still be dimly perceived. *Ressentiment* is directed at something which at the deepest level of his being the individual recognizes as good. Although there may be evil mixed with it (as in the sinful preacher), it is not the evil which is hated primarily but the good. Dwelling on the evil is *ressentiment*'s ploy for attack-ing the good.

The phenomenon of religious apostasy, still a somewhat rarified thing in Scheler's day, is now endemic. It has descended from the realm of the intellec-tuals to the general populace. There is scarcely a popular magazine, news-paper, or television series in the United States which does not manifest its ef-fects with some degree of regularity. Whereas formerly the prevailing popu-lar view was that religion is healthy and comforting, saving the individual from disorder and loss, the mass media now hold that religion is almost always a deforming neurosis, a crippler of the free human spirit, not only a deceit but a destructive one. This idea is now purveyed to the public in count-less ways.

An important test of the health of a religion is precisely its ability to pro-duce embittered apostates. Those religions which do not are not genuine. For religion, if it is true to what it is supposed to be, penetrates very deeply into the human person, and of its very essence it holds the individual up to judg-ment. Modern liberal religion has seen many of its adherents drift away, but it has produced no apostates in the true sense. There is no literature by and about ex-Unitarians. Those who do give up their religious upbringing may express varying degrees of contempt for it, but they cannot hate it and they are never obsessed with it, because it never made a deep enough impression on their personalities for *ressentiment* to develop.

It is no accident that, even in the America of a century ago, antireligious *ressentiment* clustered around the so-called "personal sins". Given the Vic-torian reticence about sex, the *Police Gazette* had alcohol as its sore point. In the past twenty years, however, traditional religion has come under ferocious assault, an assault often approaching gale force, because of its teachings about sexual behavior.

Liberal religion has diverted the gale from itself by offering a bland smile and the assurance, "We're not here to lay guilt on you." Much of its intellec-tual ingenuity has been devoted to finding ways of justifying what human beings actually do, so as to avoid having to pronounce moral judgments. On one level, the strategy has worked—the existence of a large body of "enlightened" clergy, and of entire "enlightened" denominations, is now recognized, and *ressentiment*'s attack can be concentrated on those religious figures, mostly Catholics and evangelical Protestants, who remain outside the enlightened consensus. The strategy, however, is extremely short-sighted. A religion which disturbs no one is also a religion which is of little use to anyone. It makes itself irrelevant in the very act of seeking relevance.

The spokesmen for liberal religion protest that it is indeed their aim to discomfit people, that they preach a stern gospel of righteous judgment. Their focus, however, is not on personal sin, especially sexuality, but on "social sin", which has numerous political ramifications.

If such preaching were really effective, however, society would be littered with embittered refugees from the liberal churches, endlessly picking at the scabs of their old wounds, just as apostates from the more conservative churches do now. The unadmitted secret is that few people take the social pronouncements of the liberal churches very seriously, however much lip service is paid to their alleged wisdom. Those whose political beliefs already incline them in that direction respond to such pronouncements with enthusi-asm. Others may express annoyance or outrage at what they consider a per-version of faith, but for the most part those who do not accept such judg-ments merely shrug them off.

This has nothing to do with the inherent rightness or wrongness of the judgments themselves but with the nature of social morality. Judgments about sexual morality cut deep precisely because they are judgments about individuals. Whatever excuses might be offered, in the end the individual knows that he alone is responsible for his personal behavior. When he hears a sermon about adultery, divorce, or homosexuality, it either applies or does not apply to his case. Sermons about racism, or "consumerism", or multinational corporations, on the other hand, catch everyone in the net, and since all are guilty none are. The hearer may accuse himself of sin but in a vague way only. He does not see that there is much he can do about the sin, and if everyone is implicated it somehow seems less serious, and less real. Confessing to these "social sins" may even be rather comforting, since in doing so one establishes himself as an enlightened, "honest" person.

It is a testimony to the sincerity of some religious believers, if also to their naiveté, that they think the blemishes which stain the face of the churches are the real reason why religion inspires rejection. But sincere seekers after truth have always been able to see beneath those blemishes to the beauty beneath. The argument that moralists are hypocrites is not meant to be taken literally, that is, to mean "If you behaved better I would believe in your creed." It is merely *ressentiment's* handiest weapon. It is the fact of moral authority which is hated, not its possible abuse.

Scheler made the profound observation that *ressentiment* cannot accept revelation, that is, enlightenment coming to the self from the outside. The term can be understood either naturalistically—in which one defers to the superior wisdom of another—or in the traditional Judaeo-Christian supernatural meaning of the word, and it is basic to modern liberal religion that it cannot accept the concept of divine revelation. Twentieth-century believers have still not fully understood the lesson taught by nineteenth-century atheists like Feuerbach and Nietzsche—it is not the Church which is hated but God. So long as God exists man will not be "free".

The contemporary phenomenon of *ressentiment* is not a simple division between church-members and non-church-members, however. Clergy were ridiculed in the *Police Gazette*. Now, they are eager to appear in *Playboy*. They write articles for it, are happy to be quoted in its pages, and send it letters of commendation. Ironically, it is now often from the pulpit that churchgoers imbibe attitudes of *ressentiment* toward religiously based morality.

Perceptively, Scheler identified clergy as among those people most prone to *ressentiment*. His explanation was a rather limited one—that clergy must live publicly an ethic of love and forgiveness and must therefore suppress the real feelings of anger and hostility they sometimes experience. The roots go a great deal deeper, however, for a clergyman who takes his calling seriously has an enormous burden laid on his shoulders. Not only must he serve as a vehicle of judgment pronounced on others, thus inviting their personal animosity, but he must also judge himself even more severely, precisely so that he can with sincerity talk about "we sinners". From the very nature of their calling clergy seem deeply prone to *ressentiment*, as indeed are all people who take religion seriously. The bitterest apostates are drawn from the ranks of the most devout.

The disarray into which religion has fallen in modern America owes much to this fact. *Ressentiment* in religion is unavoidable; it belongs to the very nature of faithful obedience. Traditionally, however, it has been kept under control by certain disciplines and most of all by the ideal of supernatural love, which Scheler saw as a means for transcending it. Once, however, a concept of self-fulfillment came to be accepted in religious circles, these deep-seated feelings were bound to be raked up. Much of the energy of religious "reform" in the past two decades has been negative, stemming from a systematic and often fevered assault on all previously respected authorities.

What in fact are the social conditions which encourage *ressentiment*, since it seems to be more prevalent at certain times than others? Scheler is not of the greatest help here. His observations about its sociology seem casual and rather imperceptive. He did not see, for example, what has become apparent in modern America—that a largely democratic society may stimulate the deepest and most radical expressions of *ressentiment*, even though it promotes social equality. So also recent American history suggests that *ressentiment* is by no means a function merely of suppressed animosities. Resentments freely expressed may in fact exacerbate it.

The principal case in point is the cluster of attitudes and activities which can be conveniently linked around the word "encounter". Certain psychological techniques have been perfected whereby people are encouraged and enabled to "get in touch with their feelings", of which suppressed hostilities and forbidden desires are a large part. The act of expression is supposed to be purgative and liberating. However, it is also guilt-inducing, since despite what they may believe at the conscious level, people continue to sense that certain forbidden feelings should never have been acted out. This is particularly the case where their expression has had some tangibly catastrophic effect, such as the breakup of a marriage. Thus the culture of "honesty" and self-disclosure feeds *ressentiment* in circular fashion, the cures exacerbating the disease.

The "me generation" of the 1970s can be seen as the culmination of certain trends dating back at least to World War II. One is a concept of political equality which ends by demanding the literal abolition of all social distinctions, an ideology which no longer distinguishes the moral from the political order but insists that any form of moral judgment pronounced on individual behavior is a violation of personal worth and freedom. (Hence civil liberties for pornographers and criminals become a major crusade calling forth much righteous passion.) The second trend is material prosperity, prolonged and general, which encourages the expectation that all "needs" and wants will be fulfilled. The satisfaction of every instinct comes to be viewed as a quasi-political right, and not only political but moral restrictions come to be viewed as tyrannical. No moral judgment is permitted except those the individual makes on himself, and even here a large industry has sprung up to teach people how to avoid making such judgments.

To an unrecognized degree, popular culture—through the press, television, film, and music—expresses the final surfacing of *ressentiment*, the final assault on every proclaimed moral authority. So completely has this changed from the 1950s, when popular culture celebrated conventional values, that it is truly a revolution.

Like all revolutions, it feeds on the weaknesses of the establishment, not its tyrannies. It is because the guardians of moral authority, especially the clergy but also parents, policemen, judges, and others, are visibly uncertain about their own beliefs, obviously willing to evade the responsibilities given to them, that *ressentiment* now appears so boldly. Such weakness suggests that the moral restraints against which the individual chafes are in fact invalid, disbelieved even by those who are supposed to proclaim them. This encourages overt rebellion. But the authority of the morality sustains at least a modicum of force despite the derelictions of established leaders. This feeds the *ressentiment* of the would-be escapee from morality, and it further feeds an inexplicable hatred of the very "enlightened" authorities who are so careful not to appear censorious. The victim of *ressentiment* hates those authorities for their failure to articulate a coherent moral universe to which the individual can belong, their seeming unwillingness to resolve the rackingly contradictory moral pressures to which he is subjected.

So also the social encouragement which is given not only to the overt expression of animosities but to the repudiation of personal responsibilities merely serves to deepen *ressentiment*. Parents have been told that they have no responsibility to their unborn children, and children in turn refuse to recognize responsibilities to their parents. Husbands and wives, those whose lives have been consecrated by religious vows, and others who have made solemn commitments, are systematically instructed that they have no higher duty than self-fulfillment and that whatever guilt they feel about this is merely the result of early indoctrination.

Yet, as Scheler recognized, *ressentiment* perceives the truth even as it espouses falsehood. There has occurred, in Nietzschean terms, a "transvaluation of values" whereby good is proclaimed as evil and evil as good. But even Nietzsche believed this was possible only to the rare "superman". In recent times it has been attempted by everyman, and the sometimes hysterical intensity with which it is proclaimed in popular culture shows how precarious has been the revolution.

Abortion is certainly the most dramatic example of this, both because the act itself has gone from the status (*c.* 1960) of a heinous crime to that of almost a virtue and because it is recognized by almost everyone as the chief issue over which the whole moral revolution is being fought.[3]

On the face of it the moral objections against abortion are virtually unanswerable—that the fetus is a living being who has all the appearances of being human, that in any such situation the benefit of the doubt must surely be given to the victim, that it is not consonant with justice to allow one person absolute power over the life of another, and that the law cannot remain neutral while millions of the unborn are slaughtered. At best defenders of abortion might be expected to argue rather deferentially for permission to use it in a few special instances.

Instead they make the self-evidently absurd claim that there is no moral issue involved at all and that those who raise one are willful obscurantists. It is this kind of whistling in the dark to which the bearers of *ressentiment* must resort in their efforts to effect their revolution.

That the antiabortion movement is hated with a unique ferocity goes without saying, since it shoulders the task of keeping moral authority alive in the midst of a virtual mass conspiracy to bury it. In time-honored fashion the opponents of abortion are portrayed as vicious fanatics, political troglodytes, or themselves *ressentiment*-laden enemies of sexual fulfillment. The prolife position must be declared fundamentally irrational so as to justify not even considering it objectively. (Quite literally it cannot be considered objectively, because it touches too many deep nerves which have not been safely buried.) The pregnant woman is alternately presented as a hapless victim of forces beyond her control and as a strong and independent character untrammeled by outworn rules. By a transvaluation of values the stigma is placed on the defenders of life, while virtue is ascribed to those who snuff it out.

It is important to recognize, however, that it is not the organized antiabortion movement itself which is the chief stimulant of this bitterness. It is rather the simple fact of abortion. If the moral sense is indeed rooted in human nature, then the attitude of the enlightened toward it will always be colored by *ressentiment*, and the ferocity of their crusades will be fueled from that source. (It is also a source of rather cool comfort to the defenders of life, since the greatest cause for alarm will come when defenders of abortion no longer show by their bitterness how close their moral nerves still are to the surface. Then they will have truly consolidated their revolution.)

Interestingly, Scheler also identified women as a group as especially prone to *ressentiment*, and the feminist revolution both feeds on that sentiment and further exacerbates it. However, whereas Scheler thought the male-female relationship was the basic cause—woman both acknowledges man's authority

[3] See Hitchcock, "Abortion and the Moral Revolution", below.

and resents it—modern feminism generates *ressentiment* on a deeper basis still—motherhood. Radical feminists have declared themselves independent of motherhood and motherhood itself as deforming. Less radical feminists have come to believe that the demands of motherhood can be treated casually where they conflict with the urge to self-fulfillment. Both insist that no moral guilt attaches to this repudiation and that traditional concepts of motherhood are simply outmoded. But the demands of this eternal bond are not so easily ignored, which accounts for the hysterical ferocity with which they are now denounced.

The feminist revolution and the sexual revolution meet at the point of abortion. For just as the logic of feminism demands abortion (without it a woman is never wholly "free" of the chains of motherhood), so does the logic of a "liberated" sexuality. The contraceptive revolution was supposed to obviate the need for abortion. Instead it has led to its legalization and its multiplication. The official rhetoric of the sexual revolution insists that sexual experience is wholly free and joyous. The acid test, applied and found applicable, is that it does not "hurt anybody". But in order for it to pass the test, it is necessary first that abortion simply be defined as not hurting anybody. The huge number of abortions now performed in America are a grisly testimony to the real fruits of the sexual revolution, as they are to the revolution wrought by feminism. But *ressentiment* responds to this massive reality in the only way it can—by bitter denial and denunciation of those who insist on raising the moral questions.

America in the 1970s produced a generation of materially comfortable, bored, self-obsessed individuals whose only conviction was to be "open" to all experiences. The inevitable effects of such a culture were asserted, over and over again, to be a spirit of peace, self-fulfillment, tolerance, and love. Instead the very possibility of love was destroyed, if love is thought to require unselfish devotion to another. Rather the most common product of the "me decade" (not by any means only among the young) has been aimless sensualists filled with *ressentiment*. The rhetoric of hate has risen to new heights of respectability, as in the University of Pennsylvania student newspaper columnist who expressed his chagrin that the attempt on President Reagan's life did not succeed.

America has afforded no more bemusing spectacle in recent years than the utter unbridled ferocity with which groups like the Moral Majority are now excoriated by respectable people—clergy, editors, educators, politicians. Words like "fascist" are thrown around with abandon, and the claim is made (as by a dean at Stanford University) that the Moral Majority constitutes a more serious threat to American freedom than does Communism itself.

Whatever reservations one might have about the Moral Majority, there is no proportion between its actual faults and the hysterical way in which it is attacked. When the ominous warnings of Norman Lear, for example, have been stripped of their fevered rhetoric, nothing remains except Lear's anger at the fact that someone besides himself might influence the direction of mass communications.

The Moral Majority has now become a lightning rod for all the *ressentiment* generated by the cultural revolutions of the past twenty years, a function previously served mainly by the Catholic Church. The hysteria it calls forth stems from the fact that, whatever its failings, it has chosen to remind people of moral realities they had defined out of existence, and it does so in a public and aggressive way that threatens to alter the shape of mass culture. No institution today so effectively touches those nerves which had supposedly been safely buried.

The moral revolution of recent times has been effected by playing on people's wishes to be rid of burdensome responsibilities. Like the *ressentiment* inherent in genuine religion, everyone—all parents, all spouses, all teachers and preachers—is potentially subject to this restiveness. When offered a respectable rationalization for repudiating those responsibilities, all will be tempted and many will succumb. This revolution has consolidated itself by implicating millions of individuals. Many people cannot conceive of turning back, because to do so would require the kind of unblinking look at themselves which the culture has taught them to avoid.

Scheler was probably wrong in thinking that criminals do not suffer *ressentiment* because of their overt acts of hostility toward society. This is perhaps true in situations where criminality is frankly recognized as such, even by criminals. However, as part of the contemporary moral revolution, criminality has been offered the means of endless self-justification—the criminal as victim, as social protestor, as revolutionary, as virtuoso of self-expression. Finally, if all else fails, criminality can be justified in *ressentiment*'s classic manner—who are the law-abiding that they should condemn the criminal? what are their own hidden vices? (Have you been mugged on the street? You probably cheat on your income tax.)

Ressentiment now affects not so much criminals themselves, although many have learned how to exploit it, as those respectable citizens who rationalize criminal behavior. For to minds formed in the moral revolution of recent times, criminality cannot help but have a continuing fascination, not in the old-fashioned way of love of danger or interest in the bizarre, but in the sense that the criminal is perceived, however dimly, as the ultimate moral revolutionary, the individual who has thrown off all restraints, who acknowledges no laws or taboos, who has murdered conscience. This is precisely the state to which lesser moral revolutionaries aspire. Thus they admire the criminal and seek as far as possible to protect him. Social toleration of criminality has the effect of drawing a very wide circle around all human behavior, within which less aggressive moral iconoclasts know they can live comfortably. Thus many generally law-abiding citizens, who may even be victims of criminal depredations, become apprehensive and even hysterical at demands for "law and order" because immediately they sense a challenge to their own fixed relaxed moral outlook. The criminal is a living symbol of the transvaluation of values, of evil as good (or at least as excusable) and of good (the authority of the law) as evil.

The modern moral revolution has not been solely negative, however. Half of the "playboy philosophy" was the denunciation of traditional sexual morality. The other half was Hefner's insistence, also repeated to the point of tedium, that devotees of the sexual revolution are better people — more caring, more compassionate, more humane than the "puritans". The moral iconoclasts march half the time under the banner of personal liberation, half the time under that of humanitarian concern for others.

Since humanitarian concern is now equated with involvement in fashionable causes, the claim is self-justifying. Never in the history of the world have there been so many movements claiming to work for mankind's betterment. Since genuine humanitarianism is always a rare commodity, it should be acknowledged and welcomed wherever it appears. However, here also Scheler showed himself remarkably perceptive.

Scheler, in defending the authenticity of Christian love, argued that modern humanitarianism is itself a product of *ressentiment* and feeds on it. "Love of others", and a concern for their well-being, may be an alienating experience, based on self-hatred or an inability to live with oneself. Love for the weak and oppressed may stem from hatred of the strong. Mere altruism, in Scheler's view, reflects personal emptiness.

Altruism is also, paradoxically, selfish in Scheler's view. It rests not on principled convictions about the well-being of others, which might lead sometimes to seemingly harsh actions undertaken on behalf of another's genuine welfare, but rather on feelings of empathy which are self-regarding. Stemming as it does from a rejection of any objective hierarchy of moral values, it finds a common humanity only in the lowest qualities of mankind. It is inherently materialistic and sensual.

Although the rejection of objective moral values is justified in the name of individual liberty, it instead issues in obedience to group opinion, which becomes the only reliable substitute. Scheler was among those noticing how the modern humanitarian's concern for "mankind" results in the ability to love only an abstraction, not individual people. He goes so far as to say that the concept of "mankind" is *ressentiment*'s "trump card" in its war against God.

Quite presciently, Scheler argued that in such circumstances value can be based only on utility, and utility only on pleasure. Life itself can be justified only by its utility, as it is reduced to a mere biological reality.

Scheler's strictures do not, of course, apply to all self-proclaimed humanitarians. But it is crucial to any effort to recover a genuine moral sense in society to recognize the way in which idealistic rhetoric has been preempted by the enemies of morality itself. It is basic to *ressentiment*'s strategy to proclaim its own moral superiority even as it systematically undertakes to destroy all fixed moral principles.

CHURCH, STATE, AND MORAL VALUES:
THE LIMITS OF AMERICAN PLURALISM

Through most of its history America has been perceived as a predominantly religious nation, with relatively high rates of church attendance, numerous public expressions of piety, and a general assumption that civic and private virtue depend on religious belief. The 1950s marked perhaps the peak of that diffuse religiosity: the idea of religious belief and observance was maximally honored, often apart from commitment to any of its specific forms. Billboards urged citizens to "Attend church this week", as though church-attendance were a self-evidently good thing and as though it made little difference which church one attended, or why.

Although this kind of social piety might be thought mere conformism, and as such lacking in substance, it was intended to symbolize certain realities. For one thing it was intended to affirm that America was a nation of church-going and God-fearing people, an affirmation of national commitment that transcended particular differences or particular examples of infidelity. For another, it was an affirmation of the belief that morality itself, the basis without which any civilized existence would be impossible, depended upon religion. Thus it was essential to affirm that commitment as a way of affirming one's belief in the social contract itself.

Although moral values are notoriously elusive of investigation, it also appears to be the case that until the 1960s Americans held to a fairly general consensus on such values, a consensus that was celebrated in political and civic rhetoric, extolled from a wide variety of pulpits, honored in the mass media, and to a great extent perpetuated through formal education, both public and private. This consensus included as its key factors the self-evident rightness of patriotism, self-discipline, hard work, self-reliance, family stability, personal honesty, and sensual self-restraint. However dishonored in practice, these virtues received consistent public affirmation and were usually thought of as based on religious belief.

From the beginning there has always been a fundamental ambivalence in America about the degree to which the society is and should be what is now called "pluralistic", that is, how wide a diversity of beliefs and practices are and may be tolerated. That such ambivalence has been present from the beginning is evident to anyone with even minimal knowledge of early American history. School children learn that the early settlers of New England came seeking religious freedom. As they get a little older they also learn that those same settlers denied religious freedom to others.

The temptation is to dismiss the Puritans as hypocrites. But in their own minds they were totally consistent—there was a moral obligation to tolerate religious truth, which not even kings could abridge; there was no obligation, and indeed no right, to tolerate religious error. Put in more modern and more secular terms, the earliest American settlers affirmed the desirability of greater freedom than existed in the Old World, yet believed with equal conviction that society had to rest on a common moral consensus. At various times in history this consensus has been thought to exclude Quakers, Catholics, Jews, and other religious groups. Sooner or later, however, excluded groups have been understood in such a way as to permit them to be part of the consensus. Although most Americans would probably say that there is full religious freedom in the country, certain practices dictated by religious beliefs are in fact outlawed—polygamy, snake-handling, and the withholding of medical treatment from sick children are the most obvious examples.

Whether rightly or wrongly, most Americans prior to the 1960s probably perceived a fundamental moral consensus underlying a variety of religious denominations unequalled in world history in terms of number and diversity of beliefs. Equally important, this consensus was assumed to embrace even the majority of those who had no real religious belief. Relatively few public figures would admit to such a condition, and nominal church affiliation—often with liberal groups such as the Unitarians—was a way of concealing it. Direct attacks on the broadly conceived "Judeo-Christian ethic" were rare, except perhaps in relatively protected and insulated environments such as college campuses.

The 1960s and 1970s saw a definite decline in church membership and attendance, sometimes a very sharp decline.[1] More important than the numerical fluctuation, which has tended toward a rather irregular historical pattern, has been the fact that a secular way of life is now more respectable in America than at perhaps any time in the twentieth century—understanding secularism first in the narrower sense of rejection of institutional religion and then in the broader sense of making no claim of being guided by the teachings of the historical religions. Not only do public figures now find it unnecessary to claim religious affiliation; in certain segments of society such claims are becoming increasingly rare. A frankly secularist stance enjoys a prestige equal to that of religious belief.

It would, however, be a mistake to understand what has happened in America since about 1960 as merely a division between the churched and the unchurched. The division, within each denomination, between what are often called, borrowing the vocabulary of politics, "liberal" and "conservative" elements, has been equally important. Although such divisions, in

---

[1] For a discussion of church membership and religious practice, see D. Kelly, *Why the Conservative Churches are Growing* (1973) and D. Hoge & D. Roozen, *Understanding Church Growth and Decline, 1950–78* (1979).

one form or another, have been a part of American religious life almost from the beginning, they took on unusual sharpness and deepening passion after 1960. To cite merely a few examples—the changes in the Roman Catholic Church either mandated by the Second Vatican Council of 1962–1965 or implemented in its name, the decision of the Episcopal Church to ordain women to the priesthood and to authorize a new edition of the *Book of Common Prayer*, disagreements within major Protestant bodies over the exact nature of the authority of Scripture and the extent of its inerrancy, and possibly widening divisions within Judaism over the authority of traditional religious laws and practices.

In most of these cases it could be argued with cogency that the more "liberal" groups came to be perceived as having perhaps more in common with secularists outside their framework of formal religion than with the "conservatives" within their own churches. Liberals have tended to emphasize a political agenda, for example, which is critical of the American economic system and of America's role in world affairs, an agenda shared in large measure with the secular left. Religious liberals have tended to support, quite strongly, feminism, the movement for homosexual rights, and much of what goes under the name of the "sexual revolution". One major divergence between them and the religious conservatives is precisely their attitudes toward secular movements of social change, liberals being inclined to recognize these as actual manifestations of the divine will, conservatives seeing them as frontal assaults on the Judeo-Christian ethic. Thus in 1980 certain religious leaders could join with proclaimed secularists like the television producer Norman Lear in issuing a public warning against the organization called the Moral Majority.[2] The warning was issued in response to the widespread impression that, as a new decade began, there was a "swing to the right" in which religious conservatives were once again asserting that they regarded as traditional those American values which had been transgressed.

The liberal critique of American society is in large measure the claim that, while based on the ideal of total openness or "pluralism", in practice it has always been more closed and monolithic than it should be. To what degree America was intended originally to be totally "open" is itself an open question. Through much of the nineteenth century there were legal restrictions on personal freedom which today would be regarded as intolerable, slavery being only the most obvious example. Among the Founding Fathers the commitment to civil liberties was not as complete as in retrospect civil-libertarians find it useful to believe.[3] However, history aside, it is the essence of the liberal position that the story of America is the story of the gradual extension and unfolding of that pluralism, the full encompassment of more and more

[2] A national letter went out over Lear's signature (copy in possession of the author).
[3] L. Levy, *Jefferson and Civil Liberties: The Darker Side* (1963).

diverse groups and hitherto proscribed beliefs and behavior. Liberty is regarded as capital which cannot simply be allowed to lie secure but must always be expanded, often with elements of considerable risk. Although many would have difficulty expressing the moral sources of that imperative, liberals are generally convinced that there exists a moral obligation on America to broaden continually the limits of its tolerance. So far as racial, ethnic, and religious groups are concerned this point has, at least in principle, been won completely. It has now been extended to other categories of people, such as women as a group, who are assumed to have specific rights which must be guaranteed apart from the guarantee of rights to all citizens; to cultural minorities like homosexuals; and to all those who profess "deviant" ideas or ways of life. Both the reality of and the potentiality for social conflict in these areas is, if anything, greater than it was with respect to struggles for racial equality.

In general the liberal response to this conflict is to insist that it is based on a misapprehension, which in turn is based on fear and insecurity. The purpose of an extended pluralism, the liberal argument runs, is simply to extend the rights of citizenship to all Americans, to remove all vestiges of inequality and injustice. America means equality, so the argument runs, and only when the rights of everyone are fully protected are the rights of anyone really secure. Resistance to this is then deemed to originate from one of two causes — simple bigotry, the wish to keep others in an inferior status; or unfounded fear that the extension of some people's rights will result in the constriction of one's own.

Probably not since the days of slavery has American politics confronted issues with moral roots running so deep as those now on the political agenda. Questions like abortion, the relationship between men and women, and personal sexual behavior are not easily dealt with in a political context, and instinctively politicians in times past have tried to evade questions likely to touch such deep nerves. But the commitment to a steadily expanding pluralism makes confrontation with such questions unavoidable. With most traditional struggles dealing with equality won at least in principle, the new frontiers necessarily are defined in places hitherto inaccessible to political intrusion.

This new phase of the struggle for equality will of necessity test the limits of American pluralism in ways they have never been tested before. This will occur (and indeed is already occurring) in part because it raises issues that go to the heart of deeply held and fundamental moral beliefs which cannot be easily compromised and where the mutual respect, which makes democratic dialogue possible, is often lacking. (Abortion is an obvious example. Some people regard it as one of a woman's most basic rights, others as the deliberate killing of a helpless human being. In such circumstances there is not much room for "statesmanlike" solutions.)

Another test of the limits of pluralism is the question of what unifying principle remains at the heart of a society as that society becomes more and more diverse, especially in terms of accepted moral values. A society can tolerate a certain number of positions which are antithetical to each other. Is there a limit beyond which these antitheses become socially destructive? The moral revolution since 1960 has tended to call into question, systematically, virtually one by one, every settled belief from the past. It has now become a political question whether a social order can survive based on no moral consensus. (To cite only the most obvious question, what motivates people to obey the law, and to what extent, in the absence of such a consensus?)

Thirdly, it is necessary to ask the question whether society can be indefinitely pluralistic, indefinitely tolerant of all points of view, while still maintaining genuine equality among them all. At some point does the legitimization of some positions necessarily require the constriction of others? It will be argued here that, where fundamental values are involved, this is precisely the case, and the question, which touches many areas of social life, will be considered primarily from the point of view of those issues which touch directly or indirectly on religious belief and practice.

The separationist clause of the First Amendment is admittedly very general in nature, using only ten words, and as such is subject to a number of possible interpretations. For some time after the ratification of the Constitution some of the states continued to maintain relationships between church and state which later constitutional doctrine would regard as unacceptable.[4]

Thomas Jefferson's phrase, "wall of separation of church and state", was first used, in passing, by the Supreme Court in 1878,[5] then resurrected after many decades of neglect in 1947.[6] Since the latter date it has come to be thought of as the governing metaphor in the area of church-state relations, and it has come to be the purpose of much litigation in that area of constitutional law to ferret out systematically all signs of public support of religion.

Oddly, however, in an age when few traditional assumptions have been left unchallenged, there has been relatively little discussion of why an absolute wall of church-state separation is necessary. It remains one of the few basic principles still treated as self-evidently true, even though it is far from self-evident that the First Amendment mandates such a doctrine.

Mark DeWolfe Howe argued a double tradition of church-state separation

---

[4] See, e.g., A. Stokes, *Church and State in the United States*, 3 vols. (1950); C. Antieau, A. Downey, and E. Roberts, *Freedom From Federal Establishment: Formation and Early History of the First Amendment Religion Clauses* (1964); and S. Cobb, *The Rise of Religious Liberty in the United States* (1902).

[5] Reynolds v. United States, 98 U.S. 145, 164 (1878).

[6] McCollum v. Board of Educ., 333 U.S. 203, 231 (1948).

in American history: one essentially secular, deriving from Jefferson and James Madison, and seeking to protect the public weal from the intrusion of religion; the other older, derived from colonial figures like Roger Williams, wanting to insure maximum freedom for the churches without government interference. Howe argued that the first strain has generally governed separationist thinking.[7]

Judging from the rhetoric both of some of the Founding Fathers and of later court decisions, commitment to the separationist dogma has its origins in the Enlightenment of the eighteenth century, an age highly conscious of the seemingly "irrational" passions which religion could stir up, still suffering from the aftermath of religious wars which had been common in the previous two centuries, persuaded that organized religion was almost the natural enemy of freedom.[8] The principal motive for absolute separation was to protect society from destructive religious quarrels, which were deemed uniquely intense and dangerous.

Justice Hugo Black articulated the same viewpoint in 1952:

> It was precisely because Eighteenth Century Americans were a religious people divided into many fighting sects that we were given a constitutional mandate to keep Church and State completely separate. Colonial history had already shown that, here as elsewhere, sectarians entrusted with governmental power to further their causes would sometimes torture, maim, and kill those they branded "heretics", "atheists", or "agnostics".[9]

Justice Felix Frankfurter had similarly warned that "the public school must keep scrupulously free from entanglement in the strife of sects",[10] and Justice Robert Jackson had written, "If we are to eliminate everything that is objectionable to any of these warring sects or inconsistent with any of their doctrines, we will leave public education in shreds."[11] In cases involving religion, the courts have tended to employ "sect" as a favorite synonym for organized religion, implying factionalized conflict.

If, however, the peculiar horror in which the courts seem to hold religious conflict can be seen as a holdover from eighteenth-century history and attitudes, it has assumed the character of an unquestioned assumption of eternal validity. Thus Chief Justice Warren Burger could write in 1969:

> Ordinarily political debate and division, however vigorous or even partisan, are normal and healthy manifestations of our democratic system of government, but political division along religious lines was one of the principal evils against which the First Amendment was intended to protect.[12]

[7] M. Howe, *The Garden and the Wilderness* (1962), pp. 6–7.
[8] See, e.g., R. Healy, *Jefferson on Religion and Public Education* (1962), pp. 162, 211, 216–19, 225.
[9] Zorach v. Clauson, 343 U.S. 306, 318–19 (1952).
[10] McCollum v. Board of Educ., 333 U.S. 203, 216–17 (1948).
[11] Idem., at 235.
[12] Lemon v. Kurtzman, 403 U.S. 602, 622 (1971).

A statement of this kind automatically invites the question "Why". In an age when the acceptable limits of political controversy have broadened considerably, when freedom of speech is deemed necessarily to include the expression of many divisive and potentially inflammatory ideas, it is not clear why disagreement along religious lines should be held in peculiar horror. Arguably, in the America of the 1980s political divisions along the lines of race, economic status, even perhaps gender, are actually and potentially more divisive than religious divisions. Furthermore, it hardly seems consistent with the governing spirit of liberal democracy to inhibit certain expressions of belief because these might be potentially divisive. Supposedly such "divisiveness" is not only the price paid for a real democracy but almost in a sense the very essence of that democracy, and it ought not to be the business of the courts to protect society from such disruptions.

At present it remains unproven that religious division constitutes a uniquely dangerous threat to political stability and, if it indeed is, that it is of such magnitude as to require systematic vigilance by the courts against it. Both assumptions, however, seem to lie behind the strict separationist position which the courts have accepted in large measure.

The "wall of separation" is often presented as a high constitutional principle which, perhaps reluctantly, the courts must apply even when regrettable inconveniences occur. Thus it is argued, for example, that if children attending a rural parochial school on a cold winter's morning are given a ride on a public school's bus, the entire American tradition of church-state separation is endangered.

It is worth noting that the pragmatic liberal mind does not ordinarily countenance what seem like harsh conclusions in support of abstract principles. That mind in fact prides itself on its ability to adjust principle (including law) to social reality. For this reason alone it is unlikely that abstract principle of itself governs the strict separationist position. In practice it appears that much of that position has been carved out in response to pressures from sources which regard either organized religion in general or specific religious groups as undesirable social institutions. To an extent greater than is generally realized, the separationist doctrine rests on antireligious foundations.

That Thomas Jefferson and some other of the Founding Fathers felt this hostility is well known.[13] However, it was built into law over the years in sometimes surprising ways — not until 1978 did the Supreme Court invalidate a Tennessee law, for example, prohibiting clergymen from holding public office.[14]

The personal views of the judges are scarcely irrelevant to the question. As indicated by his statement above, Justice Black, for one, seems to have regarded religious believers as uniquely likely to torture, maim, and kill in

[13] See, e.g., Healy, supra, note 8.
[14] McDaniel v. Paty, 435 U.S. 618 (1978).

the name of their beliefs and thus to be needful of restraint from so doing. His son revealed that the Justice regarded people who attended church as "hypocrites" and had a particular dislike of the Catholic Church. (As a young lawyer in Alabama, Black successfully represented a Methodist minister accused of killing a Catholic priest. The defendant's guilt was not seriously in doubt, but Black exploited the anti-Catholic sentiments of the jurors.[15])

In several of the cases involving the question of public aid to religious schools, the principle has been enunciated that the character of those schools is itself objectionable. In *Lemon v. Kurtzman*,[16] for example, Justice William O. Douglas stated that, while it was the purpose of the public schools to educate, it was the purpose of Catholic schools to indoctrinate.[17] His source for this sweeping statement was a book by a fundamentalist Protestant author claiming to make an exposé of the Catholic Church. The book claimed, among other things, that Catholic priests and religious teachers are not allowed to think, that parochial schools represent a dangerous "foreign" influence in the United States, and that they produce a disproportionate number of gangsters and juvenile delinquents. The author concluded by recommending that Catholics not be allowed to teach in public schools or hold high public office.[18] In his extrajudicial writings Douglas revealed that he was influenced by the anti-Catholic polemicist Paul Blanshard.[19]

The suspicion that teachers in religious schools cannot be relied on to teach even secular subjects in a proper manner was expressed by Chief Justice Burger and Justice Black in *Lemon*,[20] bringing from Justice White the observation that nothing in the judicial record actually showed that secular subjects were being taught improperly.[21] Justice Jackson wrote in *Everson v. Board of Education*[22]: "[o]ur public school, if not a product of Protestantism, at least is more consistent with it than with the Catholic culture and scheme of values".[23]

Prior to World War II, church-state cases before the Supreme Court were relatively rare. There was a spate of conscientious-objection cases at the start of World War II. Since then, beginning in 1947, there has been a steady flow of church-state cases, immeasurably broadening the scope of constitutional

---

[15] H. Black Jr., *My Father, A Remembrance* (1975); V. Hamilton, *Hugo Black: The Alabama Years* (1972).
[16] 403 U.S. 602 (1971).
[17] Idem., at 635.
[18] L. Boettner, *Roman Catholicism* (1962), pp. 360–63, 364, 368, 370, 379–80.
[19] W. Douglas, *The Bible and the Schools* (1966), p. 50.
[20] Lemon v. Kurtzman, 403 U.S. 602, 618, 635–36 (1971).
[21] Idem., at 667.
[22] 330 U.S. 1 (1947).
[23] Idem., at 23.

THE LIMITS OF AMERICAN PLURALISM

law in this area. In general the courts have tended toward a strict separationist position.[24]

The leading historian of the phenomenon has noted that for the most part these cases were carefully chosen and prepared and were designed to establish sweeping constitutional principles. Often they did not grow out of genuine social conflicts so much as from the desire of the plaintiffs to make a philosophical point. While skilled constitutional lawyers usually represented the plaintiffs, defendants' lawyers, especially where public agencies like school boards were concerned, rarely had much experience in constitutional matters and not infrequently had no particular commitment to the positions they were defending. In addition, strict separationists were generally on the offensive, acting as plaintiffs in fifty-three of sixty-seven major church-state cases between 1951 and 1971.[25]

Three organizations played important roles in the long-term separationist strategy: the American Civil Liberties Union (A.C.L.U.), the American Jewish Congress (A.J.C.), and Protestants and Other Americans United for Separation of Church and State (P.O.A.U.), now Americans for Separation of Church and State.[26] In all three organizations, besides constitutional principle, participants were at least sometimes motivated by antipathy to the Catholic Church and by the belief that Catholic schools are a pernicious influence in society. P.O.A.U. is the most obvious case—dating back many years, it had warned Americans, frequently in tones of alarm, that the Catholic Church constituted a threat to democracy and that Catholics could not be good Americans.[27] (Its rhetoric has moderated in recent years.) In one case brought by the A.C.L.U., the plaintiff was a woman who believed that religious education deforms minds in the same way that Chinese foot-binding deformed women's feet.[28] Leo Pfeffer, counsel for the A.J.C. and probably the most effective separationist lawyer over the past thirty years, admits to a personal dislike of Catholic schools, which he regards as undemocratic.[29]

It is arguable that the strict separationist position, which was only adopted by the courts after World War II, represents the triumph of those who regard organized religion as an actual or potential danger to the Republic.

---

[24] F. Sorauf, *The Wall of Separation: The Constitutional Politics of Church and State* (1976), p. 9, 19, 21.

[25] Idem., at 30–33, 89, 106–11, 165, 349–50.

[26] Idem., at 31–33.

[27] For an example of P.O.A.U. rhetoric, see C. Lowell, *The Great Church-State Fraud* (1973). For a sample and refutation of such rhetoric over the span of a decade, see L. Creedon & W. Falcon, *United for Separation: P.O.A.U. Assaults on Catholicism* (1959).

[28] Sorauf, op. cit., at 135.

[29] Pfeffer, "The 'Catholic' Catholic Problem", *Commonweal* (Aug. 1, 1975): 302–303.

As such it is not an even-handed application of some principle of neutrality so much as it is the enshrining in law of a particular philosophy.[30]

As it applies to religion, the First Amendment contains two clauses, the second, ensuring free exercise of religion, being only slightly shorter than the first. If the extent of the separationist clause is in some doubt, the extent of the free-exercise clause is not. From the beginning of the United States it has been clear that there were to be no restrictions of religious liberty except in very extreme cases, such as the Mormon practice of polygamy in the nineteenth century.

Liberal opinion has generally held that the two clauses are perfectly complementary to each other, that the separation clause is in fact a necessary prerequisite of the free-exercise clause, since church-state entanglement would itself pose a serious threat to religious liberty. However, in practice it has often been necessary for the courts to choose between them, and a judicial policy of remaining vigilant against church-state entanglement in practice often means the willingness to impose, or to allow others to impose, burdens on the free exercise of religion.

The dilemma would be less acute under a regnant judicial philosophy which regards the interpretation of the Constitution as a narrow and technical matter, in which it is the business of the judges to expound the law as written, whatever practical consequences might flow from that. However, for many years the reigning judicial philosophy has concerned itself quite consciously with the real or potential social effects of court decisions. The frequency with which the courts have shown a willingness to permit disabilities in the exercise of religious freedom, for the sake of maintaining strict separation, indicates what is often a deliberate choice on the judges' part.

The most obvious example is public aid to religious schools. It would be difficult to show that concrete harm comes to the body politic as a result of such aid, or that such aid necessarily would deprive religious schools of their independence. Countries with political structures comparable to the United States—Canada, Australia, and the Netherlands, for example—have maintained such aid programs for many years without serious ill effect.

The strict separationist argument rests rather on abstract principle—that such aid is in itself bad because it violates a self-evident principle. But the evident correctness of the principle is precisely what is in question. When it does not rest on abstract principle the argument against such aid is usually based on the fact that some people object to the use of their taxes for purposes of which they disapprove or in which they do not believe. But the Constitution provides no guarantee that one's taxes will only be used in ways compatible

[30] See Francis Canavan, "The Pluralist Game", *Law and Contemporary Problems* 44, no. 2 (Spring 1981): 23.

with one's beliefs. Given the immense size and complexity of the federal budget, virtually any taxpayer could discover numerous uses of tax money of which he or she morally disapproves. It appears to be only in the area of religion that the courts have recognized a quasi-right of taxpayers to object to specific uses of their tax money.

Court decisions with regard to school aid have been somewhat inconsistent. In general, however, they have tended to forbid all direct or indirect forms of such aid at the primary and secondary levels, while allowing it for the most part at the level of colleges and universities.[31] During the period when these cases were under litigation, and particularly since about 1965, many private religious schools, especially those under Catholic auspices, closed because of financial pressures. If it is assumed that church-operated schools are an important exercise of religious freedom, if it is assumed that by operating schools the churches are performing a vital social service, and if it is recognized that parents who send their children to religious schools are also taxpayers, it would seem that the state has a compelling interest in seeing to it that these schools are as good as they can be and are not starved for funds. The courts have in general tended to hold that people cannot effectively exercise their rights if they lack the financial means to do so (thus, for example, the provision of free legal services for indigent defendants). In the area of religion, however, it often appears that the courts, from a separationist standpoint, take a certain satisfaction in permitting as many financial burdens as possible to develop. The general tendency in modern society is for the state to find ways of aiding institutions which, even though private, are deemed worthy of survival, a pattern which prevails from hospitals to zoos and includes symphony orchestras and groups which provide contraceptive and abortion services. Religious schools almost alone remain outside this pattern, often because they are regarded as social institutions which should not survive or whose survival should be made difficult.

Along with school aid, the question of religious observances in the public schools has provided the bulk of the church-state cases of the past thirty-five years. While there have been some seeming inconsistencies, in general the courts have systematically banned all overt religious instruction, along with prayers, readings from Scriptures, and religious symbolism. Reluctantly, they have allowed, under certain circumstances, children in public schools to

---

[31] The principal Supreme Court cases are: Everson v. Board of Educ., 330 U.S. 1 (1947); Board of Educ. v. Allen, 392 U.S. 236 (1967); Lemon v. Kurtzman, 403 U.S. 602 (1971); Committee for Public Educ. & Religious Liberty v. Nyquist, 413 U.S. 756 (1973); Meek v. Pittenger, 421 U.S. 349, *reh. denied*, 422 U.S. 1049 (1975); Wolman v. Walter, 433 U.S. 229 (1977); Roemer v. Maryland Pub. Works Bd., 426 U.S. 736 (1976).

be released from regular classes in order to attend religious instruction off school premises.[32]

The religious elements banned from the schools have usually been studiously nondenominational in character. Thus the courts have ruled not only against the favoring of any particular religion but against the favoring of religion in general. The schools are to be scrupulously neutral where matters of religion are concerned.

How neutral they can be in practice is something which will be discussed later. There are, however, certain other aspects of this position which are questionable. Beginning in 1948, it has been a consistent claim by plaintiffs in separationist suits that their rights are violated if religious observances, however generalized, are imposed on them. One such early case, for example, held that even though children receiving religious instruction in a public school left the regular classroom, those who remained behind were subjected to embarrassment and possible harassment.[33] However, on other occasions the Supreme Court has specifically said that, in the words of Justice Jackson, "If we are to eliminate everything which is objectionable to any of these warring sects or inconsistent with any of their doctrines, we will leave public education in shreds."[34] It sometimes appears in court decisions that there exists a constitutional right on the part of nonbelievers to be protected from unpalatable impositions of religious beliefs, but no corresponding right on the part of believers to be protected from ideas which they find offensive.

The strict separationist position also seems incompatible with prevailing trends in modern education. It was more defensible when schools were regarded as having a primarily technical role—they were to teach young people skills like reading, writing, and arithmetic, which could be seen as divorced from larger questions of meaning and value. Now, however, schools tend to stress "total" education and are seen as institutions which shape young people in myriad ways, of which the strictly academic is only a part. Furthermore, it has been a general tendency in modern education to hold that children should not be insulated from controversial and even disturbing aspects of reality.

Given these views of education, any system which resolutely excludes religion is already an anomaly. If the schools are regarded as helping to shape the child's total world, then the exclusion of religion cannot help but shape a religionless world. At the most formative period of their lives, children are in effect taught that religion is unimportant or even perhaps false. They are

---

[32] The principal Supreme Court cases are: McCollum v. Board of Educ., 333 U.S. 203 (1948); Zorach v. Clauson, 343 U.S. 306 (1952); Engel v. Vitale, 370 U.S. 421 (1962); Abington School Dist. v. Schempp, 374 U.S. 203 (1963).

[33] McCollum v. Board of Educ., 333 U.S. 203 (1948).

[34] Idem., at 235.

habituated in modes of thinking and feeling in which religion plays no part. Although the school may deliberately seek to introduce the child to "controversial" subjects, religion cannot be one of these. The very exclusion itself has major symbolic importance.

Several remedies are proposed. One is that religion be taught as an academic subject, rather like geography. But in practice this does not appear to be very common and in any case does not have much bearing on an education which seeks to prepare children for "life".

More common is the assertion that religious education is properly the business of the family and the church. But this begs the question. Parents send their children to school precisely because they feel incompetent to educate them at home. And although strong family practice is probably an essential prerequisite for instilling religious belief in a child, in many homes this practice may be relatively inarticulate and unsophisticated. Churches have access to children for only a very few hours a week, not in any way comparable to the time they spend in school. There are many functions currently performed by the schools that might be performed adequately by other agencies. When any of these is in fact relegated to other agencies, the school is conveying to the child the idea that it is not really important.

Cases in which strict separationism has been applied in such a way as seemingly to limit religious freedom have become fairly common: currently under appeal to the Supreme Court is a case in which a federal circuit court permitted a student organization to use campus facilities for a Bible-study group.[35] A district court[36] had originally upheld the university's decision to forbid such use. At another state university, student religious groups are restricted in the number of meetings they may hold on campus and are required to pay rent for the facilities, conditions not imposed on other student groups. A state court upheld such restrictions and granted university authorities the right to impose prior restraint on such meetings, on the grounds that there was a "clear and present danger" of violation of the establishment clause.[37]

Such cases have arisen at a time when the overwhelming tendency of courts, and of universities and colleges themselves, has been to expand the limits of student freedom and to hold that all manner of "controversial" opinions have a right to be heard. They have also arisen in an atmosphere in which the tendency of courts has been to protect constitutional freedoms not only in narrowly procedural ways but also by seeking to identify substantive violations of freedom which may seem technically legal. The trend in church-state cases seems to go contrary to both these tendencies.

[35] Chess v. Widmar, 635 F.2d 1310 (8th Cir. 1980), cert. granted, — U.S. — (1981). The Supreme Court ultimately upheld the rights of the student religious group.
[36] Chess v. Widmar, 480 F. Supp. 907 (W.D. Mo. 1979).
[37] Dittman v. W. Washington University, No. C79-1189W (W.D. Wash., Feb. 28, 1980).

The theory of separationism holds that the state is and must be neutral in matters of religion. But, as suggested previously, such neutrality is difficult to attain in practice. There can be little doubt that present separationist safeguards do insure government neutrality among religious groups—public policy does not seem to favor Christians over Jews, for example, or Catholics over Protestants. However, it is a more substantial question whether public policy can and does maintain effective neutrality between religion and unbelief, between professed theism and other kinds of faith which can be thought of as competing with it.

To maintain that such neutrality is possible seems to require postulating that public policy is somehow arrived at in a "value-free" manner. Yet it would be difficult to show any policies which are in fact completely neutral. At the lowest level, certain policy decisions may be purely functional in that they merely involve choices as to how to achieve particular goals. Yet the goals themselves, at a higher level of policy-making, cannot be "value-free". Certain values may be assumed to be commonly shared throughout the body politic. However, it is one of the arguments here that such common assumptions are becoming fewer in number. Furthermore, even within the framework of common assumptions, important value judgments must often be made which involve sharp conflict.

A classic example, already alluded to, was the Supreme Court's 1878 decision outlawing polygamy as practiced by Mormons in the Western United States. On one level the decision was clearly a limitation on religious freedom. The Court reached its decision by positing the existence of an overriding value—the welfare of society required the support of a stable, legal family in the traditional sense, which polygamy would tend to undermine. (The court also made a distinction, which proved not to be very useful, between freedom of religious beliefs on the one hand and religious actions on the other, which might be restricted by law.[38]) The court assumed a commonly held value—the legally established nuclear family—which was one of the givens of American society. Today there are many people who would reject that given, and it seems likely that a similar case today might be decided quite differently.

The common liberal argument for pluralism at this point asserts that the law merely expands the limits of permissible belief and behavior. In the process no one suffers; people may find certain ideas distasteful or invalid, but they are not required to accept them, merely to tolerate them. With regard to polygamy, for example, some people might be permitted in law to practice it, but others could still enter into traditional marriages.

Such a philosophy, however, is totally out of step with the overwhelming tendency of modern government, which seems almost inevitably set on a

[38] Reynolds v. United States, 98 U.S. 145 (1878).

course of expansion of powers and expansion of the ways in which it intervenes in the lives of its citizens. The minimal government envisioned by classical conservative theory might conceivably claim the kind of neutrality which pluralism postulates. The modern, activist, liberal welfare state cannot be neutral and does not aim to be.

Public education, as already discussed, is a prime case in point. No responsible educator would deny that education involves the making of countless value judgments—such as in establishing curricula, choosing teachers, mandating textbooks, and setting goals. Many of these judgments involve moral choices which may be controversial. The very absence of religion is, as already argued, a judgment of this kind. Contrary to the beliefs of many people, the courts and the schools have decided that education is best carried out with no religious component at all.

One of the relatively few instances in which opponents of strict separationism have taken the offensive in litigating constitutional questions has been recent cases in which Protestants of the type generally called fundamentalist have sued school districts to force the inclusion of biblical accounts of creation alongside the theory of evolution in their curricula or, alternatively, to present evolution as merely a theory rather than a fact. Plaintiffs contend that the teaching of evolution alone violates their religious beliefs and also violates the required neutrality of the state.[39]

A more widespread and perhaps more sensitive area of conflict is over sex education in the public schools. Such programs have become all but universal and perhaps arouse more public controversy than any other aspect of education. The standard argument in favor of such programs is that they are indeed neutral—they merely impart information to students which is deemed appropriate for students to have. But the very existence of such programs involves a value judgment, since some parents oppose them on moral grounds and assert that sex education belongs to the domain of the family. Others would approve such programs, but only if they included explicit moral guidance about sexual behavior. In reality, it appears that many such programs aim at shaping children's values and attitudes with regard to sex. The general assumption behind such programs is that being "sexually active" in a variety of ways is normal and healthy for young people and that the schools should help them to do so safely and without guilt.[40] Such aims conflict directly with the moral and religious beliefs of many parents, who thus perceive the schools as directly undermining their own attempts to inculcate values in their children. Legal challenges to such programs have generally been unsuccessful. It is not even clear that courts will recognize a general right of exemption

[39] Epperson v. Arkansas, 393 U.S. 97 (1968); Daniel v. Walters, 515 F.2d 485 (6th Cir. 1975).

[40] For a critique of such programs, see Horner, "Is the New Sex Education Going Too Far?" *New York Times* Magazine (Dec. 7, 1980): 137–48.

from such programs for children whose parents disapprove.[41] In any case, in some of its earlier decisions, the Supreme Court seemed to say that it is insufficient merely to exempt certain children from programs which violate their consciences, since this may single them out for ridicule and harassment.[42]

If the public schools are the most obvious place where values clash, they are by no means the cockpit. Abortion is another classic example. The liberal position—that those who oppose abortion are free not to engage in it, while those who approve it may do so—simply begs the question, since in the minds of antiabortionists they are being asked to countenance the massive taking of human life. A possible compromise over the abortion issue would be to permit abortions to be performed by private agencies but to keep the state scrupulously neutral. Virtually no one, however, finds this acceptable. Proabortionists generally wish to see major governmental support for the practice—it is regarded as an integral part of health care, as well as an important tool in population control, and as such should be promoted by publicly funded agencies both domestically and abroad. The modern welfare state simply cannot remain neutral on such issues.

Recognizing this, proabortionists brought suit in federal court to invalidate the so-called Hyde Amendment whereby Congress forbids most expenditures of public funds for abortions. The major grounds for the suit was the claim that the law violated church-state separation because it enacted the principles of particular religions, notably the Roman Catholic Church. Under the so-called "divisiveness" doctrine, the claim was made that any legislation which could be shown to have been influenced primarily by religious believers was invalid because of its tendency to promote religious conflict in society. Plaintiffs went to the length of reading the mail of the congressional sponsor of the legislation, to determine the religious affiliation of those who wrote to him, and of submitting an affidavit about his personal religious practices. The Supreme Court ultimately rejected the argument.[43]

Had it won acceptance, it would have had immensely far-reaching consequences, since a great deal of legislation (for example, the Civil Rights Act of 1964)[44] could be shown to have been passed as a result of strong religious pressures. At some level the divisiveness doctrine—the argument that certain kinds of state action are forbidden simply because they tend to create religious controversy—is recognized by the Supreme Court, however. It was enunciated by Chief Justice Burger in one of the school-aid cases.[45] The very fact

[41] See, e.g., Cornwell v. State Board of Educ., 428 F.2d 471 (4th Cir.), cert. denied, 400 U.S. 942 (1970).

[42] See, e.g., McCollum v. Board of Educ., 333 U.S. 203, 227, 232 (1948).

[43] Harris v. McRae, 448 U.S. 297 (1980) (copy of plaintiff's brief in possession of the author).

[44] For the importance of religious influence on legislation, see J. Adams, *The Growing Church Lobby in Washington* (1970). The Civil Rights Act is considered at 1-3.

[45] Lemon v. Kurtzman, 403 U.S. 602, 622 (1971).

that the issue is raised tends to demonstrate the impossibility of the state's neutrality in matters of basic values.

Another point of conflict between the professed neutrality of the state and its actual commitment to certain values is the question whether policies to which the state is in principle committed may be enforced with regard to religious institutions which claim exemption either in terms of religious freedom or church-state separation. The Supreme Court, by a narrow margin, has ruled that the National Labor Relations Board does not have jurisdiction over teachers in religious schools. The Catholic hierarchy argued in the case that to permit such a thing would be to permit the government to intervene in disputes which might be of a purely religious nature, e.g., a decision to dismiss a teacher for failing to teach Catholic doctrine.[46] A Protestant school has successfully argued in a state court that regulations imposed on the school by the state effectively interfered with religious freedom by restricting the school's right to set its curriculum and hire teachers in accordance with its religious mission.[47] Largely unlitigated, at least at the federal level, is the question whether religious institutions, contrary to their professed beliefs, would be prohibited from discriminating against classes of persons specially protected by law, for example, by excluding women from the ranks of the clergy or refusing to hire homosexuals as teachers.

It is worth noting that certain strict separationists do not altogether regard the wall as excluding both sides equally. Leo Pfeffer, for example, notes that church and state historically have sought to dominate each other, with the state usually successful.[48] He also argues that some of the Supreme Court's decisions of the past thirty years have made the "liberalization" of the Catholic Church more likely by making parochial schools harder to maintain, thus helping those in the Church who seek a "congregational" polity independent of hierarchical control. Pfeffer believes all religions, partly as a result of court decisions, are fated to become irresistibly secularized.[49]

Through most of American history, questions of church-state relations have been fairly easy to define because there were few problems as to what constituted a church. However, the First Amendment does not mention "church" but rather "religion". Implicitly, therefore, it seems as though the amendment does not only apply to formally organized groups which designate themselves as churches. America has always been fruitful in producing

---

[46] NLRB v. Catholic Bishop of Chicago, 440 U.S. 490 (1979).

[47] Sheridan Road Baptist Church v. Michigan Dept. of Educ., Cir. Ct., Mich., No. 80-26205-AZ (Dec. 8, 1980).

[48] L. Pfeffer, *Church, State, and Freedom* (1953) p. 727.

[49] L. Pfeffer, *God, Caesar, and the Constitution: The Court as Referee of Church-State Confrontation* (1975) p. 49, 231, 250, 253, 348.

new religions, and in the past twenty years there has been a vast proliferation of them, the constitutional import of which is not clear.

Insofar as newer religious movements can be readily identified as such there is no problem, since presumably they have the same rights and are subject to the same restraints as older and more established churches. The problem emerges with respect to movements which may not declare themselves to be religions, and may in fact even deny that they are, but which others understand to be. An issue has arisen with respect to the movement called Transcendental Meditation, whose proponents claim that it is merely a technique for recollection and self-exploration, while critics claim it is a religion actually or potentially in conflict with other religions. Thus far federal courts have upheld the critics.[50]

A potentially much more divisive issue is over the "religion" of secular humanism. Many religious believers are convinced that there exists such a philosophy, which is antithetical to theism, dismissing the latter's claims as illusory and hence as personally and socially damaging to those who accept them. Secular humanism also advocates an approach to life in which human beings are encouraged to rely entirely on their own powers and to live and act as though no divine being governs the universe. Finally, certain practical consequences tend to flow from these theoretical beliefs—for example, secular humanists tend to reject the traditional, strict Judeo-Christian moral code with regard to sex and to advocate "free" and "open" attitudes toward sexuality which are morally objectionable to many religious believers.[51]

However, it is not the contention of critics that secular humanism is merely the doctrine of a particular organization having relatively few members. They rather contend that it is a widely held philosophy of life shared by many people, not all of whom would even be familiar with the name. For purposes of the First Amendment the contention is that secular humanism often functions as the governing philosophy of many public schools and other public agencies and that it is not subject to the same restraints in the name of separation that organized churches are. Thus, the argument runs, religious believers suffer violation of their rights by having an alien and unacceptable philosophy imposed on them. Thus far the courts have shown no inclination to accept this argument.[52]

That the courts should take the argument more seriously is suggested by the fact that the Supreme Court, in establishing the criteria for valid conscientious objection from military service, has itself declared secular humanism

[50] Malnak v. Yogi, 592 F.2d 197 (3d Cir. 1979).

[51] A convenient summary of secular humanist doctrine is found in the American Humanist Association's *Humanist Manifesto* I & II (1933, 1973).

[52] See e.g., Hobolth v. Greenway, 52 Mich. App. 682, 218 N.W.2d 98 (1974); Medeiros v. Kiyosaki, 52 Haw. 436, 478 P.2d 314 (1970).

to be a religion, entitled therefore to the same considerations and protections as all other religions. In one such case the Court ruled that:

> We believe that . . . the test of belief "in a relation to a Supreme Being" is whether a given belief that is sincere and meaningful occupies a place in the life of its possessor parallel to that filled by the orthodox belief in God of one who clearly qualifies for exemption.[53]

If secular humanism is indeed a religion for the Court's purposes, and if religion is to be understood as the Court thus understands it, it seems to follow that very difficult and profound questions are raised with respect to the duty of the state to be vigilant against secular humanist intrusions into the public order in the same way it is required to be vigilant against theistic intrusions. It is noteworthy that no less a personage than Leo Pfeffer argues that the courts have indeed enshrined secular humanism as the official creed.[54]

The issue raises once again the anomaly discussed in relation to the unexamined assumptions of the strict separationists, namely, why it is to be assumed that theistic creeds alone, of all the schools of thought which contend with each other in modern society, are to be singled out for special exclusions.

Instinctively the liberal mind tends to uphold individual rights, especially those based on conscience, when these conflict with law or government policy. A long tradition holds that individual rights must be scrupulously respected, and even dissent from law must be accommodated as much as possible.

It remains uncertain, however, how far the courts will go in permitting dissent on religious grounds from firmly established law or public policy. Historically the Supreme Court has gone fairly far in upholding the right of Jehovah's Witnesses, for example, not to be compelled to salute the American flag[55] or of Amish parents not to be forced to send their children to public schools.[56] However, as one constitutional scholar has somewhat cynically suggested, the courts have a record of solicitousness toward religious beliefs perceived as marginal and dissenting while tending toward strictness and vigilance with respect to "mainline" beliefs.[57]

An acute area of conflict has been the growing tendency of some Protestants to establish their own schools. Such establishments have come under attack by various government agencies, including the Internal Revenue Service

[53] United States v. Seeger, 380 U.S. 163, 165–66 (1965). See also Torcaso v. Watkins, 367 U.S. 488, 495 (1961).
[54] "Issues That Divide: The Triumph of Secular Humanism", *Journal of Church and State* (1977), 203–205.
[55] Board of Educ. v. Barnette, 319 U.S. 624 (1943).
[56] Wisconsin v. Yoder, 406 U.S. 205 (1972).
[57] W. Berns, *The First Amendment and the Future of American Democracy* (1976), p. 77–79.

(charging improper claims of tax exemption) and state departments of education demanding control of accreditation. The results so far have been rather mixed. In each case, however, the supporters of the schools in question claim that conscience, particularly relating to freedom of religion, forbids them to enroll their children in public schools.[58] More radical yet is the contention of some parents that the moral character of existing schools requires them to educate their children at home, in accord with their own beliefs. Again the judicial results have been mixed.[59]

Parents have also brought suit to overturn compulsory sex education courses in public schools, on the grounds that such courses violate the religious and moral beliefs of the parents. Such claims have been disallowed.[60]

The practice of "deprogramming" of recruits to various religious sects also raises questions of religious freedom which are far-reaching in their consequences. On the one hand the state seems to have a clear obligation to protect those who are tricked or coerced into joining groups which suppress their freedom, as in the notorious case of the People's Temple of Jim Jones. However, in the nature of things it is extremely difficult for the state to determine when an individual has indeed been subjected to techniques which negate personal freedom, and the very attempt to do so may have a "chilling" effect on religious liberty. Once the state takes it upon itself to judge when religious conversions are genuine and when the result of forced means, there would be no end to the necessary interference in matters of conscience and religious liberty.[61] It is also worth noting in this connection that some modern skeptics believe that all religious commitment is by definition irrational and therefore might be subject to automatic suspicion and review.

Attempts to "deprogram" members of religious cults are often brought by the members' parents, and the whole area of parental authority is a sensitive one in which the ground appears to be shifting. It is also a subject closely intertwined with personal religious liberty, as indicated in the instances cited above in which parents object on grounds of principle to what is taught in the public schools. The Supreme Court has already ruled that minors have a right to contraceptive and abortion services without their parents' consent,[62] a ruling which offends the consciences of many parents not only in its substance

[58] See, e.g., Kentucky State Bd. v. Rudasill, 589 S.W.2d 877 (Ky. 1979).

[59] See, e.g., Michigan v. Noble, No. 5791-0115-A (1979).

[60] Note 35, supra.

[61] Alexander v. Unification Church of America, 634 F.2d 673 (2d Cir. 1980); Peterson v. Sorlien, 299 N.W.2d 123 (Minn. 1980).

[62] Planned Parenthood of Missouri v. Danforth, 428 U.S. 52 (1976). Note, however, that the Court has recently limited Danforth. Although it remains unconstitutional to legislate an irrevocable power to parents to forbid their daughter's abortion, a state may require parental notification, when possible, of an abortion to be performed on a dependent unmarried minor. H. L. v. Matheson, 49 U.S.L.W. 4255 (U.S. March 24, 1981) (No. 79-5903).

but also in the way that it seems to establish the authority of the state above that of the parent in a highly sensitive and important area of life — the nurture of children. Some parents with traditional beliefs fear that the state will indefinitely expand the scope of children's rights so as to minimize parental authority, especially in the crucial area of moral values, and that the state will commit itself to certain policies, e.g., the encouragement of sexual activity among the young, that will directly conflict with parents' own values.

As American society, often led by its courts, has greatly widened the limits of permissible belief and behavior over the past twenty years, it has not simply enriched the "pluralism" which has always been a feature of that society. In the nature of things the decision to tolerate certain hitherto disapproved ideas or actions has often required tightening restrictions on ideas or actions previously considered orthodox. An indefinitely elastic pluralism is not possible. Expansions in some areas are likely to cause contractions in others.

In particular the unofficially privileged place which organized religion has traditionally enjoyed in American life has been eroded, often with active judicial effort toward that end. The urge to ensure that non-belief does not suffer in comparison with belief has often led to practical and theoretical restrictions placed on religion itself. The classical doctrine of strict separationism rests on an assumption that the state can and must be neutral. But in practice this is impossible. Values are necessary for the functioning of any society, and if they are not consciously adopted and publicly acknowledged they will be smuggled in surreptitiously and often unconsciously. Values are always in real or potential conflict, and the state inevitably favors some values over others.

WHY IS THE SILENT MAJORITY SILENT?

Conventional political wisdom in the 1970s held that the majority of Americans were liberal on economic issues, in general supporting the welfare state, while remaining conservative on what are called the "social" issues, encompassing sensitive areas of personal morality like sex and drugs.

The seeming contradiction is not at all mysterious. In most societies the majority of people are essentially traditional in their beliefs, and the general concept of the welfare state is now traditional, deeply imbedded in our politics for well over forty years. Until the 1960s, it would not have occurred to many that there was any inconsistency in being both economically liberal and socially conservative. Such a combination precisely defined the working-class backbone of the New Deal coalition that lasted until the student radicals of the 1960s began to call for a cultural revolution.

As late as 1972 Senator McGovern believed he was being slandered by being tagged with the trinity of "acid, amnesty, and abortion" and took pains to try to dissociate himself from it. That exercise seems almost quaint now, in the 1980s, when amnesty is largely a dead issue, abortion enjoys a privileged legal status, and many conservatives favor the "decriminalization" of marijuana. For, while the welfare state appears to have been stalled, there has occurred over the last decade an unprecedented extension of the socially and legally permissible limits of personal behavior.

The first half of this phenomenon—the reassessment of the long-entrenched welfare state—has been extensively discussed. The latter half—the growing liberalism in the field of personal behavior even as many people express alarm at the perceived deterioration of morals and moral authority—has received much less attention.

Even the phrase "personal behavior" is misleading. The day is past, possibly forever, when purely personal behavior—that is, behavior which is intended to be wholly private—attracts much public concern. And those who advocate liberalized standards of personal conduct are precisely those with a stake in ensuring that it does not remain private. What they are seeking is some form of public and official approval.

The spokesmen for sexual liberation still rely heavily on the notion of privacy. "What people do in the bedroom is no one else's business", they say. But if it were really so simple there would be no argument. The existence of organized movements for sexual freedom demonstrates that the subject has advanced far beyond the question of a right to privacy.

The question centers rather on three closely related factors, all involving government—money, social approval, and education. It is in these three areas that the supposedly conservative 1970s witnessed a social revolution unprecedented in American history.

The most basic of human relationships—between parents and children, husbands and wives, all men and all women, human beings and their physical environment—are being subjected to radical questioning and reassessment. New moral attitudes, often diametrically opposed to those commonly held twenty years ago, now permeate almost all forms of public discourse. Psychological skills are being applied to a task no less ambitious than that of wholly redefining human nature and enabling people to discover, for the first time, who they "really" are. Meanwhile, those traditional seats of authority which might be expected to provide resistance to these trends, especially the family and organized religion, either have made their peace with this "new morality" or have lapsed into demoralized impotence.

Social approval may seem at first to have little connection with public policy. However, moral values have a way of being defined politically—many people take their moral cues from government policy and cannot conceive that what is legal may nonetheless be immoral. The moral beliefs and actions of public figures also serve as cues. (Thus the revelation of the extramarital adventures of the Kennedys probably does less to diminish public respect for them than to make marital fidelity itself seem less important.) Those who speak most passionately about the right to privacy are often those who understand very well that the political arena is the most efficient place for transforming popular beliefs.

In a welfare state, no particular use of public money is precluded in principle, and none is beyond the realm of possibility. Politics is to a great extent a struggle over how the money will be distributed. Thus it is never sufficient to say merely that the law permits certain kinds of private behavior. It becomes necessary to decide whether the government will pay for abortions, whether it will distribute contraceptive devices, whether it will provide legal assistance to homosexuals who claim to have been discriminated against, whether it will mandate "affirmative action" programs in their favor.

Education is the most sensitive area of all, even more sensitive and potentially explosive than money. Shall there be sex-education programs in the schools, and what values shall they embody? (Such programs are never neutral or merely technical.) Should schools employ teachers or use textbooks that parents find morally objectionable? Is it permissible for schools to reflect the religious values of their communities?

Despite the supposed social conservatism of the times, liberal values triumphed in all these areas of conflict during the last decade, and the momentum clearly lies with those who look upon public policy as a legitimate and necessary way of extending the moral boundaries of an already permissive society. Despite occasional defeats (for example, in local referenda on homosexual rights), the moral avant-garde now sees the fulfillment of its most extravagant hopes as realistically attainable. What accounts for the apparent political impotence of the "silent majority"?

Although the basic conflict is often defined as between "intellectuals" and non-intellectuals, this very denomination is part of the strategy of the avant-garde, implying that reason is on their side, that their opponents are governed by emotion and even hysteria. But, in fact, it is articulateness, something obviously related to intelligence but not identical with it and often subversive of genuine rationality, that is really relevant here. In a fragmented and at least formally democratic society dependent on the mass media, an enormous advantage accrues to those able to define the questions, to set the terms of discourse. In such contests the defenders of traditional values more often than not appear slow-witted, stumbling, and defensive. They have lost the battle almost before it begins because they are reduced to responding to the initiatives of others.

In part the very nature of the media makes this inevitable. Their whole existence is predicated on the purveyance of "news", which gives an automatic advantage to spokesmen for any unfamiliar, and especially any iconoclastic, position. Furthermore, the journalistic profession seems overwhelmingly to attract people who want to think of themselves as advanced and enlightened. Finally, the media automatically focus on the short range. They bring the light of publicity to bear, in a particularly dramatic way, on immediate problems and questions, especially those susceptible of bipolar simplification. They seldom raise long-term questions, much less deal with them.

Given the media's importance in forming public opinion, and the corresponding decline in influence of the church and the family, even many moral traditionalists find themselves living in a mental world which has been heavily saturated by the very ideas and modes of thinking to which they feel instinctive aversion. On the assumptions of such a world, their own convictions are mere prejudices. They often cannot explain why they feel as they do and are consequently at the mercy of anyone more articulate than they.

The virtues of the traditionalists are also their vices. The classic defense of traditionalism holds that, while good and sufficient reasons can be adduced for most traditions, it is precisely of the nature of tradition not to require philosophical defense, except in extreme situations. A traditional way of life is one which takes its practical authority from custom itself, from the instinctive sense of the rightness of things which a genuinely traditional community inculcates in its members. The tree can grow because its roots are not being constantly yanked out of the ground for examination. Members of the community can live its values in a deep and authentic way because they do not agonize over whether those values are right.

But this settled way of life is, because of the very conditions which make it possible, highly vulnerable to attack. Skepticism, whatever else it is, is always a corrosive. It can dissolve existing bonds with relative ease, even when it is powerless to create new ones. The simple question "Why not?" often reduces traditionalists to uneasy silence. They are the ready-made victims of predatory intellectuals and of the media, which prefer to allow traditional ideas to be defended by visibly nervous, tongue-tied, seemingly stupid people. If objections to a novel position (for example, homosexuality as merely an "alternative lifestyle") cannot be easily stated and concretely demonstrated, then it is assumed that mere prejudice governs the objectors.

Although economic and political conservatism has its abstract thinkers and its articulate spokesmen, social conservatives have been by and large much less well equipped. They are dependent on stray scraps of philosophy and have virtually no leaders, inside or outside politics, who are able to engage the enemy on its own ground. (Powerful as the Moral Majority may have been in the last election, for example, it was not arguing in such a way as to convince anyone who did not already agree with it.)

Although they are frequently linked together, political and economic conservatism on the one hand and moral conservatism on the other are quite different things and have different modes of operation in the public realm. A certain attitude of vigilance, even aggressiveness, is built into the philosophies of political conservatives, who predicate either liberty or order as their desired goal, and of economic conservatives, who accord property that status. Both of these types of conservatives regard those ultimate values as things which need to be won and, having been won, constantly defended and even enlarged. Political and economic conservatives almost instinctively conceive of life as a battle, and of things of value as things precariously held (thus the paradox of political conservatives who mistrust strong central government yet support a large military establishment).

Moral conservatism, which can perhaps be defined as a vision of society resting on the sanctity of the family (usually, but not always, with religious roots), seeks to preserve a world of settled and stable social relations, clearly defined moral duties, and privacy. While not antithetical to politics, it is often indifferent to politics, in the sense that it regards life as most meaningful in its private (especially familial) aspects, and politics as a distraction from what is really important.

Apart from ideology, the camps of those who are liberal and those who are conservative on "social issues" are separated by their attitude toward politics itself. Since the Kennedy campaign of 1960 a conspicuous segment of the population—generally fairly young, educated, and affluent—has found in political activity the elusive sense of personal fulfillment which modern Americans have come to believe is their birthright. Such a sense transcends specific political goals. It has rather been the excitement of politics itself, especially where a glamorous candidate is concerned, that has been the essence of the experience. Often particular issues seem to be formulated as an afterthought, to give image-politics an image of substance.

Morally conservative people tend to be unenthusiastic about and even suspicious of a political style which seems appropriate to those whose lives are geared to fashion and movement and who promise continually accelerating social change. Just as they are inarticulate and at a disadvantage vis-à-vis the media, social conservatives often concede the political realm to their opponents before the struggle has even begun.

Oscar Wilde said the most cogent objection to socialism was that it consumed too many evenings; moral conservatives would agree with him. Those who become "political activists" are those who need a sense of excitement and movement in their lives. Attending meetings, serving on committees, drafting manifestos, making speeches, lobbying politicians, even filling envelopes and licking stamps are felt to be meaningful actions. Whatever philosophical convictions they may or may not hold, people attracted to such activity are almost automatically disposed toward further social change, if only because it sustains the sense of movement which they crave and provides justification for continued activity.

But social conservatism prefers a life that is settled, stable, placid, private. Looking at the liberal activists, moral traditionalists see people who, even apart from their dubious ideas, seem frenetic, willing to give up too large a part of their private selves to the demands of public activity. Conversely, the activists perceive the traditionalists' way of life as boring and trivial. (Before the late 1960s the media tended to glorify domestic tranquillity. In television comedies, for example, only minor crises were introduced, just sufficient to sustain mildly dramatic plots. Now domestic stodginess is ridiculed, and television focuses on those previously regarded as being on the margins of society—divorced persons, homosexuals, drug-users, unmarried parents, et cetera.)

Lionel Trilling once wrote that conservatism generally lacks real thought and substitutes for it what he called "irritable mental gestures". The observation is not unfair. While seldom a thinker, the liberal social innovator has usually armed himself with a whole catalogue of arguments against the status quo. The traditionalist, on the other hand, is usually taken by surprise when his beliefs are challenged. He finds it amazing and incomprehensible when values which to him are so obviously correct are questioned, and his response, at least initially, is indeed likely to be an irritable gesture, a few familiar clichés to ward off the enemy until the forces of tradition can be rallied.

At the heart of moral conservatism is a contradiction which the traditionalist dimly senses and which increases his irritation. For if the nature of traditionalism is the preference for a settled, stable, and placid personal life, then this life will necessarily be disrupted by the very act of defending it. (Moral conservatives often instinctively support their countries' wars, since they believe in patriotism as a basic virtue. Only when it is too late do they realize that wars deeply alter the social and moral fabric of the countries engaged in them.)

What is involved here is not mere laziness. Moral traditionalists often involve themselves quite deeply in the activities of their churches, their children's schools, Boy and Girl Scouts, et cetera. In other words, the traditionalist prefers to give himself to activities which are directly relevant to the family, while liberal activists see political goals, fought for in the public arena, as alone worthwhile.

The traditionalist's reluctance to commit himself fully to the political struggle is accompanied by an equal reluctance to examine the intellectual basis of his threatened values. For to undertake such an examination in a systematic way would also undermine the stable, settled character of a traditional way of life. It would involve fighting according to the enemy's rules. Thus many traditionalists tend to alternate passivity with grouching, waiting for someone else to erect and man the barricades, toward which they are willing to offer moral and sometimes financial support.

In the places where moral battles are commonly fought (in school districts, for example), while many are disturbed by evolving social trends, relatively few become actively involved. They seldom attend meetings. If they do, they usually remain silent, expressing their views candidly only to their closest friends. They are easily persuaded that certain policies they may not like are inevitable and cannot successfully be resisted.

In the moral traditionalist's world, to be identified as the leader of a cause carries with it intimations of craziness: only fanatics speak their minds publicly. A leadership vacuum thus develops, such that those who do push themselves forward as leaders often actually are oddities—shrill, unstable, slightly unsavory. Then when the cause has been discredited by its spokesmen, the genuine traditionalist retreats even deeper into passivity and privacy, embarrassed even to have his beliefs known. There are middle-class communities where it is less damaging to be known as a homosexual than to be known as one who disapproves of them.

In addition, although liberal rhetoric officially encourages passionate adherence to one's beliefs, in practice those who set the terms of public discussion see to it that only "progressive" ideas are accorded respect. That members of the bourgeoisie were once capable of staging a minor riot in protest against Stravinsky's *Sacre du Printemps* has a certain nostalgic charm. In the intervening decades, and especially in the past fifteen years, the bourgeoisie have learned that they may not resist moral and cultural change. At most they may choose not to participate in it themselves. Unlike those who propagate change, they have no right to "impose" their own values on the whole of society.

Moral traditionalists have thus been conditioned, through the schools, the media, and even the churches, to assume that their own beliefs are matters of taste, not based on anything solid or defensible. They are made to feel that they have no right to impede society's changes. An entire industry has sprung up to "help" people learn to accept with equanimity whatever happens to the world. The final result is the diminution of freedom in the name of freedom. We are liberated from the tyranny of the past — in order to accept a certain vision of the future.

The objective causes for anxiety in the present-day world — terrorism both political and criminal, the erosion of institutional authority, widening intellectual and moral confusion, the revival of magic and superstition, the decay of the cities, the possibility of war or economic disaster — more than justify alarm. But alarmist views are tolerated only from favored groups, especially so-called environmentalists and "peace" groups.

Real discussion of the future course of Western society has in effect been banned from the public sphere by the tacit judgment that certain opinions (concerning the social effects of the decline of organized religion, for example) represent merely unenlightened prejudice and are not to be taken seriously. People who are shaken by the breakdown of the family, by the breakdown of morality, or by violent crimes are assured that their alarm is based on misapprehensions. Nothing is regarded as worth becoming exercised about, since almost all social change is assumed to be for the best. The media, partial to change because change provides automatic drama, endeavor to make life a spectator sport. Rather than being deeply affected by events, people are invited to view them with detachment, to enjoy them as entertainment. What is most offensive about the phenomenon called radical chic is that it encourages wrenching kinds of social change for the sake of titillating bored people who believe that they have an undeniable right to lead "interesting" lives.

Although the word is often employed as a talisman, there is probably less genuine "pluralism" in America now than two decades ago. As the English historian E. R. Norman has observed, the authority of pluralism is mainly invoked during the period of transition from one orthodoxy to another. Liberal activists now speak of pluralism, or toleration of unpopular ideas, in the context of winning social acceptance for such things as homosexuality and "open marriage". But it is not simply toleration they seek. In reality they believe in a therapeutic norm to which all are expected to conform. Whatever one's chosen "lifestyle", no one is conceded the right to be a principled moral traditionalist. Much of the influence of the media and the educational system is bent toward bleaching out genuine cultural differences (as distinct from picturesque differences) and drawing the entire society within the folds of the liberal moral consensus, the essence of which is the willingness to ask repeatedly the question, "Why not?" and rarely to discover a persuasive answer.

What is generally called neoconservatism is a phenomenon whose significance has not yet been fully appreciated. Mainly concerned with economic and political ideas, it nonetheless takes a skeptical attitude toward almost all the prevailing liberal orthodoxies and hence at least indirectly offers support for moral traditionalism. (A few of the neoconservatives, like Daniel Bell and Robert Nisbet, have explicitly inquired into the religious and moral foundations of a viable society.)

Apart from the specific content of their thought, what may be significant about neoconservatives is the implicit lesson they convey about the role of the intellectual as outsider. Mass education and the mass media have at last created a situation in which almost everyone can be a "dissenter", mouthing "unpopular" ideas to the applause of the crowd. Neoconservatism has risen because some of the genuinely thoughtful people in society now feel alienated in a new way from the ostensible mainstream. The bourgeoisie are no longer callously complacent, impervious to, or intolerant of, new ideas. Instead they are, increasingly, eager buyers of a debased, bargain-basement kind of modernism.

The intellectual as defender of traditional values, an unfamiliar figure in the past three centuries, may become more conspicuous in the remaining two decades of this one. Conceivably, a sense of moral firmness will come to be genuinely "countercultural" amidst a populistic hedonism. However, the embers of tradition are by no means extinguished amidst the ashes of classical bourgeois culture, and an articulate neoconservatism may provide the voice, and the sense of self-confidence, which will enable many within the great American middle class to do what fashionable liberal rhetoric urges them to do—once again take control of their lives.

THE AMERICAN PRESS AND BIRTH CONTROL:
PREPARING THE GROUND FOR DISSENT

In 1964, at a time when it still supported the traditional Catholic teaching on birth control, the Jesuit magazine *America* predicted that the Church would "disappoint those who think that *aggiornamento* is the Italian word for contraception" (October 24).

The joke was an apt one because, aside from the Second Vatican Council itself, probably no aspect of Catholic life attracted wider attention in the 1960s than the Church's position on birth control. It is perhaps no exaggeration to say that for many people the willingness of Church authorities to change the traditional doctrine on this point was the single most important test of what was called "renewal". The deeper spiritual and theological dimensions of the Council were often missed, especially by the media, in favor of practical, easily definable issues which had some contemporary social relevance. Birth control admirably filled the need for such an issue.

The disappointments which have so often followed the high promise of the Council can only be understood when it is also understood to what degree the Council was a media event. By that is meant that what happened at the Council, and what finally appeared in its widely unread documents, was less important in the practical order than what people thought happened there. The majority of American Catholics—even, it might be suggested, the majority of American priests and religious—got their knowledge of the Council primarily from the media. The image of *aggiornamento* which the media projected, and the expectations which they raised, was of central importance in understanding the disappointments and disillusionments which afflicted so many Catholics in the postconciliar era.

Although the failure of either Council or pope to reverse the traditional teaching on contraception is often given as a major reason for this postconciliar demoralization, American Catholics on the eve of the Council showed little evidence of either expecting or desiring a change. *Commonweal* and *Jubilee*, two of the more intellectual and avant-garde American Catholic journals, asked prominent lay people and religious to express their hopes for the Council just prior to its opening in 1962, and the subject of birth control was scarcely mentioned. No one asked that the doctrine be changed.[1] No less an authority than Father Andrew Greeley stated in 1963 that American Catholics accepted and followed the Church's teaching.[2]

[1] See *Commonweal*, June 8, June 29, July 6, July 13, Aug. 10, Sept. 21, July 27, 1962; *Jubilee*, Oct. 1962.

[2] "Family Planning Among American Catholics", *Chicago Studies* (Spring 1963).

However, the vision of a Church changing many things which had been popularly thought to be unchangeable—Friday abstinence and the Latin liturgy being perhaps the two most obvious—inevitably stimulated curiosity, if not eager anticipation, concerning other possible changes. In addition, the moral and social climate of America in the 1960s was such that birth control would not remain long undiscussed.

The fact that many American Catholics—a substantial majority, according to some surveys—do not accept the teachings reiterated in *Humanae vitae* is often presented as though it represented the admirable and newly acquired ability of these Catholics to think for themselves, independent of hierarchical dictation. The implied model is that of the individual, in close communion with the self and perhaps a few other people, agonizingly wrestling with the conflicting demands of conscience and authority, finally emerging with a newly forged position which is the proud result of courageous and independent thought. In fact opinions are usually formed in modern culture in intensely social contexts, amidst a great deal of propaganda and strong attempts by "opinion-makers" to direct the flow of thought.

Two issues had arisen in the early 1960s which largely created the context in which public discussion was carried on. One was awareness of the possibility of an overpopulated world and the consequent need to control population, a discovery which even then gave rise to a rhetoric, largely accepted without question by the media, that was urgent, panicky, and sometimes bordering on the dictatorial. The control of population was, in countless articles and radio and television broadcasts, presented as an imperative which could neither be denied nor compromised. It soon became one of the new moral absolutes, spawning its own far-flung orthodoxies.

The second issue revolved around a series of widely proclaimed "breakthroughs" in the technology of contraception, chiefly the various "pills" that would either regulate ovulation so as to pinpoint the times of likely pregnancy or would inhibit fertilization altogether. Although from time to time over the coming years the safety of these pills from a medical point of view would be questioned (and still continues to be), the overwhelming burden of the original publicity was that these pills had solved the age-old problem of undesired pregnancies.

It is significant that a third question which would exercise the media and the public before too many years was not as yet much discussed in the early and middle 1960s. The sexual revolution had not as yet been discovered and, although some conservatives predicted that easy and effective forms of contraception would induce promiscuity, these predictions were generally dismissed as alarmist. (It is worth noting, what is common knowledge now but was not so widely recognized at the time, that the campaign for more "enlightened" attitudes toward population control, although often presented as spontaneous, was heavily financed by groups like the Rockefeller Foundation and Planned Parenthood, and the propaganda campaigns behind it were skillfully organized, often enlisting the aid of people who did not even realize they were being used.)[3]

In this context the Catholic teaching on birth control could not help but seem a major barrier to human progress, and at no point was the Church, in this new ecumenical age of general good feeling, more roundly condemned for backwardness and rigidity than here. Although it was obviously the hope of Pope Paul VI that the problem of contraception might be discussed calmly, prayerfully, and at the necessary length, the heated atmosphere surrounding the question soon made that impossible.

The first point at which a change in the Catholic position occurred was on the question of whether the sale of contraceptives should be legal. Many states prohibited such traffic through laws which had originally been enacted under Protestant influence, although in many places the laws were also widely violated. In 1965 the Supreme Court, in a case involving the state of Connecticut, ruled all such laws unconstitutional.

For the most part the Catholic response was one of cautious approval, or at least acceptance. As early as 1963 the lay magazine *Commonweal* had urged repeal (January 4, August 23), arguing that such a step in no way implied moral approval of contraception and suggesting that American Catholics were sophisticated enough to realize that fact. William Ball, a prominent Catholic attorney active in church-state questions, hailed the Connecticut decision (July 9). *America*, which was at the time uncompromising in its support for traditional Catholic doctrine, had also urged repeal (November 7) and approved the 1965 decision, taking wry satisfaction in the fact that, in postulating a "right to privacy" as the basis for forbidding the states to outlaw contraceptives, the Supreme Court had seemingly fallen back on an unacknowledged concept of natural law (July 9).

Although the reasons for Catholics acquiescing in the repeal of anticontraceptive laws might have been valid in the abstract, the episode also showed that many Catholics were overly complacent about the direction of their society and poor prognosticators of its future, to say nothing of being naive about the intentions of those whom they were increasingly loath, in the conciliar atmosphere of good will, to consider their enemies. *Commonweal*, for example, cited a New York State law prohibiting social workers from referring clients to birth-control clinics as evidence of how a compromise solution could be worked out in which Catholic consciences would be respected. The

---

[3] This and other aspects of the birth-control controversy were dealt with extensively in a book by Msgr. George A. Kelly, *Battle for the American Church* (Doubleday, 1979).

state, according to editor James O'Gara, would be "neutral" on this sensitive issue (January 4, 1963; February 7, 1964). William Ball thought the 1965 Connecticut decision presaged the possibility that the Supreme Court might eventually forbid all governmentally funded birth-control programs (July 9, 1965).

There were already some ominous signs on the horizon, however. Melvin Wulf of the American Civil Liberties Union specifically challenged William Ball's contention (*Commonweal*, August 20, 1965), and *Newsweek*, which showed a strong and consistent interest in whether the Catholic teaching might change, suggested that the bishops had already made a "strategic retreat" on the question of public funding by shifting the ground of their argument from the claim that contraceptives were immoral to merely making a claim on behalf of respect for the Catholic conscience (September 6, 1965). By 1966, *America* was chiding the bishops for their alleged silence in the face of steadily increasing government-sponsored birth-control programs (April 23), but *Commonweal* was ridiculing as hysterical and unrealistic a pamphlet, published by the Pennsylvania Catholic Conference, which warned that the state might use its authority to promote not only contraception but also euthanasia (July 22).

The secular press, not surprisingly, was quicker than the Catholic press to suggest that even the Church's position on the morality of contraception might change. In 1964 the mass-circulation magazine *Look* published two articles on the subject (July 14, September 8), followed by two more in 1965 (February 9, August 10). In 1963, *Newsweek* characterized the Catholic position as "blindly archaic" but saw evidence that the Church was becoming "modern" (September 9). The next year it characterized the Church as like a great ship whose slow turnings, when they first begin, are scarcely perceptible but are also irreversible (July 6). Progress in the technology of the pill would soon harmonize religious dogma and medical necessity, the magazine predicted (May 25). *Time*, generally more cautious than its principal rival where Catholic matters were concerned, was slower in warming to the subject. In the summer of 1963 the *New York Times*, bellwether of American newspapers, published a five-part series, four of the articles on the first page, concerning changing Catholic opinion (August 5–9).

In these early years the media were particularly alert for any signs that the Catholic monolith was cracking and, following a pattern which would become increasingly familiar in the post-conciliar years, gave lavish attention to any Catholic who took a public stand even slightly at odds with official Church teaching.

For a time the most useful of these was a rather elderly priest from the University of Notre Dame, John A. O'Brien. As early as 1961, Father O'Brien had published an article in *Look* entitled "Let's Take Birth Control out of

Politics" (October 10), in which he upheld the traditional teaching while urging that the state neither forbid nor encourage birth control. In 1963, in a perhaps unprecedented journalistic occurrence, he published an identical article simultaneously in both the Catholic journal *Ave Maria* (August 24) and the Protestant *Christian Century* (August 28). His theme was primarily a strong plea for the necessity of family planning and population control, and he concluded by urging Catholics and Protestants to join together in the task, each following the methods approved by their respective religious traditions. A few months later he returned to the *Christian Century* with an article entitled "Let's End the War over Birth Control" (November 6), in which he urged "dialogue" and "love" and warned Catholics against assuming that their views on the subject were widely shared. This time his conclusion urged a White House Conference on world population and a heavily funded government program to effect means of population control.

Father O'Brien's opinions gained wide secular attention, including a front-page article in the *Times* (October 29), in which he said the practice of birth control was morally permissible for most non-Catholics. The *Times* also supported his position in an editorial (November 9), *Newsweek* quoted encomia of Father O'Brien from the very liberal Episcopal Bishop James A. Pike and from officers of Planned Parenthood, who termed the priest's opinions "a source of joy" (September 9).

It was an irony apparently not noticed at the time that, although contraception was presumably of interest mainly to younger married people, the two most notable Catholic spokesmen for a more liberal position were elderly men. Besides Father O'Brien, the most celebrated of these was a Harvard professor of gynecology, John Rock, who almost overnight went from a fame largely confined to medical circles to a national celebrity.

His views had been published in *Good Housekeeping*, a women's magazine, as early as 1961 (July). However, real fame attended the publication in 1963 of his book *The Time Has Come: a Catholic Doctor's Proposals to End the Battle Over Birth Control*. In it he advocated that the Church accept the morality of the pill, making some gesture in the direction of theological principle but relying mainly on the threat of overpopulation and the easy availability of what he termed safe new contraceptive devices. Excerpts from the book were published in the *Saturday Evening Post* (April 20) and *Reader's Digest* (September).

Although in his many years of prominence in the gynecological field Rock had never been publicly identified as a Catholic, his position as a responsible dissenter within Church ranks now achieved enormous publicity. The *New York Times* featured his proposals on page one (April 29), and published an admiring biographical sketch of him (April 29), and the paper's leading columnist, Arthur Krock, also devoted an article to the Boston professor (April 23). He was prominently featured in *Life* magazine (May 10) and his name was invoked at least three times in *Newsweek* articles over the next year (September 9, 1963; June 8 and July 6, 1964). In one interview (July, 1964) he was quoted as saying: "They can't take my church away from me. It's as much mine as it is theirs", adding, "I'm in this fight for good." In another (June 8, 1964) he urged Catholics not to wait for a papal decision, since the press of overpopulation was too great. His book contained an introduction by Christian Herter (a Protestant), former Secretary of State and Governor of Massachusetts, indicating the importance which the political establishment attached to the question.

Rather curiously, in all the publicity given Rock's proposals, almost no one called attention to the element of self-interest in his pleadings — as a professional researcher into human reproduction he was calling for a massive commitment of government funds in that area. Rock's credibility also depended on the public impression that he was in all other respects an orthodox Catholic. Although in 1966 he was quoted by the *New York Times* (May 1) as saying that he would never prescribe or recommend abortifacients, by 1973 he was, in his role as "the father of the pill", ridiculing the Catholic doctrine on abortion and predicting that it would eventually be changed, adding gratuitously that it would certainly have changed had Pope John XXIII lived, since the Pope had sought to save the Church from "medievalism". Given the reality of malnutrition in the world, he called efforts to prevent abortions a blasphemy.[4]

Within the Church itself in 1963–64 opinion divided rather neatly along the lines of the two most prestigious journals of opinion, the lay-edited *Commonweal* and the Jesuits' *America*.

America's position was one of unremitting support for the traditional doctrine and frequent urgings that the rhythm method be quickly perfected (e.g., October 26, 1963; March 21, 1964). The magazine published a long negative review of the Rock book (April 27, 1963), questioned whether the pill would ever be morally acceptable (March 7, 1964), accused the *New York Times* series of distortion (August 17, 1963), and published a reply to Father O'Brien's articles (September 7, 1963). With regard to the Rock book the journal also called attention to the words of a reviewer in the *Times*, who, although himself in favor of contraception, had said that "Dr. Rock has made the tragic mistake of underestimating the intelligence of his own religious leaders. The Roman Catholic Church will recognize sugar-coating and reject it as artifice."[5] *America* (July 11, 1964) also welcomed a statement by Pope Paul reaffirming the traditional doctrine and said that it put an end to discussion which was threatening to undermine the Church's teaching authority.

[4] Quoted in the *Boston Globe Sunday Magazine*, reprinted in the *St. Louis Post-Dispatch*, Aug. 20, 1973, p. 2B.
[5] Robert E. Hall, M.D., in the *Times Book Review*, May 5, 1963.

Commonweal's position in those years was somewhat more complex, although, as the most notable organ of liberal Catholic thought in America, there was considerable public expectation that it would take an advanced position. In 1963 (August 23) the editors disclaimed any interest in persuading the Church to change its teaching, stating that this was outside their competence. They urged a perfecting of the rhythm method. Their response to the Rock book (May 17, 1963) was cool, noting serious deficiencies in the work but admitting that it had raised important questions. In most of its pronouncements during this period the magazine urged Catholics above all to be calm and rational on what easily became an emotional subject.

The following year, however, *Commonweal* published a book review by Robert Francoeur (October 16) which asserted that the traditional teaching was no longer tenable. (Francoeur, a diocesan priest, was then on the faculty of Fordham University. He later left the priesthood and became one of the leading apologists for the "sexual revolution" of the 1970s.)[6] Growing bolder, the editors suggested (November 13) that the teaching would change, that the old arguments were being discredited, and that a consensus was developing among the laity. An entire issue (June 5) was devoted to the subject of contraception, with each article suggesting, at least cautiously, the possibility and necessity of the Church's approving the pill.

American Catholicism in the conciliar years had a reputation for being highly orthodox, ultramontane, and cautious, a character which for some American Catholics was an embarrassment, and the Council was among other things a vehicle by which they hoped this "narrowness" might be overcome. Beginning in 1963 increasing attention was given to developments in European theology which, it was suggested, showed the unnecessary rigidity of moral attitudes prevailing in the American Church. A Belgian theologian, Louis Janssens, had written an article, in an obscure professional journal, cautiously endorsing use of the pill, and a Dutch bishop, Willem Bekkers, had urged a reconsideration of the traditional doctrine. *Time* (April 10, 1964) gave major publicity to both statements and pronounced the rhythm method unreliable. *Commonweal* (April 26, 1963) reprinted Bishop Bekkers' address. *America* (April 18, 1964) found statements by the Dutch bishops disturbing and unclear but thought that in part they had merely been distorted by the media.

Michael Novak, then a graduate student at Harvard, most clearly articulated the sense of some American Catholic intellectuals that European thought was more open and progressive than what prevailed in America. Criticizing those American theologians like John Ford, S.J., who had rejected Canon Janssens' proposals (*Commonweal*, April 24, 1964), he stated

[6] See, for example, his book *Utopian Motherhood* (New York, 1972).

bluntly that "European moralists regard themselves as teachers of the popes and bishops, as those who blaze a trail and go out ahead, 'rethinking the natural law' and also the past statements of the popes."

Novak was one of the first people to raise an issue which advocates of a changed doctrine on contraception had good reason to keep buried—the question of authority in the Church. Since there was a powerful feeling on the part of many Catholics that the Church's teaching authority would be undermined by such a change, revisionists generally tried to focus the issue as narrowly as possible and minimize the broader implications of what they proposed.

Newsweek, however, showed both a perspicacious understanding of the real issues and an apparent desire to use birth control as a wedge for prying open a number of other closed doors. "The specter of the Church leadership following its flock and responding to pressures from below cannot soon be forgotten", the magazine commented on one occasion (July 6, 1964) and said that married couples wanted to be "rightful participants in the Church's magisterium". A few months later (November 9) it ended an article with a rhetorical quotation from Cardinal Alfredo Ottaviani, "Is it possible that the Church has erred for centuries?", implying an answer opposite from the cardinal's intended one. Ten years after *Humanae vitae* one of the leading American dissenters from the encyclical, Father Charles Curran of the Catholic University of America, admitted that the traditionalists had been more correct than the innovators in sensing the full implications of any change. Although insisting that the revisionists had been sincere, he observed that they had been short-sighted in arguing their case merely in terms of the development of doctrine, without recognizing that what was required was a negation of past doctrine and past papal authority.[7]

During the conciliar and immediately postconciliar years a spate of books appeared arguing for a change in Catholic teaching with varying degrees of caution or boldness. These included, besides the Rock book, a symposium edited by William Birmingham entitled *What Modern Catholics Think About Birth Control* (1964); *Contraception and Holiness* (1964), by the retired Jesuit archbishop of Bombay, Thomas Roberts; *Contraception and Catholics* (1964), by the Georgetown philosopher Louis Dupré; and—a few years later—Daniel Callahan's *The Catholic Case for Contraception* (1969). In addition a major historical work appeared—John T. Noonan, Junior's *Contraception: A History of Its Treatment by the Catholic Theologians and Canonists* (1965), which established the consistency of the doctrine throughout the centuries but whose author stated publicly that he saw grounds for permitting a change. All these books achieved a good deal of notice in both the secular and the religious press, and Archbishop Roberts became something of a cult figure, thus adding

[7] "Ten Years Later", *Commonweal* (July 7, 1978): 426–30.

a further instance to the odd phenomenon in which elderly males played a major role in giving birth control respectability in Catholic eyes.

Those who hoped that the Council itself would modify or reverse the traditional doctrine were inevitably disappointed and were reduced virtually to grasping at straws. In 1964 much significance was attached to the fact that three prelates — Cardinal Paul-Emile Leger of Montreal, Cardinal Leo-Josef Suenens of Malines-Brussels, and Patriarch Maximos IV Saigh of Antioch — had urged exploration of a new approach to the question. *Newsweek* (November 9) thought their intervention might be a possible "mandate" to the papal commission then studying the question. *Time* (November 6) proclaimed the intervention a "watershed" and a "turning point" in the Council. The *New York Times* featured it on page one (October 30), where it often published news suggesting a possible change in the doctrine.

In the end the Council in its allegedly most "progressive" decree, *Gaudium et Spes*, urged couples to accept the possibility of large families (I, 50), insisted that the subjectivity of conscience was not sufficient basis for moral decision, and said that couples must respect previous prohibitions by the Church of certain methods of limiting procreation (I, 51). It also spoke of "illicit practices against human generation" (I, 47).

Writing in *Commonweal*, (November 20, 1964), the Canadian theologian Gregory Baum stated that in the draft scheme of the document the Council fathers "did not pretend that the Church knew the answers to the urgent questions which married people all over the world ask". Catholics were mistaken, he suggested, in thinking that the Church had committed itself on the question of contraception — if the teaching was actually questioned in a solemn council it obviously could not be infallible. Warming to a theme which would be increasingly dominant in his work in the years ahead, he asserted that the real issue was one's attitude toward the world — it should not be regarded as an enemy. The next year, writing in the same journal (December 24), he formulated the position which came to be adopted by all those who sought to appropriate the Council's authority as the basis for change — since the Council had not adopted the traditional terminology of the primary and secondary ends of marriage, it could be assumed to be leaving open the possibility of birth control, and the official teaching was therefore in doubt.

The Council had generated immense ecumenical enthusiasm and an eagerness on the part of Protestants and Catholics to overcome old differences, to understand each other's traditions with sympathy and respect. Birth control, however, was notably one area where no such ecumenical gestures were made, despite the fact that the commitment of most Protestant bodies to the idea of family planning was a relatively recent one. One of the leading Protestant ecumenists, Robert McAfee Brown, a Presbyterian and an official observer at the Council, welcomed the Rock book, for example, taking the opportunity to urge a massive publicly funded program of birth control.[8] The leading liberal Protestant journal in America, the *Christian Century*, returned to the subject again and again, often in tones bordering on anti-Catholic.[9] Claims on behalf of rhythm and the potential of the world to feed an expanding population were dismissed out of hand, and rhythm was labelled as "unnatural" (September 16, 1964). The journal gave space to Michael Novak (April 14, 1965) for an article contending that the Church had simply erred and should admit as much, and it also acclaimed Dr. Rock's book (May 29, 1963). The editors' tone was often flippant and near to being contemptuous, as in an editorial entitled "Will Rome Take the Pill?" In 1966, when the American bishops criticized the expenditure of federal funds to promote birth control, both the *Times* (November 23, page one) and *Time* magazine (December 2) gave prominence to the fact that various Protestant leaders had issued a counterstatement supporting such programs.

By 1965 the pattern of press treatment of contraception, insofar as it related to the Church, was established—although defenders of the traditional doctrine were given some exposure (most frequently quoted was Msgr. George A. Kelly, director of the Family Life Bureau of the Archdiocese of New York), far more space and prominence were given to the growing body of dissenters. From the standpoint of objective and honest journalism, traditionalists were also sometimes treated unfairly. For example, *Newsweek*, after quoting Msgr. Kelly on one occasion (July 6, 1964), gave its own gloss on what he had said: "Msgr. Kelly's fears are justified: sex is more fun with oral contraceptives."

The objectivity of the journalistic approach was questionable even without such blatant editorializing, however. The key concept was that of supposed "trends" that were developing and which the press was merely reporting. To establish such trends, however, it was necessary either to ignore all evidence against them (the probability, for example, that the majority of American theologians still supported the traditional doctrine in 1965, and almost certainly all the bishops did) or to treat it as unimportant. The postulation of a trend—in this case that the Catholic teaching on birth control was in the process of changing—was at best a guess on the part of the reporters, rendered all the more dubious by the obvious desire of most of the press that such a change should take place. The wishful thinking of the authors and journalists was offered as "news" to readers who were presumably indulging in similar wishful thinking or, if they were not, were supposed to.

[8] Ibid., *Commonweal* (July 5, 1963): 395–97.
[9] See, for example, July 6 and Nov. 16, 1966, Jan. 18, 1967, and Jan. 18 and Dec. 6, 1967.

A brief survey of the *New York Times* demonstrates the pattern. Although traditionalists were interviewed and quoted, they usually appeared on obscure pages of the paper or in the midst of long articles primarily devoted to dissenting opinions. Meanwhile, prominence was given to other opinions. In 1964, for example, the paper reported that a Jesuit sociologist, John L. Thomas, was the first priest to attend a Planned Parenthood convention and that he predicted a change in the Catholic teaching (May 1). Front-page coverage was given to a statement by the German theologian Bernard Häring that the Council supported family limitation (June 3). A front-page exposure was given to a series of meetings at the University of Notre Dame, sponsored by the Ford Foundation, which led to a qualified approval of contraception by the priests and lay people present. John Cogley, a former editor of *Commonweal* and now an editor of the *Times*, wrote several articles for the paper discussing changing Catholic thought on the subject (June 20 and August 26, 1965). Another favored journalistic technique was to present upholders of the traditional doctrine in as unattractive a light as possible, while idealizing its critics. For example, in an article on James Drane, an Arkansas priest suspended by his bishop for publicly attacking the doctrine, *Life* (September 8, 1967) photographed him laughing and buying ice cream for children at an amusement park.

During 1965 the most important new development on the subject was reports that the official papal commission charged with making recommendations to the Holy Father was badly split and was having difficulty reaching a conclusion. *Time* reported this fact (April 2), as did the *Times* (April 6). *Newsweek* characteristically drew a larger lesson from the division, quoting an anonymous theologian as saying that "Just as with Vatican II . . . the moderates now are prepared to go beyond achieving a limited goal (in this case, birth control) to a re-evaluation of doctrine (sexual morality)" (April 12).

Interest in the Church's dilemma also began to spread beyond the major organs of news and opinion. *U.S. News and World Report*, a generally conservative publication, returned to the subject briefly and periodically, always pointing out the difficulties of the traditional doctrine and holding out the possibility of change (September 9, 1963; July 6, 1964; April 12, 1965; May 1, 1967). A women's magazine, *Redbook*, published an article purportedly by a Catholic mother entitled "This Baby Will Be My Last" (July 1965), and another women's magazine, *Ladies Home Journal*, reported on "The Secret Drama behind the Pope's Momentous Decision on Birth Control" (March 1966). In 1965–66, *Look* published articles with titles like "The Catholic Revolution" (February 9, 1965), "Lady Doctor Defies Her Church" (August 10, 1965), and "The Pope's Unsolvable Problem" (December 13, 1966). The *Saturday Evening Post* published a testimonial by Rosemary Ruether entitled

"A Catholic Mother Tells Why 'I Believe in Birth Control' " (April 4, 1964), in which she declared that rhythm "does great psychological damage". (Some years later Professor Ruether revealed that while still an undergraduate she had ceased to be an orthodox Catholic in any ordinary sense of the term and had found meaning in the worship of ancient pagan deities as well as the Judaeo-Christian God.)[10]

In 1964–65, the leading American moral theologians either supported the traditional teaching or refrained from supporting change. Writing in *America*, for example, (January 11, 1964), the Jesuit Richard McCormick discussed marital love as something encompassing more than the intention to procreate but warned that it was a mistake to assume that birth control was therefore necessarily appropriate. Father Charles Curran, writing in *Jubilee* (August 1964), surveyed the opinions of those advocating a change and concluded that they were insufficiently probable to be followed in good conscience.

By 1966, however, it seems fair to say that the propaganda battle over birth control had already been lost in the United States. (The year 1966 seems to have been the crucial one in other respects. Research by the author into liturgical change in America also shows that ideas about worship changed radically beginning in that year.)[11]

Early in the year (January 28) the Benedictine scholar Paul Marx asked the editors of *Commonweal* who would determine what constituted "the serious circumstances" for the use of birth control which they stated would justify such use. The editors replied that a properly drawn papal document would make that distinction. Later in the year (July), the editors boldly pronounced that "the Church has already reversed its position on contraception; now it is up to the magisterium to bring its teaching in line with that change." Having predicted in 1965 (April 16) that a papal statement would be forthcoming by Easter, the editors noted in the fall of 1966 (November 11) that the Holy Father had again postponed his decision and concluded that the official teaching was obviously in a state of doubt. The following spring (April 28) the editors said that they wanted to belong to a Church willing to admit its errors. During 1965 (March 27), *America* had insisted that the Church could not bow to social pressures, although it also published an article (February 20) by the director of family life for the diocese of Cleveland, Msgr. Francis Carney, in which he stated rather ambiguously that the Church was discerning human needs "under the sociological pressures of this decade and the inspiration of the Holy Spirit". The journal still advocated the rhythm method and warned its readers that the official teaching might not change (April 10). In the fall (November 13) the editors anticipated an imminent encyclical,

[10] See her autobiographical article in *Journeys*, ed. Gregory Baum (New York, 1977).
[11] See Hitchcock, *The Recovery of the Sacred* (New York, 1974), especially chapter 1.

which it predicted would reaffirm traditional doctrine, and meanwhile it supported that teaching (April 24).

However, when in the spring of 1966 (May 21) the journal published an article by one of its editors, Francis Canavan, S.J., asking whether the liberalizing of laws on birth control and abortion would lead to the legalization of euthanasia by 1984, the article was noted as being merely the author's own opinion. In the fall (November 12) the announcement that a papal decision had again been delayed was greeted by *America*'s editors as "puzzling". For the first time they refrained from supporting the traditional doctrine but, significantly, noted that doubts about that teaching were becoming more widespread and were harder and harder to dispel. Priests in the confessional were giving penitents permission to use contraceptives.

In 1967 the magazine published articles by two Jesuit theologians, Robert Y. O'Brien (March 4) and Theodore Mackin (July 15), favoring a new approach. O'Brien denied that the Church had any "pipeline to heaven" on moral questions and asserted that Catholic couples were mature enough to distinguish between a responsible use of contraceptives and "the contraceptive mentality symptomatic of a sick civilization". Mackin argued that the Council documents authorized responsible parenthood and seemed to negate the rhythm method by suggesting that prolonged sexual abstinence was unhealthy in marriage.

The editors of *America* remained silent during most of 1967. However, in the fall (September 30) an editorial reported certain Catholic doctors as saying that contraceptives were necessary for a healthy marriage. After first defending the doctors from the charge of having challenged the teaching of the Church, the editors went on to endorse this opinion and said that it was an urgent question fit for discussion by the coming synod of bishops. The revolution was now complete, although *America*'s editors did not acknowledge that any had taken place. The most influential secular and religious journals in the United States now all favored a change in the traditional doctrine.

The divisions within the ranks of the papal commission, and the repeated delays in the issuance of an authoritative papal statement, were widely interpreted in the United States as evidence of the doubtfulness of the traditional doctrine, and given that opinion it is reasonable to assume that many Catholics not only granted themselves the benefit of the doubt in their marital practice but also altered their beliefs as well. *Time* reported on the split in the commission in some detail (April 22) and invoked the principle *"lex dubia non obligat"* — a doubtful law does not bind — a solution to the dilemma which was repeated a few months later (November 18), when it became apparent that no papal statement was imminent. *Newsweek* (February 14, 1966) also noted that more and more priests were authorizing the use of contraceptives and cited Gregory Baum, Richard McCormick, Charles Curran, and other theologians as to the practical state of doubt which existed and the nonbinding nature of the teaching. The magazine, referring to the Holy Father, made the point that "the longer he waits, the more onerous the decision will be, for as time goes by, more and more Catholic couples will feel free to make their own responsible decisions." Meanwhile the *New York Times* continued to give steady publicity to the failure of the Church to reach a decision, the growing instances of Catholic disregard for the traditional doctrine, and the increasingly bold statements by some Catholics justifying a change.[12] When the Holy Father indicated late in 1966 that the traditional teaching was still in effect the newspaper editorially disapproved of his action (November 3), which it feared would set back the clock in the Church, and a few weeks later (November 17) it also denied a charge by the American bishops that the government was using coercion in the other direction. In the spring of 1967 (March 29), a front-page article suggested that the recently issued encyclical *Populorum progressio* might permit governmentally promoted birth-control projects, and a subsequent denial of this by the Vatican press office (April 1) was buried deep inside the paper.

In the midst of the developing debate over birth control in the American Church a new publication had appeared which played a major role in the controversy. The *National Catholic Reporter* had been founded in 1964 and, as one of the liveliest and most controversial journals in the Church, was widely read and had especial influence among restless priests and religious. The paper regularly published articles with titles like "Around the World Seeds of Ferment" (May 3, 1967), "Church Accused of Callous Neglect on Birth Control" (May 22, 1968), and "Experts See Consensus for Change in TV Discussions of Birth Control" (May 10, 1967). In the spring of 1967 (April 19) the paper published the texts of the differing majority and minority reports of the papal birth-control commission, confidential documents which had presumably been given to the paper by a member of the commission. The fact that the majority of the commission favored a change in the traditional doctrine received wide attention and was urged as a strong reason why a change should be made. *Time* (April 28) diagnosed the unauthorized publication of the reports as an attempt to pressure the Holy Father into issuing the desired statement and suggested that it might have the opposite effect. *Newsweek* characterized those who opposed the majority recommendation as merely a "conservative clique" (May 1).

In that same spring of 1967 (March 20), *Newsweek* also published an extensive

---

[12] See, for example, Jan. 1, Feb. 17, Mar. 31, May 1, June 4, Oct. 20, Oct. 30, Nov. 3, Nov. 24, Dec. 3, 1966; Jan. 17, Apr. 19, May 11, Sept. 23, Oct. 14, Oct. 18, Oct. 23, 1967. A number of these articles appeared on the first page.

survey of American Catholicism, including opinion polls on a variety of subjects. The survey found not only a sharp increase in the number of Catholics who approved of contraception (about 73 percent) but also a measurable change of opinion about abortion, divorce, and clerical celibacy. Although the magazine did not draw the conclusion, it appeared that the effects of the "sexual revolution" had begun to seep deep into the American Church.

The year leading up to the issuance of *Humanae vitae* in July of 1968 was largely anticlimactic. On June 21, *Time* reported that a *motu proprio* which the Holy Father was about to issue had been withdrawn at the urgent entreaties of several European bishops. The same month the journal *U.S. Catholic* published a lengthy article asserting that the traditional doctrine was no longer in effect, and only a few days before the encyclical was issued on July 25 Father John Thomas was reported as predicting in a public lecture that the Church would accept all medically approved methods of birth control except sterilization.[13]

The issuance of the encyclical initiated a battle in the press even more intense and prolonged than the one which has been surveyed here and would require at least as much space to detail. In the pages of *Newsweek*, for example, it gave rise to a vicious vendetta against Pope Paul VI which lasted for at least five years.[14] One final example of media involvement must be noted, however, because it reveals how radically the opinions of certain people had changed in a few years' time and how effectively they had learned to exploit the media for their own purposes. Several hundred American Catholic theologians announced their dissent from the encyclical, under the leadership of Father Charles Curran. A decade later Father Curran described the process by which that dissent was mounted:

> In July rumors began to fly that an encyclical condemning artificial contraception was imminent. I was in frequent contact with colleagues at Catholic University and throughout the country. The strike at Catholic University the year before had the effect of catapulting me into a very prominent leadership role on this question of artificial contraception and the Roman Catholic Church.
>
> We tried in vain to raise enough publicity to prevent the issuance of any encyclical. It was my judgment that an encyclical at that time reaffirming the older teaching would be catastrophic. Many people would think that they could no longer be loyal Roman Catholics because of their decision to practice artificial contraception. Priests would be searching for guidance and would also be thrown into great crises of conscience. I was convinced that most Catholics and priests did not even know about the right to dissent from authoritative, noninfallible, hierarchical teaching. Plans then began to take shape to formulate a response to the encyclical that was rumored to be imminent.

[13] Reported in the *National Catholic Reporter*, July 24, 1968.
[14] See Hitchcock, "Bigotry in the Press: the Example of *Newsweek*", *The Alternative* (now *The American Spectator*), (Oct., 1976): 19–21.

On Sunday evening, July 28th, it was reliably reported on radio and television that an encyclical would be issued on Monday, July 29th. The encyclical was released in Rome on that Monday morning (at 4:30 A.M. New York time). I already had contingency reservations to fly back to Washington about noon on Monday. After numerous phone calls Sunday evening and Monday morning, a meeting was set for Caldwell Hall (my residence) at Catholic University that afternoon for a group of theologians to assemble and discuss a response to the encyclical. Copies of the encyclical were promised to us at that time. Other calls were made to theologians around the country telling them that a statement would be forthcoming and asking them to be prepared for a phone call later that evening asking them to sign the statement.

A group of about ten theologians met in Caldwell Hall, read the encyclical, and discussed a response. I insisted that the statement could not hedge, but would have to meet head on the question of dissent. . . . It was agreed to hold a press conference Tuesday morning to announce the statement, and in the meantime we telephoned the other theologians around the country to get their names for the statement. At the press conference I was the spokesman for the group and issued the statement in the name of eighty-seven American theologians. The number later swelled to over 600 signatures of people qualified in the sacred sciences as a result of a mailing to members of various professional organizations. Naturally this response became headline news throughout the United States and in all the television media. In fact we were able to hold subsequent press conferences in the next few days in an attempt to obtain as much coverage as possible.

Our quick, forceful response supported by so many theologians accomplished its purpose. The day after the encyclical was promulgated American Catholics could read in their morning papers about their right to dissent and the fact that Catholics could in theory and practice disagree with the papal teaching and still be loyal Roman Catholics. Other theologians around the world joined in and also even individual bishops and later some conferences of bishops. But our response as a quick, well-organized, collegial effort was unique. This, I hope, solved some problems for many Catholics, although I am sure that it also created problems for many other Catholics, who could not understand this type of dissent.

. . . In the ensuing furor, two false charges tended to ruffle me more than usual. Some claimed that we never read the encyclical. (It is true that our response was published before even many bishops had received the encyclical.) Such a charge is not only false, but anyone who read our short critique had to be convinced that it was a direct response to the reasoning of the encyclical itself. Others claim that our action was precipitous. My answer to that is: What is the virtue in delay? Our statement has stood the test of time much better than many that were written weeks or even months later. No, it was imperative to act both with speed and theological accuracy to accomplish our purpose. There was absolutely no virtue in delay.[15]

There are numerous lessons which might be drawn from this narrative. The crucial point, however, pertains to the often repeated claim that American

[15] See the essay by Father Curran in *Journeys* (ed. Baum).

Catholics massively rejected *Humanae vitae* and that their rejection was the occasion of a growing alienation from the Church.

Several points seem relevant. One is the fact, often lost sight of, that the rejection of *Humanae vitae*, to the extent that it occurred, was hardly spontaneous. It was preceded by at least five years when the most influential segments of the press, secular and Catholic, propagandized intensely and unremittingly for a change in the official teaching. Although there was much talk of "dialogue" and "pluralism", in fact the discussion was remarkably one-sided. It was the first major test of a phenomenon which has grown increasingly familiar—the question how, in modern society, it is possible for any group, especially a religious group, to teach and maintain doctrines toward which the most influential organs of that culture are hostile. How can a church prevent itself from being effectively excluded from making its voice heard in society above the din of contrary voices?

The second point is that the divisions within the official papal commission and the consequent delays which attend the issuance of an authoritative papal statement virtually doomed the encyclical to the kind of reception which it received. Long before the summer of 1968 the relevant questions had become settled in the minds of many. Delay was equated with doubt and doubt with permission to dispense with the doctrine. In the minds of many people an expectation had been built up that the teaching would change. One American member of the papal commission, Dr. John R. Cavanagh, had in 1965 bluntly warned clergy and other Church leaders that they should be preparing their people for the fact that the teaching would not change.[16] There is little evidence that his warning was heeded. The expectation of change which was built up in many minds not only led to widespread rejection of the encyclical when it finally appeared but also to a good deal of bitterness.

Finally, the significant fact should be noticed that at every stage the tendency of the advocates of change—in most cases probably sincere—was to minimize the full implications of their positions. The word "abortion" was scarcely ever mentioned, for example. The reaction to *Humanae vitae* was undoubtedly one of the most traumatic and damaging events in the history of American Catholicism, its repercussions still affecting the Church in innumerable ways. The prelude to this reaction shows the American Catholics, including some of their leaders, making almost every mistake it is humanly possible to make. It is not at all clear that the appropriate lessons have even yet been learned.

[16] *Jubilee* (Dec., 1965): 40–41.

POSTMORTEM ON A REBIRTH:
THE CATHOLIC INTELLECTUAL RENAISSANCE

In the summer of 1907, Pope Pius X, later to be canonized a saint, issued two documents, *Lamentabili sane exitu* ("With Truly Lamentable Effect") and *Pascendi Dominici gregis* ("Feeding the Lord's Flock"), both in condemnation of a theological movement which he called modernism. Among the doctrines condemned were denials of the historical reliability of Scripture and the Church's authority to interpret it, and denials of immutable truth. The drift of modernism, as the Pope condemned it, was that religion was an essentially human phenomenon, the product of the evolving creative consciousness of the human race.

Whether all the modernists held to all the positions condemned has been a matter of debate ever since. It is a judgment which is difficult to make because to some extent the modernists were either supported or condemned for wishing to introduce more historical studies into theology, and it is not clear how far all of them wished to carry the historical method. The principal targets of the condemnation (which, like most such papal documents, did not single out individuals) were undoubtedly the French priest Alfred Loisy and the Irish former Jesuit George Tyrrell. The most eminent names associated with the movement were those of laymen — Baron Friedrich von Hügel and Maurice Blondel. Both of the latter were sharply critical of some aspects of the modernists' work, and the degree to which they should be considered modernists has also been the source of continuing controversy.

Conventional wisdom in Catholic intellectual circles of the 1970s holds that the condemnation of modernism brought an end to serious Catholic thought for more than fifty years, ushering in a reign of terror which inhibited intellectuals until the benign pontificate of Pope John XXIII (1958–63) and the dramatic changes of the Second Vatican Council (1962–65).

Oddly, however, an obscure event the year before the modernist condemnation had already signaled the beginning of possibly the brightest period of modern Catholic thought. In June 1906, in Montmartre, the young Jacques and Raïssa Maritain, both former agnostics — he from a liberal Protestant background, she of Russian-Jewish birth — received baptism. To the degree that they were aware of modernism at all (they may not have become aware of it until some time later), they approved Pius X's condemnation.

The Maritain conversion can be looked at from one standpoint as another in a series of such occurrences stretching back to the time of Romanticism, a process involving the conscious rejection of the rational skepticism of the Enlightenment. John Henry Newman was the chief nineteenth-century figure in the drama. From another standpoint, however, the twentieth-century conversion phenomenon, lasting practically down to 1960, was a distinct phase which owed relatively little to the earlier ones.

Perhaps the most remarkable thing about Catholic thought in the twentieth century has been precisely the fact that most of its eminent figures were converts. That men suckled in a creed outworn should grow up prepared to elaborate and defend it is not surprising. That brilliant skeptics should ultimately be attracted to it is surprising. Ironically, even in France, the "eldest daughter of the Church", most of the great twentieth-century Catholic intellectuals—the Maritains, Paul Claudel, Léon Bloy, Charles Péguy, Gabriel Marcel, Edith Stein—were converts, either actually or in the sense of born Catholics who rejected childhood faith but later returned to the Church with a passion. There were also the near-converts, like Henri Bergson and Simone Weil.

England, where the Catholic population, other than poor Irish, was quite small, naturally needed convert thinkers even more, and a supply was always available: G. K. Chesterton, Christopher Dawson, Ronald Knox, Graham Greene, and Evelyn Waugh. Even Anglo-Catholicism gained its principal luminaries—T. S. Eliot, W. H. Auden, C. S. Lewis—from convert ranks.

Modernism, treated for over fifty years like a minor and altogether uninteresting event, now returns to haunt Catholicism like a repressed desire, and it has become customary to say that the questions which the modernists raised now constitute the present Catholic intellectual agenda. Also customary is the lament that condemnation of the movement cut off the Church's most promising effort to make its doctrines credible to modern skeptics. Yet the remarkable fact is that the distinguished converts of the twentieth century were attracted to the Church, not in spite of the condemnation, but almost, in some cases, because of it. What they found attractive and credible in it were precisely those things which Pius X sought to protect with his condemnation, and they found the characteristic doctrines of modernism either false or uninteresting.

A little-noticed aspect of modern intellectual history is that although liberal religion, whether Christian or Jewish, was created with the aim of making the old faith credible to modern doubters, it rarely does so. Such liberalizations, rather, appeal primarily to those who were raised in the old creed, have become restive under it, and are often in the process of abandoning it. Intellectual converts are almost always attracted to rather traditional and even rigorous versions of religion, probably because liberalized religion merely confirms the skeptic's suspicion that the traditional faith was false.

For whatever reason, France and England were the centers of this Catholic intellectual revival, quite possibly because of the necessary confrontation with a hostile culture which was a permanent feature of Catholic life in those countries. (France, while nominally Catholic, harbors a continuing tradition of antireligious skepticism dating from the eighteenth century.) The flowerings in Spain and Italy were much less brilliant and, while there was much activity in America, most of it was dependent on European models. The Church in Germany had a brilliant intellectual life, but Catholic energies there were focused primarily on questions of internal Catholic concern and made less contact with the wider culture, at least outside the German-speaking lands (the chief exceptions being Romano Guardini, Josef Pieper, and the Swiss theologian Hans Urs von Balthasar).

Catholicism inspired an especially fruitful literary creativity, including not only Waugh, Greene, Georges Bernanos, and François Mauriac but even a major Catholic novelist in a most unlikely place, Norway's Sigrid Undset. Perhaps only in literature was the American contribution, while modest, nonetheless significant, embracing a generation of writers — Flannery O'Connor, J. F. Powers, Walker Percy — younger than the European masters and essentially independent of them. (Catholic writers roughly contemporaneous with the Europeans, like F. Scott Fitzgerald and James T. Farrell, found largely negative inspiration in their childhood faith.) America has also had its noted literary converts — Robert Lowell, Thomas Merton, and Tennessee Williams — although Catholicism's influence on Williams' writing is scarcely detectable.

That Catholicism should have proved fruitful in the twentieth-century literary context is not surprising for several reasons, not the least important of which is the fundamental dramatic tensions which it generates: sin and redemption, authority and freedom, tradition and experience. Modern culture, as it grows simultaneously more open and more uniform, takes on a certain flatness which renders novelistic creation in particular quite problematical. For those who took Catholicism seriously, however, there was never any lack of enticing possibilities.

An important measure of Catholicism's spiritual and intellectual collapse since 1960 is that whatever literary inspiration it now provides is once again a largely negative one (for example, the Americans Tom McHale and Mary Gordon and the Australians Thomas Kenneally and Colleen McCullough), sometimes verging on hate. The classic Catholic novelists of the "preconciliar period" — that is, the period of the "unreformed" Church before the Second Vatican Council — found a resolution of tensions in ways which reaffirmed the essential validity of belief. The sufferings endured and the perplexities explored finally yielded an experience of richness and profundity previously only glimpsed. Nowhere, perhaps, did Catholic novelists move more resolutely against the cultural grain than in their willingness to propose the redemptive value of renunciation. Oddly, despite the rich comic possibilities inherent in Catholicism's relationship to modern culture, only Evelyn Waugh, among the major Catholic writers of the classical period (ca. 1930–60), systematically exploited them. He was also the most rigorously orthodox of all and the least accepting of modern secularity.

A major unsolved mystery is why Christianity, and especially Catholicism, has never ceased to inspire composers all the way down to the present, while overtly religious painting, among major artists, virtually ceased in the seventeenth century. In the twentieth century alone, the list of composers who took inspiration from Catholic liturgy includes Bruckner, Stravinsky, Poulenc, Dupré, Duruflé, and Messiaen, alongside Anglicans like Vaughan Williams and Britten. Among painters, however, Georges Rouault stands almost alone as an identifiably Catholic artist.

A Catholic presence in the arts could perhaps have been predicted in the century of science; at least since the time of Pascal the ground of religious affirmation in the West has been shifting from the objective to the subjective, from formal argumentation to the seemingly ineradicable religious sense which is found in human beings. In the world of imagination, virtually no belief seems impossible, and religious themes have often been used by artists having no belief in the doctrines behind them. (Among major writers of the Catholic revival perhaps only Graham Greene is open to this suspicion, although, as he describes his development, he moved only gradually away from the orthodoxy which he had embraced at the time of his conversion in the 1920s.)

In its most powerful and influential expressions, however, the Catholic revival sought to meet the rationalists on their own ground. While not insensitive to the artistic and the intuitive (both Maritain and Gilson wrote aesthetic treatises), the dominant Catholic thinkers of the age were determined that the phenomenon of belief should be placed on a rigorously constructed foundation. It was scholastic philosophy and theology that would receive the major investment of Catholic intellectual resources.

Despite general impressions to the contrary, the authority of Thomas Aquinas did not dominate Catholic thought through all the centuries following his death. Although his name was revered in the nineteenth century, other thinkers, notably the sixteenth-century Jesuit Francisco Suárez, were probably more influential. The modern Thomistic revival dates essentially from the authoritative exhortations of Pope Leo XIII in the 1880s.

Any number of modern people, beginning with Machiavelli, have asserted that Christianity is useful, and the Romantics managed to restore its respectability by proclaiming its beauty. But to the converts of the early twentieth century one question alone mattered: was it true? The conversion of the Maritains stemmed from their conviction that it was. Their dilemma was the age-old metaphysical one—whether life has meaning—and faith was the only alternative to the fulfillment of a suicide pact they had made with one another. In the skeptical and positivistic atmosphere of the Sorbonne of 1900, religious beliefs alone seemed hopeful and truly humane.

Initially the Maritains may have been what the Church calls "fideists", a position that is widespread even though officially condemned. It means religious belief which is self-validating, an understanding of belief which is essentially nonrational and even irrational, without philosophical foundation. Groping for something more, the Maritains passed under the influence of Bergson. But it was the discovery of Aquinas that proved to be a revelation almost as great as that of Catholicism itself. "Woe unto me if I should fail to Thomisticize", Jacques Maritain quipped in a paraphrase of Saint Paul. Gilson came to Thomism via a much cooler and somewhat later route. He discovered the medieval philosophical heritage while researching Descartes's intellectual antecedents.

The scholastic revival predated Maritain and Gilson, but without them it would probably have remained a wholly Catholic thing. Instead, by the eve of World War II, a kind of scholasticism was being taught even in some secular colleges, among them the University of Chicago under Mortimer Adler and Richard McKeon, where the joke ran that atheist professors taught Catholic philosophy to Jewish students. Even where it did not command assent, scholasticism was taken seriously. Gilson, for example, gave his series of lectures on *Medieval Universalism and Its Present Value* in conjunction with the Harvard tercentenary of 1936 and in 1943 lectured at Rutgers on *Dogmatism and Tolerance*. His *The Unity of Philosophical Experience* was also based on Harvard lectures, and *Reason and Revelation in the Middle Ages* was a series of lectures given at the University of Virginia. Maritain was welcome at a number of American universities, notably Princeton. Suggestive of a not altogether positive kind of change which has occurred in American academic circles over the past few decades is the fact that such lectures on such subjects would not be likely to gain sponsorship today and, if they did, would probably attract little interest.

Against the positivistic and skeptical spirit of the dominant American philosophies, the apostles of neo-scholasticism asserted the possibility of genuine metaphysical knowledge, a perennial truth valid and knowable in all historical periods. Toward this end, they proposed Aristotelian logic and epistemology as constitutive of the method, and their ultimate conclusions were also essentially Aristotelian, albeit in Thomistic form. It was a system of thought which began with sense experience, proceeded to a metaphysical understanding of what was experienced, and reasoned through a series of causes to the Final Cause, God.

The openness which many nonbelievers showed toward neo-scholasticism may have owed something to the religious revival among Western intellectuals that began as early as T. S. Eliot's conversion in 1928 and came to flower after World War II. However, the neo-scholastics were emphatically not calling for a revival of faith, or at least not primarily. They took their stand on the foundation of reason, and their critique of modern thought — put forth most boldly in Maritain's *Three Reformers* and Gilson's *The Unity of Philosophical Experience* — was that it either rejected reason or misused it. All forms of irrationalism, whether fideistic, romantic, psychological, or existential, were criticized, as were uses of reason that were merely instrumental or analytic and failed to grasp reality in all its fullness.

At the same time, the neo-scholastics also insisted that a genuine rationality would inevitably lead to God, understood first as the ultimate cause of all things. Reason, while it did not inevitably lead to faith, nonetheless showed that faith was not irrational. The act of believing was itself not unnatural, a recognition finally that reason had been pushed to its limits and that there were more things in the universe than could be dreamed of in philosophy.

The fideistic tradition in Christianity, which also had a long pedigree, was sternly read out of court, and much of Catholic intellectual life came to be characterized by a kind of hyperrationalism in which the passion for logical proof and argumentation was dominant. This led to a strange and ultimately very damaging anomaly in Catholic higher education, whereby theology was often not taught at all or was taught badly, while major effort was concentrated on the teaching of philosophy. In this respect Gilson was far less rigid than some of the lesser neo-scholastics, and he aroused controversy by his insistence that, in Aquinas, philosophy and theology were not distinct disciplines, that Aquinas's philosophical positions had been directly influenced by his religious faith (for example, his assertion of God as "pure being" having been inspired by God's self-revelation to Moses in the burning bush: "I am Who am"). Maritain, while of deep faith, was more inclined to operate within a strictly philosophical framework. (A probably apocryphal story has Raïssa Maritain asking a woman, "Are you a Thomist?" "No, but I'm a Catholic." "Well, at least that's a start.")

The neo-scholastics were naturally vulnerable to the charge of being romantic nostalgists, of being religiously motivated to return to the Middle Ages. Whatever elements of truth there may have been in that charge, it seems likely that they were attracted less by the idea of a perfect age of faith than by a rationally based philosophy which was more comprehensive than anything modernity could offer — reason not primarily as skeptical and analytical but as creative and systematic. Gilson in particular was antiromantic in his repeated insistence that many self-proclaimed Thomists really misunderstood the nature of scholasticism and read it in ways that were subtly corrupted by precisely those modern philosophical errors which they were ostensibly rejecting. (The key point for both Maritain and Gilson was the apprehension of the "act of existence" itself — the question whether or not a thing really exists, and how, not merely the general or abstract conception of it in the mind.)

Gilson was a historian who ventured only occasionally into fields of contemporary controversy. His historical work was monumental: a series of studies of Augustine, Bernard of Clairvaux, Héloise and Abelard, Aquinas, Bonaventure, Duns Scotus, and Dante, culminating in the magisterial *History of Christian Philosophy in the Middle Ages*. Rarely has one man dominated a scholarly field as long as Gilson did from the Medieval Institute at the University of Toronto.

The neo-scholastics made a bold and unfashionable but certainly not unreasonable claim: that the process of human thought culminates at certain points in history, arriving at a peak whose achievements are forever valid. Their peak was the thirteenth century and the work of Aquinas, whose synthesis of faith and reason was to be taken as the most profound intellectual account of the depth and complexity of existence. The history of late scholasticism, loosely lumped together under the title of nominalism, was then the history of the disintegration of that synthesis, the prelude to and cause of the modern Western cultural breakdown. (When the scholarly reaction to Gilson set in, it centered primarily on two things—a more positive evaluation of late scholasticism and the charge that Gilson underestimated the influence of Plato on the whole scholastic enterprise.)

Gilson did occasionally venture into battles of the moment. In *Dogmatism and Tolerance*, for example, he made a case similar to one made by Hannah Arendt—that totalitarianism does not aim to instill, but to destroy, convictions in people—and went on to argue that certain kinds of dogmatically held beliefs would be a bulwark against the modern totalitarian state. (Earlier, in one of his Harvard lectures, he had joked that the spirit of relativism could hardly become more tolerant than to welcome the dogmatist into its midst, a congratulatory remark which would have much less applicability in contemporary academia.)

However, it was primarily Maritain who undertook to demonstrate the relevance of Thomism to the twentieth century, publishing five books on aesthetics and five on politics, as well as formal philosophical works and other assorted projects. For some years he lived in Princeton and for a time served as French ambassador to the Vatican. In the 1920s he had given his support (as had T. S. Eliot) to Action Française, the French movement which, under the atheist Charles Maurras, advocated a revival of the prerevolutionary alliance of throne and altar. But Maritain became disillusioned with the movement even before it was condemned by Pope Pius XI in 1926. By World War II, Maritain had become a convinced democrat and, living in the United States during the Pétain regime, found himself increasingly attracted to the American political system. Unlike in France, democracy in the New World was not contaminated by anticlericalism and official secularist ideology. He thought that separation of church and state had obviated church-state conflict.

In *Scholasticism and Politics*, written during World War II, Maritain expressed discouragement at the pessimism and lack of self-confidence characteristic of the Western democracies, and in the postwar world he joined enthusiastically in the resurgence of that confidence. While stopping short of asserting that democracy as a political system flowed directly from correct philosophical principles, he nonetheless dismissed Fascism and Communism as inherently irrational. Bourgeois individualism was, however, implicitly immoral and, by breaking down all sense of community and shared moral values, would inevitably end in some form of statism: order imposed from above. In *Integral Humanism* (1936) and later works, he developed a systematic critique of the prevailing modern political ideologies and argued that a workable political order, which might appropriately be democracy, depended on a correct understanding of human nature and of natural moral law.

Maritain became something of an Americanophile, seeking to counter not only what he regarded as European misconceptions about America but also the Americans' own self-deprecation. In *Reflections on America* (1958), he argued that Americans were not really materialistic but were the most idealistic people in the world, although theirs was an idealism often unformed and lacking in philosophical bases. America, he thought, offered perhaps the best contemporary prospect for the emergence of a truly Christian civilization, based not on governmental decree but on the gradual realization of Christian values on the part of a majority of the population. American saints were coming, he predicted.

But his postulation of a possible Christian civilization in America did not in any way temper his optimistic political liberalism—a facet of his thought which caused him to be held in suspicion by some of his fellow Catholics in the 1950s. The Dominican chaplain at Princeton, for example, refused to allow him to address the Catholic students. (One of the exquisite ironies of recent Catholic history was that Maritain in his last books was acerbically critical of secularizing priests, while the Dominican chaplain resigned from the priesthood and ended his days as a real estate salesman in Florida.)

No doubt in part because of Raïssa's background, Maritain had an enduring interest in anti-Semitism, which he analyzed and criticized in two books, and he was one of the principal influences in the effort to establish better Jewish-Catholic relations. Racism he regarded as America's most severe flaw. As early as 1958 he was praising Martin Luther King, Jr., and the Chicago neighborhood organizer Saul Alinsky.

Maritain and, to a lesser extent, Gilson provided the program for a bold kind of Catholic intellectuality—an appropriation of medieval thought for modern use, not so much a medieval revival as a demonstration of the perennial relevance of the medieval philosophical achievement. The modern mind was to be brought back to its Catholic roots, not by the simple disparagement of modernity or by emphasis on the subjective necessity of faith, but by a rigorous and demanding appeal to reason. In the process, scholastic principles would be applied in new and often daring ways.

In the end the gamble failed. Despite promising signs in the 1940s, secular thinkers did not finally find the scholastic appeal persuasive. And, as is inevitable when an intellectual community is dominated so thoroughly by a single system of thought, a restiveness was building up in Catholic circles. Although Maritain insisted that Thomism, because of the central importance it gave to the act of existence, was the true existentialism, Catholic intellectuals of the 1950s were attracted to the movement which more usually went by that name; and Gabriel Marcel, a Catholic existentialist of the same generation as Gilson and Maritain, was available to mediate between faith and anguish. Catholic colleges in America were hospitable to existentialist and phenomenological currents at a time when few secular institutions were, and what Catholics sought there was primarily a philosophy which was serious about the metaphysical questions of existence, yet not as rationalistic, rigid, and abstract as scholasticism often seemed to be.

The neo-scholastics were often accused of not taking history seriously—a charge which could not but have a good deal of truth to it, given the fact that medieval philosophy had not recognized history as a properly scientific discipline and given the relentless scholastic urge to discern fixed principles amidst the flux of change.

Although Catholic historians were numerous enough even in neo-scholasticism's heyday, only one major Catholic thinker approached the understanding of his religion from a primarily historical standpoint. Christopher Dawson was, like so many others, a convert. Raised in an apparently serene Anglicanism and entering the Church of Rome while in his twenties, he seems not to have passed through the crucible of doubt. A prolific writer despite a rather late start, he achieved a certain celebrity in both Catholic and non-Catholic circles, and his work in cultural history was praised by, among others, Arnold Toynbee, Harry Elmer Barnes, Crane Brinton, and George Lichtheim.

It was customary for neo-scholastics to speak rather patronizingly of Dawson's work, since he was doing mere history, where generalizations were of a lower order of significance than those supplied by metaphysics. Although Dawson was read and listened to, conventional opinion both inside and outside the Church had agreed to treat neo-scholasticism as the single most authentic expression of Catholic thought, and Dawson was thus regarded somewhat as an interesting anomaly. Whereas Gilson and Maritain were published almost exclusively by prestigious secular publishers, most of Dawson's books were brought out by the Catholic house of Sheed and Ward. In 1958 he was the first appointee to the new chair of Roman Catholic Studies at Harvard, but by that time he was in ill health and his influence was rather limited.

While religious faith as such was more overtly present in his work than in Maritain's, Dawson too asked to be judged primarily on scholarly grounds. His central thesis, elaborated with great sophistication and detail through numerous books, was that historically human cultures have always rested on some religious foundation and that the modern West is unique in the history of the world in attempting to dispense with that foundation. As a general thesis it seems close to being indisputable and, if it has not been taken sufficiently seriously by historians, this is probably because of their own discomfort in the presence of religious phenomena.

Yet Dawson did not claim to be only a historian and, although his learning was immense, he rarely engaged in the kind of original research which is the basic stuff of modern historiography. In compensation he demonstrated a formidable grasp of the most diverse cultural phenomena — art, theology, politics, economics, sociology — from practically all of the world's cultures. Long before it had become fashionable in academia to decry narrow disciplinary specialization and Western cultural provincialism, Dawson was showing precisely how a historian could, and indeed had to, account for all available data.

Nonbelievers could not accept Dawson's work, perhaps less because of his assertion of religion's historical importance — a contention that could hardly be denied — than because of his analysis of the likely future consequences of nonbelief. The loss of spiritual roots, he argued, would induce not only moral crises but political and cultural crises as well. Like Maritain, but more systematically and with much greater historical awareness, he predicted that modern bourgeois liberalism, left purely to its own devices, would drift toward some kind of totalitarianism, or else would prove incapable of withstanding totalitarianism's appeal. As early as the 1950s Dawson argued that the end of colonialism would not lead to the revival of native Asian and African cultures but to the beginnings of worldwide political uniformity based on the Western Marxist ideology.

Dawson's characteristic differences from the neo-scholastics were revealed in his treatment of the Protestant Reformation, which he, unlike Maritain, did not see primarily as the breakdown of the theological synthesis and the triumph of an irrational subjectivity; rather, he saw it as the triumph of a new worldliness made possible by the abolition of monasticism. Although he revered the Middle Ages, Dawson was more attracted to the culture of the baroque, the almost miraculous survival of deep and creative religious faith into the modern secular milieu. Both the Protestant north, with its austere religion of individual and interior faith, and a Catholic France, which had resisted the Counter-Reformation, were the seedbeds of modern secularity through their detaching of reason from both faith and imagination, thus liberating it for purely instrumental purposes.

Whereas Dawson for the most part stayed aloof from contemporary political controversies, he was the kind of conservative whose principles could have radical implications. He was coolly critical of both capitalism and nationalism, for example, seeing them as products of the modern secular bourgeois state, and nationalism in particular as a substitute religion. He advanced these judgments at a time when American Catholics tended to be ardent patriots and when free-enterprise capitalism enjoyed a generally good Catholic press.

If Maritain was politically liberal, professing his fundamental faith in Western democracy while urging a deepening of the moral and philosophical basis of that democracy, Dawson's critique of the political order went a good deal deeper. (Given the religious assumptions of both men, it could also be argued that Dawson was the more clear-eyed and consistent.) Opposed to Fascism and Communism as corruptions of the religious sense, he was cool toward democracy as based on illusions and as ultimately unable to withstand totalitarianism. Although his criticisms were muted (Dawson was rarely polemical in any overt way), there was a sense of his strong reservations about the American experiment.

His was not a sentimental medievalism, nor even a sentimental evocation of the baroque, but rather a vision of a social order based on explicit moral and religious values deeply embedded in the mental habits of the population and in social institutions. Reared in a quiet rural environment near the border of Wales and Herefordshire, he regretted the passing of the genuinely traditional and closely knit communities of his youth. He did not, however, propose a revival of older values, recognizing the impossibility of all such revivals. Rather, like Maritain and Gilson, he proposed the appropriation of certain older values for the purpose of creating a new social order, one which he recognized might look quite different from anything in the past.

If Dawson was held in suspicion in secular circles because of his overt Christianity, he was also held in suspicion by some Catholics because of his refusal to make neo-scholasticism, or indeed any philosophy, the center of the Catholic intellectual enterprise. Most neo-scholastics may have accepted his historical analysis, yet there was a prevalent feeling that, by basing the Christian case on history, he was weakening it. In *The Crisis of Western Education* (1961), he advocated a reinvigoration of the classical liberal arts tradition, but broadened and deepened by the inclusion both of modern and of non-Western components. Its purpose, he argued, was to put students in touch with the mainsprings of their own civilization, which alone could stem the Western cultural drift. His system stopped short of seeking to inculcate religious belief, although that might well have been one of its by-products. Instead, it aimed to make students appreciate and understand the religious roots of the modern West, and he thought that the Catholic colleges were heirs to a much deeper and richer culture than the secular schools had access to.

Dawson's proposals for educational reform were tried in a few small Catholic colleges but had only slight influence on the major institutions, where neo-scholasticism was the heart and soul of the curriculum. In private correspondence during the 1950s Dawson expressed serious doubts about this situation, offering the judgment that philosophy and theology were suitable subjects only for those who were already educated, and suggesting that the medieval universities had ultimately been killed by the dominance of scholasticism. He considered Maritain a Romantic and complained that he approached literary works in an ahistorical way.

When Dawson made these judgments, in 1955, neo-scholasticism appeared to be impregnably self-confident and dominant in Catholic higher education, its attitude toward its critics either haughtily condemnatory or condescendingly tolerant. Many things came together in the next decade to shake that confidence, the most important being a religious event—the Second Vatican Council and what surrounded it. The Council attempted to define a new Catholic relationship to the world, and its pronouncements were also used by some people in much more radical ways than were ever intended.

The initial result was, for the first time, to give respectability to modes of philosophical inquiry other than the scholastic. Like most forms of pluralism, this was not limited to peaceful coexistence. By 1965 the dominance of scholasticism was severely shaken; it found itself retreating from movements which had the advantages of appearing youthful, progressive, and outside the establishment. By 1975, despite occasional flurries of renewed interest, scholasticism had come close to disappearing in most Catholic colleges and universities, and virtually nowhere had it survived as a systematic, methodical quest for truth at the heart of the curriculum.

There are many reasons for this. Among the most important is the fact that the scholastic mode of thinking is probably suitable only for relatively few people; it is a highly technical, subtle discipline, not easily grasped or assimilated. Generations of Catholics, including priests, learned it almost by rote, often ending with a set of abstract propositions which they could not easily relate to the world or to history. Dawson's pedagogy had proposed instead that Catholics (and others too) be drawn imaginatively back into the Christian past. Then, when they had made that past a part of themselves, they could undertake the search for enduring philosophical truth. In retrospect it might be argued that neo-scholasticism, while it gave its disciples a sense of the rightness of their position, often failed to impart to them a love for it, something which Dawson's approach to education might have accomplished. Gilson himself, in *The Spirit of Thomism* (1964), criticized some of its practitioners for fashioning a "static" and "sterile" philosophy.

The Catholic intellectual landscape has been unimaginably changed over a twenty-year period—so changed, in fact, that it can hardly even be mapped. Today eclecticism reigns supreme, not only in the choice of philosophies but in matters of Church doctrine as well. The contemporary Catholic intellectual's relationship to his own traditions is at best confused and ambivalent. The subjectivity which neo-scholasticism held at bay for so long has come rushing forth with a vengeance and Catholics are most receptive to every kind of psychological nostrum. In the process, the institutional supports for Catholic intellectual life have themselves been eroded; colleges have been closing their doors, and most of those that survive face an uncertain future. In the meantime they have, for the most part, ceased even to try to form in their students any distinctive way of thinking about the world. A number of Catholic journals have ceased publication, and most others find their subscription lists declining. In commercial terms, no market for serious Catholic intellectual work is being created, and the outlets to such markets as do exist are constricted. Most of the books of the twentieth-century revival have gone out of print.

As is usually the case when dominant figures die, a reaction has set in against the leading lights of the revival they impelled. Since so many of them were extraordinarily long-lived (Maritain, 1882–1973; Gilson, 1884–1978; Dawson, 1889–1970; Marcel, 1889–1973), the reaction set in even before their deaths. As early as 1965, for example, Sheed and Ward began to be cool toward publishing Dawson. Maritain's later works that were critical of the "new Church", especially *The Peasant of the Garonne* (1968), were sometimes savaged by Catholic reviewers. The present generation of Catholic college students scarcely knows Gilson, Maritain, Dawson, Mauriac, Waugh, or Bernanos even as names in a textbook.

Almost without exception the leaders of this revival had no quarrel with basic Catholic doctrine and rarely had any even with Catholic practice—a phenomenon not entirely due to neo-scholasticism. The existentialist Marcel, for example, gave lectures in the United States in the early 1960s in which he offered poetic, almost mystical support to the ideal of noncontraceptive sex. The phenomenologist Dietrich von Hildebrand, another convert, became the most ardent champion of orthodoxy. Most of the great figures of the revival (Graham Greene alone excepted) expressed greater or less degrees of misgivings about the changes that occurred in the Church after the Second Vatican Council—which was also true of most of the leading theologians whose work had prepared the way for the Council, notably Henri de Lubac, Jean Daniélou, Louis Bouyer, and Hans Urs von Balthasar.

There are several intriguing ironies in this slaying of the fathers which has occurred since the Council. Contemporary Catholicism wishes to be relevant to the world, and not to rest secure in an ecclesiastical ghetto. Yet no recent Catholic thinker has attempted to explore social and political realities with anything like the comprehensiveness and trenchancy of Maritain or Dawson. It wishes to be taken seriously in secular intellectual circles, yet no Catholic thinker alive today has the respectability in those circles which Gilson, Maritain, Dawson, Mauriac, or Waugh enjoyed. It proclaims the age of the laity, emancipated from clerical dominance. Yet the leading lights of the revival were almost all lay people, while the three most influential thinkers in the contemporary Church — Pierre Teilhard de Chardin, Karl Rahner, and Bernard Lonergan (the last still alive) — are Jesuits. (Teilhard's quasi-mystical writings have lent themselves to all kinds of interpretation, and his long-range significance is still uncertain. Rahner and Lonergan represent a branch of Thomism which Gilson and Maritain regarded as inauthentic, since it undertakes a dialogue with Kantianism rather than affirming that Thomistic epistemology escapes Kant's strictures. Called "Transcendental Thomism", it has been largely a Jesuit movement.)

The Catholic intellectual revival, apart from its specific content, represented a unique twentieth-century cultural phenomenon — an approach to truth based on the supposition of the normative correctness of certain traditions, and intellectual activity directed primarily at a more profound penetration and exposition of those traditions. The dominant style of modern thought has been contestation of all traditions, and it was largely the Catholic intellectual community's belated reception of that mode of operation which led it to declare irrelevant its own richest flowering.

DOES CHRISTIANITY HAVE A FUTURE?

A believing Christian cannot think that Christianity will ever disappear completely. However, faith does not know the exact form its survival will take in any particular age of history, nor does it guarantee that the Church need be more than a tiny remnant.

Christianity, even more than the theater, deserves the epithet, "the fabulous invalid". In purely historical and sociological terms, extrapolating from present trends, the following prediction seems not unreasonable: by the beginning of the twenty-first century most of what are presently considered the "mainline" Protestant denominations in America (Episcopal, Presbyterian, United Church of Christ, Methodist, along with some branches of the Baptists and the Lutherans) will either have ceased to exist or ceased to claim any distinctively Christian character for themselves. The Roman Catholic Church may continue in a condition of stagnation and confusion, although there are now hearty signs of revival. Whatever lively Christian presence exists in America (and it may be very lively) will be centered in those denominations presently considered peripheral and not quite respectable — those which are called, pejoratively, fundamentalist and which call themselves Evangelical. Christianity as a whole will be a distinct minority position in most of the Western world, its adherents kept on the defensive much of the time by a hostile culture.

The major Protestant denominations have been experiencing a decline in membership for some years, even as the more "conservative" denominations continue to grow. However, these statistics, while obviously relevant, are not the main point — a church which is smaller but stronger might be precisely what Christianity needs to carry it into the next millennium. Rather, the point is that this numerical decline has been accompanied (and perhaps caused) by a continuing process of internal confusion, demoralization, and self-destructive attempts to capture an elusive "relevance".

Some of the existing churches in America will not survive simply because there is no reason why they should. They possess no doctrine, worship, structure, spirit, or morality that is indispensable to the world. This is not to say that they do no good, and especially it is not to deny that there are many good people in them. Rather, the good they do is increasingly of a kind which is done better by many other social agencies. These churches now mainly offer their members psychological help, vaguely humanitarian guidance, and political exhortation. To the degree that people find these things desirable, there are other institutions better equipped to supply them. To call oneself a Methodist or a Presbyterian comes to seem increasingly arbitrary

117

when the purposes these churches seem to serve have no discernible connection with what these names have meant historically.

The anomie of certain of the churches can be most graphically comprehended if a series of questions is put to them, questions which the great majority of Christians throughout history would have regarded as central to their faith: Who was Jesus Christ? Was he indeed the Son of God and did he rise from the dead? Does he really offer eternal life to those who believe in him? Is the Word of God in Scripture a genuine self-revelation of God and does it speak with authority? Does Christianity provide firm moral principles by which people can live their lives and do these principles also partake of divine authority? Are human beings faced with the possibilities of salvation and damnation?

Some within the churches would unhesitatingly answer these questions in the negative, thus fixing an unbridgeable gulf between themselves and all the generations of Christians who came before them. Many more, however, would find the questions themselves embarrassing and perhaps presumptuous. They immediately begin reformulating them in such a way as to avoid having to give answers. Still others seek to be affirmative on each point, but their answers betray a preference for vague and metaphorical language, a reformulation which also marks a radical break with the Christian past but lacks the honesty to acknowledge this fact. (Often a form of self-delusion is involved.) When asked what in their faith they can affirm with enthusiasm and conviction, many modern Christians are only able to repeat the clichés of avant-garde politics or well-meaning humanitarianism.

Even the most "liberal" denominations would at least claim to be Christian in the sense that they recognize the figure of Jesus Christ (however understood) as somehow central to their lives. Yet even that vague affirmation is eroding, as it was fated to do once these same churches agreed that doctrines about Christ are unimportant. To assert the centrality of Christ comes to seem more and more arbitrary, a mere concession to tradition; bolder spirits within the churches are even now asserting that God (however that word is to be understood) is manifest with equal power in Hinduism, Buddhism, American Indian religions, and many other cults. Indeed, contemporary "liberal" theology is so eager to see God in human beings, in historical events, and in nature that a formal religion of any kind is rendered superfluous; it makes little sense to affirm that God was present in Jesus any more than he is present in, say, the hands of a great artist.

Having jettisoned so many doctrines and beliefs in the twentieth century, having in fact become virtuosi of such renunciations, the liberal churches will before long find the "courage" to assert that the name Christian is a narrow and constraining one. To the degree that these churches exist at all a quarter century hence, they will probably exist as general community centers. They will keep themselves relevant because, while there are many specialized groups addressing themselves to politics, human potential, and humanitarian uplift, they will have the facilities to offer a home to the widest variety of such activities. Worship, if it is carried on at all, will be regarded as one aspect of a broad program, a specialized activity like macramé or drug counseling.

The appeal of the "conservative"churches has been identified as their ability to provide meaning for life. Whereas "liberal" clergy, when confronted with basic questions of right and wrong, truth and falsehood, are likely to pronounce that life is, after all, a continuous search in which no one has any final answers, the conservative churches do offer answers, and answers hallowed by the powerful traditions of two thousand years. Furthermore, although they are often accused of merely comforting people rather than challenging them, they tend in fact to make rather strong and precise demands on their members, which is also part of their appeal. (One sign of the emptiness of "liberal" religious denominations is that they offer no means of predicting the probable beliefs or behavior of their members.)

The demonstrable appeal of conservative forms of Christianity, including some rather recently founded groups like Mormonism and Jehovah's Witnesses, immediately presents a serious challenge to one of the unquestioned dogmas of liberal Christians—that "modern man" finds traditional beliefs incredible and that the churches can hope to survive only by adapting their teachings accordingly.

But who is modern man? Rudolf Bultmann said that no one who uses an electric light can possibly believe in the miracles of the New Testament. Yet countless people do precisely that, and they believe even a great deal more. The liberal apologist then shifts ground slightly—not everyone alive in the late twentieth century, even in the West, is truly modern. But the original assertion has thus been rendered tautological—modern men do not believe in miracles only because modern men have been defined as those who do not believe in miracles.

At present the favored liberal explanation of the popularity of conservative religion is that it is attracting all those people who cannot cope with modernity and especially those troubled by the rapid social changes of the past two decades. As such they are catering to a gradually disappearing clientele. There are several flaws in this contention. One is the fact that the mainstream of Protestant Evangelicalism is increasingly characterized by a sophisticated intellectuality, self-confidence, and a determination to confront the secular world, not flee from it. A large number of young people, some of them from the most prestigious colleges and universities, have flocked to Evangelicalism.

Modern liberal religion, along with modern philosophical humanism, holds that traditional Christianity has been rendered incredible in three ways:

scientific rationality, which undermines dogma; humanitarian ethics, which regards man's life on earth as alone important; and democratic politics, which brooks no religious authority. In this view Christianity is a mere anachronism, which will gradually disappear or else will survive by shedding its supernatural baggage and accepting a purely worldly mission for itself.

But those who subscribe to the tenets of orthodox belief are often people quite at home in modern technological society. (They seem to be among those least inclined to join antitechnological crusades.) They appear to have no quarrel with democracy. (Some of them celebrate its virtues with religious enthusiasm.) And some of the greatest modern humanitarians (notably Mother Teresa of Calcutta) have been motivated precisely by a traditional and even childlike faith. Interestingly, lovers of antiques and those whose passion is to preserve old buildings seem to be mainly secular in outlook. Religiously traditional people are more likely to be living in the most up-to-date suburbs.

That much of the Western world is now thoroughly secularized can hardly be doubted. A secular viewpoint, in which religion is treated as at best a curiosity, permeates the media and much of the educational system, for example, and it is difficult to identify how in practice religious beliefs influence social behavior. It is the fact of this secularity that looms so large in the minds of liberal Christians and which dictates that they make their faith endlessly adaptable. But although secularity is often treated as an inexorable result of the modernization process of the West, against which the churches struggle in vain, in fact liberal religion itself is now the most important agent of secularization in America. Further, it is the liberal clergy and other religious professionals who are likely to be more secular than their laity and more committed to disseminating secular attitudes.

Although it is customary to speak about liberal religion, what goes by that name is usually the antithesis of religion. For religion, in almost all times and places, has meant submitting oneself to the highest powers of the universe. Liberal religion tends first of all to deny the existence of higher powers. It prefers to think of God as the deepest dimension of reality, and in so doing it leaves open the question whether God even exists as a being distinct from and superior to the universe. Furthermore, liberal religion anathematizes the very idea of submission. Self-fulfillment, properly understood, is deemed the proper goal of human existence. Religion in its root meaning indicates a "binding", and it is almost the essence of the liberal religious mentality not to wish to be bound by anything.

At first it may appear that Christianity has suffered severely in modern times primarily because of the triumph of philosophical relativism, which makes religious dogma, and eventually any kind of religious belief, no longer credible. If Christianity is seen as merely one possible world view among many, then its force and its authority are soon lost. However, it can be argued that in the past quarter century the problem has not been too much relativism but too little. Secularists, while insisting that all creeds and all ideas are only provisional, have nonetheless sought to establish the secularist perspective on the world as the only plausible one, the only one suitable for rational human beings. Religious belief has been negated, ignored, or treated as a purely subjective phenomenon, rather like falling in love. Where faith once kept unbelief on the defensive, it is now the latter which is intolerant and imperialistic. Yet many secular intellectuals are unequipped to think seriously about religious questions and do not care to. Their unbelief is an unexamined dogma, a mere mental habit.

A genuine relativism, a genuine "pluralism" in the sense of admitting the validity of multiple world views, would acknowledge traditional religious orthodoxy as just as legitimate as either liberal religion or nonbelief. Since no world view could be either proved or disproved conclusively, secularism would enjoy no privileged position with respect to belief. But in fact the opposite situation has prevailed, and the rhetoric of relativism has been used to discredit religion while establishing skepticism as normative.

The public schools, which most children attend, are by law prohibited even from allowing religious teaching or practice to take place on their premises. Although the purpose of this is supposed to be to make the schools neutral toward all creeds, in practice it helps inculcate the impression that secularism is the normal way of looking at the world. The secularist bias exists not only in the schools, where it is built into law, but also in other agencies where it is not. Children's television, for example, rarely if ever shows examples of living religious faith, even in situations where it would be natural, such as among the Spanish-speaking characters of *The Electric Company* and *Sesame Street*.

At the elementary and secondary levels, religious belief is ignored but rarely attacked as it is in the nation's colleges and universities. In recent years, departments of religious studies have been established in a number of secular colleges, including some state institutions. However, many more continue to regard this basic phenomenon of human existence as worth notice only, if at all, in whatever passing fashion departments of history, sociology, art, or philosophy may choose to address it. Antireligious propaganda, sometimes in asides, sometimes as frontal polemics, has been a common feature of college classrooms for many decades, and it has enjoyed much greater respectability than any suspected form of religious proselytization ever could. (The University of Kansas reorganized its Integrated Humanities Program, in part because the professors in it were accused of having a Catholic bias. Yet charges of antireligious propagandizing have been made against college faculty members for many years and have almost always been rejected on the grounds of academic freedom. If many college students have abandoned religious belief, this has been taken not as a sign of their having been propagandized but of intellectual growth.)

One result of all this is a widespread religious illiteracy in America, which it might be assumed the churches would be at pains to overcome. It is remarkable, however, how little of the resources of the mainline churches are used to counteract antireligious prejudice. To peruse the agenda of national church meetings, or to read the statements of church leaders, one would never infer that militant and often intolerant unbelief even exists in America.

Even within their own sanctuaries many local churches do little to counteract religious illiteracy among their members. Even when religious education programs are vigorous and well organized, they have tended for years to ignore most of the traditional doctrines of their respective denominations in favor of instruction which is humanistic and primarily contemporary in emphasis. (In recent years this has increasingly been true even of conservative churches like the Roman Catholic Church.) If doctrines are taught at all, they are taught purely as information and not in such a way as to be able to claim assent.

The circular character of the problem of belief is revealed at this point. Liberal clergy commonly assert that the Church can no longer emphasize doctrines like the Trinity and the divinity of Christ, miracles, or sin and redemption, because modern people, even church members, no longer find these things meaningful. But it is more precise to say rather that the majority of church members (to say nothing of the unchurched) have never had these teachings expounded to them. Doctrines are indeed couched in a language that is increasingly opaque to most people, but this is largely due to the fact that those who might be expected to teach them how to penetrate it have largely abandoned their task.

T. S. Eliot once said that in modern culture "paganism has all the best advertising space". What he meant by this, among other things, was that non-Christian, sometimes even anti-Christian, categories of thought so dominate the media, the educational system, politics, and the other major areas of modern life that Christian ideas can scarcely even be heard and understood. This is a situation to which many of the clergy now appear willing to acquiesce.

The ease with which they accept the contention that theological language is irrelevant and meaningless is the best possible indication of the internal demoralization of Christianity. For strong and self-confident movements — psychology, for example, or the youth culture of the recent past — are not at all reluctant to employ a language that is unfamiliar and even shocking to the general public. They force that public to learn the new terminology, which before long passes into general usage. The process by which theological language has come to be regarded as inappropriate to public discourse is a precise index of the wider process by which religion itself has been relegated to an ever narrower compartment of modern life.

Among the religiously illiterate in America there are evidently many people who experience religious stirrings of one kind or another. Often their understanding of religion is so slight that they do not even comprehend what it is they are seeking, and there are numerous secular movements whose spirit is essentially religious. Many of those who are searching are eventually attracted to the constantly widening fringes of contemporary religion, to cults of greater or less degrees of bizarreness.

Some, however, do make their way to one or other of the mainline churches, and here they are likely to be frustrated. Looking for some answer to the mystery of human existence, some revelation of a reality beyond the mundane, they are likely to be told merely that being a Christian means being kind to other people and respectful and loving of oneself. This advice, and the form it takes, will not be greatly different in content or spirit from many brands of humanism available from many secular vendors. God's name will be invoked, to be sure, but often in such a way as to leave in doubt who God is and whether his name is not simply a convenient metaphor. The example and teaching of Jesus will be held up, but not in such a way as to show how Jesus is finally more important than, say, Socrates or Gandhi. The central mysteries of historical Christianity are likely to be passed over in silence, as is any genuinely distinctive Christian moral belief, especially with regard to sex.

Many of those thus disappointed in their religious search seem now to move on to the Evangelical groups—the 1970s have been a period in American history when the incidence of sometimes highly emotional conversions to Christ was at a peak, often among people previously without any real faith. Others fall back into a vaguely unsatisfying secularism or remain disciples of an equally unsatisfying, and equally vague, Christianity.

The resurgence of Evangelical Christianity was the most important religious phenomenon of the 1970s. It takes many forms, of which the charismatic or Pentecostal movement has been the most influential, cutting across denominational boundaries to include Catholics, Eastern Orthodox, and members of the more liberal Protestant bodies, as well as those from Evangelical or fundamentalist backgrounds. The religious prophets of the 1960s (most notably Harvey Cox, in his immensely influential and wholly wrongheaded book *The Secular City*) foresaw a future in which only a liberal faith, concentrated primarily on ethical questions, would have any validity. Instead it is precisely such a faith that appears to be losing appeal among those who have any interest in religion at all. Evangelical Christianity has also displaced the liturgical churches, mainly the Anglican and the Roman Catholic, which seemed to show the most vigorous life and the best ability to attract converts from about 1945 to about 1965.

In 1971 the president of the Unitarian Universalist Association, Robert N. West, told the press that no religious group would survive unless it assumed a liberal stance similar to that of his own denomination. The next year, however, the Unitarian Universalists reported one of the largest membership declines of any American denomination. The fundamental error of the religious liberals is the failure to ask the question why people who have given up most traditional Christian beliefs should feel a need for any church at all. As the whole society grows more secular, it is not likely that those churches will attract members who have most successfully accommodated themselves to secularity, because secularity means for many people the discovery that they do not need or want a church of any kind.

For nearly two hundred years liberal religious leaders have been especially anxious to gain the respect of those whom the German theologian Friedrich Daniel Schleiermacher called the "cultured despisers" of Christianity, namely, the intellectuals. The effort to make Christianity intellectually "respectable" continues despite the remarkable irony that extremely few intellectuals have ever converted to the liberal brand of Christianity. Virtually all the notable intellectual and artistic converts—men like T. S. Eliot, W. H. Auden, Evelyn Waugh, C. S. Lewis, as well as near-converts like Henri Bergson and Simone Weil—have been drawn to the traditional hierarchical and liturgical churches and have generally opposed all modernizing tendencies within those churches. The point the liberalizers always miss is that, while agnostic intellectuals may admire the courage of revisionist Christians, they also regard their revisionism as merely a confirmation of their own skepticism. Thus they have little motive to take Christianity seriously.

But in a way liberal Christians have not missed the point, because, despite all the rhetoric to this effect, the purpose of religious revisionism is not to attract nonbelievers. (For many liberals the very idea of convert-making is distasteful in any case.) Rather it is to meet the desires of the liberals themselves—those within each denomination who for various reasons are disaffected with their particular traditions and only feel comfortable when they have deprived those traditions of all authority. (Once they have been rendered impotent, they can be reinstated as picturesque, which helps explain why religious liberals are often devotees of architectural and ethnic preservationism.)

Liberals within each denomination warn that the church will lose its credibility among "modern men" unless it changes radically, and they consequently acquire a vested interest in showing that modern men are indeed unreceptive to traditional Christianity. But orthodox faith—including such touchstones as belief in the divinity of Christ and his bodily Resurrection, the inspired historical truth of the Bible, life after death, and the reality of miracles—would be far more widespread than it is if the full weight of clerical authority were not so often used to beat down all signs of "fundamentalism" in the churches. Religious leaders who would never dream of saying a negative word about any non-Christian religion often allow themselves full license to treat conservatives within their own churches as though they were merely malicious troglodytes. It is in this sense that liberal theology is perhaps the single most important force for secularization in modern society.

Except among Evangelicals, there is no aggressive antisecularizing campaign currently being mounted in America, and most "liberal" religious leaders would be embarrassed and alarmed if one were to develop. This malaise is also found among Roman Catholics, though papal initiatives could well produce changes in the future. Rather than converting nonbelievers, liberal religious leaders see their principal task as that of converting their own people, a conversion process which involves helping their people overcome their religious "hangups" and learning to live comfortably in an unbelieving world. Many of these liberals are content with whatever crumbs their churches are tossed from the secular table, and the most insistent point they make to their people is "Don't resist change!" Clergy, like the late Episcopal Bishop James A. Pike, who desert the church to become part of the secular mainstream are commonly applauded, even within their own churches, for their "courage" and "honesty".

On the face of it such a situation is fantastic—in most organizations the leadership is more firmly committed to the group's principles than is the membership at large and must often struggle to safeguard the fidelity of the members. It might be assumed, by one unfamiliar with the churches, that the laity would be particularly susceptible to secularizing tendencies, since they live immersed in the world, while the clergy, partially insulated in an ecclesiastical ghetto, would try to hold the line againt erosion. That the opposite condition prevails is due primarily to two factors: the system under which clergy are educated and the kind of clerical subculture that has come into being in the major denominations.

The dream of liberal Christianity in each age has been that, if certain doctrines or practices are discarded which are deemed by nonbelievers to be false or pernicious, the remaining layers of faith will be secured against attack. Instead, in each generation the attack penetrates deeper and still more is surrendered until, in the late twentieth century, liberal Protestantism has scarcely any doctrine left. The secular world continually devises tests to determine how much the liberal churches will swallow, and by now it has become apparent that there is practically nothing they will not swallow.

Since Protestantism enshrined the Bible as the central authority of faith, it has naturally been in Scripture studies that the greatest crisis has occurred, beginning with the German "higher criticism" of the nineteenth century. By now, demythologizing has become a preferred way of intellectual life for many, because it frees them from an authority they very much wish to be freed from. There are no longer any dramatic crises of faith possible in liberal Christianity, and the snares of doubt no longer threaten. Instead liberal Christians feel much more threatened by incipient slides back into "fundamentalism". Many Catholics have similarly learned to demythologize their ecclesiastical traditions.

Seminaries and divinity schools are in more and more instances institutions whose primary effect is to produce graduates fully formed in the mentality of the prevailing secular intellectual milieu. This extends quite widely to include opinions about politics and sex, for example, but in particular it applies to the future clergyman's ingrained attitudes of reserve, skepticism, even outright disbelief and antagonism toward the official teachings of his own denomination. Not uncommonly, pious young people from religiously conservative families find the seminary an experience designed to alienate them from their cultural roots, and many seminaries effectively bleach out most of the orthodoxy and fervor their students bring with them. Although formerly this was not true of Catholic seminaries, in the past decade it was increasingly the case as American Catholicism adopted more and more of the dominant attitudes of liberal Protestantism.

Although the purpose of this kind of education is supposedly to make people "open-minded" and respectful of diverse viewpoints, in practice it inculcates a mentality that is closed to anything outside the purview of existing secular orthodoxies. For many future clergy, and many seminary professors, it becomes imaginatively impossible to think in terms other than those that dominate in secular academic circles. The clergy and other professional churchmen form a special and self-perpetuating subgroup within each denomination largely committed to a particular world view.

Clergy, therefore, not uncommonly embark upon their work as missionaries, not however as missionaries to the unbelieving but as missionaries to their own flocks, agents of the general liberal consensus. Their primary task is understood as helping their people overcome their "backward" and "narrow" attitudes, many of which derive from the central traditions of the denominations to which they belong. Odd though it may seem, the clergyman, by virtue of his education, is often a spiritual and psychological outsider in the denomination. Especially in the past decade, many clergy have left church work to become teachers, counselors, social workers, or bureaucrats in public and private social agencies, occupations unhampered by the necessity of maintaining even a residual religious identity.

A second place of refuge for clergy who feel cramped in the parish ministry has been the denominational bureaucracies themselves—the offices of education or social action, for example—where contact with ordinary church members is minimal, where like-minded fellow bureaucrats provide a supportive atmosphere, and where programs can be formulated in accordance with the best current wisdom. (Directors of religious education, for example, are likely to show far more veneration for the words of theorists like Piaget, Kohlberg, and Simon than for the Bible. Where accepted secular wisdom is concerned, they are uncompromising fundamentalists.) The situation of the modern churches, and especially the situation of the clergy, cannot be understood unless the clergy are understood as what they increasingly are—a species of modern bureaucrat. This is true even of many of the parish clergy.

There is a now-outdated stereotype of bureaucracy that regards it as rigid, traditional, dogmatic, and the enemy of change. Genuinely modern bureaucracies, however, are almost the reverse of these things. Bureaucrats in modern government and private agencies are far more likely to regard themselves as "change agents", people who have made shrewd estimates of how much change society can stand and at what pace. Within those limits, they are usually willing to support all possible change and even to initiate it. Especially in the churches this involves the use of authority to undermine authority.

The bureaucrat is someone who is part of a network much larger than the particular agency he administers. He belongs to professional organizations, attends national meetings, reads specialized publications. More and more he conceives his task as one of implementing, within his own domain, the governing ideas of his profession, which in turn derive from prevailing intellectual orthodoxies, especially in the social sciences. By definition a bureaucrat is someone who is "ahead" of his people; otherwise his training would be wasted and his very function dubious.

The official ecumenical movement owes a great deal to the bureaucratic mentality. Denominational officers tend to be more ecumenical than most church members, precisely because they have successfully relativized the official beliefs of their denomination in a way those church members have not. It is of the nature of modern bureaucracy that its personnel are essentially interchangeable from one agency to another. Thus modern clergy cultivate a style that allows them to function equally as well in secular social agencies as in the church, and that would allow them to function as well in one denomination as in another.

The modern professional's principal constituency is not those below him, the people he presumably serves, nor those above him, his nominal supervisors. It is rather his fellow professionals, for, if he loses one position for displeasing those below or above him, he can still survive in his profession, whereas to become an outsider within the profession is to doom oneself to an institutionally marginal existence. (In all liberal denominations there are orthodox clergy out of step with their brethren. Their influence outside their own parishes is often negligible, and they are often treated as pariahs by other clergy.)

To some extent, Protestant denominations tend to be conservative in their teachings and practice roughly in proportion to how democratic they are, the Baptists being among the more conservative. The reason for this paradox is simply that in such situations lay opinion effectively reins in on clerical influence. In a number of churches, for example, a kind of tithe-payers' revolt has forced the curtailment of certain programs sponsored by national church offices. However, all the liberal churches have at least a quasi-democratic structure, and their liberalism can be attributed to what might be called the McGovern Syndrome — a well-organized, articulate, confident, and determined minority overcoming the passive resistance of the more conservative elements in the community and dominating its machinery. The Episcopal Church is a prime example of this. The traditionally conservative Roman Catholic Church presents a unique situation — its clergy, including nuns and lay professionals, have become increasingly liberal, while its highest officers in Rome remain firmly orthodox. In America its bishops at present represent a spectrum between these two poles, one result of which is that as a body they have become virtually immobile. The Church's national bureaucracies are now apparently beyond episcopal control and sometimes work actively to undermine official doctrine. Here again, the remarkable leadership of Pope John Paul II is likely soon to begin inducing changes. There is much dissatisfaction, on all levels of the Church, with this situation, and papal initiative is certain to communicate itself to every level during this decade. One result may be that certain liberals decide that they are not happy operating as Catholics after all.

In general, although they employ a rhetoric that emphasizes the need to identify with the poor and oppressed, the clergy feel most at home with the professional upper-middle class. Avant-garde ideas originate and become fashionable primarily in that class. In the end, no matter how determinedly they espouse the economic and political cause of the oppressed, it is doubtful whether liberal Christians can identify with them religiously. Those Christians who talk earnestly about the need to respect African culture are not likely to start believing in devils, for example, although most fundamentalists do. Despite the suspicion and hostility that separates them, blacks and poor whites often share an unquestioning veneration for the Bible which the liberal upper-middle class finds embarrassing. After discovering the importance of the black church, liberal white Christians have had to pretend that poor blacks are like themselves in employing the Scriptures only metaphorically and symbolically. Some Roman Catholic missionaries from the United States have abandoned their work in Latin America precisely because their people expected them to be too priestly, too identified with a cultic and ritual role, and did not accept them as agents of social change.

This liberal core within each denomination is made up of people who have come to accept change as the only certitude, the only security. They are socially, and often geographically and occupationally, quite mobile, and they welcome innovation in all areas of life, generally equating it with progress. (The anticapitalist ideology of many liberal church people is faintly ludicrous, because their own thoughts are a flowering of the late-capitalist consumer mentality, especially their unspoken belief in planned obsolescence in ideas, and their assumption that self-fulfillment rather than self-denial is the purpose of religion.)

T. S. Eliot observed forty years ago that liberal religion is adept at releasing energy, freeing people from established obligations and prohibitions, but not at refocusing it. It specializes in what the sociologist Philip Rieff calls the "remissive mode", that is, giving people permission to think and do things that previously Christianity had forbidden. Many people in liberal churches seem to find meaning primarily in that. They experience a sense of excitement, relief, and perhaps even mild ecstasy at discovering one by one that all the old taboos can now be broken. Inevitably, it has been in the crucial area of sexuality that the most important battles have been fought. Although advanced Christians now employ the high-flown rhetoric of Marxism to justify their departures from religious orthodoxy, for many the playboy philosophy has been far more influential. (As *Playboy* sought to establish its respectability in the 1960s, liberal clergy were happy to write for it.)

All kinds of causes—the rights of racial minorities, the antiwar movement, labor disputes, the needs of "third-world" societies, ecology, women's liberation, and homosexuals' rights—might be compatible with the mission of one or other of the churches. However, for the contemporary liberal denominations these are virtually the only things worth serious attention. What skeptical philosophers have called "God talk" has been dismissed even by the clergy as a distraction from the real business of living. Social and political causes are literal godsends, because they alone provide the churches with the momentum that gives them the appearance of vitality. They have life only to the degree that they can latch onto already moving vehicles, and any sign that the vehicle is slowing down—a "conservative backlash"—engenders panic and a rush to seek for new movements.

It is again indicative of the superficiality of the "Marxism" of many advanced Christians that they fail to appreciate the class basis of their own preferred religious style—the system of clerical education in most denominations seems almost designed to create an elite that is alienated from the common people. (Most Catholic priests and nuns in America probably come from blue-collar families, and many pride themselves on how far they have "progressed" beyond their parents' world. The reaction against the Catholic past is to a great extent a reaction against a blue-collar church on the part of people who have entered the professional upper-middle class.)

Although liberal Christianity takes its cues from the secular intellectual world, it is incorrigibly middle-brow, in the sense of being aware of only certain sets of ideas. Rejecting what they regard as the narrow anti-intellectualism of the orthodox, many liberal Christians are unaware that a respectable case for tradition can be made at all. What is called the neoconservative movement — represented by people like Daniel Bell, Irving Kristol, Daniel Patrick Moynihan, and James Q. Wilson — has largely passed them by, and they seem unaware of the very existence of philosophical conservatives such as Leo Strauss, Eric Voeglin, and Michael Oakeshott. The point is not that these conservatives are necessarily correct and the liberals wrong but that those liberal Christians who pride themselves on being open-minded and rational cannot really come to grips with any conservatism other than the most simplistic.

Since liberal Christians accept the secularist agenda virtually without question, they insure that by definition the churches will always be "behind" the world and frantically struggling to catch up. "Energy Ethics Reaches the Church's Agenda" is a typical article in a Protestant journal.

Although most liberal Christians would probably rank freedom high on their list of desirable values, what they end up promoting is often something quite different. For although they lend their voices to the chorus of those who announce liberation from all past restraints, what they also preach is submission to the movement of history, the willingness to allow oneself to be effortlessly carried along by social change. They break down resistance to change in part by telling their people that such resistance is futile. This helps explain the appeal totalitarian states like China and Cuba have for many Christians. Conversely, although there is also much talk about compassion, advanced Christians commonly feel no necessity to have compassion for those who stubbornly resist change and are tossed on the scrap heap of history.

The crusade for social justice, understood almost exclusively in terms of currently fashionable causes, is the natural culmination of the decay of Western Christianity, not because the causes themselves are necessarily misdirected or because they are incompatible with Christianity but because a fanatical, almost exclusive attachment to such causes is a confession of religious bankruptcy. The liberal churches have nothing to say except to add their voices to the already loud chorus of protest.

Many lay people, even many who are ordinarily inclined to vote for liberal political candidates, are troubled by the liberal political ideology of the churches because they perceive it, correctly in many instances, not as the natural expression of basic Christian faith but as a substitute for it. What troubles them is less the particular stands the clergy and the national church offices take than the fact that the taking of such stands seems to absorb most of the attention, energy, and passion the church possesses. Most people probably join churches to have their religious needs met, and they find that these needs are treated by the official church either as nonexistent or as dangerous distractions from social involvement.

Most lay people probably associate their church with the nexus of traditional moral values by which they seek to live their lives—it is linked with the family and with ideals of personal probity and integrity. Yet the influence of what is broadly called "situation ethics" has been so pervasive in the liberal churches that they can give little support to such values and often end by helping undermine them. One of the strangest paradoxes of contemporary religious life is the manner in which the relativist perspective on morality, which is essentially what situation ethics is, is turned on and off to suit particular situations.

From the earliest times, for example, sexual morality has been closely linked to religion, and Christianity in particular has had a highly developed ethics of sexual behavior. Yet the contemporary liberal churchman is likely to believe that the church has nothing firm to say on that subject. He tends to avoid questions of sexual behavior as much as possible and becomes impatient if they are asked too insistently by the laity. In the end the only statement he can make with confidence is that sexual behavior involves so many various and unpredictable factors that no general rules can be set down.

Many clergy also treat the central teachings of Christianity in the same way. They do not like to be pressed concerning the identity of Jesus, the authority of the Scriptures, or other doctrinal points, and are content, even eager, to tolerate a wide variety of opinions on these subjects, on the grounds that close certitude is impossible and undesirable.

It might be assumed, therefore, that those moral questions that are even further from the traditional heart of faith, that are uniquely contemporary and involve innumerable variables (some of which are highly technical), would be even less susceptible to an authoritative Christian stance. Instead, however, as modern clergy become less and less able to speak with authority on matters of religious doctrine, they find it increasingly possible to take passionate and uncompromising stands on issues like African politics, the Panama Canal treaty, nuclear energy, and various American labor disputes.

Social ethics has become for liberal Christians the last frontier of the absolute, from which they rigorously exclude situation ethics. No liberal clergyman is likely to tell his people that they have a right to make up their own minds about racial segregation, for example. They do not encourage an ecumenical perspective on these issues—militant blacks are not urged to dialogue with Klan members, liberated women with male chauvinists, pacifists with American Legion officers. There is little disposition to believe that truth lies on both sides of these divisions, that conflict is unnecessary and based largely on misunderstanding. So absolutist is the moral perspective employed here that many liberal Christians are inexorably attracted to those authoritarian regimes, like China and Cuba, that claim to have eliminated injustice, even if the cost has been personal freedom. For many liberal Christians the idea of a worldwide movement for social justice, even if Marxist in character, is the last great cause to which they can give themselves, a substitute for their own failed religious faith.

The liberal churches increasingly seem to aim their message at those whom Peter Berger calls "the religiously tone deaf", those for whom religious questions, religious needs, and religious beliefs are simply unreal. For many such people life, and particularly religion, has become weightless — it is possible to make endless revisions, negations, reinterpretations of traditional beliefs without any particular consequence, much as one rearranges furniture or buys a new wardrobe.

Periodic religious revivals are announced, and there is now more public talk about religion than there perhaps was a decade ago. However, the new religiosity does not seem, for the most part, to believe in a real God, really existing, to whom creatures must submit. It is rather a metaphorical way of talking about human existence, and it has given rise to what might be called religious epicureanism: recognizing that there is a spiritual side to their existence, many materially comfortable Americans want to experience the pleasures of the soul as well, and they approach the historic religions of the world as though they were smorgasbords, choosing and consuming whatever looks delectable.

The doctrines and symbols of historical Christianity are now being divorced from their matrices and given independent existence. However, this independence is merely a prelude to their being reabsorbed into some new religious synthesis. Two millenia ago Christianity, imbued with a sense of its own authority, took from classical paganism whatever it found useful, confident of its ability to transform those borrowings in accordance with its own needs. Now Christianity finds itself at the opposite end of that process, redefined rather than doing the redefining, lacking either the power or the will to resist.

Although liberal clergy sometimes accuse their conservative flocks of being too church-centered, too taken with the needs of the institution itself, it is in fact they who are the true idolaters of the institution, since they wish it to continue existing even as it loses its historical reasons for doing so.

Finally, however, the 1980s may prove to be a much more hopeful time for American Christianity than the two decades that preceded them. In part this may be merely because a contracting economy is inducing a new sobriety in people, a new sense of the finitude of human existence, which renders the extravagant and self-centered religiosity of the earlier period less and less psychically tenable.

By the end of the 1970s it was also apparent that the most important religious "fact" in American society was the resurgence of Evangelicalism, not only in terms of numbers but also in popular impact (especially through the electronic media) and apparent sense of social identity. Paralleling this has been the growth of sophisticated forms of Evangelical theology and social thought, all of which require that Evangelicalism be taken very seriously in the 1980s.

In many ways the firm orthodox Catholicism of Pope John Paul II seems to have little in common with American Evangelical Protestantism. Yet there are some close affinities with respect to morality, for example, as well as the eager willingness to affirm ageless and fundamental Christian beliefs like the divinity of Christ.

Most importantly, however, both authentic Catholicism and authentic Protestantism share a belief in a genuine divine revelation, religion as coming from God and not merely as an emanation of man's own creative impulses, and it is this which is the ultimate dividing point in contemporary Christianity. The charismatic movement may play an important role in bringing orthodox Catholics and orthodox Protestants together.

From one standpoint ecumenism may seem to have run its course, to be in fact a symptom of liberal Christianity's spiritual bankruptcy. But from another perspective the genuine ecumenical age may scarcely have begun. God undoubtedly has in store for his people surprises of which they have scarcely even dreamt.

ETERNITY'S ABIDING PRESENCE

It is a measure of our times that, when a question like "Why am I a Catholic?" is asked, the answers that instinctively come to mind tend to be pragmatic ones: because being a Catholic helps me to find meaning in life or to express myself fully as a person, or because Catholicism helps to make a better world or alleviates the sufferings of those in need.

Such assertions, while not irrelevant, fall a good deal short of answering the question. Our unmetaphysical age (one might even say antimetaphysical age) seems not to want to address itself to the most obvious answer that can and must be given to such a question. "I am a Catholic because I believe Catholicism is true." Whatever validity other answers may have, they have none in and of themselves. They are meaningful only if the truth of Catholic teaching is first accepted.

I say that these common responses are a measure of our times because I think they show how deeply certain very un-Catholic modes of thinking have come to be almost unquestioningly accepted in the Church in a short period of time. Prior to the Second Vatican Council few Catholics would have doubted that an assertion of doctrinal truth was basic to the Church's claims; we were, if anything, perhaps ultrarationalistic, too much taken with argument and logical persuasion. However, the influence of romanticism with its assertion that Christianity is beautiful, or liberal Protestantism with its conviction that it can be practically useful, has now seeped into our bones. We are awash in the therapeutic habit of mind which cares only about what a thing means "for me" and not what it is or may be in itself.

Having said this, I am somewhat embarrassed, since I am neither by profession nor by temperament a metaphysician. To the degree that I understand it, I would subscribe to Cardinal Newman's *Essay in Aid of a Grammar of Assent* as perhaps the best statement of a Christian (and ultimately Catholic) apologetic that I know of. I find classical scholastic argumentation more or less convincing on a formal level, but ("for me") somewhat lacking in ultimate persuasion.

The question "Why am I a Catholic?" immediately confronts us with one of the classic paradoxes of Christianity, for which we have no answer. In the last analysis, if we take Christian doctrine seriously, we have to say that we do not know the answer to that question, for the answer lies in the realm of God's grace and his providence. As Catholics we do not believe in the classic formulation of the doctrine of predestination, yet it is also clear that tangible, comprehensible, human explanations of the presence of faith in certain lives take us only so far. Another of the dangers of our time is the tendency to think almost exclusively in human terms, as though we could instill faith in our children, for example, by creating the proper familial and educational environment. We have less of a sense than we used to have of how much we depend on God's dispositions of our requests and desires. That faith is a gift, and that we must pray for its reception and preservation, is something we often now lose sight of.

At first glance the idea contained in Christ's awful admonition, "You have not chosen me; I have chosen you", may seem self-serving and flattering to the ego of the one chosen, and certainly there has been no lack of Christians, throughout history, who have taken it as a guarantee of privilege and status. But the reverse is, of course, really true—the gift of faith is a humbling thing not only because of the awareness it brings of one's unworthiness but also because it cannot help but dawn on any normally sensitive person that it is, from a human standpoint, a gift bestowed almost arbitrarily. As recipients of this gift we are less like victors in a race than winners in a lottery, although God must indeed have his own purposes.

In the past fifteen years, one of the great periods of crisis in the Church's history, I have been struck over and over again at the number of people whose faith was, evidently, more intense, better informed, and more fruitful than mine, who nonetheless seemed to lose it, or give it up, or willingly exchange it for something inferior. I can find no particular personal merit in my own perseverance in faith: God makes use of whatever instruments he chooses.

There is much effort expended in our time trying to remake Catholicism in such a way as to render it "relevant to modern man", or to alleviate the objections which certain modern men may have to it. I think this activity is misconceived on several grounds. It is, quite obviously, a strategic error—the history of modern Christianity shows rather conclusively that, while efforts to redefine belief may be meaningful to people who are already Christians and who are experiencing problems of faith, they do little to attract skeptics into the churches. On the contrary, they merely serve to confirm the skeptics in their conviction that Christianity is indeed outmoded and irrelevant, because believers themselves are willing to jettison so much of its historical baggage.

There is also a fundamental objection to this modernizing process which arises from the nature of Catholicism itself and of its claims to truth. Catholicism is perhaps the boldest of all religions precisely in hazarding so much on those claims. It is not content to be accepted for its utility or the beautiful poetry of its symbols, although there have always been people who have approached it primarily for such reasons. It rather insists that it stands or falls on its claims to teach truth, an assertion that in one sense renders it highly vulnerable in a skeptical age and that also suggests that attempts to relativize its doctrines are not acts of courage, as they are often presented, but flights to security. If the doctrines of the Church are true, then most of the practical objections made against it are essentially irrelevant; while, if they are not true, the Church has been party to a gigantic historical fraud and can not and should not be rehabilitated by any "updating" process.

There is a scholastic or metaphysical approach to Catholicism that establishes its essence from an examination of doctrinal statements made over the centuries. Such an approach is now often dismissed as dependent on modes of thinking which are no longer valid. Without entering into that particular controversy, it seems to me that one arrives at a very similar understanding of the Church by employing a purely historical (perhaps even phenomenological) method. Whatever else it is, the Catholic Church is a historical entity which has manifested a particular identity throughout history. Like all historical entities, it is what it is and it cannot be arbitrarily redefined as something else. Much contemporary talk about the Church, by very well-meaning people, suffers from the apparent delusion that it is possible to define that church merely as one would like it to be, without regard for what it really is and has been.

Looking at the Church both as a historian and as one who has lived within it for forty years, I see it as manifesting certain very obvious characteristics which cannot be ignored or wished away. Among the most important of these are: a conviction of the importance of dogma and of dogmatic formulations, hence of doctrinal orthodoxy; the irrepressible propensity to express its beliefs through ritual and symbol; a clearly defined and detailed moral code; an unwavering conviction that the meaning of time is found only in eternity; a strong respect for tradition; and a hierarchical structure. Whatever does not possess these characteristics, however good and desirable it may be in itself, cannot be called authentically Catholic.

Personally I find fideism — the idea that God's truth is so far above human reason that all we can do is humbly believe, however little such belief may correspond to our own rational perceptions — rather appealing. I think it also must be recognized that some kind of fideism has, throughout history, had a very powerful appeal to some very great minds and personalities, the sense that one must simply submit — the intellect, the will, the whole person — to the divine being. The characteristics of historical Catholicism which I have outlined above are things which do not appear to have inherent appeal or plausibility to many people in our own age. Words like dogma and hierarchy seem almost guaranteed to provoke negative reactions. I am tempted at this point to take a purely fideistic stance and to say that, precisely because they are uncongenial and even offensive, they must be taken all the more seriously, that ultimately what God requires of us is our submission.

However, I stop just short of saying this because, while submission is (historically considered) an essential element of all religion and one which contemporary Christianity tries to wish away, God is also love and he is truth. It is not blind obedience that he seeks from his people.

I am enough a child of my times to understand why some people are horrified at the very thought of a dogmatic, traditional, hierarchical institution like the Catholic Church. At the same time I have to say that for me these aspects of its existence have never been sources of great offense or anguish. Had I not been born a Catholic, or had my experiences within the Church been different, perhaps I would now feel differently. Once again such vagaries of history are somehow within the scope of God's mysterious providence. However, while insisting that one's personal feelings are ultimately not the appropriate standard of judgment concerning right and wrong, truth and falsehood, I also ask those who are severely offended by what the historical Catholic Church is and always has been to consider whether their experience is necessarily the only possible one.

Probably no feature of the Catholic Church arouses so much immediate antagonism as the idea of dogma and its accompanying idea of authority. To claim to be able to define truths with certitude, to pronounce that certain formulations are erroneous and even heretical, to insist that there exists an authority which is able to distinguish truth from falsehood, is to invite total rejection from those segments of the world which consider themselves modern, even within the Church itself.

I have nothing new to say on this subject. If the idea of dogma, and its accompaniments, is to be declared false, this must surely be done on some grounds more profound than the tastes of a particular age. The circumstances of dogma's rejection themselves point toward its importance. Leaving aside the claim of divine authority (without which, of course, it is ultimately meaningless), dogma is surely important precisely because it protects us from the unrestrained enthusiasm of a particular historical period. Humanly speaking, dogma is the means by which a community like the Church endeavors to salvage as much as possible from the wreck of each particular historical epoch, the almost fanatical drive which each epoch manifests to remold all of reality to suit its own specifications. In proclaiming dogmas, the Church is telling us something very hopeful—that there is a truth which we can know despite the inevitable limitations of our own perceptions, and that our knowledge of this truth can withstand shifting historical patterns. We are not mere prisoners of history but have the freedom of those to whom the truth has been revealed.

The word dogma almost inevitably conjures up negative reactions in our time, but it is worth recalling that not so many years ago the fact of Catholic dogma was for many people an integral part of the Church's appeal and credibility. This was especially true of so many of the great intellectual converts of the past century and a half, beginning with John Henry Newman. The radical reversal of mood among the intellectual classes which has led to dogma's present discredit should be treated as precisely that—a mood, a possibly quite temporary shift in feeling that may well reverse itself once again. Political dogmatism is never out of fashion for very long in intellectual circles.

If I were given a word-association test with regard to the Catholic Church, I think the word that would leap most immediately to mind would be "richness". Instinctively I sense Catholicism as representative of a far more complex, profound, and variegated kind of reality than any other creed with which I am familiar. If the word dogma calls forth hostility from the modern mind, the word heresy is almost guaranteed to summon benign feelings. A heretic, after all, is someone who insists on uttering inconvenient truths which those in authority would rather not hear. He dares to assert the sacredness of individual conscience in the face of repressive authority. How can modern man not admire and respect such a person?

We forget, however, that a heretic, from the Church's standpoint, means someone who picks and chooses, who deliberately takes the part for the whole. I have never found heresy attractive (although particular heresies may have attractive things about them), because it means the impoverishment of richness, the emptying of the depths, the rendering simplistic of what is and ought to be complex. So also it seems to me that there cannot be anything of grandeur about heresy, although individual heretics may be brave and sincere people, because heresy always stubbornly tends toward reductionism, energizes its sometimes fanatic zeal on behalf of a narrowed and impoverished view of reality. Instinctively I feel that what is individualistic, what pits private judgment against communal wisdom, is likely to be destructive and corrosive of truth and goodness.

In a sense I think that contemporary heresies, understood as either attacks on or radical modifications of established Catholic dogma, are among the least interesting in the entire history of the Church. The classic doctrinal controversies, such as those early ones surrounding the nature and identity of Christ, were courageous ventures onto uncharted waters by bold and powerful minds. What passes for an equivalent boldness today often seems to emanate from personal pique of some kind, which is quickly rewarded by media adulation, and it is the familiar attempt to take the rich stew which is historical Catholicism and reduce it to a supposedly more palatable thin soup.

This reduction directly relates to another of the basic notes of Catholicism which I have identified—its preoccupation with eternity. It seems to me that, if the pressures to "renew" the Church in our time can be reduced to a single idea, it is the wish to foreswear eternity, not to permit it to intrude into the comfortable confines of mundane life, to "explain" the doctrines and symbols of the Church in purely human and temporal ways. In Dwight McDonald's phrase from a slightly different context, it aims "to turn down the voltage so as not to blow a fuse". It caters to the apparent desire of many people for a comfortable, even a cozy, kind of religion.

In insisting on the reality of eternity, and not only its reality but also its central significance to human life, the Church is taking an enormous gamble. I suspect that even in the staunchest "ages of faith" many people have often felt themselves so deeply immersed in the undeniable denseness of daily life that the notion of eternal life seemed to them extremely remote and improbable. We cannot evade the central necessity of faith—ultimately our conviction that we have an eternal destiny rests not on whatever "intimations of immortality" we may experience but on the promises of Christ, of which our experiences may not necessarily give much of an inkling.

In speaking about the reality of eternity I do not merely refer to personal immortality, to life after death, but also to the idea that there exists a transcendent eternal realm within which our time-bound existences are, as it were, a kind of parenthesis. There are the staggering implications of the doctrine of the Trinity—the eternal generation of the Word from the Father, and that love between them which is the Holy Spirit—and the (if possible) even more staggering implications of the doctrine of the Incarnation—that at some precise historical moment the Word took flesh and dwelt among us. There are finally the immense implications of the idea of revelation, that the eternal God chose to reveal something of himself to us and that we therefore have knowledge of this transcendent, eternal realm in a way that infinitely surpasses all merely human glimpses of eternity.

There is an immense gamble here, as there is with regard to the Church's stance of dogmatic certitude, because if this assertion concerning eternity is deemed incredible, then the Church's entire existence is rendered inauthentic. It cannot be rescued by appeals to its supposed practical or worldly utility.

But, on the other hand, if this teaching is true, then it is the most significant statement about our existence with which we will ever be confronted. One cannot be indifferent to the possibility of eternity, nor, having once accepted it truly, can its existence fail continually to cast beams of the brightest light into our darkness. Those who are disciples of the Incarnate Word and who believe in his promises necessarily must see all aspects of existence differently. Conversely, those who lack this faith must necessarily be seen as lacking essential understanding of the nature of human existence.

The question immediately arises: Are those who do not believe to be consigned to perdition? Are they debarred from leading good and meaningful human lives? The answer is of course no, and it has been a positive aspect of the development of modern Christianity that it has enabled us to see this fact. There is also an advantage in our being enabled to see that there is a distinction to be made (although not a separation) between religion and morality, heretical though that proposition may seem to some people. Put crudely, there is a great deal about religion which is not useful in any discernible or measurable sense.

Kierkegaard, a Protestant whose writings I found inspiring and very helpful at one point in my life, distinguished the category of faith from the category of the ethical and dared to suggest that Abraham's sacrifice of his son Isaac was a manifestation of pure faith, of pure response to the greatness and authority of God transcending all ethical notions. Ultimately, although I find it tempting, I do not think this can be true, and it is certainly not a Catholic idea. But there is a kernel of truth in it.

What contemporary Christianity is most in danger of losing sight of is what might be called the esthetic dimension of religion—the fact that genuine religion ultimately means a human response to what is recognized as great, holy, powerful, good, and beautiful. As with art, a much lesser instance of the same kind of experience, this response is not primarily useful. It is indeed useless, because it is primarily recognition, response, acknowledgment. It tends to express itself in praise, but often it is silent and even immobile before the thing perceived. In ultimate terms contemplation has primacy over action.

I do not think historical Catholicism can be fairly accused of discouraging activity in the world, or of fostering the idea that ethics and religion have nothing to do with one another. In fact, some of the most powerful attacks against the Church, especially at the time of the Reformation, were directed against its alleged overemphasis on good works. Catholicism is in some ways a very pragmatic religion, always tending to form organizations, to throw up structures, to provide work for people to do.

But its real greatness lies in its sustained ability, over many centuries and in so many cultures and climates, to keep alive in men's hearts the sense of eternity and the sense of the reality of the all-powerful and all-loving God. The "useless" response to the beauty and greatness of God is what we call worship, and the Church has masterfully created conditions in all times and places in which worship can occur.

The dissatisfaction with Catholic worship which has been so marked a feature of postconciliar times has much to do with the prevailing dissatisfaction with the idea of worship itself. Catholic ritual has been criticized not because it is not an effective vehicle for worship but because it is—what certain modern people object to is a ritual which is "for God" rather than "for me".

Next to dogma, ritual is probably that aspect of the Catholic phenomenon most guaranteed to provoke negative responses, and the term "meaningless ritual" is now itself routinely employed as a meaningless ritual, as though all ritual were meaningless.

But it is again enlightening to recall how recently—as recently as fifteen years ago—traditional Catholic ritual was deemed to be one of the Church's strongest points, the source of a great deal of its appeal among both simple and sophisticated people. In the practical order, it was ritual which perhaps better than anything else gave to many people, including some who came to it as unbelievers, a sense of the reality of eternity, of the beauty and majesty of God, and of the possibility of an appropriate human response to God.

Ritual becomes meaningless in one of two ways—by people ceasing to believe in those things which the ritual is meant to effect and symbolize or by their expecting from the ritual the kind of pragmatic effects which it was never intended to bring about. The first danger is that of estheticism, a heresy which can be devastating in its consequences but fortunately tends to be confined to rather small elements of the population. The second, now at least, is much more widespread.

To me, authentic Catholic ritual reverberates with intimations of eternity, and it has had this aspect for me for as long as I can remember. As does dogma, ritual presents a world larger, deeper, and richer than that of our experience. It summons and focuses our attention, however briefly, on eternity. When either dogma or ritual is thought of as necessarily leading to certain practical results—a greater human sensitivity, for example, or a new dedication to helping others—it is misconceived. The connection is short-circuited. The rich stew is once again reduced to the soup of the day.

The sacramental religion which is Catholicism seems to me the only kind appropriate to the Incarnation, and as a consequence I have never been particularly attracted to the Protestant churches. But the sacraments have meaning only as vessels of eternal life, not as mere venerable and dramatic ceremonies or as expressions of present human needs and triumphs. If we represent them as anything other than what they are, we effectively cheat people.

In our time there are many people who accept the importance of ritual in the abstract but in effect ask why we need these particular rituals. They are offended by the seemingly arbitrary nature of a prescribed ritual, when it seems to them that there are many ways available to improve it, or even to make use of original liturgical compositions.

The "arbitrary" character of Catholicism, and indeed of all of Christianity, seems to me something very basic to it and something which must be accepted and recognized. It is a character imparted by Catholicism's being a historical religion. For if the objection were taken far enough, we would have to ask in effect why God chose to become man at the particular time and place he did. Most of us could probably conceive of other times and places, perhaps even other personages, which would seem to us more appropriate for the Incarnation and more conducive to its effects. The Church itself represents a similar "scandal of particularity", and throughout history it has been the repeated contention of the Church's critics and enemies that Christ could not have founded a Church like this one, by which they mean that he ought not to have.

Anything which is historical, and which is allowed to have its true historical character, developing organically through time, comes to have a circumscribed and particular identity which it cannot lose and is not free to surrender. The scandal of particularity, which begins by questioning why the Church's rituals need to be observed in this particular arbitrary way or why certain dogmas are expressed in this form rather than in some other, soon moves on to wondering why it is not possible to have a Church quite different from this one. The final point of such speculation, at which some have already arrived, is to question the once-and-for-all character of God's sending his Divine Son. Could there not be many such incarnations, in many different cultures? Given certain assumptions, it becomes virtually necessary to think so.

Paradoxically, it seems to me that the "arbitrary" character of Catholicism is precisely what saves it from being truly arbitrary. Of course the Son of God could have been incarnated under different conditions. Of course we might have a Church different from the one we have. Of course our rituals or our dogmas might have taken quite different form. But in the order of history they have not. God has somehow willed them to be what they are.

Romanticism has been defined as "split religion", and in the past few years there has been a "rediscovery" of religion by people who were previously indifferent or hostile to it. However, it is a discovery which is basically inimical to Christianity precisely because it has to do with religion in general, while Christianity, as an incarnational and historical faith, is very much religion in particular. A church which allows free expression to all manner of doctrinal, liturgical, and moral impulses is a church which soon falls victim to the spirit of the age. It becomes a vehicle for the expression of the favored "religious" impulses of a particular culture, but to that very extent it can no longer lay claim to being the proper expression of divine revelation. It ceases to be a revealed religion. It becomes a primarily worldly entity, echoing and reechoing the world's voices.

Thus far I have said little very specifically about tradition, but I think its presence is detectable in everything I have said. There is a specific danger in intertwining the arguments for the importance of tradition and the truth of Christianity, just as there is a specific danger in emphasizing the esthetic character of religion. Paralleling the heresy of estheticism is the heresy of traditionalism, in which whatever is old is deemed good and in which the preservation of historic Christianity is necessary because Christianity is one of the foundation stones on which civilization is built. For a Catholic, the assertion of truth is something to which we must return again and again.

However, it also seems to me that the traditionalism of the Catholic Church is no accident—and for several reasons. First, to be a historical religion means not only that the Catholic faith develops through time but also that it looks back, unabashedly, for its validation and its source somewhere in the past, embarrassing though this notion may be to some people. If we take the Incarnation seriously, then we must accept the fact that the high point of human history is a specific event which can be dated and located with a fair degree of precision. Our "story", such as we have, is essentially the fleshing out of that story. We look forward to Christ's coming again, but equally we look backward to his having already come. We are barred from being the "now generation".

There is a cheap kind of traditionalism in which outdated language and dress, musty old buildings, and old-fashioned ideas conjure up a sense of permanence and stability. This is not the kind of traditionalism which Catholicism can countenance, although from time to time attempts are made to co-opt it for that purpose. However, it is also appropriate that the Church should seem, from the world's viewpoint, an unnaturally stable and even outdated institution. For the Church, if it truly speaks from the perspective of eternity, must always manage to distance itself from the prevailing spirit of each particular age, must always speak in ways which will strike the world as strange. And in the process of its long historical development, it is also inevitable that the Church will discover certain forms of expression — verbal, symbolical, or institutional — which it will recognize as having enduring and permanent validity and which it will continue from age to age. (Put another way, not every age is equally penetrating in its religious understanding or creative in its expressions of that understanding. My feeling is that our own age is particularly impoverished, especially in its sense of liturgical and symbolic expression.)

But what then are we to make of hierarchy? It can be defended in terms of tradition, but I think it is necessary to give it a more solid grounding than that. I am not among those who regard religion as a quasi-aristocratic phenomenon which ordinary people cannot be trusted to understand and which must be upheld by the "leaders" of society in the same way that, for example, the value of high art is so upheld. In fact I think the history of Catholicism shows a religion which penetrated very deeply into the life of the common people, a situation which endured until after the Second Vatican Council. That there has occurred an estrangement of the elite from the masses in the postconciliar Church has been due largely, I think, to the determination of some of the elite to move farther and faster than most ordinary believers were willing to do.

However, since the Church speaks from the perspective of eternity, it is true that democracy, like all other political systems, is essentially irrelevant to its life. It is free to incorporate elements of the democratic system into its structure, as it has generally incorporated elements of whatever political system has prevailed at any particular time, but it is not obligated to do so. Hence the continued existence of a hierarchical system is no embarrassment to the Church and can even be taken as a laudable sign of its independence from prevailing customs.

Hierarchy as it functions in the Church can be conceived in at least two ways. One is hierarchy as principality and privilege, the system whereby bishops and other prelates live in luxury and require that a kind of servile deference be paid to them. Clearly this is the remnant of the cultural mores of certain past ages and has no relevance to our own time.

However, it is also true that the problem of hierarchical authority cannot be solved by an easy appeal to the "authority of service" or other concepts devised to help avoid the hard questions. The bishop remains, in the root meaning of his title, an overseer. He is not merely a presiding officer or chairman, still less a kindly grandfather who always praises and never scolds. If the Church claims to teach truth, it cannot avoid the question of where the authentic power to articulate that truth lies. Catholic doctrine and tradition concede the key role in the process to the bishops, individually and collectively, and classical theories of popular consensus, as developed by Cardinal Newman, for example, necessarily limit the role of that consensus. Any bishop who truly seeks to do his duty in times as disturbed and confused as our own will find ample occasions to warn, correct, and teach with authority. For some, this necessary exercise of office will inevitably seem tyrannical and oppressive.

So far I have talked of "Catholicism" in terms general enough to apply to Eastern Orthodoxy and to Anglo-Catholicism as well as to the Church of Rome. In fact I have a good deal of sympathy for the view of Catholicism which defines it widely enough to encompass these other churches and which speaks of Catholic Christianity in terms of the identity which emerged during the first four or five centuries of the Church's history.

But the papacy still looms very large and, contrary to what many people feel, for me it looms even larger in our own day. If we accept historical development in the Church, then we must accept the fact that with every development certain doors are shut for the future, even as other doors may be opened. The papal office is one such door. The full maturation of the papal office has shut many doors even as it has opened others. Following the First Vatican Council, and following what the Second Vatican Council said about papal authority, it is not possible to pretend that the papal primacy is not integral to Catholicism or that its development is reversible.

A decade ago I was inclined to minimize the importance of that office, since I believed that whatever was essential to Catholicism was found in conciliar decrees as well as in the general traditions of the Church. In the meantime, however, I have come to a deepened appreciation of the importance of the papacy, and in fact I regard it as indispensable to the future of Christianity.

Eastern Orthodoxy and the worldwide Anglican communion are the essential test cases for the viability of a Catholicism which rests on the consensus of the whole Church, expressed primarily through the collective body of the episcopacy. Orthodoxy seems to preserve this Catholicity very well. However, it is so closely tied to ethnic identities that it is difficult to judge how well it would survive independent of those identities. Unlike Roman Catholicism, it has not attempted to penetrate to all corners of the world or to bring into its fold all those, of whatever diverse nations, races, and cultures, who will listen to its teachings. Anglicanism, meanwhile, seems increasingly vulnerable to modernism in all its forms, a fact which is especially notable in its moral teachings. Despite staunch pockets of orthodoxy within its ample folds, Anglicanism seems vulnerable to modernistic onslaughts at its highest levels of leadership, including many of its bishops.

I agree with those commentators who identify *Humanae vitae*, the 1968 encyclical on contraception and related matters which was issued by Pope Paul VI, as an important watershed in the history of attitudes toward the papacy. However, unlike most of those who make this point in order to argue that the encyclical was a disaster from the point of view of papal credibility, I think that in the long run the prestige of the papal office will be immensely enhanced by it.

Having said that, I must confess to having been among those who were made unhappy by its original issuance and who hoped that somehow a "compromise" settlement could have been worked out. But much has happened in ten years' time, and it is becoming more and more clear (and frighteningly so) what the full implications are of an attitude which deliberately divorces human sexual activity from the purposes of procreation.

Looking merely at the history of the papacy in the twentieth century, I find it highly impressive that, although the wisdom or advisability of this or that practical papal policy might be questioned, on matters of formal teaching ranging from sex to social justice, as well as more general doctrinal questions, the popes have been unerring in their understanding of the real issues at stake and their courageous willingness to speak even when their speaking has predictably provoked a storm of abusive protest. While "the institutional Church" is often dismissed as stodgy, cautious, and mired in routine, I find on the contrary that the popes have been and continue to be truly prophetic.

The mention of *Humanae vitae* leads immediately to that remaining characteristic of historic Catholicism which I identified earlier as essential to it—namely, its clear and well-defined moral teaching; and it is precisely because of those teachings, especially those having to do with sexual behavior, that the Church is now under such severe attack from so many quarters and is in fact actively hated.

It is often said that the preconciliar Church overemphasized sexual morality, and that may well have been true on the practical level, although attention to the papal encyclicals of the past century would suggest that this imbalance did not affect the highest levels of Church leadership. In the abstract it is easy to say that sexual sins are less serious than matters of social injustice, yet sex has a way of continually intruding itself into public consciousness. It is a subject that will not go away, mainly because our sexual identity and the behavior which flows from it is so basic to all our personalities and all of us feel that sexual rights and wrongs have a lot to do with who we are and who we ought to be.

It is not possible to discuss the complexities of the sexual revolution in this short space. However, I think that what goes by that name is based on a whole series of false assumptions about human nature and the nature of morality, assumptions which cannot help but result in disasters for those who make them, and ultimately for the whole society within which they are made. It seems to me that authentic Catholic teaching about sex in our times reveals a wisdom, a sanity, and a balance which "the world" sadly lacks and many other religious bodies seem eager to throw away as quickly as possible. (Absent a hierarchy, and especially a papacy, the Church of Rome might be easily stampeded in the same direction.)

Preconciliar Catholics are also often accused of having been overly sin-conscious, our religion too negative and built upon notions of guilt. Again, in the practical order this may well have been true for some people, although I am convinced that it is a reality which has been greatly exaggerated for sensationalistic purposes. There are several dimensions of the question which are commonly ignored, however. One is the fact that, however much the Church may be accused of having exaggerated the element of moral guilt, this very exaggeration was a compliment to human nature, by its attributing of moral responsibility to man. Free will was taken seriously, which meant that both sanctity and damnation were regarded as real possibilities, within reach of all. Human actions and human decisions had real moral weight. The new spirit of "liberation", while it talks a great deal about maturity and adulthood, often ends by casting people in the role of permanent adolescents who are never fully responsible for what they do but are constantly excused and indulged.

Traditional Catholic moral theology, including the often excoriated casuistry, seems to me to have been based on an acute realism about human nature and a nicely wrought balance between a clear-eyed awareness of what people are prone to do on the one hand and what they are capable of on the other. The moral law as explicated by the Catholic Church was always a nice balance between justice and mercy. For many generations of people it made the reality of moral choice, and the drama of that choice, immediate and real, just as it made the prospect of eternity, and of an incarnate Second Person of the Trinity, immediate and real.

In the postconciliar Church much energy has gone into the task of refashioning Catholicism in such a way that no one can be harmed by it, that none of the distortions and deformations which are alleged to have been so common a feature of the preconciliar Church can ever recur. Such an enterprise, while the motives behind it are understandable, seems to me profoundly misconceived. A religion which contains within it no possible sources of deformation, which does not harbor elements that can be misused for destruction, is also a religion incapable of any profound good. It is a religion which is simply weak and impotent.

Historically the Church has always been aware of the possiblility of such deformations, of scrupulosity, for example. But it has, in its divine origins and its sense of historic mission, chosen to hazard this possibility. Without the possibility of hate, there is no love. Without the danger of despair there can be no hope. Without sin there is no redemption. The Church which seeks to uncover in people the image and likeness of their Creator, to point out to them the path of imitation of their Savior, must demand a great deal and, like a great surgeon, always confront the possibility that the operation will fail, that the patient will emerge worse for the experience.

In summary, Catholicism seems to me unique in the world today in the consistency with which it has made vivid and accessible the prospect of eternal life and of life in the world lived in the light of eternity. Its worldly achievements, including its actions on behalf of social justice, are not inconsiderable. But it is not for this primarily that it lays claim to distinction. Religion in its root meaning is a binding, a process by which individuals surrender themselves to something greater than themselves, something worthy of their surrender. It is an all-or-nothing proposition in which salvation is at stake. For nearly two millennia the Roman Catholic Church has mediated this awareness to the world, in innumerable and varied ways. The crisis through which it is now passing is one of the three greatest in its history, along with the Arian crisis of the fourth century and the Reformation of the sixteenth. It is part of an authentic Catholic faith to be confident that, however much it may be buffeted in this crisis, however deeply wounded, it will not only survive but emerge stronger. For if God's ways are not our ways, then his ways for his Church are likewise not ours, and its future is already determined, not by what we do to this Church or fail to do for it, but by his own plan for it and the destiny with which he endowed it from its very foundation.

BEYOND 1984: BIG BROTHER VERSUS THE FAMILY

The most comforting lesson that can be learned from history is that it is full of surprises. Although many of these are unpleasant, on balance the happy surprises perhaps outweigh them. Historians who are conscious of abstract "social forces" can discover numerous times in the history of societies when seemingly ineluctable pressures tended toward the utter annihilation of civilized life. Most of the time something happened—some twist in the anticipated events—which kept life at least tolerable and provided the basis for an eventual renaissance.

This lesson of history is especially comforting because any rational extrapolation from current trends in American society is likely to yield a dismal picture of the moral quality of life in the year 2000, whether or not America copes with the energy crisis and its other material problems.

What follows, therefore, while quite logical in terms of what is presently happening in America (and indeed most of the West), should not be taken as suggesting some iron historical law. Pessimism on this point can induce passivity, which itself would be one of the chief conditions for the fulfillment of this prophecy. What is threatened is human freedom, and the determined exercise of human freedom is the ultimate antidote.

In one sense the scenario here set forth culminates in a familiar event—the triumph of Big Brother—upon which every intelligent adolescent can discourse at length. But perhaps worse than failing to anticipate future dangers is the tendency to expect them from the wrong quarter. For a long time there has been an expectation that Big Brother will emerge, if at all, from a vaguely "right-wing" context—an alliance of big business and big government, a strong military, police engaged in surveillance of citizens and forcible suppression of dissent, and disregard for established civil liberties.

All these dangers are perhaps potentially real. But by sounding so many alarms over so many years liberals have probably significantly reduced the likelihood of their occurring. Those in a position to mold public opinion are quick to grasp the implication of new phenomena like, for example, the use made of personal financial data deposited in credit records, and they are quick to propose safeguards against abuse. For decades the momentum of politics has been in the direction of systematically rectifying all such real or imaginary abuses, and remedies are not difficult to devise.

In theory liberals recognize the possibility that Big Brother might come from the left. However, they tend to regard this as merely an academic possibility. The array of totalitarian leftist states in the world is perceived as the unfortunate effect of archaic social orders which were unable to "modernize"

148

in a democratic fashion and which slipped from one kind of tyranny into another. Since this dynamic has little relevance to the Western democracies, liberals tend to be complacent about the totalitarian threat from the left.

The very familiarity of George Orwell's prophecies about 1984 has perhaps robbed them of much of their sting, not only in the way that what is familiar inevitably becomes what is tolerable, but also in the sense that the evils Orwell portrayed have so dramatically impressed themselves on the Western imagination that many people would recognize them only in the form in which Orwell presented them. Put another way, Orwell's fictional world is evidently evil. What many sincere and well-meaning people cannot imaginatively grasp is the possibility that such a totalitarian regime might emerge gradually and incrementally, as the outcome of a whole series of decisions motivated largely by benign intentions and carrying an intimidating moral weight behind them. The big brothers of the future will not be recognizably evil people; they will look instead like rational idealists.

Part of the deficiency of the popular Orwellian view of a totalitarian future is its generally individualistic bias. The horrors of a totally controlled society are comprehended primarily in terms of the restrictions placed on individual people — their speech, their reading, even their love-making. Partly in consequence of this, defenders of freedom have come to regard individual rights as the cornerstone of all liberty and have a willingness to exalt individual rights without much regard for other social consequences. (One obvious example is the determination to protect accused criminals from all possibility of unjust treatment, to the point where it has become much easier for social predators to trample on the rights of their fellow citizens.)

However, the greatest failure of the individualistic approach to human rights has been the inability to recognize how an ardent concern for freedom, understood in a particular way, can itself contribute, in the long run, to the undermining of freedom. The argument here is a familiar one, but no less true for all its familiarity — the systematic "liberation" of individuals from their membership in all traditional social groups in the end leaves them naked and vulnerable, no protection intervening between themselves and the all-powerful state. The two social groups which have suffered most from this distorted notion of freedom are the church and the family, especially the latter.

Some analysts have argued that the most ominous shift in American social policy in recent years has been from an emphasis on liberty to an emphasis on equality and, beyond that, from an emphasis on equality of opportunity to an emphasis on equality of results; there is no doubt that this shift has had significant consequences. The argument is again familiar but true — if equality matters more than liberty, then the liberty of some people will have to be restricted to prevent them from gaining advantages, by whatever means, over their fellows. And if equality of result is taken to be the only true test of equality of opportunity, then even more severe restrictions necessarily follow.

The relevance of this argument to the rights of the family is obvious. All kinds of research have demonstrated that the family is the single greatest factor determining a child's likely success or failure in life. This is true not only in terms of the family's material condition—how expensive an education can the child be given, for example—but perhaps even more in terms of the quality of love, support, and encouragement which children receive at home. Further, although these advantages are usually understood in ways that have tangible bearings on career opportunities—whether parents encourage ambition in their children, for example, or promote intellectually stimulating family activities—intangible moral factors are perhaps even more important. Who can weigh the immense advantages which accrue to a child from a loving, stable home life or from being nurtured in a firm and coherent moral universe?

Thus sooner or later a militantly egalitarian social philosophy will come to identify the family, even more than the school, as the greatest single obstacle to true equality, a fact at least dimly recognized already by the dogmatically egalitarian ancient Spartans. So long as attempts to overcome this inequality concentrate on trying to help children of disadvantaged families—through remedial education, for example—they may be welcomed. The dogmatic spirit is so deeply ingrained in the champions of equality, however, that sooner or later such remedies will not be enough. They will attempt to strike at the root of the problem by removing children from family influence as early as possible and as thoroughly as possible. Only uniform, state-controlled nurturing facilities will be deemed truly protective against the "unfair" advantages which some families give their children.

But it would be a mistake to regard the battle as solely one between champions of equality and champions of liberty. Paradoxically, as dogmatic egalitarianism grows in influence, so also does an almost anarchistic notion of personal liberty. It is not accidental that the long-standing popularity of quasi-collectivist philosophies in America is now matched by the growing popularity of a doctrinaire libertarianism, and not merely as a reaction. What both philosophies share is an antipathy to mediating communities. Libertarianism is badly mistaken in thinking that an extreme emphasis on individual freedom is the best bulwark against political tyranny. Instead such a philosophy precisely helps bring about the situation alluded to previously— the lone individual standing naked before the all-encompassing state.

If anything, the contemporary Western understanding of liberty poses an even greater threat to the family than does egalitarianism, for while total equality is an ideal which lacks general appeal (most people probably think of themselves as at least potentially above average), total freedom is a seductive promise indeed. Most important, the dangerous growth of the power of the state has been accomplished in modern America by persuading people that the state's power is far more benign than that of the lesser institutions it seeks to supplant, a claim which in many instances has been true. By now, however, the momentum in the direction of expanding state power is almost irresistible, and the automatic solution to virtually every perceived social problem is yet a further expansion of that power. Only occasionally does the citizenry seriously ask whether the cure is not worse than the disease, and as yet there has been no serious and sustained political debate on the question. (As clear-headed analysts have pointed out, opinion polls show people deeply distrustful of government bureaucracies but also inclined to support politicians and policies likely to swell those bureaucracies even more.)

One of the great advantages that enemies of the family have is the fact that the family is by far the most intrusive of all social institutions, precisely because it is the most basic and the most nurturing. Everyone who has ever been part of a family at one time or another has experienced a sense of constriction and limitation. The family which protects and warms also seems to inhibit exploration of all the myriad opportunities seductively held out by the great world beyond. This feeling is especially acute among adolescents, but it is by no means unknown among middle-aged parents. The claim that the family is inherently a tyrannical institution gains immediate response from unthinking people who cannot distinguish between tyranny and inconvenience.

Far more alarming than legal efforts to restrict the family is the fact that so many people, including parents, seem willing to surrender familial rights voluntarily. A simple case in point is the enormous increase in the number of mothers of small children who are working outside the home not only because of economic "necessity" (often defined as the "need" to maintain two cars, a summer house, et cetera) but also for the sake of self-fulfillment. The arguments about the effects of this on small children are complex. But there is a strong sense that most women who have chosen to entrust their children's nurture to professionals have not seriously considered the implications. They have been told by some professionals that the practice is not only harmless but positively beneficial, and they are not interested in other respectable opinions. Contemporary popular literature, including the women's magazines, is full of exhortations to live for oneself and on occasion frankly admits that children are a serious crimp in one's freedom. There is a full social continuum here, with large numbers of people choosing not to have children at all.

The rejection of marriage by large numbers of people is equally troubling, and for similar reasons. The decision to enter into unmarried cohabitation is presented as a purely personal one, of interest to no one but the participants.

But the point of such arrangements, whether or not consciously recognized, is precisely the rejection of the family as a basic unit of society, the refusal to assume the responsibilities which accompany family life. Despite romantic talk about not wanting to encumber a beautiful relationship with mere legalism, the point of unmarried liaisons remains the fact that they can be slipped out of at will. The refusal to marry, even in an age when marriage itself is a relationship rather easily gotten out of, signifies the refusal to make a commitment, and especially the refusal to take long-term responsibility for the welfare of children. It is a relationship devised precisely for those whose sense of their own "needs" completely overrides any sense of responsibility they may have toward others.

In the debates over social policy and public morality not enough attention has been paid to the personal lifestyles of the participants in the debate. Those who are truly committed to family life are hampered by that very commitment, since they are rarely free to devote large blocks of their time to political activity. On the other side are arrayed those — social workers, academics, journalists, lawyers, government bureaucrats — who have given their careers first place in their lives. Not only do many of these people have a professional interest in expanding the power of social agencies at the expense of the family, their own chosen way of life inclines them in the same direction. The numerous professional women who inhabit these territories, or the professional men married to professional women, cannot help but insist that the arrangements they have worked out for themselves and their children are the best possible ones and that those who cling too closely to the traditional family are simply backward and timid.

Family structure breaks down for a variety of reasons, but one of the most important, now, is the willing response made by some parents to the blandishments of "liberation" from their responsibilities. The progressive surrender of more and more familial authority to the state or to private social agencies is welcomed by these parents as a wholly positive thing, since its immediate effect is to free them from certain burdens. They then become ardent lobbyists, in the social and political arena, for the general expansion of state authority at the expense of the family. (The distinction between state agencies and private ones becomes less and less relevant as private agencies are increasingly funded by the government and operated in accordance with uniform governmental rules.)

Imagine the following picture of American life in the year 2000, a picture not at all unrealistic in terms of a projection of current trends.

— Virtually all private social agencies have disappeared. All health care, counseling, recreational programs, et cetera, are under goverment auspices, a condition brought about partly through coercive legal action but in large measure by the voluntary surrender by private agencies of their autonomy, in exchange for tax support and official certification. Those few agencies not susceptible to those blandishments have been driven out of existence by the sheer impossibility of competing with publicly funded institutions, or by the legal necessity of conforming to governmentally imposed standards. (For example, all hospitals will be required to provide "comprehensive" health services, including abortion and sterilization, and all counseling offices will be required to refer clients to agencies providing those services. Homes for the elderly will be required to proselytize their residents on behalf of the "living will".)

— All education is also governmentally controlled. Most private schools have been driven out of existence by inflation, and by the fact that even the wealthiest could not compete with publicly funded institutions. Those few surviving were subject to so many governmental rules that their independence was in effect destroyed. (The government, for example, closely regulated who could be admitted to particular schools, who could teach in them, what could be taught, et cetera. The deliberate effect of this regulation was to force all schools to be "comprehensive", meaning that schools could not be organized along religious lines, for example, or could not offer curricula greatly at variance with those officially approved by the Department of Education.)

— Personnel in these institutions — teachers, social workers, psychologists, et cetera — are all required to adhere to general philosophies and practical programs which are in conformity with accepted Federal guidelines. There will be no dissenting voices. Adherence to positions on, for example, abortion or euthanasia at variance with official ones will be taken as evidence of professional incompetence.

— Vigilant government agencies exist to protect individual "rights" in such a way that institutions like families and churches have no authority over their members. Building upon the beginnings made in Sweden in the 1970s, these agencies will have constantly expanded their authority to intervene between parents and children, not only in cases of demonstrable cruelty but also by continually expanding the definition of cruelty. Just as egalitarians will seek to undermine the family because it provides some children with a better foundation for life than others, so self-proclaimed friends of liberty will worry constantly that the family restricts its members too much. Elaborate bureaucratic machinery will exist by which children are encouraged to make complaints about their parents, spouses about each other, and neighbors to be vigilant against undetected abuses in other people's families. (If this seems farfetched, it is well to recall that in 1976 a member of President-elect Carter's inner circle of advisors, Greg Schneiders, proposed that children be encouraged to monitor the thermostats in their homes and report parents who wasted energy.) In any apparent conflict between individual rights and communal authority, the presumption will always lie with the individual.

—The churches will have shrunk to a wholly private and unobtrusive status, their adherents a diminishing minority of the population. Secularist philosophy will be so pervasive in the schools, the media, and government agencies, and family influence so weak, that most people will find religion, in anything like its traditional forms, exotic and incredible. The social status of practicing Catholics, for example, will be not much different from that of Mennonites in 1980.

Churches, and individual church members, may still possess the legal right to dissent from official policy. However, the combination of inflation and revised tax policies (enthusiastically promoted by civil-libertarians) will leave most churches without resources. They will have no access to the media, and even their own organs of communication will have largely disappeared through bankruptcy. Taxation of church property will mean that few new buildings are put up for religious purposes, and most old ones are gradually lost. Churches will be mainly composed of people with few financial resources, who have made significant worldly sacrifices—in terms of careers, for example—to preserve their faith.

A series of court decisions involving the First Amendment will have helped to bring this situation about. Tax exemption for churches will be declared unconstitutional, and the government will remain fanatically vigilant to expunge all traces of religious influence from schools and other social agencies. Parents will probably be denied the legal right to educate their children in religious schools, on the grounds that such an education is a violation of the children's rights to equality of opportunity. If religious schooling is still permitted, those who attend such schools will in fact pay a heavy penalty in terms of worldly opportunities open to them. (Again, this is not far-fetched. In a case involving the Amish, *Wisconsin* v. *Yoder*, Justice William O. Douglas, whose opinions for many liberals have the force of divine revelation, questioned whether religious groups had the right to impose their "narrow" ways of life on their children. The full implications of this principle are staggering.)

The totalitarian state of the future will not seek to outlaw religion, since it does not wish to create martyrs and since it will find other methods of discouragement more effective. In fact it will even encourage a generalized, vague, humanistic kind of religion, in which the rituals, the symbols, even some of the creeds of traditional churches will be used, indiscriminately intermingled with one another, to create a church which is really a form of therapy. People will be encouraged to participate in these churchly activities as yet another way of finding themselves, or expressing themselves, or whatever else it is they wish to do. But such religion will be understood to have reference only to the individual psyche and the "needs" of the person, not to a real God who really exists and who passes judgment on the nations.

—The family, in the traditional sense (which is the only legitimate sense), will also have shrunk to decided minority status. The breeding of children will have been transferred in large measure to laboratories, and individuals may require governmental permission to beget offspring. In this situation the permanent commitment implied in marriage will seem to have less and less point, and social agencies will promote temporary liaisons as psychologically healthier. The absence of permanent and unbreakable personal ties will be viewed by those in power as a positive social good, anatomizing individual citizens even further. People will retain the legal right to marry and to remain permanently faithful to one another, but to do so will be to invite social suspicion and official disapproval.

—The concept of "health", in a greatly expanded and indeed revolutionized sense, will be the key to the changes that will have taken place by the year 2000. Rather than referring merely to identifiable maladies, the new idea of health, embracing psychological as well as physical factors, will refer to the total well-being of the individual, the realization of each person's full potential. (This definition is already in use by the World Health Organization.)

The philosophy of self-fulfillment, which conquered large segments of the American middle class during the 1970s, will become enshrined in official social agencies and quite possibly defined as a constitutional right. Much legislation and governmental rule-making will be devoted to making self-fulfillment available to the greatest number of people.

It is under the rubric of health, thus understood, that the state will claim the right to intervene in the relationship between parents and children. Not only will parents be prevented from physically mistreating their children but a form of "mental cruelty" to children will be defined which will include, for example, inculcating them with inappropriately "rigid" and "outmoded" moral ideas. The state may institute psychological testing for parents, and those who fail could have their children taken away from them or be forbidden to beget any more children. Among those declared to have failed such tests would be those who believe, for example, in the divine authority of the Scriptures, miracles in a supernatural sense, absolute moral laws, et cetera. All such beliefs will be declared unscientific and therefore inappropriate for children to learn in a scientific age. Holding them will be regarded as evidence of psychological maladjustment and rigidity of personality.

—Sexual beliefs and behavior will be taken as a special index of health and an important criterion of proper attitudes. In effect the "playboy philosophy" of the 1960s—casual sex for pleasure, the absence of all guilt, continuous experimentation to achieve more and more satisfying sexual experiences—will be officially adopted as constitutive of health. This will be due in part to its almost universal acceptance within the therapeutic professions themselves, in part because it will be the chosen life-style of most of the bureaucrats who will make the rules in the year 2000 and in part because an increasingly totalitarian state will regard recreational sex, disconnected from all possibility of producing children, as an important way of keeping the majority of the populace occupied and happy.

There will be deeper reasons at work as well. Although many liberals, especially religious liberals, now argue that "personal" morality is unimportant in comparison with "social" morality, those with any depth of insight into the human soul realize how closely sexual behavior, and beliefs about sexual behavior, are bound to the inner core of identity of each person, which is the chief reason sexual morality has remained a sensitive subject through the centuries despite repeated attempts to declare it insignificant. People who change their sexual beliefs and behavior in any significant way, especially if they are persuaded or seduced into changing against their better judgments, usually undergo other kinds of personality changes. The social engineers of the future will understand quite well that people who have been indoctrinated into holding flexible opinions on so basic and intimate a subject as sex are unlikely to have firm convictions on very many other subjects. Above all they are unlikely to be committed to any kind of religious creed which compels them to resist the state in its intrusion into sensitive moral areas or to accept martyrdom.

— A positivistic and secularistic moral relativism will be the officially mandated philosophy of the schools and social agencies of all kinds, as well as the overwhelmingly dominant philosophy of the media. Overtly religious philosophy will be excluded from most agencies by a rigid interpretation of the First Amendment. Where it exists it will be purely private and ineffectual, about on the level of belief in reincarnation at the present time. Relativism will be doubly blessed in that it will be regarded as a sign of mental health and because, in the absence of any permanent and transcendent moral principles, official government policy alone will define right and wrong. In the 1960s a president of Yale asked rhetorically, "What has happened to our morality?" and one of his professors answered sardonically, "We're drowning in it." But despite the prodigal moralizing of that decade, in the end the iconoclastic self-assertiveness spawned by the New Left won out over any commitment to high principle, so that the "me decade" of the 1970s followed. The politics of the year 2000 may have permanently ratified this victory of the self-justifying, self-gratifying self. Morality will have been abolished.

— The twin concerns of population control and energy conservation have greater potential for totalitarian control than perhaps any other political imperatives, a fact which many people naively fail to recognize but which others recognize quite well and are eager to exploit. There could be no more blatant and complete violation of personal liberty than the kind of interference in people's lives which would be necessary to determine who is or is not fit to produce offspring, and how many. Some population-control zealots already admit that they would accept enforced sterilization or enforced abortion if necessary, and in the world of social engineering today's extremism becomes tomorrow's conventional wisdom. Such measures will be accepted by people who now justify abortion on the grounds that the state has no right to interfere in the privacy of a woman's reproductive life. Both population control and energy conservation will be proposed as practical absolutes, since they relate to survival, or at least to the survival of that "quality of life" which the state has determined is appropriate to its citizens. Normal questions about civil liberties will be declared inapplicable to these emergency areas.

To those who regard the above scenario as improbable and fanciful, it should be pointed out that certain important elements of it have already occurred. In particular, in the past two decades those institutions most likely to provide resistance to such developments have been either neutralized or co-opted into the service of this emergent totalitarianism. Those institutions are the churches, the schools, the media, and the family itself.

In speaking of "the churches", one speaks of a much more diverse phenomenon than often appears at first glance. Yet those churches which by common consent occupy the "mainstream" of American society, roughly those affiliated with the National Council of Churches, plus the Catholic Church and reformed and conservative Jews, are at present pathetically unable even to comprehend what is happening in America, much less to mount any kind of effective response to it.

Many religious people are simply passive and confused. They may feel vaguely uneasy about things they see going on around them, but they are unable to analyze what is happening with any depth or acuity. Furthermore, in many instances they have been indoctrinated by their religious leaders into a reflective stance of permanent embarrassment over the alleged "backwardness" of the churches and the fear that religion is the enemy of freedom and progress. Thus they have been conditioned to accept every kind of social and moral change, no matter how much they may personally dislike it.

Many denominational leaders, clergy in particular, can visualize themselves in almost any kind of social role except one where they might be mistaken for Cotton Mather. They are constitutionally incapable of opposing the drift toward secularism, relativism, and hedonism, because to do so would be to do violence to their carefully cultivated self-image as open, progressive, sophisticated, freedom-loving men. Thus many of them deny or minimize what is happening, when they do not actually endorse it. Some have also calculated that their own people are so heavily influenced by these trends that the churches dare not oppose them.

For various rather complex reasons, leaders of "mainstream" denominations also find it remarkably easy to become whole-hearted apostles on behalf of the new — any moral crusade which lifts the banner of "freedom" and "justice" automatically enlists their support, whether it is the antiwar movement or "gay rights". The credal vacuum which now lies at the heart of liberal religion groans until it is filled, and what it is usually filled with is messianic political and social dogmas. In many churches the professionals, lay and clerical, have adopted a social engineering mentality which will make them allies of the government bureaucrats who will effect the scenario for the year 2000 which is described above. (A revealing case is that of the Catholic Church in America. Many of its clergy, religious, and professional laymen hold positions on controversial social issues like homosexuality which are quite at variance with the Church's official doctrines. Except for abortion, the Church's official bureaucracies tend to give at least passive support to the ominous tendencies noted above, and altogether its American leaders appear to be timid and confused.)

Concerning the schools, two facts so fundamental as to be usually overlooked need to be recalled in order to understand what has happened and is likely to happen. One is that formal education, of its very nature, implies a certain inadequacy in the family. Otherwise children would not be sent out of the home for long periods of time to acquire knowledge which presumably they cannot acquire anywhere else. Thus schools are always potentially in conflict with the family, and various methods have been devised to permit ultimate lay control over education, generally through elected school boards. By now, however, the mystique of professional expertise is so strong that parents probably have less influence over what is taught in schools than at almost any time in the past. The educational profession increasingly regards only its own philosophies and practices as valid and has developed institutionalized means for repulsing outside criticism. The professionalism of the educators is also linked to the professionalism of psychologists and others working in sensitive moral areas, so that positions inimical to familial authority and traditional morality come to permeate the schools more and more. The National Education Association and the Department of Education will extend these even further.

The overlooked fact about education is that it is always ultimately moral and religious in nature, whether or not it aspires to be. This is true even of the most narrowly practical kind of education, which imparts a view of the world and of human action in the world by what it omits and what it encourages students to regard as important.

A generally unrecognized fact about American public education is that it worked tolerably well down to the 1960s mainly because it did have an unacknowledged religious basis — a kind of nondenominational Protestantism. However, with the collapse of Protestantism and the emergence of an aggressive secularizing movement dedicated to expunging all traces of religion from the schools, this situation ended abruptly. (All the court cases imposing strict secularity on the public schools date from the post-1945 period. Some of the most important were only decided in the 1960s and 1970s.)

But, as noted, all education has a moral and religious vision at its heart, whether or not this is intended. Given the current legal and moral climate of American society, this vision can only come from the philosophy broadly called secular humanism, a philosophy which proceeds on the working assumption that there is no God (one may privately believe in God so long as this does not influence one's conduct), all moral principles are relative, utilitarian considerations ultimately govern moral decisions, and the maximization of one's own "self-fulfillment" is the proper goal of existence. Once again a moral vacuum has been created in the schools, partly by the courts, partly by the education profession itself, and something inevitably rushes in to fill it.

The media also have undergone a remarkably radical transformation in about a decade's time. Formerly the media at least paid hypocritical respect to religious and moral values, even if media personnel were often privately cynical about them. However, the confusion and demoralization (in a double sense) which has affected American society in the past fifteen years has led these same personnel to calculate that they can offend against those values with impunity, a calculation which so far seems correct.

The reasons why the media choose to do this are complex and not altogether clear. In part the simple need for constant novelty, titillation, and entertainment provided through the systematic breaking of all taboos, seems to govern. This is true in "news" as well as entertainment, and the news is now largely purveyed in categories which proclaim constant "breakthroughs" and which habitually contrast the stodgy old (whether consumer products, medical procedures, or moral practices) with the enlightened and efficient new. It also appears to be the case that the media attract disproportionate numbers of alienated and iconoclastic people, who often seem to harbor a perpetual grudge against "straight" society. (Phil Donahue and Tom Snyder, both graduates of Catholic universities, are cases in point.) Whatever the reasons, iconoclastic moral values now saturate the media, often more through ridicule and attack directed at traditional values than by the purveyance of any positive new vision. But the overwhelming message which the media drum into their audiences is, "Do your own thing. Rules are made to be broken."

It is unfortunately the case that many otherwise morally conservative people are almost mesmerized by the media, especially television and, among younger people, popular music. The frankly pagan values which are celebrated are often not recognized or, if they are recognized, are treated as though they were entertainment only and had no effect on anyone's moral character. Yet it is probably the case that the "stars" of the entertainment industry have more moral influence, especially on impressionable young people, than any other kind of public figure.

The media like to think of themselves as antiestablishment and as the watchdogs of the state, and it will be interesting to see whether, if the scenario sketched above starts to unfold, they will attempt to counteract it. In all likelihood they will not, in part because the values which this future totalitarian state espouses will be the values most media people are comfortable with. It will also be the case that, given the disintegration of traditional social groups like churches and families, there will be no independent sources of value in the society of the future and little basis, other than personal taste, from which anyone can criticize the dominant ideology. This will be especially true if, as seems likely, this totalitarian state claims to provide maximum personal happiness for all its citizens, happiness being understood mainly as pleasure.

Much of the blame for the problems outlined above falls on the shoulders of those who believe, or profess to believe, in traditional moral values. Among such people there is an extraordinary amount of passivity, timidity, and sheer lack of awareness of what is going on around them. Many of them would like to see a savior, someone who would rescue them from what they at least dimly perceive as a peril, provided no effort, and especially no risk, would be required of them. In case after case the moral iconoclasts have won victories because their erstwhile opponents failed to mount effective resistance. There are many traditionalists who allowed themselves to be lulled into complacency by reassuring verbal formulas explaining that what looks like radical change is not that at all.

Ordinarily religion would provide the major focus of resistance to this emergent totalitarianism. However, a whole generation of Christians has now been raised with no real knowledge of the faith they profess. They remain ignorant of the Bible, of historical creeds, of the very categories of thought in which Christian belief has historically expressed itself. As a result they lack even the vocabulary with which to counter their enemies. Confronted in the media by caricatures of Christianity, they may be affronted but do not know enough even to counter the caricature effectively. What they have been given by their religious teachers is a sentimental humanism which often leaves them intellectually vulnerable to any movement which claims to promote human betterment, even when that movement is anti-Christian. They may feel that something is deeply wrong but, lacking the means to articulate their feelings, they are easily persuaded that these are mere prejudices which they should overcome. Pagan values are often mistaken for Christian. (In a Midwestern newspaper a woman wrote: "The Bible commands every woman to rid herself of anything that prevents her from fulfilling what she feels is her role in life.")

Twenty years ago, when the threats to traditional moral values were far less ominous than they are today, traditionalists were far more effectively vigilant, and ordinary people were much more quickly shocked and roused to outrage. Paradoxically, the vigilance and the outrage have declined as the reasons to be alarmed have increased. The very pervasiveness of the "new morality", the degree to which it saturates public discourse, gives it a familiarity which leads many people to accept it as normal and inevitable. Many people have trained themselves not to become alarmed or shocked any longer, since this is the only way they can maintain their peace of mind.

Although most of the impetus for moral change comes from those quarters which can be broadly called "liberal", it is by no means the case that the people called "conservatives" are always reliable allies against such changes. Since conservatives in general oppose the expansion of government bureaucracies, on balance they provide some objective protection against the kind of totalitarianism described above. But many conservatives are preoccupied with economic or military-diplomatic issues and do not see the importance of moral or social questions. Many conservatives share with many liberals an apparent conviction that economic issues are paramount in public life. The standard liberal response to the breakdown of the family, for example, is to propose larger government programs aimed at funneling money to families in need, as though poverty alone were the cause of family problems. Many conservatives give the impression that they believe that in a free-market economy all such problems would solve themselves. Virtually all the leading conservative candidates for president seem to treat the moral crisis of the age as a mere afterthought, while the leading liberal candidates can be counted on to advance the totalitarian scenario sketched above. (With regard to both liberal and conservative politicians there is a distasteful question which must nonetheless be raised: in advanced political circles, especially in Washington, a kind of hedonistic life-style seems to flourish which attracts people regardless of their ideologies. High-pressure politics often puts severe strains on family bonds. It seems likely, therefore, that many politicians are personally in the camp of the moral iconoclasts and are unlikely to oppose with conviction the kinds of changes outlined above.)

Conventional wisdom suggests that the 1980s are a traditionalist decade. After the frenetic political climate of the 1960s and the frenetic moral climate of the 1970s, people once again seek peace, order, and stability. If true, however, this is only partial comfort. If the traditionalism of the 1980s is mainly a reaction to what went before, one more swing of the pendulum, it will merely prepare for yet another decade of iconoclasm in the 1990s, a pretext (the "repressive '80s") for a final assault on traditional values.

Those who are called traditionalists (the name itself is quite inadequate) must find some basis for their position besides what might appear to be merely a sentimental attachment to the past or nervous anxiety about the future. To say this is to say that a genuine moral and religious revival must occur, one whose fruits must be effectively communicated to masses of people. The task will be difficult given the inhospitability of the schools, the media, and many of the churches.

Yet a new religious realignment may be taking place. The growing influence of the evangelical Protestants, who appear to be becoming more sophisticated as they become more visible, is probably the single most important religious fact in contemporary America. Catholicism, under Pope John Paul II, may be in the process of recovering both its will and its intellect, both having atrophied together. Orthodox Judaism is growing, is increasingly militant, and also shows considerable sophistication. It is precisely these groups which the media have sought to discredit and isolate, to declare in effect to be marginal and unbalanced. (Thus the media constantly draw the distinction between "good" Catholics who oppose the Pope and the other kind who are too timid to do so.)

One of the interesting developments of the next decade may be the emergence of a new, broadly-based political coalition involving people (for example, Catholics, Baptists, and Orthodox Jews) who ordinarily would have little to do with one another but who can unite around certain issues, especially those involving the family. The numerical potential of such a coalition is immense. In addition, as it demonstrates its strength, it will inevitably draw politicians, conservative and liberal, into its orbit. One of its greatest challenges, and the major test of its effectiveness, will be its ability to reach its potential constituency, given the almost universal hostility of established institutions, both religious and secular.

This is a constituency, and a platform, whose outlines are only beginning to become visible. It heralds a politics which has few precedents in American history. But the stakes, perhaps precisely because of their elusiveness in ordinary political terms, are also without precedent.

ABORTION AND THE MORAL REVOLUTION

The act of abortion is sometimes characterized as a tragic necessity, in the classical sense of a situation in which two undeniable goods conflict with one another, one or both fated to give way in the face of the requirements of the other.

Yet in practice those who advocate the morality of abortion rarely treat it as though it were tragic in any sense at all. A utilitarian calculus in which the needs of the mother are weighed against the needs of the unborn child and in which the former is given precedence is, however unacceptable, at least comprehensible. But such a calculus, if truly employed, could not help but induce in its users a profound sense of ambivalence. Recognizing the legitimate claims of the child, the mother could never feel altogether justified in her choice, however necessary she might believe it to be. For a truly moral person, no matter how much persuaded that abortion is sometimes permissible, the act could never leave behind a wholly peaceful conscience.

In fact, however, the present cultural attitude toward abortion in no way includes this ambivalence. Although the word "tragic" is bandied about by those who seek merely a convenient verbal formula for disposing of scruples, the possibility that the child has rights is never seriously considered and is routinely and implicitly denied. The regular employment of the utilitarian calculus would actually mark a moral improvement, since it would bring the question at least to the point of admitting that the child's rights must be consciously weighed.

The ploys by which these rights have been denied are too well known to require discussion — the use of terms like "product of pregnancy" and "evacuation of the womb" to obscure what is really happening, the assertion that the fetus is merely a parasite on the mother, and the absolutist claim (made by ostensible moral relativists) that the mother's rights alone matter.

In any moral social atmosphere those who support the permissibility of abortion would treat antiabortionists with at least a certain deference, admitting that hard moral choices are involved and that those who insist on asking pointed questions are right to do so. They would recognize that the general moral sense of society is protected from atrophy by those who demand that acts like abortion not slip into the realm of unexamined routine. In the end they would be prepared to say at least that antiabortionists are right in the abstract, even if their ethic is too demanding and must be compromised in practice.

It would then follow that those who support abortion would feel a strong obligation to minimize its use. Having identified certain cases where they

163

believe abortion is the lesser of two evils, they would be at great pains to insure that it was resorted to only in such cases, and they would exercise rigorous vigilance to prevent its becoming a routine practice. (If there is truly a parallel between abortion and capital punishment, the equivalent would be for the defenders of the latter to be determined that no innocent people should be executed.)

Instead a quite different situation prevails. Although legal abortion was advocated on the basis of the familiar "hard cases"—in this instance rape, incest, and danger to the mother's life—virtually all knowledgeable people now admit that such cases are rare. Abortion has indeed become routine and, as many even of its defenders now admit, is simply used as the ultimate method of contraception.

Women who seek abortions need not demonstrate any motive greater than an aversion to inconvenience. In no way does this situation seem to embarrass proabortionists; most seem to welcome it as a sign of progress.

Despite what is often asserted, the debate over abortion is not a conflict between two opposed moralities, not even between an absolutist valuing of human life and a relativist one. In a quite literal sense those who support abortion have no moral position. Their position is based precisely on the denial of morality, at least in this instance. Their greatest crime is, in one sense, not their willingness to countenance and even encourage abortion but their determination not to permit the morality of the question even to be discussed. In the interest of securing the practice against attack, they are prepared to suppress all considerations of morality whatever.

Antiabortionists see parallels between themselves and the antislavery abolitionists before the Civil War, and the parallel is nowhere more pronounced than at this point. Although some defenders of slavery may have regarded it as a tragic necessity, and although some slaveholders (like Thomas Jefferson) had bad consciences over the practice, the burden of proslavery opinion came to be a flat denial that any moral question was even involved. With slavery as with abortion, those who insisted on raising the moral questions were themselves attacked as immoral. In both cases an act which, morally speaking, could be characterized as at best dubious was elevated to the status of a virtue.

In the case of slaveholders, vested property interests, plus the legitimacy which any long-standing social practice automatically enjoys, largely explains the determination to defend the indefensible. Here the parallel with abortion diverges. Except for those who actually perform abortions, no one has an economic stake in the practice and, far from enjoying the sanction of custom, legalized abortion is a shockingly new and radical idea. What then accounts for the ferocity with which its defenders insist that evil is good?

Mere convenience seems inadequate to explain the passion involved, even though convenience may be the single most common motive for women seeking abortions. Many morally dubious things are done for the sake of convenience, but such actions are usually justified, if at all, without much apparent conviction, indeed almost furtively. Why do many people passionately support a woman's "right" to kill her unborn offspring even when they themselves will probably never be in a position to seek an abortion?

Much of the passion, the ferocity which shades into hate, can perhaps be taken as a hopeful sign. Surely in many cases it indicates that there is indeed a conscience at work, a conscience which does not permit the easy acceptance of a horrendous deed and which gives the individual a semblance of peace only to the degree that the moral tables are turned. The defender of human life must be cast as the aggressor, the taker of innocent life, the victim. When the ferocious passions of the proabortionists have subsided, when they no longer trouble to vilify their opponents, the cause for worry will be much greater, because it will signify the final disappearance of even the residue of moral sense on the question.

The practical questions surrounding abortion, especially of course the huge number of human lives lost, are enormous. However, it is crucial to the antiabortion cause to recognize also how the practical questions are increasingly overshadowed by the symbolic. Defenders of abortion are not interested in the question whether fetuses are human and whether, therefore, it is moral to kill them. They dismiss such questions as unanswerable, which means that they do not wish to examine them in any serious way. But the very word "abortion" carries resonances of a kind which accompany few other terms in the language. Stating one's position on this single issue has the effect of calling into play a whole range of moral and social attitudes, and people are now often for or against abortion apart from any consideration of its concrete effects.

A preliminary distinction can be made between right-wing and left-wing proabortion sentiment. The former, which is found among many people of conservative beliefs, rests on the perception that legal (and governmentally funded) abortions help solve certain social problems—there will be fewer "unwanted" children, hence less social pathology and less need for expensive welfare programs. People who accept this largely utilitarian principle are usually not militant on the subject of abortion, however, and are not actively part of the group which presses constantly to push back the established limits of protection for human life (euthanasia and infanticide being obviously related issues).

Left-wing proabortionists are by definition part of the moral avant-garde of society, and it is their beliefs which are most influential and effective in establishing public policy. Their opinions, in fact, dominate the media, academic life, and the majority of public and private social agencies. Utilitarian considerations certainly enter their thoughts, and utilitarian arguments are especially used to attract popular support. But for most such people the symbolic issues are finally more important than the practical. (Thus liberals remain unmoved by the charge that governmentally funded abortion programs serve to restrict the black population. They are not primarily interested in the practical results of such programs.)

The symbolic issues exist in a series of concentric circles which support and complement one another. The outermost of these circles is that of class conflict — the perception that antiabortionists are uneducated, crude, and irrational, while their opponents are enlightened and civilized.[1] Although this stereotype is deliberately concocted for propaganda purposes — it is a stereotype which the media are only too glad to propagate — those who employ it probably also believe it.

It is a generally unrecognized fact about contemporary social life that virtually all change, no matter what populist banner it marches behind, achieves success or failure largely on the basis of what response it evokes from the educated and articulate segments of the middle class. (The black civil rights movement is a classic example.) In fact, very few movements in contemporary life do have populist roots. Most often, movements which appear populist are really the creation of an educated elite.

Abortion is a major instance of this phenomenon. Public support for abortion was initially solicited in the form of sympathy for the "victim" of restrictive laws — allegedly young, poor women either butchered in back alleys or forced to bear unwanted children, while rich mothers flew to safe clinics in foreign countries. Yet the number of women who actually could and did go to foreign countries for abortions was always very small, and the drive for legalized abortion aimed to provide a convenient service for well-off middle-class women. The middle-class couple who have decided that they want no more children or who, should their daughter become pregnant outside wedlock, would not want her life to be "ruined", are the backbone of proabortion opinion in America. All the "needs" of the poor are asserted largely as a rationale for middle-class benefits.

In recent years, holding the correct political and social opinions, and associating oneself with the right kind of causes, has become an important badge of middle-class fashion in America, a phenomenon with which attitudes on abortion are intimately involved. Growing out of the civil-rights and antiwar movements, a conflict has been postulated between an allegedly narrow, bigoted, violent, and irrational white lower and lower-middle class and an educated, enlightened, and progressive upper-middle class. Although in fact social and political attitudes cannot be predicted with nearly such

---

[1] See Peter Skerry, "The Class Conflict over Abortion", *The Public Interest* (Summer 1978); reprinted in *The Human Life Review* no. 4 (Fall 1978): 34–41.

neatness, this image is an important part of the self-esteem of many educated people who take their superior economic status for granted but especially pride themselves on their advanced social views. In particular such people have fallen into the habit of assuming that every belief sanctioned by tradition is likely to be false and that the well-being of the human race is carried forward by constant intellectual and moral innovation.

Such people see themselves as the "cutting edge" of social change in America, and to be associated with avant-garde (and slightly daring) movements is for many of them a psychological necessity. Apart from the specifics of the issue, they see antiabortion sentiment as representing all those backward attitudes which society must seek to erase. (Liberals who complain about the alleged right-wing dominance of the antiabortion movement miss the most obvious point—if liberals themselves were to espouse the cause with vigor, conservatives would automatically be deprived of an issue.) Because the antiabortion movement is as close to a genuinely populist cause as can be found in America, it is hated with special ferocity.

The English historian E. R. Norman has remarked that there is talk about "pluralism" only during the period of transition from one orthodoxy to another. Once the new orthodoxy has become established, its defenders no longer show any interest in the values of tolerance and multiple viewpoints which they previously extolled.

Defenders of traditional orthodoxies have frequently used overt censorship to inhibit the spread of heterodox ideas. Defenders of the new orthodoxies recognize that this is often counter-productive. Much more effective is the kind of censorship they practice, which consists in creating a climate of opinion in which people have the bare legal right to express dissenting views but in which such views are made to seem so eccentric as to be literally incredible. For example, on almost all questions pertaining to sexual behavior—contraception, abortion, extramarital sex, unmarried cohabitation, homosexuality—defenders of traditional values have, within less than a decade's time, been put on the defensive, their beliefs stigmatized in the media and the educational system as symptomatic merely of narrow and insecure personalities.

Although the rhetoric of change emphasizes merely the right of each "alternative life style" to be tolerated, the struggle is never merely for toleration. Of necessity the media, the schools, and public and private social agencies must take positions with regard to all controversial belief and behavior, and it is the aim of the apostles of the avant-garde to insure that these institutions adopt their own beliefs as normative, relegating traditional values to the closet.

Although the rhetoric of relativism is freely used—the assertion that no absolutes exist and that all beliefs are therefore equally valid—in practice a new absolutism is espoused. Those who believe in sexual "liberation", for example, commonly do not recognize sexual abstinence as a valid way of life.

At most they concede it a legal right to exist, and they generate massive social pressures against it.

The new orthodoxy fits closely with the reality of class conflict, already discussed, in that this orthodoxy is essentially located in what has often been called the "new class" — those persons who regard themselves as enlightened and emancipated in their opinions and who are maximally receptive of new ideas. In essence these people believe that moral belief, although necessary to society, is also dangerous because of the passions it arouses. Publicly they espouse the idea of relativism and equal toleration of all opinions, in order to dampen possible outbreaks of moral passions of which they disapprove. In practice, however, they concede to themselves the sole right to have moral passions, the sole right to mount moral crusades. Moral passion is treated as a dangerous substance which must in effect be licensed.

Since the late 1960s there has been talk of a "conscience constituency" in American politics, meaning an element among the voters which shuns traditional party loyalties and traditional considerations of economic self-interest in favor of political behavior based on the perceived moral importance of particular issues. These are issues — war, racism, poverty, ecology, the "Third World" — which ordinary politics either takes little interest in or seeks to avoid, precisely because they are emotional and divisive.

The intense hatred which many "new politics" people have for the antiabortion movement stems from their feeling that the kind of people who are opposed to abortion, especially if they are demonstrably religious, have no right engaging in moral crusades. Such crusading is permissible only if directed toward subjects which have been certified as genuine issues of conscience. Conceiving themselves as the authentic keepers of the public conscience, such people are rendered angry and frightened at the prospect of others — the wrong kind of people — claiming the authority of conscience for their own concerns.

Those "single-issue" voters who have allowed their political loyalties to be guided solely by considerations involving, say, war or the Equal Rights Amendment, are commonly admired, within the "conscience constituency", for their purity, even if their single-mindedness is sometimes thought a bit short-sighted. Those who cast their ballots solely on the question of abortion, however, are accused of being dangerous fanatics and threats to the democratic system, the remedy for such a threat being a renewed sense of party loyalty, in which antiabortion voters would not hold politicians accountable for betraying them.

During the antiwar movement those who engaged in acts of civil disobedience were treated as heroes by most of the "enlightened" element in America, and those who went beyond disobedience to acts of destruction were usually "understood" even if not precisely condoned. In the late 1970s it has been antiabortionists, and especially young antiabortionists, who have shown a comparable willingness to risk themselves and their futures. Yet their witness has been largely ignored, or else dismissed as mere fanaticism, and acts of destruction directed against abortion clinics, even when there has been no evidence as to who perpetrated them, have been treated as almost sacrilegious, proof of the fundamental immorality of the antiabortionists.

The moral avant-garde requires, in politics, a constant series of symbolic victories, which both serve to proclaim the triumph of the enlightened class of people over the backward and the continued and progressive triumph of advanced opinions over traditional beliefs. The terms of permissible public discourse, and the permissible style of those who engage in public discourse, are defined to that end, and supporters of the new manage thereby to keep the momentum always with themselves, their opponents constantly on the defensive.[2]

With regard to abortion, as on other questions, what is being tested in part is the media's ability to mold public opinion, and much of the media's hostility to the antiabortion movement stems from that movement's stubborn refusal to allow the media to instruct it in correct opinions.

Two other concentric circles are perhaps really dimensions of the previous one. They are constituted by two particular orthodoxies which have, within a decade, managed to establish themselves as beyond question. Their fortuitous coming together accounts almost entirely for the sudden triumph of the proabortion position in the public realm.

The first of these is the population question, the assertion that the world is threatened by the prospect of too many people and that all means of population control, including abortion, should be unstintingly used. The ramifications of this contention are too vast to be adequately discussed here. However, two relevant points can be noted. One is that, consciously or otherwise, the mentality of Zero Population Growth and the related philosophy of eugenics expresses the traditional elitist idea that the world would be a better place if there were fewer people and if those few were also more carefully selected. In short, it envisions a world in which only those who fit into the enlightened consensus have a right to exist. Secondly—a point which is rather obvious, though seldom noted—there could be no more effective road to totalitarian control in the democratic West than by invoking draconian measures to ensure the survival of the race. Furthermore, through such measures (especially as they affect the sacred area of sexual behavior), the enlightened elite can compel the backward masses to behave correctly. Many ardent civil-libertarians show an odd ambivalence toward proposals forcibly to regulate human breeding. (So also, few alarmists on the subject of population

---

[2] See Hitchcock, "The Dynamics of Popular Intellectual Change", below, and "Power to the Eloquent", *Yale Review* 46, no. 3 (Spring 1977): 347–87.

seem to be alarmed at the prospect of life created in the laboratory. The symbolism of yet another astonishing "breakthrough" far outweighs the practical demands of their cause. Many of them would probably prefer a society in which all life were created in the laboratory and little was left to human activity.)

The second unimpeachable orthodoxy is feminism, which neatly complements population control in its tendency to denigrate motherhood as at best a specialized talent suitable for a relative few, and at worst a form of tyranny. Again the complete ramifications of this orthodoxy are too large for discussion. However, feminists who are opposed to abortion (as some sincerely are) are rather in the same position as Catholics who support it—the official doctrine of feminism does not treat abortion as peripheral, negotiable, or even debatable. The unrestricted right to an abortion is rather taken as basic to any authentic feminism.

There is compelling logic in this, in the sense that the shattering of the hitherto sacred bond between mother and child is necessary for creating the kind of "freedom" that orthodox feminism seeks. Arguably, all aspects of women's traditional social role stem ultimately from either the fact of or the potentiality for motherhood, and it is crucial to the orthodox feminist position that women be able to deny any finally binding obligations which they have toward children. Orthodox feminism is an especially militant manifestation of a larger, and increasingly prevalent, social philosophy which holds that the "needs" of the individual are self-validating and that no person or institution may restrict those needs. Abortion is perceived by many feminists as the acid test of real commitment to the cause—if even that deeply rooted scruple can be overcome, then the individual is indeed a true believer. With feminism as with other fashionable political causes, no considerations of mere morality can be allowed to dilute the degree of commitment to the movement.

The innermost circle, the very core of the militant proabortion position, is the simple act of moral iconoclasm itself, and it is the fanaticism which this act breeds which fuels the passions motivating the other circles.

The "conscience constituency" engages in moral innovation in two opposite ways. On the one hand it seeks to define as immoral actions that most people do not think of as such—driving automobiles, building dams, smoking tobacco, eating steak—while on the other it declares permissible and even virtuous certain actions that are commonly deemed immoral—using drugs for enjoyment, homosexual relations, abortion, viewing pornography. The assumption beneath both sets of positions is that the moral perceptions of ordinary people are not only distorted but topsy-turvy, and that it is the duty of the avant-garde precisely to effect a "transvaluation of values". Crucial to this revolution is the necessity of keeping the pressure high. One or two radical moral ideas are likely to suffer the fate of social isolation and be rejected. A moral revolution occurring on all fronts simultaneously will, however, so weaken the public sense of self-confidence, so distort the overall moral perspective, as to make virtually any idea seem plausible, so long as it is advanced with sufficient eloquence.

The pragmatic arguments for abortion, including the "hard cases" alluded to above, were never intended to be final. Rather they were necessary tactical preludes to the central symbolic act of iconoclasm, the assault on two of the most deeply rooted of all human moral institutions—the imperative to protect defenseless life and the sacred bond between mother and child.

Antiabortionists wonder how two such profound moral instincts, both supported by powerful and ancient religious, legal, and social taboos, could possibly be discarded so cavalierly, how the act of abortion could be so swiftly transformed from a heinous crime into a work of charity. The answer is that it is precisely because of the sacredness of the prohibition that such a transformation had to occur. The avant-garde mentality is not content simply to transgress moral prohibitions when they are inconvenient, which has been done in all ages of history. Rather the avant-garde recognizes only one wholly-binding moral imperative, namely, in the words of the sociologist Philip Rieff, "the systematic hunting down of all settled convictions". Precisely because the act of aborting is widely perceived as immoral, it must be defiantly asserted. It is the crucial test case to demonstrate that traditional moral values, especially those which have roots in religion, shall not prevail.

The sometimes grotesque contortions through which the moral implications of abortion are denied are indication enough that a large residue of guilt still plagues those who insist that this is a surgical procedure merely equivalent to extracting inflamed tonsils. There have been some notable public conversions by people who began with a belief in the rightness of abortion but whose consciences would finally no longer permit this rationalization.

However, there is only limited comfort to be had from the existence of this moral residue, because it is precisely of the nature of the avant-garde mind to treat guilt as an atavism, an admittedly powerful force which must be systematically rooted out. Only when people suffer no guilt for their acts will they feel truly free. Abortion is the most important test case to determine whether, given massive propaganda doses, people can be made to overcome their deepest inhibitions. It is an experiment with immense relevance for the future.

The ultimate aim of this moral iconoclasm is the establishment of a morality which is wholly a human creation, not only in the sense of having no divine referent but also in the sense of being precisely a creation, that is, an emanation from the self, an exercise of the sovereign human will.[3]

---

[3] See Hitchcock, "The Roots of American Violence", below.

The final result of this exercise—a result already achieved by many of the avant-garde—is that morality as such ceases to exist. This fact is generally overlooked because of the intense moralizing in which many of these same avant-garde indulge. But when the same law that withdraws its protection from unborn children subsequently extends it to snail darters, and when these legal decrees are hailed by enlightened opinion as signs of moral progress, it is clear that what is operative is not moral sense but mere fashion. There is no longer any right or wrong except that which has become enshrined in the ebbing and flowing of approved causes.

The struggle over the legal and moral status of abortion in America extends far beyond the lives of the millions of unborn, important though those lives are. It is finally a struggle over whether morality as such will endure and will be allowed to make its claims on the way human beings live.

FAMILY IS AS FAMILY DOES

Deciphering coded terminology was a major prerequisite for understanding the White House Conference on Families held in three different regional meetings in the summer of 1980.

For example, when conference officials talked about "takeovers", they did not mean, contrary to what many people might have thought, a process by which state steering committees appointed delegates to the conference solely to satisfy their own view of who should be represented. Rather they meant situations where various groups of citizens, fearful that the conference would turn out as disastrously as the International Women's Year meeting in Houston in 1978, organized themselves to elect the kinds of delegates they preferred. Whatever might be said of these elections, they were the closest the conference ever got to democratic accountability, and conference officials sometimes seemed to regret that there were any elections at all.

"Special interest groups", also contrary to what might have been assumed, were not, for example, movements for homosexual rights or publicly-funded abortions, nor were they the social workers and educators who had a vested interest in encouraging new government programs of all kinds. The term was rather reserved for people who resisted these things and who, as family members, proclaimed in effect, "Let us alone." From the beginning conference officials perceived the latter people as somehow sinister.

With words thus defined in an Alice-in-Wonderland fashion, it is hardly surprising that the White House Conference on Families literally did not know what it was talking about. Originally it was supposed to be about "the Family". This was changed to the plural in order to signify, as the organizers never tired of repeating, that there is no single model valid for all families.

Up to a point, almost everyone could accept this. No one, for example, would be likely to condemn either the "nuclear" or the "extended" family as traditionally understood. No one, either, wants to read single-parent families out of polite society. But the conferences's hidden agenda could not stop there. The term had to be kept as elastic as possible, to include by implication any group of people sharing the same household, including homosexuals. Given numerous opportunities to indicate that by family they meant something which at least approximated the traditional definition of people related to each other by blood, marriage, or adoption, conference officials pointedly refused to do so. Obviously their intent was to use the word "family" as a peg on which to hang anything.

This being the case, those who tried to define family were treated as prissy and quarrelsome scholastics determined to split hairs in fruitless controversy

173

while troubled people cried out for help. There was a curious kind of role reversal as a result—educated professionals, the kind of people who pride themselves on clear thinking and the avoidance of slogans, kept insisting that it made no difference what people meant by the word, while those who are often dismissed as ignorant and muddleheaded hysterics were the ones who thought it important for the conference to state exactly what it was all about.

The refusal to define family inevitably gave rise to basic confusion as to the conference's very purpose. Sometimes it seemed to be predicated on the assumption that families are "in trouble" and need help, help being perceived almost always as new or expanded government programs. At other times, however, conference leaders proclaimed defiantly that "the family is alive and well in America" and implied that the conference had been summoned to celebrate its well-being.

Writing some time before the conference, the sociologist Allan C. Carlson anticipated the flaws which would vitiate its thinking. Among other things, he noted that if the family is not defined and an acceptable model agreed upon there will be no way of judging whether families are healthy or not.[1] Given this uncertainty, how could the conference say anything meaningful, or on what basis could it prescribe remedies for the family's various deficiencies?

At the deepest level the refusal to define family seemed to be motivated by a tenacious resistance to morality itself, an assumed agnostic relativism so taken for granted that any overt reference to moral criteria was treated as a dangerous atavism, rather like a recurrence of the bubonic plague. Those who sought a definition were suspected of trying to impose their own narrow view, probably religiously motivated, on the rich diversity of American life. It was thus possible to see such people as sinister "special interest groups" bent on perpetrating a "takeover", and it became not only permissible but almost mandatory to manipulate the process to prevent this from occurring. The underlying spirit of the conference, as officially organized and controlled, was a classic instance of the secularistic society, not only in the general exclusion of religious considerations (aside from a few token benedictions and moments of silence) but, more importantly, in the helplessly complacent assumption that one view is exactly as good as another.

The problem went a good deal deeper than specific issues, like abortion, which might be thought of as divisive in a sectarian way. It worked to invalidate anything which smacked of the kind of judgment which would, by implication, include some and exclude others.

A whole series of such judgments could be easily conceived. Is it better for people to enter into relationships with persons of the opposite sex rather

---

[1] "Families, Sex, and the Liberal Agenda", *The Public Interest*, 58 (Winter 1980): 66. Reprinted in *The Human Life Review* Vol. 6, no. 3 (Summer 1980).

than the same sex? Is it desirable that such relationships be based on mutual respect and affection and be enduring? Is it important that such enduring relationships be ratified and symbolized by a formal and legal commitment? Should such commitments be sustained permanently if at all possible? Is one of the important purposes of such relationships the procreation of children? Do those who bring children into the world have special obligations for their personal and moral formulation, and do they also possess certain rights as a result? Should society seek to create an atmosphere in which commitments and responsibilities of this kind are supported and helped?

By its silence, and sometimes by its speech, the White House Conference was unable to give answers to any of these questions. Those who raised them too persistently were accused of disruptiveness, and the answers themselves were treated as unimportant.

The point is not, as it was often suggested, that to answer such questions would be to interfere in the personal lives of those who do not measure up to a certain ideal of family life. The point is that the conference was summoned mainly to recommend public policy. As was its destiny from the beginning, it found itself unable to say either that the well-being of American society in any way depended on particular answers to these and other questions, or that public policy should be aimed in one direction (for example, to support stable nuclear families) rather than another. To take certain extreme cases, if America should become a predominantly homosexual society, if the institution of marriage should virtually disappear from lack of use, if sexual promiscuity came to be statistically normal behavior, if most couples ceased producing children or neglected those they did beget, there would be few bases, in the results of the White House Conference, for regarding these developments as undesirable or seeking to reverse them. (It is indicative of the extent of the moral revolution that has occurred in recent years that, while those who would answer an unequivocal yes to the questions proposed above are now commonly dismissed as "fundamentalists", until a very few years ago the social sciences themselves overwhelmingly gave the same answers. Not only have several millennia of religious and moral wisdom been discarded, but also the insights of classical sociology and psychology.)

A revealing index of the studied moral neutrality of the conference is the almost total absence of a particular word from the reams of documents it generated — the word "divorce". Surely the incidence of divorce has something to do with the moral health of the family. When the divorce rate continues to rise steeply, when more and more marriages end abruptly, often with the effect of separating children from one of their parents at a crucial time in their lives, this ought surely to be of concern to those who take the well-being of the family as their primary task. Yet the subject was scarcely even discussed in the conference. By implication it too was treated as irrelevant.

In the mentality of the conference organizers, which was also, given its organization, the apparent mentality of a majority of the delegates at all three sessions, divorce was a taboo subject because of its implied judgment on people who have been divorced. (There was some amusing symbolism here. The original designated chairman of the conference was a divorced woman, who resigned when she was asked to accept a married man as co-chairman. President Carter then appointed as chairman Jim Guy Tucker, who has never been divorced but whose wife has been, thus presumably making him the right kind of compromise appointee.)

But the issue obviously goes well beyond anyone's possible desire to point accusing fingers at the divorced. Divorce, which is the dissolution of a marriage, surely says something important about the condition of marriage. It is surely not a matter of indifference whether people remain married or not, whether or not children continue to live with both their parents, whether marital commitments are understood to be permanent in nature. Morality aside, there are important psychological and sociological issues here. Yet the demands of their zealous agnosticism required that conference delegates, highly educated though many of them were, render themselves oblivious to the most pressing kinds of questions.

The same studied insensitivity was practiced with regard to a whole range of elementary questions about family life. Had someone made a slashing frontal assault on the very idea of the family, charging that throughout history it has been a deforming and tyrannical institution deserving of annihilation, the conference would have had no moral or intellectual basis from which to meet the attack. What it had come to celebrate, insofar as it had any definable subject, was "people interacting with people", in whatever ways that occurs.

Many profamily[2] people suspected that the conference was rigged to give support to avant-garde moral ideas like abortion and homosexuality — and there were certainly delegates who worked assiduously to that end, tasting success at least in the Baltimore and Los Angeles meetings, achieving a stalemate in Minneapolis. However, the organizers were probably sincere in saying, as they frequently did, that they hoped the conference would not get "bogged down" with such issues. Given the vagueness of the idea of family, it was inevitable, however, that both profamily people and champions of "alternative life styles" would each struggle to give some discernible shape to the subject under consideration.

The real hidden agenda, however, was not moral iconoclasm, tolerable

---

[2] The term "profamily" was disputed on the grounds that all participants in the conference were profamily but simply had different understandings of the family. However, the self-styled profamily people were justified at least to the extent that they were the only group at the conference explicitly committed to the conventional definition of the family as people related to one another by blood, marriage, or adoption.

though such iconoclasm was to the organizers. Rather, it was an approach to social life ("family" in the broadest possible sense) which was studiously materialistic, largely economic, and fundamentally political.

Americans are now accustomed to the fact that their courts look upon religious division and disagreement with a peculiar horror, to be contained and sanitized at all costs. Pluralism is increasingly a misnomer in a society where genuine religious differences must be kept muted, and American secularism is now based not on the necessity of maintaining strict neutrality among all sects but rather on the government's equal suspicion of all. Political, economic, racial, ethnic, or sexual conflicts, no matter how bitter or divisive they become, are officially taken as signs of a healthy democracy and as such are encouraged. Moral and religious controversy, however, is viewed as merely destructive. Thus the most fundamental questions about human existence, which inevitably intrude at every point of civilized life, cannot be confronted.

Moral and religious questions, no matter how obviously relevant to family matters, therefore had to be systematically excluded from the White House Conference. Its organizers, in setting forth their guidelines for discussion, gave no encouragement to anyone's possible belief that the family's crisis is essentially a moral one. Such an opinion was frequently expressed by citizens in attendance at regional hearings in each state, but even when such concerns were forwarded to Washington as reflective of the popular mind, they were passed over in silence as the national steering committee attempted to discern the *vox populi*.

Ostensibly religious people themselves played an essential role in this exclusion. The religious groups (including the United States Catholic Conference) which joined in the Coalition for the White House Conference on Families, a strange umbrella organization offering its public endorsement of the conference, did little or nothing to insure that religious and moral concerns were given proper weight. The chief Catholic spokesman, Auxiliary Bishop J. Francis Stafford of Baltimore, gave a speech in which he affirmed that the primary questions were spiritual and asked whether the conference could transcend the materialism of American culture. Yet the same speech dealt almost exclusively with poverty and unemployment. At the Minneapolis meeting, where the percentage of overtly religious delegates was probably higher than at the other two conferences, any public mention of religion or God was likely to be met by someone's leaping up to proclaim, "Personally religion means a great deal to me. But it has no place in the public arena." (One of the reasons the USCC belatedly withdrew from the Coalition, after the Minneapolis meeting, was the fact that the Coalition urged the defeat of all resolutions perceived as having any kind of "sectarian" bias, including antiabortion statements. Most were indeed defeated.)

Profamily people tried to point out that the Supreme Court, in certain cases dealing with conscientious objection to war, has noted the elasticity of the term "religion" and has declared that secular humanism enjoys that status. But careful thinking was not exactly characteristic of the majority of delegates, and the point was brushed aside unexamined. In Minneapolis a resolution requiring that the moral and religious values of parents be given equal consideration in the schools with the operative philosophy of secular humanism was defeated at an intermediate stage of the conference, although by a narrow margin. A majority of the delegates, Christian clergymen though some of them were, clung to their fond belief that secularism is a benignly neutral system of values.

An adequate analysis of the problems of the family would surely have to take account of the cultural phenomenon variously called the "me generation", the "culture of narcissism", or the "imperial self". Far from being a reactionary and sectarian ideal, this phenomenon has been noticed quite widely by essentially secular commentators, like the socialist historian Christopher Lasch.

In this view of society, what has happened to the family in recent years is merely one aspect of a much larger phenomenon — a general breakdown of a sense of responsibility, as people have come to regard it as their birthright to experience "self-fulfillment" and have systematically, and with encouragement from many of the principal organs of the culture, abandoned familial and other responsibilities which are felt to be too constricting. Men and women refuse to make permanent commitments to each other and often refuse to have children. The care and training of children are increasingly passed to outside agencies. To an extent such things have always gone on. What is new in the past two decades is the fact that they have not only become respectable, they have become in certain circles almost mandatory. The now deeply ingrained expectation of self-gratification virtually insures, in many cases, that the spirit of self-sacrifice necessary to all successful human relationships cannot be summoned. The General Mills Corporation circulated to each delegate the results of extensive surveying the company had done of family members, demonstrating among other things the existence of "new-breed parents" who specifically reject the idea of sacrificing for their children. The conference never so much as discussed the implications of this.

A corollary to this is the kind of moral revolution which has taken place in America, which has had the effect of creating a system of values, especially in the sensitive area of sexual behavior, deeply at odds with traditional values which are themselves overtly family-centered. Values being purveyed in the mass media, and increasingly also in the educational system, are now at odds with traditional values. The result is to weaken the moral authority of the family quite drastically and to set up a system of values which competes with parents for the allegiance of their children. Not only does this weaken the entire fabric of family life, it often throws children into intolerably confusing situations and robs them of any firm system of beliefs by which they might lead their lives. Rather astonishingly, the conference also failed to address itself to questions like the rising rate of adolescent suicide.

Even if the above analysis is not accepted in its entirety, it is obvious that it contains important insights into the nature of the crisis facing American families. But it is also a perspective which was fundamentally taboo to the kind of people who organized and dominated the White House Conference. By implication the family was denied to be a primarily moral entity, and moral perspectives on the family were implicitly declared irrelevant. Once again the result was willful stupidity fostered by ostensibly intelligent people—they had to pretend not to notice glaring features of the subject they were discussing, because otherwise the discussion would have been taken in directions where they did not wish to go.

Many delegates were at best ambivalent as to whether the family should be treated as having any kind of moral authority at all. The closest the conference came to recognizing this authority specifically was at Minneapolis, where a comprehensive resolution concerning parents' primary authority for the education of their children was, by a close vote, discarded in favor of a vague and innocuous affirmation of parental "participation" in the formation of educational policy. A resolution requiring parental consent to enroll children in morally controversial educational programs was defeated by one vote, the margin of defeat being provided by a Jesuit priest from Missouri, Father Michael Garanzini.

Both in Baltimore and Los Angeles the conference passed vague resolutions expressing concern over the effect of the media on children, which was as close as the conference came to acknowledging the possibility that the culture itself may be antifamily, or that a broad cultural crisis may have something to do with the family's problems. However, the Baltimore resolution concerned itself mainly with racial, ethnic, and religious stereotyping, and cautioned that the media should give favorable portrayal to the family "in its diverse forms", the favorite code expression of those without much affection for the traditional family.

As could have been predicted, the conference found it difficult to identify religion as an important source of the family's strength. The Baltimore meeting gave it the barest of nods—a twelve word statement easily lost in the welter of longer and more passionate affirmations. The Minneapolis meeting, in a close vote, rejected a motion requiring that theism be given equal weight with secular humanism in public institutions, especially schools. However, the same meeting rather inconsistently passed another resolution opposing the imposition of secular humanism on public institutions. It ranked fiftieth out of fifty-six issues on the meeting's list of priorities.

If, however, the churches were defeated at the conference, they were for the most part willing victims. With a few exceptions, those who were prominently identified as representatives of the churches either actively supported the secularist agenda or failed to take a firm stand against it. One Catholic priest, for example, Father Thomas D. Weise, vicar for charities for the Diocese of Mobile, was enthusiastic in his praise of the Baltimore meeting and described for the *Washington Post* how he had reached an agreement with Betty Freidan on the subject of abortion. At the Minneapolis meeting he gave public witness by telling the delegates that "this has been the most exciting experience of my life since I first fell in love." Perhaps most remarkable was the fact that the churches themselves did not try to insist that the conference needed to recognize the moral and religious dimensions of the family. An official interdenominational statement prior to the conference included the familiar warning about a "takeover" by "special interest groups" and then concentrated almost exclusively on the economic and material problems of family life. It was signed by official representatives of the Roman Catholic, United Methodist, Southern Baptist, and American Baptist churches and the Lutheran Church in America. Whatever visible religious strength appeared at the conference came mainly from evangelical Protestants (and some Catholic antiabortionists) acting as individuals.

Often during the course of the conference the strange realization dawned that the family was being discussed, and its future planned, by people who were its enemies. What was for some people evidence of family pathology—divorce, separation, unmarried cohabitation, homosexuality, estrangement of children from parents—was, for these others, evidence of hopeful progress toward liberation, and the conference refused to adjudicate between these two views. Had someone proposed that public policy encourage incest, the conference would have found it difficult to find a basis on which to take a stand.

Yet in the end this did not induce immobility in the delegates, as might logically have been expected. The carefully tended agnosticism on basic questions merely served to inspire a greater certainty and sense of righteousness about less ultimate issues. For the real agenda of the conference, intuitively shared by organizers and a majority of delegates, was based on an agreement to treat the family essentially as an economic unit, to define its pathologies as almost entirely economic in nature and therefore susceptible to economic cures. The hidden aims of the conference were in the direction of stimulating political support for new or expanded government programs addressed to all kinds of economic needs. In this context the word "family" was merely a convenient propaganda label attached to favored programs, most of which could have been formulated without any particular references to the family as such.

Conference rules specified that no more than half the delegates were to be professionals, a category defined as those who acquire more than half their income from activities related to family matters. This in itself seemed an excessively high ceiling. At public hearings in Missouri one witness suggested that the conference could be most productive if the organizers tried to identify men and women who had been successful in raising their own families, and drew on their own expertise. It was the kind of advice that the organizers did not want to receive, however. No one knows for certain what proportion of the delegates were professionals. What is certain is that a rather high proportion were people who would benefit, in some tangible way, from new or expanded government programs of various kinds. Educators, social workers, employees of private social agencies, medical personnel, and various other professionals were conspicuous at the three meetings. (Representative of the broad pattern were public-school teachers and administrators. On every troubled point of family life the delegates reached for the predictable liberal solution—more and better "education". The scope and influence of the schools would increase enormously if every resolution were taken seriously. The Baltimore conference called for support of the public schools, conspicuously omitting mention of the private schools. At Minneapolis a resolution affirming parents' rights to educate their children in private schools "without financial penalty" was the casualty of a close vote.)

What might be called the professionalistic orientation of the conference helps account for the position of the churches. Many clergy seem now to have a professionalized mentality which causes them automatically to gravitate toward other professionals rather than toward their own parishioners. They share the unexamined assumption that more and better professional services are the solution to all problems, and the general professional aversion to making moral judgments. More tangibly, many church agencies are beneficiaries to one degree or another of government programs and are being drawn more and more into the public orbit, however private they may still be in theory. The National Conference of Catholic Charities, for example, was represented at the conference by its executive director, Monsignor Lawrence Corcoran, who was critical of the profamily movement. Significantly, Catholic agencies officially withdrew from the Coalition for the White House Conference on Families not only because of its stand on abortion but also because of its opposition to public aid to parochial schools.

Not surprisingly, the greatest degree of consensus at the conferences came on noncontroversial but obviously important problems like drug and alcohol abuse and care for the aged, although with some disagreement over how these problems were to be approached. The sharpest battle lines were not between liberals and conservatives as traditionally understood, that is, in conflict over economic issues. Liberal resolutions on economic questions tended to pass by larger margins than resolutions having controversial moral implications.

At Baltimore the fifteen issues given highest priority by the delegates involved: drug and alcohol abuse, the care of the aged, parental work schedules, taxation, child care, health, care of the handicapped, unemployment, family violence, adoption and foster care, education, and teenage pregnancy. The list at Minneapolis was not appreciably different. In both instances delegates showed a propensity for identifying tangible, physical problems ostensibly susceptible to equally tangible and physical solutions requiring heavy public financing. Obviously, no one can be indifferent to problems like drug abuse, care of the aged, or the plight of the handicapped. But it is worth pointing out that such problems are not always family problems, involving as they often do individuals who do not belong to any family. The eagerness with which the conference identified them as of the highest priority sprang not only from the relief of discovering things which were noncontroversial but also from the willingness to use the word "family" simply as a slogan under which to file all sorts of perceived social needs.

Since the conference chose not to treat the family as a moral institution, it was perhaps inevitable that it would ultimately fall back on an essentially mechanistic model. Thus the documents are studded with terms like "stress", "dysfunction", "support", "reinforcement", and "system". Apparently, the majority of delegates were most comfortable with the belief that the family is a complex mechanism that fails mainly because of impersonal forces which press on it at particular points. If the pressure can be relieved or redirected, if countervailing pressure can be established, or if pressure points can be reinforced, the family will once again begin to function correctly, without any regard for troublesome questions about the role of moral values and human choice in its life.

The inadequacies of the materialistic model are so obvious that it cannot be supposed that intelligent people fail to perceive them. For example, a sociological study out of Rutgers University confirmed what unsystematic observation had already concluded—teenagers in affluent American suburbs often suffer from "malaise" and "alienation" and seek relief in drugs and promiscuous sex.[3] But the White House Conference assumed that most social problems are traceable to poverty and those which are not are attributable to inadequate social services or inferior education. Yet on these assumptions it is impossible to explain why the affluent suburban family is as much beset by troubles as the poor urban family. Failure to address the question was not merely a sin of omission on the part of the conference, however. As Allan

[3] Ralph W. Larkin, *Suburban Youth in Cultural Crisis* (New York: Oxford University Press, 1979). The work is vitiated in part by the author's trendy and unproven political explanation of the phenomenon.

Carlson has observed, ". . . the liberal family-policy agenda cannot over-come—for in some ways it actually reflects—the shallowness and confusion of prevailing cultural norms and the personal hedonism dominating American life."[4] The White House Conference gave Americans little reason to suppose that any of their problems are in any way their own fault or amenable to responsible, willed decisions on their part. Instead they are en-couraged, at whatever social level, to think of themselves as passive victims of a process from which they will be rescued by better public programs. In a sense the conference, reflecting the dominant ideas of an avant-garde American culture, offered people the bribe of nonresponsibility—no matter what dubious personal choices they may make with whatever disastrous con-sequences for their families, there will be publicly supported programs to rescue them. (Thus, for example, there need be no discussion of the delicate and explosive question of whether small children need the attention of full-time mothers.)

Given the proclaimed American "shift to the right", and given President Carter's own professed concern for the health of the family, how did the White House Conference arrive at the point it did? How could it go so con-trary to the perceived mood of the nation? The answer is both simple—the conference was stacked—and deceptively complex. It repays close attention because it has implications for the whole future of American democracy.

There were various ways in which its organizers could control the con-ference's drift—by the membership of its national steering committee (in one count only *one* member out of forty-one was unequivocally profamily), by the guidelines issued for public discussion, by the selection of state steering com-mittees, by the choice of delegates, by the state steering committees' readings of the summaries of public hearings (in Missouri, a strong antiabortion state, the state committee chaired by Father Garanzini arbitrarily ignored all testimony about abortion), by the appointment of "facilitators" and section chairmen at each of the three national meetings, and finally by the meeting in late August when the resolutions were to be collated in Washington and a final report issued. Anyone unable to effect a predetermined outcome through this process would have to be a poor politician indeed.

So many profamily complaints centered on the process of selecting dele-gates that it is worth noting a few of the more egregious examples of manipu-lation:

—Besides the delegates from each state, the national steering committee ap-pointed "at large" delegates who had voting rights at each of the three meetings. At Minneapolis, for example, there were 119 "at large" delegates out of a total of about 630.

4 "Families, Sex, and the Liberal Agenda", p. 79.

—The governors of Indiana and Alabama, disapproving of the apparent drift of the conference, decided not to send delegations. The national steering committee then in effect appointed delegations of its own choosing from both states.

—In seven states—California, Kansas, Maine, North Carolina, Pennsylvania, South Carolina, and Texas—none of the delegates were elected. All were appointed either by the governors or the state steering committees or, in a few cases, chosen by lot. Originally the conference rules specified that a minimum number of delegates be elected. However, after an early profamily victory in the Virginia elections this requirement was dropped.

—In Tennessee voting was restricted to 200 specially-selected delegates nominated by various organizations. Prolife and profamily organizations complained that they did not receive notices until the deadline for nominations was past.

—In the state of Washington an antiabortion woman was twice elected chairman of the state delegation by mass meetings of interested citizens. However, the state steering committee not only overturned her election but refused even to certify her as a delegate. Eleven of the fifteen members of the committee were state employees and four were associated with Planned Parenthood. An appeals court judge recognized serious irregularities in the procedures but ruled that he had no legal authority to compel fairness.

—In Kansas, after first announcing that delegates would be elected at a state meeting, the steering committee instead had names drawn out of several boxes. As critics pointed out, no one except the committee was sure what names were in the boxes.

—In New York City a nominating committee culled 48 names from an original list of 520, and a member of the committee charged that people of prolife or profamily sympathies were systematically eliminated. Voting, held at Fordham University, was restricted to those who had applied in writing and been given authorization by the steering committee on the basis of whether there was sufficient room. Profamily groups again charged that they were shut out. As a result, elected delegates included former officers of the National Organization of Women, Catholics for a Free Choice, and Lesbians over Forty; the attorney who argued the case against the Hyde Amendment in federal court; and the wives of various proabortion politicians.

The importance of these manipulations goes beyond ordinary political maneuvering, since it was the more or less openly stated position of the organizers of the conference that majority rule was unacceptable and that a "fair" representation of delegates had to include a noticeable proportion of people outside the normal patterns of family life. Once established, this rule easily translated itself in some cases into a virtual exclusion from state delegations of people with traditional family perspectives.

Someone has remarked that there is nobody so self-righteous as a bishop when he is doing something trendy, and the comment seemed appropriate to Jim Guy Tucker at the Minneapolis meeting, when the unrepresentative character of much of the delegate membership was challenged. Ordinarily cultivating a relaxed and affable manner, Tucker summoned up all the reserves of his Southern Protestant heritage to give the objector a stern lecture on justice, implying that the criticism was aimed at black representation and the critic was probably a racist, although Tucker and everyone else knew that the point of the objection was not racial at all.

Tucker's reference to race had the effect of recalling one of the interesting ironies of the situation—although there was a general assumption by trendy white liberals that the blacks stood with them on their agenda, at least in Minneapolis there was a notable representation of black evangelical Protestants, who were firmly profamily and refused the condescending implication that their interests were solely economic. Everyone recognizes the importance of evangelical religion in the black community, and these were people who insisted that it be taken seriously. (Predictably, the Minneapolis television stations, given the opportunity of showing a dialogue about abortion between a black male proabortionist and a black female prolifer, chose instead an exchange between the black male and a white, male, Southern prolifer. To have shown the first exchange would have shaken too many of the stereotypes which the media have cultivated for so long.)

The symbolism of Tucker's chairmanship extended beyond the ambiguity of his status with respect to divorce. Like "Jimmy" Carter, he is a Southerner whose very name and accent seemed to identify him solidly with traditional, down-to-earth, rural American values. But the irony has not been sufficiently noticed that, whereas George McGovern was, perhaps prematurely, tagged with "acid, amnesty, and abortion" in 1972, President Carter was able, precisely because of his reassuring Southern qualities, to preside over the greening of American public life. It was through his administration that the counter-culture came into its own. The White House Conference was one of the means by which this was effected, and Jim Guy Tucker was a serviceable instrument for this purpose.

Despite the strong traditionalism and family-centeredness of Hispanic culture, most Hispanic delegates to the conference seemed to support the antifamily agenda. Black delegates were probably expected to do the same but did not always fulfill expectations. (Polls consistently show, for example, that blacks tend to be more opposed to abortion than whites.) What ethnic minorities were invited to do, in the conference as well as on the larger political and social scene, was to accept the leadership of the avant-garde white middle class and allow themselves to be co-opted for its agenda.

This, finally, was the real point of the manipulation of the conference. It was to ensure that those people who are assumed to represent the wave of the future would dominate its proceedings. At bottom the conference assumed that the traditional family is passing out of existence and, while it was not exactly prepared to celebrate that event, it was nonetheless determined that no time be wasted in mourning it. The political implications of this are far-reaching and require nothing less than the abolition of truly democratic procedures, lest "backward" people retard progress. The White House Conference was an example of how Congress would probably be chosen if certain influential people had their way. The growing reliance on the courts rather than the legislatures is, of course, a major instance of the same thing.

Ostensibly the beneficiaries of the nuclear family's decline are the extended family, the single-parent family, the childless couple, the unmarried couple, possibly the homosexual couple or the commune. But the real beneficiary, as most delegates knew, dimly or sharply, is the government. In the end the White House Conference was called to ratify the process by which the state assumes most of the functions the family has traditionally discharged. The vast majority of resolutions at all three meetings called on government to take some kind of aggressive action and, although there were occasional warnings against government action detrimental to the family, most criticisms of government were for its failure to act.

Insofar as the majority of resolutions were economic in nature, this was a familiar pattern. It was the relatively few who recognized that not all problems are economic that occasioned the most controversy and alarm and seemed to promise the greatest threats to the family's independence.

The scenario by which government intervention in private life is justified is by now a familiar one. First, a certain kind of social problem is identified. Either it is a hitherto unrecognized problem or a problem whose seriousness is alleged to have been greatly underestimated. Through professional organizations, civic groups, the media, the churches, et cetera, the prevalence of the problem is endlessly emphasized. Something like a sense of urgency is finally created. Next the complexity of the problem is also asserted. Ordinary measures will not do, especially measures which attack symptoms rather than causes. A massive, systematic, highly sophisticated attack must be mounted. A large part of the problem is said to be due to public ignorance. Consequently a massive "educational" campaign—through the media and the schools—must also be mounted. People's attitudes toward the problem must be changed. Often erroneous popular attitudes are said to be the result of some deeper-seated misconceptions about the nature of reality, which must also be changed. Finally, because of the complexity and massiveness of the problem, only governmentally sponsored programs are deemed sufficient. It is the government which alone has the resources to finance the programs, coordinate the efforts on all levels, certify those who will administer the programs, and evaluate the results.

The tragedy of the situation is that the problems themselves are usually real enough and cry out for some kind of action. However, the good will of an awakened public is then exploited, first, to make people think that they have no power themselves to solve their problems, and second, to induce them to put themselves passively into the hands of increasingly intrusive bureaucracies.

A few randomly selected issues will illustrate the point:

—*Child and spouse abuse*. The occurrences are real, and shocking. Unquestionably there are times when government intervention is justified. However, it takes no fevered imagination to realize that, if the government chooses to become systematically alert to intra-family abuse, it will inevitably claim for itself far-ranging powers of intervention. The very definition of abuse will continually expand and will be the means by which particular philosophies of childraising will be imposed by law. What, for example, is psychological abuse? Does it include parents who are deemed too rigid, too backward, too authoritarian, or too moralistic in their attitudes and are therefore conceived as damaging their children?

—*Promotion of health*. Health too is an infinitely elastic concept. Already it is interpreted as implying the "right" of minor children to contraceptive and abortion services, no matter what their parents' wishes. The new emphasis is on "preventive" health care, including preventive psychological care. If health is defined, as it sometimes now is, as the total physical and mental well-being of the individual, what will it not include? Not only, for example, will children be deemed to have a right to be "sexually active", the question will be seriously raised whether in most cases such activity is not a prerequisite for healthy development. It will become the duty of the state to promote and facilitate such activity, as well as to inculcate in children the proper kinds of "flexible", "open", "tolerant" attitudes toward all kinds of human behavior.

—*Minority rights*. Such rights always go beyond merely a legal guarantee of nondiscrimination in employment, housing, education, or political participation. Inevitably they come to mean also that the government must actively promote minorities' well-being, and this means among other things that it must seek actively to promote tolerance. This in turn means that the power and authority of the state, especially through its schools, will be used to make "alternative life styles" like homosexuality seem normal, natural, even desirable. Private agencies like religious schools will be pressured into conforming to the same mold.

—*Help for distressed families*. Economic help is one issue, the merits of which have been debated for many years. However, the White House Conference also envisioned family members as lacking the basic skills to live their lives successfully. Several resolutions called on government and private agencies to help them acquire such skills, in parenting, in personal relationships, in preparation for marriage, et cetera. It once again takes no great imagination to see how such programs would quickly become the means by which particular values relating to marriage, parenthood, or sexuality would be in effect frozen into bureaucratic practice, actively promoted by the authority of the government, even embodied in law.

Perhaps most revealingly, delegates to the three meetings showed almost no propensity for thinking that government itself may often be the enemy of the family,[5] and no inclination to scrutinize the actions of public agencies or the courts (for example, in recent cases allowing children to "divorce" their parents for sometimes trivial reasons). Where government was criticized it was almost always for doing too little. There was, to be fair, talk about government's developing "family impact" statements which would calculate the probable effects of public policies on family life. But if no one can say what a family is and if no one can meaningfully distinguish family health from family pathology, such statements will have little meaning. They could even be themselves a further means whereby government imposes its own notions of family life, contrary to those of its citizens.

The refusal to define the family is not unrelated to the ominous future which the White House Conference portends. As the distinguished historian of civilization Kenneth Clark has remarked, "authoritarian governments don't like dictionaries. They live by lies and bamboozling abstractions, and can't afford to have words accurately defined."[6] America is far from having such a government at present. However, one of the most dismaying aspects of the White House Conference was precisely the sense that so many delegates, chiefly those in the "helping professions", live their lives amidst words and jargonized phrases which float freely, endlessly combined and recombined to mean whatever their users want them to mean.

The family, throughout history, has been the chief zone of personal privacy and freedom in society, the place where the most intimate bonds of personal devotion and loyalty are forged, bonds stronger than any the state itself can claim. It was the pathos of the White House Conference that most of the delegates seemed both unaware of and indifferent to this fundamental reality.

[5] See Hitchcock, "Beyond 1984: Big Brother Versus the Family", above.
[6] *Civilization, a Personal View* (New York: Harper and Row, 1969), p. 257.

THE NOT-SO-NEW ANTI-CATHOLICISM

In the midst of the Democratic National Convention in July, 1976, Roman Catholic Archbishop Joseph L. Bernardin of Cincinnati spoke out publicly against the party's recently adopted platform plank favoring legal abortions. The plank, he said, was offensive to many Catholics.

Stuart Eizenstat, a key aide to Governor Jimmy Carter, who was about to become the party's presidential nominee, told the press that the archbishop's statement "was not from the hierarchy". "My understanding is that many in the hierarchy were extremely upset and in effect told him to cool it. No one has come to his support. I think that fellow went out on a limb."

Archbishop Bernardin was in fact the elected president of the American bishops and was speaking in their name. After numerous telegrams from bishops protesting Eizenstat's remark, he apologized, explaining that he had not known who Archbishop Bernardin was.

The explanation was more astounding than the original comment, revealing as it did that the Carter staff had not taken the trouble to acquaint themselves with even the most elementary facts about a minority group — Roman Catholics — who have traditionally been one of the major sources of electoral support for the Democratic party. It is inconceivable that the official leader of any other minority, no matter how small, would be contemptuously dismissed as "that fellow" by the aide to a man who hoped to be elected president of the United States. (Eizenstat became assistant to the president for domestic policy.)

The situation had not improved when, a short time later, candidate Carter admitted publicly that he might, perhaps, be perceived as having a "Catholic problem", but pointed to the presence on his staff of another key aide, Joseph Duffey, who would keep him in touch with Catholic concerns. Carter was probably aware that Duffey had a record of proabortion activity. Misled by an Irish name, however, he was evidently unaware that Duffey is an ordained Congregationalist minister.

In early December, not long after the Carter victory, still another aide, Greg Schneiders, gave an interview to the *Washington Post* in which he described the Catholic Church as a "farce" and said, "I think the Catholic Church does a better job of screwing people up than any other institution." He also told the *Post* that he was Carter's advisor on Catholic affairs. After the predictable protests, Schneiders issued an apology of sorts, characterizing his words as "ill chosen", "poorly stated", and "a mistake", but not retracting the substance of what would seem to have represented his true feelings. President-elect Carter, who had just been elected with substantial Catholic support, felt no need to repudiate publicly what Schneiders had said, and Schneiders continued as part of the Carter team.

Incidents as strange as these might ordinarily be supposed to signal electoral disaster for the candidate unlucky enough to have such aides. After all, in 1884 the Republican party met defeat in part because a Protestant minister tried to tag the Democrats as the party of "rum, romanism, and rebellion". That nothing happened in 1976, and that candidate Carter did not even feel any apparent discomfort, signaled the Carter force's recognition of something that is a badly kept secret in contemporary American life: Roman Catholics are the major minority group against whom it is still respectable to express prejudice and contempt. What the historian Arthur Schlesinger, Sr., once called the "most deeply rooted of American prejudices" is still alive and well.

The mere suggestion of such a thing is likely to provoke incredulous dismissals, since it runs contrary to a widely believed myth, held even by some Catholics who ought to know better. According to this myth, anti-Catholicism was a force operating in the earlier history of the country, deriving from its Protestant roots and fueled by nativistic hostility to immigrants. Since World War II, so the myth runs, such prejudice has largely disappeared. The "melting pot" smoothed out ethnic differences. As the country grew more sophisticated it also grew more tolerant. Finally, in 1960, Catholics symbolically came of age when one of their number was elected president. The spirit of ecumenism now rules, and old religious animosities are rapidly dying out.

The "era of good feeling" that characterized the early 1960s—the age of John Kennedy and Pope John XXIII—was an unusual and temporary parenthesis in the history of anti-Catholicism. President Kennedy's career reveals why this was so. Despite earlier attempts to canonize him, it is now rather widely acknowledged that John F. Kennedy was at best a marginal Catholic. His close identification with Irish-American Catholicism was useful in Massachusetts politics, but the closer he got to national office the more expedient he found it to minimize his religious loyalties. Privately, some of his intimates have revealed, he had little understanding of Catholic teachings and even less sympathy with them.

The climax of the process was his humiliating meeting with the Protestant clergy of Houston during the 1960 campaign, during which he was forced to give repeated assurances that he was a loyal American and that his religion would not interfere with his duties under the Constitution. Kennedy's Houston speech was reportedly written by John Cogley, a journalist often called "Mr. Catholic" in those years but who later revealed that as early as 1957 he had considered becoming an Episcopalian, which he finally did.

President Kennedy was able to have the best of both worlds. Many Catholics rallied to him enthusiastically as one of their own, while knowledgeable observers believed there was little chance he would behave in a "Catholic" way once elected. The election of a Catholic president was contingent on a widespread perception that he would relegate his religion to a totally ceremonial function in his life. To a great extent that rule still prevails: Catholic politicians who hope to succeed nationally are often required to make symbolic gestures dissociating themselves from the Church, with endorsement of legalized abortion now the minimum gesture required. A black, a Jew, a woman, or a Chicano elected to office is not expected to eschew support for matters of concern to his or her particular group. Often, however, a Catholic politician cannot afford to be identified with Catholic causes to even a slight degree. Despite the fact that he is not a regularly practicing Catholic, Governor Jerry Brown of California was treated by much of the press as a religious freak, and his actions are frequently explained by his once having been a Jesuit. (According to *Parade* magazine, "He is the most Aquinistic governor in California history", whatever that means.)

The pontificate of Pope John XXIII (1958–63) and the Second Vatican Council (1962–65) aroused enormous worldwide interest in things Catholic, and much of that interest was sympathetic to a degree never before manifest. In retrospect, however, it is possible to see the peculiar slant that sympathy took, and why the sympathy itself serves as the basis for some of the new anti-Catholicism. John XXIII was turned into a mythical figure allegedly transcending the "narrowness" of his Church, a figure bearing little resemblance to the real man of staunch peasant piety. More important, the Second Vatican Council was misunderstood to be a process by which the Church was admitting that it was an antiquated and rigid institution and was systematically bringing itself into conformity with modern society. Indeed, decrees of the Council bear no such interpretation, but this is the way they were presented to the world by the media, with assistance from Catholics who wished that it had been so.

The new philo-Catholicism thus rested on the expectation that the Church was surrendering its historic identity and, although the term was rarely used, becoming Protestant. Nuns left off their habits. The Mass was translated into the vernacular. Friday abstinence was abolished. All this gave rise to the expectation that the Church was also ready to discard its "inhumane" and "incredible" doctrines, and when this failed to happen, it simply aroused renewed animosity against an institution so willfully backward. Much contemporary anti-Catholic feeling is directed, quite simply, at the Church's refusal to die.

Unlike other minority groups, Catholics are ill-equipped to defend themselves. The Catholic League for Religious and Civil Rights, for example, was founded only in 1973 and is small and understaffed in comparison with a group like the Jewish Anti-Defamation League. Many Catholics are also psychologically unprepared to strike back because, having been told so often that Catholics have finally been accepted in America, they wish desperately to believe it is so, shrinking into passivity when faced with evidence to the contrary. Among some of its intellectuals and professionals American Catholicism has more than its share of Uncle Toms.

The new bigotry has its own distinctively modern forms, a current favorite being the sacrilegious use of Catholic symbols in pornography, a new sport even in some college papers. The *Observation Post* of City College, New York, printed a cartoon of a nun masturbating with a crucifix, and the student paper at Harrisburg Area Community College in Pennsylvania had a cartoon on the "carnalization" of Mother Elizabeth Seton, the first canonized American saint. As products of public colleges, the latter two items were at least indirectly subsidized by public funds.

Consider the *St. Louis Post-Dispatch*, a paper with a national reputation for liberalism and open-mindedness. For several years the *Post-Dispatch* published thrice-weekly columns of opinion by a modernized version of a familiar figure in American history—the professional ex-Catholic. Jake McCarthy, a one-time public relations man for the Archdiocese of St. Louis, became disenchanted with the Church since discovering the sexual revolution and other things not generally taught in parochial schools. In the first few years of his column McCarthy made the evils of Roman Catholicism his main subject. Later, he seemed to have lost interest in religion, although he also claimed to stay away from the subject because he was shocked at the "intemperate" mail it generated.

A typical McCarthy column explained that Irish priests came to the United States "to earn a living from the pockets of honest bricklayers and dishonest politicians. Thievery was cleaner in the sight of God than the body of a woman." Diatribes against clerical celibacy were a recurring feature along with the contention, never accompanied by proof, that the same people who oppose abortion also oppose gun control and favor capital punishment. Often critical of the churches' failure to address themselves to social issues, he deplored Catholic "meddling" in politics on the abortion issue. In a column on Good Friday he contended that all churchgoers were hypocrites and that truly religious people like himself would stay at home that day. The same column made a favorable reference to the Jewish *seder*, and it is inconceivable that the *Post-Dispatch* would give space to a columnist who insulted Jews on their high holy days. The cardinal archbishop of St. Louis was never mentioned in McCarthy's columns except demeaningly, but various Protestant clergy (and former Catholic priests) were sometimes praised.

Although McCarthy often characterized Catholic doctrines as "outmoded", he is not a rationalist. He has exclaimed over the truth revealed by ouija boards and once defended abortion on the grounds that the souls of aborted fetuses are probably reincarnated in a happier state. In common with some other anti-Catholic Catholics, such as Jimmy Breslin, he is sympathetic to the Irish Republican Army. McCarthy's regular presence in the *Post-Dispatch* demonstrates the chief difference between anti-Catholicism and other kinds of bigotry such as anti-Semitism or racism: It is respectable. McCarthy has been given an award by the American Civil Liberties Union and boasts of being asked to speak from Protestant pulpits. Periodically he printed letters of praise from ministers. In truth a whole stable of writers has developed—Breslin, Pete Hamill, Thomas McHale, Thomas Fleming, John Powers—whose stock-in-trade includes the theme of how deforming a Catholic upbringing is to the human personality, how cruel and inhumane is the Church. If this is a point of view that deserves a public hearing, it is also true that media have not even attempted a balanced perspective. (Numerous articles about convent life of the "I leapt over the wall" variety have seen print, but the fact is ignored that certain traditional orders of nuns are now almost the only ones attracting and keeping novices.)

Much religious journalism, as it applies to the Catholic Church, is open editorializing masquerading as reporting. Examples abound.

—When a group of Croatian nationalists hijacked a TWA jetliner a while back, wire services gave prominent play to the claims of Dick Maurice, a Las Vegas newspaper columnist, that the bishop of Peoria, Edward O'Rourke, had frightened the passengers more than the hijackers had. The bishop's offense, as it turned out, was that he urged people to pray and pronounced forgiveness of sins. It was later revealed that Bishop O'Rourke had been elected by the passengers as their spokesman. Some may have found his words comforting, but this was not even suggested in the wire service dispatches.

—The Associated Press in 1974 sent out two lengthy articles by Bill O'Shea, an AP reporter and former priest, featuring the history of his 1967 ordination class at the Chicago archdiocesan seminary. O'Shea's picture of the seminary was unrelievedly bleak; he descended to ridiculing the way his former seminary rector pronounced his words. One former classmate who professed to be happy in the priesthood was described as "plugged into the sources of power and advancement in the Church" and, O'Shea strongly hinted, was mainly interested in security. The overall impression was that no humane and sensitive person could possibly function as a priest.

—On December 3, 1971, the day on which thirteen Catholics were killed in a pub bombing in Belfast, the *Chicago Daily News* wire service distributed an article identifying the Catholic Church as the principal obstacle to Irish unity. Irish Catholicism was identified (by unnamed "experts") as the chief cause of mental illness and alcoholism in Ireland, and the clear implication was that the Ulster Protestants had good reasons for fearing and disliking Catholics.

—Marquis Childs, a widely syndicated Washington journalist, characterized antibusing demonstrators in South Boston as "Hail Mary-praying", while failing to apply the same epithet to the Irish Catholic judge who ordered the busing.

—*The Congressional Quarterly* published an article on the abortion question in which the name of each Catholic congressman was starred with an asterisk, a form of identification not given for any other denomination or on any other issue. (The irrelevance of the designation was demonstrated by the starring itself, which failed to reveal a significant pattern of Catholic voting.)

—A *New York Times* television critic, John J. O'Connor, told his readers that the structure of the Nazi S.S. was "patterned on Jesuit hierarchical concepts".

—When an abortion clinic was fire-bombed in Cleveland, the *Cleveland Plain Dealer* gave prominent front-page coverage to the demand of a professional anti-Catholic, William Baird, that non-Catholics retaliate by attacking churches and other Catholic institutions. No evidence was offered that Catholics were responsible for the firebombing.

—The National News Council has upheld complaints of religious stereotyping against both the *New York Times* and Walter Cronkite of CBS. The newspaper was censured for consistently identifying legislators as Catholics, even when their votes on abortion issues were at odds with Catholic teaching, while not offering religious identifications of other legislators. Cronkite was cited for accepting proabortion stereotypes and labeling the prolife position as "the Catholic view".

—Over a period of seven years (1968–75) *Newsweek* magazine kept up a running attack on the leadership of the Church because of its failure to rescind "outmoded" teachings. American bishops were characterized as "personally underdeveloped", and when a small minority of Chicago priests voted to "censure" the city's bishops, the magazine hailed the event as "of historic significance". Pope Paul VI, during the same period, was never once referred to positively in *Newsweek*'s religion pages and was at various times characterized as "a puppet of the papal household" and the "main attraction" of a "Catholic carnival". For two years in succession the magazine openly speculated on the pope's supposedly imminent death, and managed to find a psychiatrist who pronounced him unfit to exercise his duties.

—Murray Kempton, celebrated "liberal" columnist for the *New York Post*, reflects the perduring link between nativism and anti-Catholicism. "The Irish are most fit to govern in functions that place them candidly on the side of the oppressors. What benevolence they have comes out best on the side of despotism. . . ." He urges that the Irish be thought of "as the finks the essential story of their rise in our society has instructed us that they are. . . ."

The essence of bigotry is stereotyping, taking attributes of a particular group (the lazy black, the grasping Jew, the hysterical woman) that are not entirely absent from some of its members and allowing these to stand as accurate symbols of the whole group. Jimmy Breslin's novels portray, as one reviewer has admiringly summed it up, "the narrowness, alcoholism, ignorance, and barrenness of lower-middle-class Irish Catholic life in America", and a large part of the educated population of America has accepted stereotypes according to which to be a believing Catholic is to invite personal disaster and stunted growth.

Many otherwise knowledgeable people refuse to admit that anti-Catholicism even exists. In recent years such diverse social groups as women, blacks, Jews, homosexuals, and Chicanos have succeeded in "raising the consciousness" of the media and the public generally about stereotypic thinking. A process of self-censorship takes place to avoid offending those whom it is unfashionable to offend. Perhaps because offending Catholics is still very fashionable, much of this suppressed hostility is now directed at them. Protests against anti-Catholic bigotry are likely to elicit only prim warnings about censorship and the need to air "controversial opinions" so that the bigot ends by casting himself as a virtuous and righteous defender of American liberties.

Had Murray Kempton written about blacks as he wrote about Irish, no respectable newspaper in the country would have given him space. The respectability of anti-Catholicism continues unabated. In 1974, for example, the prestigious Xerox Corporation published a booklet, aimed at elementary and secondary-school students, which characterized Pope Paul's teaching on birth control as "immoral" and asked students to discuss whether the Church should be tried before an international tribunal for its "crimes". In response to protests from the Catholic League for Religious and Civil Rights, Xerox at first denied there was anything offensive in the booklet but finally withdrew it from circulation. It still occasionally surfaces in schools around the country, bought with public money.

A good deal of current anti-Catholic sentiment has surfaced because of the continuing controversy over abortion, but it is probably more accurate to say that abortion has not so much fomented anti-Catholic feeling as it has provided a rationale for feelings already there. Proabortionists freely employ words like "medieval" and "inquisition", which are guaranteed to provoke Pavlovian responses in a society with a long history of anti-Catholicism. (Critics of the Catholic doctrine manage to have it both ways, calling it "medieval" and also insisting that it was not adopted until the nineteenth century.)

During the 1976 presidential campaign a Protestant theologian from Yale, William Lee Miller, who was also a strong Carter supporter, published an open letter to the Catholic bishops of the United States chiding them for the way antiabortion pickets were "harassing" the Democratic candidate. What made the letter interesting was the variety of anti-Catholic notes it sounded. First Miller professed not to know by what title to address the bishops and spent several paragraphs lecturing them on the emptiness of all titles, a solid Protestant blow against the pretensions of prelates. Then he complained because a priest who picketed Governor Carter was "still dressed in black in a way the priests I know today are not". The antiabortionists were denied any real moral concern and were said to represent "power" and a "threat". Most significant was Miller's assumption that antiabortion pickets in Indiana could be stopped by an appeal to the collective body of bishops, a view of the antiabortion movement that sees Catholics as the hierarchy's puppets. (In fact many antiabortionists regard the bishops as timid and vacillating on the issue.)

Innumerable proabortionists have sought to refute the opposition through no more sophisticated a tactic than identifying that opposition as Catholic. (Public opinion polls about abortion vary greatly in their results, depending on how the questions are phrased. One Gallup poll shows 45 percent of the population favoring some kind of antiabortion amendment to the Constitution, 49 percent opposed. Legalized abortion has been voted down in the only two states where a referendum has been held—Michigan and North Dakota.) Arthur Flemming, chairman of the Civil Rights Commission, has gone so far as to assert that the Constitution ought not to be amended when the amendment flows from "wholly or partially nonsecular, or religious, motives", and a suit is now pending in federal court seeking to invalidate legislation supposedly enacted under religious influence (the "divisiveness" doctrine).

The absurdity of this contention becomes apparent when it is recalled that every civil rights gain since the Civil War has been brought about at least partially by strong religious pressure and that the formula would have precluded Martin Luther King, Jr., for one, from seeking to influence legislative matters. What such individuals really mean, at least in some cases, is that Catholic influence should not be tolerated.

The argument that, by opposing abortion, the Catholic Church is seeking to impose its morality on the nation and is violating the First Amendment is never balanced by the charge that Protestant and Jewish groups that approve abortion are doing the same thing. When, shortly after the Democratic convention in 1976, Archbishop Bernardin announced that the bishops were "encouraged" by President Ford's stand on abortion and "disappointed" in Governor Carter's, there was a hurricane of outrage in the media to which the bishops finally succumbed, in effect repudiating their original statement. There was no such reaction, however, when a month later the General Convention of the Episcopal Church officially opposed an antiabortion amendment to the Constitution, thus in effect endorsing the Democratic stand and repudiating the Republican. The media have rarely pointed out that the majority opinion written by Justice Blackmun in the crucial *Roe* v. *Wade* decision of 1973 established a governmental policy on abortion very close to what the United Methodist Church, to which Justice Blackmun belongs, thinks that policy should be. (A St. Paul abortion rights activist, Gerri Rassmussen, has explained to the press how her lobbying efforts stem directly from her religious commitments and her Methodist upbringing, an admission that did not deter her from once more castigating the Catholic Church for "intruding" itself into politics.)

Proabortion media regularly characterize antiabortion activities as the work of "highly organized, well-financed pressure groups", a description that could be applied with equal validity to almost any political-action group that has even minimal hope of success. If organized religion indeed threatens to "impose" its values on American society, a greater threat would seem to emanate from a group like the Religious Coalition for Abortion Rights, which lobbies vigorously in Washington and claims to represent twenty-three Protestant and Jewish organizations. (In the 1972 Michigan referendum on abortion the Board of Social Concerns of the United Methodist Church provided over half the funds to the unsuccessful campaign for legalization.) Yet the Catholic "intrusion" on the abortion question has been placed in a special category and judged by standards that seem to apply nowhere else.

In 1976 proabortion groups in Minnesota, including the student newspaper at the University of Minnesota, strongly opposed the candidacy of a Catholic doctor to head the obstetrics and gynecology department of the university hospital, despite his promise not to allow personal views to influence his policies. The doctor was finally approved, but the opposition to his appointment was a blatant appeal for religious discrimination in hiring, which is contrary to the 1964 Civil Rights Act. Senator Richard S. Schweiker (R., Pa.) has introduced legislation to prohibit medical schools from discriminating against applicants for admission who oppose abortion, a bill that Congress failed to pass in 1978, although a survey by a Chicago doctor has shown that two medical schools admit discriminating against such applicants, thirteen others state that antiabortion beliefs create "administrative problems", and a majority of medical schools question applicants about their beliefs on the subject. It does not appear to be an issue high on the civil libertarian's list of priorities.

In the past thirty years probably the most persistent source of irritation with respect to church and state has been court decisions concerning public aid to private schools, in which judges have consistently refused, on constitutional grounds, to allow anything more than peripheral aid. Many Catholics have become rather cynical about these decisions, believing that if the majority of parochial schools were not Catholic the courts would long ago have found a way to aid them. (In fact the courts have now found a way to aid religiously affiliated colleges, the majority of which are not Catholic.) Since the time of the New Deal, the Constitution has been regarded as a very flexible instrument, capable of yielding principles appropriate to the social needs of the age. Thus, if the courts stand by the idea of a rigid "wall of separation" between church and state, it seems reasonable to assume that they do not regard the survival of parochial schools as a desirable social good.

Although often the argument is advanced that, however much it might be desirable to aid parochial schools, the principles of the Constitution forbid it, the facts indicate an immense animosity directed at the parochial schools simply because they are Catholic, and their survival is deemed by many people to be socially undesirable:

— The late Supreme Court Justice Hugo Black, as is widely known, belonged to the Ku Klux Klan before his elevation to the court. Somewhat less widely known is the fact that his political rise in Alabama was aided by his successful defense of a Protestant minister who had killed a Catholic priest. The fact of the shooting was never in doubt, but Black got his client acquitted by blatant appeals to anti-Catholic bigotry.

Justice Black never apologized for his role in the case, but it is generally assumed that he rose above the prejudices of his earlier life. However, his son, Hugo Black, Jr., has written that "the Ku Klux Klan and Daddy, so far as I could tell, only had one thing in common. He suspected the Catholic Church. He used to read all of Paul Blanshard's books exposing power abuse in the Catholic Church."

— In *Lemon v. Kurtzman* (1970), Justice William O. Douglas voted against even limited aid to parochial schools, partly on the grounds that "zealous" teachers in those schools "may use any opportunity to indoctrinate a class". In a footnote Douglas established to his satisfaction that "in the parochial schools Roman Catholic indoctrination is included in every subject" by citing a work called *Roman Catholicism* by Loraine Boettner. The book is nothing more than an anti-Catholic diatribe, without even pretensions to objectivity, published under fundamentalist Protestant auspices. Justice Douglas's citation of the book was evidently an example of the principle of "any stick to beat the dog", since the justice ordinarily manifested little sympathy for religious fundamentalism.

— One of the principal architects of court cases denying government aid to parochial schools has been Leo Pfeffer, longtime counsel for the American Jewish Congress. In a 1975 article Pfeffer stated bluntly: "I did not like the Catholic Church." He also reported that his daughter, when annoyed at him, used to threaten to marry "a Roman Catholic army officer from Alabama". Finally he revealed that his animus against parochial schools began when he first saw school children in uniforms and nuns in habits lined up in a school yard. When predictable protests followed his article, he replied primly that "epithets contribute little to the communication of ideas, but they can be quite destructive to civilized conversation or the search for truth." (One can imagine the public reaction if a prominent Catholic attorney were to express distaste at the sight of Jewish boys in *yarmulkes*.)

Anti-Catholicism, as exemplified in Justice Douglas's 1973 *Lemon* opinion, brings together strange bedfellows indeed—conservative Protestants and liberal humanists who are ordinarily anathema to one another. Throughout American history it has been militant Protestantism that has mainly nourished anti-Catholic sentiments in America, but increasingly in recent years the most bitter prejudice has originated in secular circles that see the Catholic Church as the last remaining bastion of traditional religion and therefore to be opposed at all costs. (The tactical alliance some conservative Protestants make with such people is therefore extremely short-sighted on their part.)

The career of Paul Blanshard is instructive. Although his anti-Catholic attacks were always cast in terms of true Americanism and concern for separation of church and state, Blanshard reveals in his autobiography, *Personal and Controversial*, that he was an "utterly typical example of the sexual revolution of the 1920s" and that he was first stirred to write about the Catholic Church when he chanced upon a book about Catholic sexual morality.

Blanshard is the quintessential example of the humanist who considers his own philosophy as normative for society and who sincerely believes that someone who espouses his "enlightened" creed could never be bigoted, because, he says, he belonged to "liberal and tolerant groups far removed from the intolerant Know-Nothing school of thought". This particular form of bigotry rests on the assumption that no rational person could possibly be a religious believer. Hence all religious education has to be "indoctrination", while humanistic education is "enlightenment". Blanshard is gleeful that parochial schools are being driven out of existence by financial troubles. "If we must have a rightist bloc in American elementary education, let the rightists pay for it", is his rather eccentric gloss on the First Amendment.

Paul Kurtz, editor of *The Humanist* and a professor at a state university, has noted that "the philosophy of secular humanism is becoming the dominant point of view in America and also in a good part of the Western world." There is an implicit assumption by many humanists that their philosophy is not a religion in the traditional sense and so ought to dominate the public forum, while the First Amendment conveniently excludes churches from fully entering the same arena.

Again, the late Justice Black once told his son that church attendance was for lesser breeds of people who "got to be scared into doing the right thing". Black also described those who favor prayers in the public schools as "pure hypocrites who never pray anywhere but in public for the credit of it". (Via such profound thoughts are high constitutional principles discovered.)

In Kansas Protestant, Jewish, and humanist elements have joined forces in attempting to effect the abolition of the Integrated Humanities Program at the University of Kansas, which has a heavy emphasis on the classics and medieval culture and which is accused of being Catholic-dominated. Whatever merit the charge of Catholic bias may have, it is significant that it is taken seriously, since charges of Marxist, atheist, or liberal bias in academia are routinely repulsed as threats to academic freedom.

Anti-Catholicism can be expected to continue, especially in the form of propaganda in the media and even in the educational system, a concerted attempt to deprive Catholics of moral and intellectual legitimacy in the public eye. Perhaps it is only fitting to give the last word to Paul Blanshard, who did so much to make anti-Catholicism newly respectable after World War II: "Why allow Christian salvationism to flourish side by side with scrupulously accurate science as if they were legitimate twins in our culture, when you know that the Christian doctrine of salvation is untrue?" It is not farfetched to think it just possible that the clear threat implied in Blanshard's words might someday be carried out in a thoroughly "enlightened" America.

THE ROOTS OF AMERICAN VIOLENCE

Conventional opinion about the 1960s is wrong about two major contentions: that the essential thrust of '60s politics was a program for social change based on "idealism", and that this thrust was essentially frustrated. In fact a revolution of major significance did occur in that decade, and its repercussions grow increasingly stronger. In certain important ways the would-be revolutionaries of the '60s won their war without realizing it, because the revolution they succeeded in bringing about was not the revolution to which they had officially committed themselves.

One of the least-discussed yet most significant facts of recent American history has been the process by which the morally "idealistic" middle class began by joining hands with the underprivileged lower class to improve the lot of the poor but ended by learning to see itself as the truly oppressed class and its *own* grievances as deserving of its major expenditure of moral energy. The campus revolts, with the assertion of "the student as nigger", began the process. Women's liberation, homosexual rights, the sexual revolution, legalized abortion, the drive to legalize drug use, the "human potential" movement, and the broad-fronted crusade on behalf of every variety of "alternative life style" have followed. In an important sense, even though its clientele come mostly from the lower classes, the prisoners' rights movement is part of the same revolution.

Far from being in a period of conservative retreat, America is now in the midst of the harvest season of ideas which were planted in the heyday of the New Left. The communications media, the schools, the churches, the "enlightened" segment of the middle class, the courts, and a not-inconsiderable number of politicians are responsive to all these causes. The "revolution" dreamt of in the 1960s continues in ways not predictable in Marxist categories. But it may be winning the battle for minds.

What seems to be occurring is the triumph of a perception which the literary historian Quentin Anderson has shown to be persistent and recurrent in American culture—the "Imperial Self". Anderson regards Ralph Waldo Emerson as the seminal articulator of the belief that "realized human greatness consists in a demand for the immediate realization of our widest vision . . . . Our momentary sensations of omnipotence and omniscience tell us what we ought to become, what state is appropriate for us." The truly realized individual seeks finally for "the power to dispose of the whole felt and imagined world as a woman arranges her skirts". The 1960s were not the first time in American history when people dreamt of "the act not of identifying oneself with the fathers, but of catching up all their powers into the self, asserting that there need be no more generations, no more history, but simply the swelling diapason of the expanding self".

In a misleading way American society appears now to be overly politicized, in the sense that every conceivable social question inspires its own ideology and fuses together its own coterie of warriors, who mount the demand for ostensibly political actions in relief of their stated needs. But on a more important level, what has occurred has been the abandonment of politics, or its annihilation, in favor of public and organized forms of therapy. Emphasis is less and less on the general material needs of the citizens, with which the state has some possibility of coping, and more and more on the formerly private, personal, and subjective aspects of their lives, which the state is expected, somehow, to respond to in symbolically comforting ways. What the New Left primarily accomplished was to establish a particular style of public discourse which enables emotionally frustrated people to express themselves in cathartic ways. It provided the mechanisms by which inhibitions were systematically shed.

The virtual youth-worship characteristic of the past decade is by no means accidental (given the romantic, and now normatively modern, conception of the young as free, spontaneous, open, and as yet unformed and undeformed by society). The adolescent personality has been enshrined as the ideal model of human behavior, by which standard what has usually been thought of as growth can only be decline, and authentic human life is only achievable through rejuvenation.

The Janus-like character of the adolescent personality has not been formally acknowledged, but it has, perhaps unconsciously, imprinted itself on the behavior of those who regard themselves as the culture's advance guard. Officially committed to an ideology of love, joy, freedom, tenderness, and peace, they often behave with petulance, hostility, and violent aggressiveness. (At his trial in San Francisco for kidnapping and armed robbery, the upper-class guerrilla, William Harris, shouted out in court that "Che Guevara once said a true revolutionary is guided by feelings of love. In whatever Emily and I did we did not abandon that important ideal.")

Characteristically adolescent attitudes are now endemic to much of what passes for adult politics. There is a persistent love-hate relationship with authority figures, so that conventional authorities are routinely rejected as oppressive while incense is offered to distant but symbolically potent figures like the late Chairman Mao. There is a constant high-pitched demand for freedom, rarely accompanied by any consideration of how competing demands can be reconciled with one another. Boredom comes easily, despite a multiplication of the kinds of diversions available. One's maturity and adulthood are militantly asserted, but one's failings are commonly blamed on others. Courage and independence of mind are celebrated, but peer approval and passing fashion largely determine beliefs.

Lines like the following are recognizable and perennially adolescent, including the mechanical repetition of clichés meant to suggest original thought: "I am unhappy when my spontaneity and creativity are stifled. . . . I need to have control of my life. I need the freedom to lead myself in directions that spring from my heart, not in the directions chosen by others. . . . I have a wonderful mind, can see thousands of possibilities before me, but I feel trapped in a bureaucratic and heartless system." As a high school student's lament it is a pure example of a familiar genre. When a fifty-year-old columnist for a major daily newspaper reprints it to illustrate the truth about society it is indicative of willful personal regression.

The pseudo-politics of the present moment creates many of the "problems" which it then endeavors to solve in precisely the way that unthinking parents and counsellors create "problems" in certain adolescents—by constantly encouraging a preoccupation with self, a compulsively repetitive introspection which will always discover something over which to agonize. To the often-repeated assertion that institutions no longer work as they once did, it might be retorted that they perhaps work better than in the past. What has changed are the expectations people have of these institutions, expectations which are often vague, highly unrealistic, and constantly increasing.

The central problem of contemporary culture is a threatening solipsism— the failure to realize and accept the existence of other beings distinct from oneself. The political effects of this have been significant and deleterious, and the ultimate logic of solipsism is necessarily the dissolution of all politics. Quentin Anderson writes of

> a drastic reduction in the capacity to imagine that encounters with others will further a definition of self. For our visionaries, their most inclusive sense of the world is not at risk in encounters with others; the self has been walled off by the faith that it cannot be defined by its reciprocal relationship. . . . A part of the process of becoming a self in such a culture is precisely the need to deny the efficacy of the operative familial and social constraints in fixing a sense of the self."[1]

Contemporary solipsism manifests itself most dramatically in the evidently common experience of social forms as merely threatening and oppressive. No part of the self is invested in society, which therefore assumes a wholly alien and sinister visage. Furthermore, the imagination is unable to conceive of the real existence of other persons so different from oneself that society might in fact have legitimacy in their eyes. Social forms are recognized only as giant conspiracies which impose themselves on individual egos. Hence personal survival depends on a continued and frantic resistance to this attempted invasion of self.

[1] Quentin Anderson, *The Imperial Self* (New York: Alfred A. Knopf, Inc., 1971). The quotations in this paragraph are from pages 24, 56, and 58. See also by the same author, "Practical and Visionary Americans", *The American Scholar* (Summer 1976): 408.

Classically, justification for revolution has been sought in the measurable material conditions of life — extreme poverty, despotic rulers, palpable social injustice. Now, however, the call for "revolution" looks for its legitimacy only in the subjective sense of grievance which certain people have, even if they live in relative material comfort and political freedom. "Repression" is an essentially personal experience, the reality of which cannot be legitimately questioned.

Although often unrecognized, the dominant model of political life now operative for many people is the Hobbesian war of all against all, not only in the sense that society is experienced as a great devouring beast but also in that the natural posture of man is thought to be self-assertion, the end result of which is a cacophony of contending egos. To a degree that would have seemed horrifying twenty years ago, aggressive hostility has been accepted by many people as natural to the most basic human relationships, such as families.

At no time in history has there been so much celebration of "love", "community", "commitment", "concern", and "involvement". At no time have so many people claimed to have found the elusive keys to such joys and been so eager to share them with others. Yet in the midst of this celebration personal bonds of all kinds continue to dissolve quite visibly, often precisely among that segment of the population which claims to have at last discovered how to live. Herbert Hendin, in his book *The Age of Sensation*, has graphically anatomized the pathological inability to love or sustain commitments on the part of many young people, their fear of others, and their varied efforts to withdraw from all demanding personal relationships. It is perhaps not coincidental that a paranoid style of politics, in which people were encouraged to believe that murderous conspiracies ultimately governed the social order, should finally issue in an inability to trust even one's supposed allies and friends. In many ways the favored political style of the past decade has served simply to legitimize hatred. Rarely have people shown themselves so ready to believe the worst of each other.

Solipsism feeds on the sense of an empty universe waiting to be filled by an infinitely expanding and expansive self. Life becomes weightless, in that nothing concrete and tangible is allowed to impinge from the outside, to define the limits within which one must live. (Drugs are used deliberately to eliminate all such boundaries, and the concept of human existence revealed in that use tends to govern other areas of behavior also.) What begins as "idealism" often ends as nihilism precisely because of the need to annihilate everything objective and weighty which impedes the expansion of the self. Rebellion is often a deliberate testing of boundaries, a probe to see exactly how far the impingement of reality can be rolled back. (The unexpected flimsiness of social constraints is then the occasion for antinomian exhilaration, followed by even more severe disorientation and need for self-assertion.)

In this atmosphere legalized abortion is an issue of almost incalculable symbolic significance, precisely because the decision to abort is one of the most radical assertions of the solipsistic mind — the denial of one of the most sacred bonds linking human beings to one another. Motherhood is reduced to an inconvenience, and apologists for abortion go to great lengths to deny any responsibility which the mother may have, even to denying the humanness of the fetus. Given certain prevailing cultural assumptions, the notion of the fetus as a "parasite" or an "invader" in the womb has a perverse logic to it.

Despite what some of its defenders claim, abortion is no longer regarded as the lesser of two evils, which may be reluctantly chosen in certain difficult situations. There has been an almost maniacal drive to remove all hint of moral stigma from it, to elevate it to an almost privileged position among medical actions (a situation reflected in several court decisions, for example). The contention that the helpless unborn child can make binding claims on its mother must not only be denied but eradicated. In the process the will of the mother is rendered fully sovereign, answerable to no other person.

Increasingly in recent times ideas have been evaluated for their beauty rather than their truth. The mundane process by which general assertions are measured against discernible realities has been scornfully dismissed in favor of criteria which primarily value "creativity", "daring", and "originality", the willingness to think the unthinkable, to make assertions no one has ever before dared make (often because the assertions are demonstrably untrue). Susan Brownmiller's contention, for example, that rape is the means by which all men seek to keep all women in subjection,[2] is not defended by her admirers as literally true but seems rather to be enjoyed as a particularly choice, because outrageous, example of political "thinking". Political positions scarcely need to be justified rationally since they are simply aspects of style, the way in which the self presents itself to the world.

If no necessary binding nexus exists between self and society, then even the possibility of a real politics is foreclosed and all of what passes for political activity is merely, in one form or another, a dramatization of self. (Lionel Trilling wrote of a culture which has a "principled indifference to the intellectual and moral forms in which the self chooses to be presented".)[3] Often now, terrorism is excused not merely on utilitarian grounds but because of the sincerity and idealism of the terrorist: it is his "statement" and therefore must be treated with respect.

[2] See Susan Brownmiller, *Against Our Will: Men, Women, and Rape* (New York: Simon and Schuster, 1975). Also see M. J. Sobran's "Men, Women, and Miss Brownmiller", *The Human Life Review* I, no. I (Winter 1976): 89–98.
[3] Lionel Trilling, "The Uncertain Future of the Humanistic Educational Ideal", *The American Scholar* (Winter 1974): 65.

The ability of the Imperial Self to make continually more outrageous assertions implies the ability of the audience, largely composed of other would-be imperial selves, to accept everything outrageous with equanimity. The culture of the past twenty years has worked hard to exorcise from people even the ability to be shocked, to break down all sense of a distinction between appropriate and inappropriate assertions. (The destruction of legal barriers to such expression is often intended as a means toward the destruction of psychological barriers as well.) The justification for the freest possible speech is not made primarily in terms of society's need to hear unpalatable truths but in terms of the individual's need to express his or her inner needs. Since all such needs are subjective and purely personal, there is finally no basis for distinguishing between true and false statements. The act of expression is its own justification.

The educated classes have consequently developed in recent years the fine ability to provide justification for every kind of idea and action, often on the flimsiest of rational bases, since the right to self-expression — however bizarre — has come to be the central political issue of the day. Public questions are more and more symbolic rather than substantive, a conflict of style and personality rather than of definable programs. Antisocial deeds increasingly abound as expressions of the burgeoning power of the self, as in the prevalence of gratuitous vandalism as a protest against the obdurate thingness of reality, the need visibly to reduce order to chaos by an act of the will.

The rage which seems to lie close to the surface of many people's lives, and which renders social life tense and strained, is an expression of the inability to tolerate the existence of anything larger than the self, the compulsive need to reduce everything to one's own size, to manipulate cultural symbols without regard for the matrix out of which they grow, solely for one's own convenience. Bored adults and impressionable adolescents are especially prone to such feelings, often reinforcing one another.

The supreme social irony of the past fifteen years is the fact that a broad-fronted movement which promised a society that would be loving, non-competitive, gentle, and communitarian has resulted in one characterized by stridency, suspicion, hostility, rampant egotism, and the breakdown of all social bonds. The line from the ideal to the reality is perhaps straighter than it might at first seem, however, because what links the two is essentially the stance of self-assertiveness, the conviction of one's own rectitude defiantly flung up against all constraining social limitations. Genuine idealists did not reflect that such passions, cultivated and marshalled in the service of good causes, might become for many people simply a way of life.

The identification of show-business personalities like Jane Fonda and star athletes like Bill Walton with leftist causes has been one of the symptomatic cultural shifts of the past decade. But on reflection it should not have been surprising, since athletes and movie stars have long been privileged persons whose egotism has been indulged and applauded, and for whom social rules were always made to be broken. Their support of "radical" causes, in the sense of systematic attacks on the legitimacy of society, are thus quite natural. True virtuosi of the self are no longer content with the limited opportunities presented by one profession or cultural role. (When New-left lawyer William Kunstler spoke at a Midwestern university and attracted only thirty listeners, he pronounced the campus "sick" and said, "You ripped the heart out of me tonight. . . . I didn't want to come out here, but I thought of the money.")[4] There is a continuing need for such persons to escalate their outrageousness in order to maintain an image of specialness.

Extremist political movements, whether of the left or the right, usually fail to provide the promised better society, in part because of the kind of people attracted to them. Those who resent most bitterly the tyranny imposed by an existing society are often those with the strongest sense of their own worth and power, and if they succeed in overturning the oppressor they can scarcely resist imposing their own wills in turn. The ultimate goals of peace and love are belied by the turbulent personalities of those committed to achieving them. Even a superficial acquaintance with American leftist groups reveals an abundance of authoritarian personalities. (Alan Adelson, a worshipful chronicler of Students for a Democratic Society, described a Columbia University member who had been expelled from the fifth grade for kicking a teacher who disagreed with him over the interpretation of a book and who became depressed whenever fights and violence were not materializing on the campus.)[5] The familiar phenomenon of upper-class leftism is perhaps not unrelated to similar authoritarian urges. Those whose birthright is to command are the least inclined to obey.

Sara Jane Moore, the "idealistic, religious" woman who attempted to assassinate President Ford, said at the time of her sentencing to prison that she regretted her act because "it accomplished little except to throw away the rest of my life." She added, however, that "at the time it seemed a correct expression of my anger".[6] Earlier she had told reporters that "there comes a time when the only way you can make a statement is to pick up a gun." Characteristically, the aristocrats of terrorism regard other lives taken as of no consequence, for the felt needs of their own existences are of surpassing value. Murder, often for no definable political advantage, is the ultimate expression of the Imperial Self, the self for whom the very existence of certain other people is a blight on one's own happiness. Karleton Armstrong, who killed a student by bombing a laboratory at the University of Wisconsin,

[4] St. Louis *Post-Dispatch*, April 7, 1976, p. 1G.

[5] Alan Adelson, *SDS: A Profile* (New York: Charles Scribner's Sons, 1972), pp. 124, 130.

[6] *New York Times* News Service Dispatch, January 16, 1976.

complained after his arrest that the press treated him as "a mad bomber who doesn't have any scruples" and asserted that charges against him should be dismissed. He also complained of "the crimes committed against me in Canada, where officials kept me in isolation for months".[7]

Taken in this context, the concern for the rights of both accused and convicted criminals, which is now so important a cause for American liberals, has somewhat disquieting implications. There is much to be said for such concern — the rights of accused persons must be safeguarded, and neither society nor the prisoner gains from a needlessly harsh penal system. But concern for the rights of accused persons has now moved beyond the insistance that established legal procedures be followed. Individuals accused of crimes which have even slightly political overtones now automatically become cult figures. Prestigious committees rush to their defense, and the question of their guilt or innocence becomes largely irrelevant to a determination not to allow society to crush a free spirit. When an accused criminal is acquitted, even if there is strong suspicion of his guilt, the triumph of justice is proclaimed. The conviction of even heinous offenders is met with silence or regret.

Conventional liberal theory about criminality, which is only beginning to be seriously challenged, in effect holds that criminal behavior can be significantly inhibited only if potential criminals are persuaded (through education, therapy, or social reforms) voluntarily to refrain from antisocial acts. The autocracy of the individual will is thereby conceded, and attempts to forcibly restrain criminal behavior are either proclaimed as unworkable (contrary to a good deal of evidence) or cast under a moral cloud. During the "Zebra killings" in San Francisco in 1974, when citizens were being shot down on the streets at random, the articulate liberal community mainly expressed outrage at the police dragnet set up to question suspects. There appeared to be far more emotional concern over the potentiality of a "police state" than over recurring actual murders.[8]

Philosophical distinctions are sometimes made between "political" crime and "ordinary" crime, with a special moral advantage conceded to the former. But it is a short step (already taken by some) for all crime to become political, in the sense that criminals are by definition rebelling against an oppressive society. Why else would they act as they do? The feminist ideologue Ti-Grace Atkinson, who at one time would not be seen in the company of males, later bestowed an "honorary sisterhood" on the reputed Mafioso Joseph A. Colombo, Sr. "Criminals don't identify with the establishment, and it's the establishment that oppresses women", Ms. Atkinson explained.[9]

Bourgeois society, often ridiculed for its hysteria over the counter-culture,

---

[7] *AP* Dispatch, May 13, 1973.

[8] *AP* and *UPI* Dispatches, April 19–20, 1974.

[9] St. Louis *Post-Dispatch*, September 1, 1974, p. 41.

was correct in sensing certain murderous realities beneath the official talk about love. The speedy deterioration of hippie ghettos into burnt-out centers of vice and violent crime is well known, a result, evidently, both of a naive belief that law was unnecessary and of the systematic indulgence of every kind of personal "need". A classic confrontation between the "straight" and hippie worlds took place in the small Missouri town of Harrisonville in 1972. For some months a group of long-haired young people loitered around the streets, allegedly harassing passersby and being in turn harassed by the police. One evening a 25-year-old man, who earlier had told police that "Simpson's my name and revolution's my game", without warning shot and killed two policemen, wounded four other people, and then killed himself. One of his friends explained to reporters that Simpson had simply come to feel too much pressure from "the system", adding that "liberal ideas don't reach a small town for some time".[10]

The special concern which many "enlightened" people have over the treatment of criminals perhaps has something to do with a sneaking admiration—conscious in some cases, less so in others—for the individual who has made the ultimate act of self-assertion. Relatively few people openly defend criminal behavior. But condemnations of even the most atrocious crimes are commonly formal, restrained, and without evident deep conviction, while true passion and outrage are reserved for real or alleged violations of the rights of the accused and the convicted.

The favored sociological explanation for crime—that it occurs primarily because people are poor and thus is motivated chiefly by the need to support one's self and one's dependents—is called into question merely by a glance at newspaper headlines randomly culled over the period of a few years: "Man Kills Widow, 71, by Setting Her Afire." "Boy, 12, Beats and Kills 83-Year-Old Woman." "Charged in Killing of Girl to Win Bet." "Gangs Attack and Kill Motorist Stranded in Flood." "Girl Thrown Off Roof Again. Father Held." "Acid Tossed into Crowd. 40 Burned." "Baby Mugged When Mother Resists Holdup." "Youths Beat, Rob Legless War Veteran." "Two Girls Set Afire after Rape." "Victims Tortured, Killed in Utah Robbery."

American society at present harbors people for whom the very existence of others is apparently an affront and for whom the temptation to annihilate those who affront them is overwhelming. Fathomless and motiveless malice obviously underlies such crimes, and liberal social theory cannot begin to come to terms with such reality, nor does it appear to wish to.

Most champions of convicted criminals obviously do not condone heinous deeds. They rather put them out of their minds. But that in itself is a political act of enormous importance, since the extreme solipsism of the violent criminal

[10] Ibid, May 7, 1972, pp. 1, 10J.

appears to take precisely the form of sundering all connection between his own deeds and the punishment which society visits on him, so that he can sincerely conceive of himself as an arbitrarily chosen victim of official persecution. In Missouri, for example, a convicted rapist filed 219 suits against the state, complaining among other things that he was not allowed to have a cassette tape recorder. Another prisoner, who in attempting to escape kicked a policeman in the groin and the abdomen and killed two persons with his car while speeding, filed a one-million-dollar suit against the state for police brutality.[11] When the Supreme Court restored the death penalty, several convicted murderers pronounced it "barbaric" and "medieval", and one Oklahoma prisoner proclaimed that no man has a right to kill another, excusing his own murdering of his wife on the grounds that "I did this under great emotional strain. I was not quite all myself."[12]

A revealing insight into the mind of the murderer was provided by an inmate of Arizona's death row, in the act of trying to arouse sympathy for his plight. Repeatedly insisting that men are sentenced "only because they are poor, black, Mexican, or friendless", he saw no necessity to inform his readers of what specific crimes they may have been convicted or even to bother asserting their innocence. His entire case, charged with righteous indignation, was based upon the supposed noble characters of the inmates and the contrasting meanness and malevolence of their keepers. Most significantly, his diatribe unwittingly almost turned into a case for capital punishment rather than against it, since he attributed the ennobling of his companions to the harrowing experience of having been condemned to death.[13] Proponents of capital punishment might find this account suggestive of the proverbial need to get the mule's attention by first hitting him in the head — some people only begin to develop character when catastrophe threatens them.

The absence from this prisoner's jeremiad of any acknowledgment of actual crimes actually committed points to the most basic flaw in most contemporary liberal writing about penology — the implicit denial that repentance and restitution are a necessary part of any "rehabilitation" process, the concentration on prisoners' grievances to the point where society's right to punish or to protect itself from marauders is virtually denied. That incarcerated criminals should brood over their sufferings to the point of forgetting why they are being punished is understandable. It is much less understandable that sophisticated outsiders should connive in that forgetfulness.

Richard Harris, a journalist specializing in legal and judicial matters for the *New Yorker*, could contrast the "interests of the state" and the interests of the defendants in Boston police court as though the state were a wholly

[11] Ibid, April 13, 1975, p. 1F; September 30, 1975, p. 1B; September 2, 1976, p. 8B.
[12] *AP* and *UPI* Dispatches, July 3, 1976.
[13] Charles Doss, "Miracle on Death Row", *St. Louis Post-Dispatch*, May 29, 1975, p. 2D.

abstract entity and as though countless citizens, many of them poorer than those who terrorize them, do not also have an interest in restraining and punishing predatory behavior.[14] Advocates like Jessica Mitford and Murray Kempton seem to feel that criminal justice merely enshrines class prejudices, as though most crimes would be wholly tolerable if only the bourgeoisie would expand its imagination. Tom Wicker hypothesizes a muddled pseudo-historical rationale for punishment, deriving it from the Puritan habit of dividing the world into the saved and the damned.[15] (He seems to forget that every society in the history of the world has imposed penalties on criminals, most of them a great deal harsher than our own.) Karl Menninger goes so far as to assert that respectable citizens label others as criminals out of a need to project their own evil impulses.[16]

What can be said about all such theses is that they are fundamentally frivolous, blatant examples of the ability of the mind to become mesmerized by the elegance and ingenuity of its own constructions. As such they are symptoms of the most fundamental malaise of our culture—the inability to appreciate the real bonds linking one person to another and the inability therefore to accept the real consequences of personal acts. For too long a pro-claimed "compassion" has been allowed to intimidate all resistance to acts of naked aggression, and in this atmosphere violence of all kinds can only con-tinue to increase.

[14] Richard Harris, "Annals of the Law", *New Yorker*, April 14, 1973, pp. 44 et seq.
[15] See Tom Wicker, *A Time to Die* (New York: Quadrangle, 1975).
[16] See Karl Menninger, *The Crime of Punishment* (New York: Viking Press, 1968).

THE CATHOLIC COLLEGE IN AN AGE OF IRONY

American Catholic colleges, having traveled farther and faster in twenty years' time than most of their secular counterparts, are among the most interesting of current academic institutions. They are also, contrary to the situation of three decades ago, among the most diverse.

Prior to about 1965, differences among Catholic schools stemmed primarily from what might be called sociological factors: size, geographic location, the social origins of the students, the particular religious orders running them, and whether or not they were coeducational.

At the undergraduate level, Catholic colleges were remarkably uniform in educational philosophy and practice, including a core liberal arts curriculum dominated by scholastic philosophy and theology, paternalistic administrations, compulsory religious exercises, strict rules of personal behavior, and a pervasive and strong emphasis on religious orthodoxy and loyalty to the Church.

To summarize the history of their transformation in a few years would be as impossible as to encapsulate the overall cultural history of the past frenzied decades. The changes in Catholic schools were intimately connected with that frenzied period; in addition, they felt the impact of a related but primarily Catholic event — the Second Vatican Council of 1962–65 — and the train of momentous religious changes which it set in motion all over the Catholic world.

Like many of their secular counterparts, a number of small Catholic colleges have simply ceased to exist, and others will doubtlessly follow them into oblivion. Their problems, primarily financial, have probably not been appreciably different from those of the small secular colleges, although often a closing has been intimately related to an internal crisis in the religious order running the school. Changes in church and society have been so rapid and drastic that some colleges no longer have an obvious purpose and have difficulty finding one.

Other institutions have chosen the bold route of secularization. The first and most celebrated was Webster College in St. Louis, under Sister Jacqueline Grennan (later Jacqueline Grennan Wexler, president of Hunter College). Manhattanville College in Westchester County, New York, was an elite girls' school operated by the Sisters of the Sacred Heart. In the 1970s it dropped its religious affiliation and admitted men, its nun-president left the convent, and it chose a black Protestant male as its new head.

The response of other Catholic institutions has varied widely. In New York State two universities run by the Vincentian Order — St. John's in Queens and Niagara in Buffalo—have insisted on their Catholic identity to the extent of refusing state money which might compromise that identity. Laypeople dissatisfied with secularizing trends in the established schools have founded a few small, traditional places like Newman in St. Louis, Christendom in Virginia, and Thomas Aquinas in California. Even many self-proclaimed Catholic institutions are no longer under legal clerical control, however, having established lay majorities on their boards of trustees some time ago.

Internally, changes have been massive. Compulsory religious activities for students have been dropped almost everywhere. Philosophy and theology curricula are often experimental and far from orthodox. Drugs and sexual freedom may be somewhat less prevalent than at many secular schools (a judgment which is of necessity highly impressionistic), but they are scarcely absent. Coed dormitories have been set up on a number of campuses, and administrators, for the most part, have ceased trying to regulate student morals. Faculty complaints about administrators are less likely to have anything to do with ecclesiastical authoritarianism and more likely to center on universal grievances such as parsimony and bureaucracy.

The transformation of the American Catholic college is conventionally dated from the publication in 1956 of *American Catholics and the Intellectual Life* by the distinguished church historian John Tracy Ellis. Although the criticisms voiced by Msgr. Ellis were not entirely new, that essay served as the major public expression of the hopes and misgivings which were to dominate Catholic educational thought for the next fifteen years.

Msgr. Ellis stimulated a growing spirit of self-criticism within Catholic higher education that centered on four basic charges against the colleges and universities—dogmatism, moralism, anti-intellectualism, and mediocrity. Although denied for a time, the justice of these criticisms finally came to be widely accepted and, linked with the profound changes of the Second Vatican Council, acted upon. In all probability, the Catholic colleges changed more significantly during the 1960s than at any previous time in their history.

The charge of dogmatism held that the theological commitments of the colleges prevented a genuinely free exploration of ideas. The schools were officially wedded to Catholic orthodoxy, usually in the form of Thomistic theology and philosophy, and divergent positions were either not taught or else presented in unfair, negative ways. In some schools students had to obtain written permission to read books which were on the official Roman Index.

Moralism was the tacit assumption that the major purpose of the colleges was to form the character of their students, a process to which purely intellectual training was subordinated and sometimes sacrificed. A college was generally deemed successful if its students and alumni were conspicuous for their piety, loyalty to the Church, and strict personal morality, even if they did not particularly distinguish themselves in professional or scholarly life.

Anti-intellectualism flowed inevitably from the first two. It was not uncommon, even twenty years ago, to hear Catholic educators denigrate the intellectual achievements of the most prestigious secular schools on the grounds that they provided little for their students in the way of moral guidance. Their apparent brilliance was sometimes dismissed as mere pyrotechnics, since it failed to lead to ultimate Truth. Students were much safer, it was often implied, if they did not take too seriously the pursuit of knowledge, since it might involve snares with which they were unprepared to cope and was, in any case, unnecessary for a happy and productive life. (There was also a somewhat contradictory implication that the students had been equipped to counter effectively every conceivable challenge to their faith.)

Inhabitants of the Catholic schools were understandably loath to acknowledge them as mediocre, but by most measurable conventional criteria they were—in the number and quality of the doctorates on their faculties, faculty publications, library holdings, and fellowships awarded to graduates, for example. Studies in the late 1950s showed that Catholics were statistically underrepresented in most scholarly and scientific fields. More serious perhaps than the facts themselves was the attitude behind the facts—a continuing complacency, an indisposition to try to improve academic quality, frequently fostered by people who were frankly at home in a mediocre educational environment and would have felt uncomfortable in more demanding circumstances.

The Catholic schools' most serious problem in the 1950s went largely unrecognized: the fact that they often failed to perform successfully those tasks which they had set for themselves; that their achievements were questionable, even within their self-defined limits.

Contrary to the impression of outsiders, theology did not dominate the curriculum; philosophy did. This was not only evident in the fact that at many schools students were required to take more hours in philosophy than in theology, but also in the fact that greater care seemed to be lavished on instruction in the former discipline than in the latter. Philosophy professors were commonly among the most brilliant on the faculty and might have been trained under demanding masters like the Thomists at the University of Toronto. Theology teachers were frequently clerics deemed qualified merely on the basis of their seminary educations; sometimes they were individuals thought of by their superiors as doubtful prospects for advanced work in a secular discipline. Students got the subtle message that theology was not at the heart of things.

Like any discipline which is highly technical and closely reasoned, Thomistic philosophy was, at least potentially, intellectually challenging. There is no doubt that, for those students whose abilities and temperament suited them for it, Thomistic philosophy was a valuable and unique educational experience.

At the same time, however, the blunt truth, rarely alluded to during Thomism's ascendancy, was that most students had great difficulty grasping the complexities of the system, and few made it a real part of themselves. Thomism possessed an authoritative and impressive aura, but it is highly doubtful whether many Catholic alumni, ten years after graduation, could give any coherent account of its principles or could honestly say that they had built their lives upon those principles.

The operative heart of Catholic higher education, before the era of reform, was not the rigorous Thomistic system, but a certain moral vision, absorbed from the very air of the schools and glimpsed in the lives of its personnel. Its major components were a fervent and sometimes simple piety and traditional family-centered values. The vision was powerful and pervasive and had an immense influence on generations of students; it was the chief thing they took away from their college experience. This vision was inadequately articulated and defended in an intellectual way, however, and this helped ensure its vulnerability in the cynical atmosphere of the 1960s.

Finally, the most serious failure of the older model of Catholic higher education was not its parochialism, its dogmatism, or its anti-intellectualism, accurate as these charges were, but that having chosen a distinctive pattern for itself, having deliberately dissented from the dominant American educational model, it failed to create a first-class example of the genre. There was no Catholic institution of the quality and prestige of other deviant American colleges like Antioch, Bennington, St. John's of Annapolis, or Chicago. (St. Michael's College of the University of Toronto perhaps came closest.)

The transformation of the Catholic schools in the 1960s was the result of both religious and educational factors. The Second Vatican Council forced a basic reassessment of theological positions and wrought changes in the character of religious instruction which were nothing short of revolutionary. Simultaneously, however, there was occurring that drive in secular education summarized under the catchword "excellence" which led to a general improvement of quality across the country—emphasis on scholarly achievement, rigorous standards, and identifying and encouraging the most capable students. By a fortuitous conjunction, both Church and culture seemed to be calling for fundamental changes in the Catholic colleges: greater openness and flexibility in thought, and a more serious and less defensive engagement with modern culture.

The requirements of change provoked an identity crisis far more serious than those usually caused by institutional reform, however. On the one hand, many colleges began hiring substantial numbers of non-Catholic faculty for the first time, both to demonstrate their openness and out of a sincere desire to find the best people. The goal of academic excellence was pursued in many institutions with little regard for its relation to the religious character of the schools, and by the end of the 1960s some of these schools found that the number of faculty actively committed to the institution's stated religious principles had fallen below the necessary critical mass. Sometimes entire departments which had undergone spectacular growth in the previous decade emerged as pockets of dissent from these principles.

On the other hand, the conscientious attempt to improve the quality of theological instruction sometimes floundered on the rocks of a massive religious crisis pervading the whole Church. Eager young nuns and priests poured into the schools armed with the most up-to-date theology, and just as quickly they abandoned their vocations for a return to secular life. (Some continue to teach in Catholic schools.) No matter how "renewed", theology could not keep up with the dizzying cultural shifts of the decade, and large numbers of students (half or more on some Catholic campuses) seemed to lose all interest in religion. No discipline was more plagued by confusion and faddism after 1965 than was theology.

The atmosphere of the Catholic schools circa 1970 was often eerie. Many administrators and faculty (especially clerical) who had presided serenely over their ghetto schools only a few years before now disbelieved those things to which previously they had been committed. They were now prepared to follow with equal faith every new educational nostrum or else they had no vision and allowed their institutions to drift into a practical secularization. There was a loss not only of identity but also of self-confidence and will. This was sometimes painful to observe and experience. There was a comparable crisis engulfing the whole Church, of which this was merely a manifestation, and it interlocked with the crisis also affecting secular academia. Many Catholic educators seemed to doubt that they had moral or intellectual credentials.

Reaffirming the Catholic identity has again become fashionable, after a period when such identity was often muted without being denied. But making the affirmation is inevitably easier than defining it. The frankly and rigorously traditional schools will probably continue to serve a clientele. For the rest, reaffirming Catholicism may be largely a matter of putting scattered pieces back together again or sealing up major cracks.

The dominance of the Thomistic system has broken everywhere, and in many schools an extreme reaction has all but driven Thomism out. Nothing has replaced it, however, as the intellectual center of the curriculum. Perhaps Teilhard de Chardin, for a time, came closest to gaining universal popularity, but his star appears to be on the wane. What is designated now as "Catholic theology" varies widely from school to school and even within a single department. Some schools debate whether they should teach "theology", implying some kind of commitment of faith, or simply "religious studies", in which religion is treated essentially like other academic disciplines.

The practical, often unreflective, moral vision which undergirded the old order has also evaporated. Probably on the whole, students at Catholic schools are somewhat more traditional in their moral views than their secular counterparts (again a highly subjective judgment), but compared with twenty years ago they are quite radical and diverse in their opinions. There is still to be found, however, a good deal of residual moral seriousness left behind when the theological flood waters recede. It tends to express itself in activities similar to those engaged in on secular campuses—peace groups and ghetto tutoring, for example—with the difference that these are often self-consciously Christian in motivation and spirit and part of a deliberate search for religious meaning. Certain Catholic models like Cesar Chavez, Dorothy Day, Mother Teresa, and Archbishop Helder Camara are invoked, but not more than non-Catholics like Martin Luther King and Gandhi. Pentecostalism has had an impact on some campuses, and there is probably more interest in prayer and religious meaning now than there was during the height of the antireligious reaction a decade ago.

Everywhere the spirit of reconstruction is muted, tentative, and uncertain. There are traditionalists who think the Catholic past is still highly relevant and needs only to be courageously reaffirmed. At the opposite end are those frankly hostile to the idea of a Catholic college. Laypeople and members of religious orders are in both groups. Many faculty and students are simply uninterested in talk about identity and approach education in a simple, pragmatic spirit. Those institutions which achieve a viable religious identity are likely to rely heavily on what the secular-minded will call luck and what the faithful will call divine grace.

The agony of the Catholic colleges was paralleled by the agony of secular higher education, and the dominating irony of the situation was the fact that the Catholic schools were struggling to conform to a model of education which was being attacked and undermined by secular critics even as Catholics came close to implementing it in their own institutions. Put simply, by the end of the 1960s it was no longer a universal conviction that the Ivy League represented the summit toward which other schools struggled; "excellence" no longer commanded universal respect. Catholic colleges began discovering that they had invested their life savings in a possibly obsolete product.

In a turn so swift, violent, and unexpected as to be bizarre, precisely those things which critics like John Tracy Ellis had said were wrong with the Catholic schools of the 1950s gained a new respectability in avant-garde educational circles and came even to be highly ranked on some lists of reforms. There were, to be sure, significant differences also—no contemporary theorist is likely to advocate a renewed paternalism like that which permeated the old style Catholic schools. However, it can be argued without exaggeration that dogmatism, moralism, anti-intellectualism, and mediocrity now enjoy a vogue which the most farseeing prophet could not have predicted in 1960.

Early in the 1970s the political scientist James Q. Wilson observed wryly that of the three major institutions with which he had been involved in his adult years—the U.S. Navy, the Catholic Church, and Harvard University—the last was no longer self-evidently the most liberal of the three, the most hospitable to dissenting ideas. From one standpoint, the often successful attempts to intimidate professors and guest speakers on the nation's most prestigious campuses have perhaps been aberrations. But they have not lacked respectable apologists, and although a majority of faculty and students may disapprove of such actions, there has been a remarkable amount of confusion and passivity about them. Liberal Catholics would have been outraged and mortified to the limits of their endurance if in 1960 Fordham students had physically (and with faculty support) driven "immoral" speakers off campus, showering them with missiles and obscenities. When it happened at Columbia a few years later, many of these same liberals were wholly uncertain how to react. The ideal of the totally open, free, civilized, and rational campus was suddenly no longer believed in by its erstwhile liberal guardians.

The more extreme examples of mob action are not the main issue, however. More significant is a new educational ideology of which moralism is the heart, the conviction that certain moral positions are so important and so evidently right that the colleges must commit themselves to them totally and failure to do so is evidence that the institution has lost its legitimacy.

Thus anti-intellectualism and dogmatism assert themselves, not only in the physical harassment of speakers and the occasional book-burnings, but also in the insistence that certain questions (e.g., the influence of heredity on human intelligence) ought not even to be raised. The traditional liberal assertion that error cannot withstand rational scrutiny has lost its force. Hostility to the life of the mind was also manifest in the widespread contempt for "mere" scholarship which spread over the campuses, even among faculty, during the period of the New Left's ascendancy. Thinking and writing came to be regarded as effete luxuries, unless put directly at the service of the proper causes.

Moralism reasserts itself not only in a political context, however, but also in the renewed demand that education make students into good people, provide them with values by which to live their lives, and not simply teach them to ask endless questions, perpetually suspending commitment in an attitude of detached criticism.

A renewed appreciation of mediocrity is also reflected in the fact that the primary purpose of higher education is no longer thought to be that of identifying the most talented students and helping them to develop their full potential. It is, rather, the education of all who desire something from the schools, and institutions and faculty who appear to devote themselves to an academic elite have come under suspicion. As many Catholic educators would have said in the 1950s, there is now thought to be nothing wrong with a "mediocre" institution, so long as it serves its students' needs.

Although few people now on campus would wish to return to the conditions existing in the Catholic colleges of twenty years ago, the ironies of history have suddenly made many educators appreciative of certain qualities which did exist in the old style Catholic schools and which have been bred out, along with whatever was stunting and oppressive.

A central moral vision, the ability to transmit lived values to students and not simply impart information or sharpen intellects, is perhaps the first of these, although the substance of that older vision would be rejected. The reformed Catholic schools now talk about values, but it is questionable how much more effective they now are in this regard than secular schools.

The demand for a "committed" scholarship, for academic programs in the service of social needs, was also anticipated by the Catholic schools, in however halting and ineffective a way. If Thomistic philosophy was frequently Olympian in its "irrelevance", it was nonetheless true that subjects like sociology and economics were usually taught on Catholic campuses within an explicit, moral framework. Liberal critics insisted that these disciplines were scarcely taught at all, because the respectable secular model of descriptive, "value-free" social science was neglected in favor of moralizing. But, here as elsewhere, what was considered liberal in 1960 was far different from what would bear the same name in the 1970s.

The Catholic schools prior to the 1960s were also characterized by the personal element now so highly prized in faculty-student relationships. This was not an accident, but was dictated by the perceived moral purpose of the colleges, in which faculty (clergy in particular) sought to know students well so as to identify their problems and generally exert a positive influence. Some clergy of questionable scholarship or teaching justified their presence on campus precisely in these terms, and many alumni remember these relationships as the most important aspects of their entire college careers. There was no deliberate repudiation of this personalism in the 1960s, but schools in pursuit of academic excellence often lowered it on their scale of values.

Finally, with some exceptions (Georgetown, Holy Cross, Notre Dame, Manhattanville), Catholic schools were generally democratic and egalitarian institutions whose clientele were typically the first in their families to attend college. At a time when large cities often had no state university branch, these schools educated countless students who might otherwise not have attended college. Liberal dissatisfaction with these schools was, to an unrecognized degree, dissatisfaction with their lower middle class milieu. Catholic liberals rarely adverted to the fact that the colleges they admired as academically prestigious were generally socially prestigious as well or that there was a connection between the two. Catholic colleges had significant experience with the education of urban working class and lower middle class students long before secular educators got concerned.

Whether the Catholic schools can now recover their authentic traditions, both religious and cultural, is problematic. An undiscussed obstacle is the fact that the moral and spiritual center of these schools, for better or for worse, has always been the religious orders running them. In some cases these orders have virtually collapsed; in other cases they are suffering identity crises which affect the schools in profound ways. Whether authentic Catholic colleges can exist without vigorous religious communities infusing them is doubtful.

The question of how "open" a college can be and still call itself Catholic is one which many institutions are understandably reluctant to face. It seems certain, however, that important moral and spiritual values (as distinct from purely intellectual values) are best transmitted and kept vital when rooted in a culture and a community. How such cultures and communities can be formed and sustained under present conditions of disintegration and anomie is not at all clear, however.

At present many Catholic colleges are, paradoxically, failing most conspicuously in conveying to their students a sense of historic Catholic culture, an awareness of the ancient tradition of which they are supposedly a part. There is a disposition to pay little attention to anything having to do with religion in the period between the New Testament and the Second Vatican Council. For most students, Aquinas is no more than a name in the freshman history textbook.

John Tracy Ellis's remarks of nearly three decades ago are generally cited as the historical charter of Catholic educational reform. Yet commonly, only that part of his critique in which he dissected the obscurantism and backwardness of the colleges is remembered. His diagnosis — that most often the Catholic schools have forgotten their own authentic heritage in pursuing modern fads like vocational training, the booster spirit, and professionalized athletics — is largely forgotten. Whether the colleges of the future will compile a better record in this regard than their predecessors is something on which, at present, no prudent person would care to wager.

PROPHECY AND POLITICS:
ABORTION IN THE ELECTION OF 1976

Whether religion significantly influenced the results of the 1976 presidential election, and specifically whether Jimmy Carter had a "Catholic problem" stemming from the abortion issue or other less tangible considerations, was much debated. The election did, however, raise other kinds of questions regarding the relationship between religion and politics that have scarcely been recognized but that may have serious meanings for the future of religion in America.

Symptomatic of the spirit of the age is that the issue in 1976 was discussed largely in terms of the "intrusion" of religion into the election campaign, an implicit acceptance of the secularist thesis that the two realms should have nothing to do with one another. Numerous pundits regretted or deplored the religious questions that attached themselves mainly to Governor Carter's candidacy. Those who strove to remain neutral nonetheless betrayed by their tone the feeling that a bizarre and thoroughly unpredictable planet had suddenly appeared in the tidy political universe.

Scarcely noticed, and not at all discussed, was a phenomenon of equal significance—the "intrusion" of politics into religion. This was evident in the powerful and well-orchestrated attempt to overbear religious scruples, especially on the abortion issue, in the interests of party loyalty and ideological correctness.

The height of concern over the church-state question was reached in September, when a committee of Catholic bishops met with both major presidential candidates and questioned them about, among other things, abortion. The bishops' statement following these meetings—that they had been "encouraged" by Ford's stand and "disappointed" by Governor Carter's—set off a massive reaction in much of the secular and some parts of the religious media. The bishops ended up issuing several "clarifying" statements that deemphasized the significance of their initial comments and left matters in a state of general confusion.

Objections to the bishops' original statement were understandable and, from certain points of view, justifiable. The bishops' meetings with the candidates were unacceptable to those who, for example, believe in an absolute wall of separation between church and state and who think the churches should have nothing whatever to say about political questions. The meetings were also unacceptable to those who regard abortion as an illegitimate political issue, wrongly "interjected" into the campaign. On either or both these grounds it was not surprising that the secular media censured the bishops in stern language. The *Kansas City Times* warned of "fanaticism" and predicted a "harsh" reaction on the part of the voters. A Catholic on the *New York Times* editorial board, William V. Shannon, wrote a syndicated column chiding the bishops for, among other things, offending against "the spirit of charity and tolerance" by stirring up "fanatical" antiabortionists against Governor Carter. Both papers seemed to imply that ordinarily political campaigns are exercises in polite philosophical discussion.

More surprising, however, was the reaction of some of those who professed themselves to be opposed to abortion on moral grounds and even to favor a constitutional amendment prohibiting it. *Commonweal*'s was among the milder reactions. It considered the bishops' statements ill-advised and also warned against backlash. Father James Rattigan, president of the National Federation of Priests' Councils, went on national televison to express "deep concern" that abortion was being overstressed. Donald J. Thorman, publisher of the *National Catholic Reporter*, wrote an angry editorial decrying the "damage" the bishops had done to the American church and quoted approvingly from the *Kansas City Times'* strident editorial.

Objections by Catholics to the bishops' statement were varied and never subjected to close analysis in the heat of the presidential campaign. Some, like Donald Thorman, counseled in effect a realistic acquiescence in the futility of fighting abortion — no amendment was likely to be passed, he thought, and Catholics should turn their attention to other matters. The same point was made, avuncularly, by James Reston of the *Times*. It is the kind of advice ordinarily called self-fulfilling prophecy.

More common was the argument from priorities. The Davenport (Iowa) *Messenger*, an official diocesan newspaper, articulated a common attitude when it argued that the rights of the unborn were not in themselves sufficiently important to determine one's vote and that abortion had to be measured against a whole range of moral concerns. This was an arguable position, but one that failed to take account of the consciences of those who might in fact regard abortion as the single overriding moral question of the day. Liberals who warned solemnly against being "one-issue voters" were not likely to have taken the same attitude toward, for example, civil rights or war when these were "divisive" political questions. It was also true that interest in "a broad range of moral concerns" was usually a code-expression meaning support for the Democratic platform.

Some Catholics also invoked the separationist argument, charging in effect that the bishops were "meddling" in politics. It was a strange position, however, held by those who had welcomed church intervention on a wide variety of social issues for years. Numerous priests and nuns openly supported Governor Carter, and the implication of the separationist argument seemed to be that political activity was suitable for the lower clergy but not for the hierarchy, possibly a defensible position but one that seemed to have been formulated merely to meet an immediate need. There had been no liberal protest when, for example, Bishop Thomas J. Gumbleton of Detroit endorsed Senator George McGovern in 1972.

The antiabortion voter had no happy choice to make on November 2. Both candidates had expressed their personal moral disapproval of abortion, a common political position that is meaningless; it is politicians' actions that matter and not their private beliefs when we evaluate their qualifications for office. President Ford endorsed an amendment allowing each state to legislate about abortion, but many antiabortionists regard this as an unacceptable compromise, since it would merely shift abortion activity across state lines. The President's stand was also regarded by many as a sop, and looming always in the background was the memory of Mrs. Ford's ecstatic praise for the Supreme Court's *Roe* v. *Wade* decision. Although Donald Thorman speculated that the real purpose of the bishops' strategy was to reelect Mr. Ford, in fact few antiabortionists were enthusiastic about him, and some antiabortion groups advised their members to vote for neither major candidate.

Governor Carter's position remained fuzzy throughout the campaign. In a foreward he wrote in 1972 to the book *Women In Need* he seemed to endorse unlimited legal rights to abortion. But early in 1976 he told Iowa voters that he favored "legislation" to prohibit abortion, later rendering that assertion meaningless by explaining he did not favor a constitutional amendment. At the Convention his agents put through a platform plank opposing such an amendment, but later the Governor tried to disown the plank. Meanwhile, he surrounded himself with advisors who were either proabortion or opposed to a constitutional amendment.

Many of those opposed to abortion thus felt little urgency about reelecting Gerald Ford but did experience a sense of urgency about defeating Jimmy Carter. Several of the Governor's staff members, notably his pollster, Patrick Caddell, repeatedly said in public that abortion was an insignificant issue that could be ignored with impunity. Thus a Carter victory, whatever the candidates' ultimate personal position, would be interpreted as an important symbolic defeat for the antiabortion movement, a sign that the issue was exhausted. A Ford victory would keep the question alive at least.

This situation produced a classic confrontation with American Catholicism that has implications for other churches as well. The split was essentially between two camps, each motivated by high moral principle: those who identified abortion as the overriding issue of public life and thus tended to oppose Governor Carter, and those who in general approved the Democratic platform, apart from its abortion plank, and thus supported him.

Ordinarily such a split might have issued in a charitable agreement to disagree by the two groups. But antiabortionists realize that high visibility and unrelenting pressure are necessary for their success. In the early days especially, pickets dogged Governor Carter. On the other side, numerous priests and nuns became actively involved on the Governor's behalf. Their support led to a sophisticated and well-organized campaign from inside the Church to neutralize abortion as an issue in the hope of electing the Democratic candidate. (At one of Governor Carter's appearances in North Dakota, four priests sat in the front row and applauded when he stated that he did not favor an antiabortion amendment.)

Instances of obvious partisanship abounded. When the Republican Convention adopted an antiabortion plank, the *National Catholic Reporter* headlined its news story " 'Conservative' GOP Convention Defends Rights Selectively — Fetuses Have Them, Hungry Don't." Those delegates who opposed the plank were interviewed at length and portrayed as courageous dissenters. In early October, relying mainly on Patrick Caddell, the newspaper announced that abortion was a dead issue. The National Coalition of American Nuns gave blanket endorsement to the Democratic platform, not even dissenting from its abortion plank. In an appearance before the National Conference of Catholic Charities (NCCC), Governor Carter was repeatedly cheered, and the delegates, strongly supportive of the Democrats' economic planks, refused to endorse an antiabortion amendment because, in the words of an NCCC official, they were "turned off by the way abortion had intruded itself into the presidential campaign". The NCCC president, Monsignor Lawrence Corcoran, then in effect endorsed Carter for President.

Anyone even remotely alert to the political situation could have predicted three years before that abortion as an issue might threaten traditional Catholic support for the Democratic Party. For more than a year Jim Castelli of National Catholic News, an official agency, had worked to discredit the antiabortion movement. A typical Castelli story asserted that "widely respected members of the American hierarchy" (not mentioned by name) were upset over the "heavily political aspect of the Church's involvement". He asserted that "some people [again mostly unidentified] think partisan politics is creeping into the antiabortion movement" and cited anonymous complaints about "force and ideological purity". Already in the fall of 1975 he had set up a hypothetical election between two candidates, one of whom opposed abortion but lacked broader social concerns, the other of whom took the reverse stance. The Church, Castelli argued, without telling people how to vote, should "educate" them in such a way that they would incline toward the second candidate. The article was obviously preparing the ground, a year ahead of time, for the probability that some liberal candidates would favor legalized abortion in 1976.

After his nomination Governor Carter gave Castelli an exclusive interview in which he has been quoted as saying he might support an antiabortion amendment under some circumstances, a statement nowhere else attributed to him. Castelli also explained away the foreword to *Women In Need*, and after the election reported that Governor Carter had not had a "Catholic problem" after all.

Following the bishops' meeting with the two candidates, Castelli wrote a story focusing exclusively on the criticisms directed at the bishops and concluded with a demand that they redress the "imbalance" their statements had created. He predicted that in retaliation various Catholic organizations would endorse Governor Carter. At the same time, the *New York Times* reported that unnamed key staff members at the United States Catholic Conference (USCC) in Washington, the Church's central administrative agency, had threatened to resign if the bishops did not back down from their "dangerous involvement with partisanship". The bishops subsequently issued the first of their "clarifying" statements that in effect blunted whatever force their original statement may have had.

The charge of partisanship against the bishops was ironic because their original statements about the two candidates had been mild and would have gone largely unnoticed if the pro-Carter media had not reacted with alarm. Meanwhile, those who condemned this "partisanship" most sternly were either announced Carter supporters or proclaimed admirers of the Democratic platform. No significant "neutral" voice spoke out, either in the media or in the Church. Those most conspicuously disturbed by the bishops' actions were without exception those who feared harm to their own favored candidate. The type of bias present in the USCC was suggested by the fact that Governor Carter, following his meeting with the bishops, added to his staff a former key USCC aide, Terry Sundy, who obligingly announced his opposition to an antiabortion amendment. (If the bishops had interrogated both candidates on, for example, unemployment, and had pronounced themselves "disappointed" in President Ford, it is likely they would have been hailed for their courage and compassion.)

The open partisanship of some of the clergy was not denied but was often cloaked in a mantle of disinterested moral concern. In Pittsburgh the executive secretary of the Capuchins' regional province, Father Charles Chaput, at first rebuked antiabortion pickets because "it hurts the cause" [of antiabortion], but in a subsequent heated exchange with a picket admitted that "I'm very pro-Carter." The Yale theologian, William Lee Miller, a Protestant, published an "Open Letter to the Catholic Bishops of America" in which he lectured them on the inappropriateness and ineffectiveness of sign carriers who had picketed Governor Carter in Indiana. Reading the letter carefully yielded a hint that Miller had actually been part of the candidate's entourage, and he expressed concern that the Governor had to endure "a lot of nonsense brought on by his religion". The letter was published in the

Christian Century, whose editor had been an early Carter supporter and chairman of his campaign in Illinois.

A vice-president of the National Federation of Priests' Councils, Father "Marty" Peter of Indianapolis, published in September an open letter denouncing the "polemics" of the antiabortion movement in general and of the supporters of Ellen McCormick in particular. (Mrs. McCormick had been an antiabortion candidate for the Democratic nomination for President.) Father Peter's main concern, however, seemed to be to defuse Catholic opposition to Senator Birch Bayh of Indiana by reminding them that they should not be "single-issue" voters. (Senator Bayh has in fact been more responsible than perhaps any other senator for obstructing the progress of an antiabortion amendment in the Senate. This did not prevent Network, a lobbying group of nuns, from giving him their highest rating during his brief bid for the Presidency.) Openly expressed clerical partisanship on behalf of one presidential candidate was at a higher level in 1976 than at any time in the history of the American Catholic Church. (Clerical support for President Ford, to the extent it existed, was largely local and personal.) This in itself was not the most significant religious implication of the campaign, however.

Former British Prime Minister Harold Macmillan once made a remark that has become famous: "If the people want moral leadership let them go to their archbishops." In a dramatic reversal of this principle Catholics in 1976 were being urged insistently by many of their clergy to seek moral guidance not from the anointed leaders of their Church but from the duly crowned head of one of the major political parties. Governor Carter's clerical supporters did not deny that morality was relevant to politics. Instead, they stated boldly that the Democratic platform was a moral document of such power and purity as to override whatever private scruples people might have about abortion. The official leadership of the Church, and the many ordinary Church members greatly exercised over this question, were termed "myopic" (Father Peter's word) and urged to support unhesitatingly the reemerging New Deal coalition.

Believers in absolute separation of church and state have a tendency to be far more vigilant against religious encroachments into politics than the reverse, and a similar pattern of thinking exists with respect to religion as a "divisive" force. Numerous observers worried over the "intrusion" of religion in the 1976 campaign; few noticed the opposite process also taking place. In fact, once the Democratic Party had adopted its proabortion plank, flying in the face of one of its major traditional constituencies, it became incumbent on the Party's supporters to exploit division within the Church, for fear that the official teaching on abortion would detach too many voters. *Commonweal* editorialized that candidates "might do well to associate themselves with or consult Catholic leaders and Catholic intellectuals", implying that such would be more fruitful than meeting with bishops (who were, evidently, not to be considered "leaders"). The columnist Garry Wills urged Governor Carter to "get acquainted with Catholics. That will teach him not to pay attention to their bishops." The *St. Louis Post-Dispatch* reported in September that the Governor had decided to appeal to Catholics over the bishops' heads, on the assumption that they had little influence with their people.

Pressure on Catholics to fall into line politically came from two opposite wings of the Party. The most articulate were clergy, many of them relative newcomers to politics and still flushed with the enthusiasm of untarnished idealism, who wanted the Catholic vote to be determined by position papers emanating from groups like Network and the Center for Concern. On the other side was Mayor Daley of Chicago, who, while paying his respects to Cardinal Cody, pronounced that "there are more important questions for the citizens of America than abortion." Both groups, for quite different reasons, had a stake in keeping Catholics as a safe delivery vote within the Democratic fold. Both discouraged the possible independent-mindedness of the "single-issue voter".

Two contradictory images of the Catholic bishops were invoked alternately during the campaign, depending on the situation: that they exercised sinister influence over their people and were a threat to democracy, or that they were pious windbags who could be safely ignored. In either version, Catholics who chose to vote for Governor Carter were deemed to be manifesting a laudable spirit of freedom and striking a healthy blow for separation of church and state.

One of the most serious questions arising from the 1976 campaign experience is one of vital concern to all churches (and indeed to all people who value genuine pluralism) but has been scarcely recognized: How can any religious group sustain doctrines contrary to prevailing opinions articulated in the media? Most church members read their daily newspapers more assiduously than their weekly religious press. Church leaders have little access to the electronic media, and a Sunday sermon is no substitute. The educational system is indifferent or hostile toward traditional religious values, by and large. In such a situation church members, except the most fanatical or resolute, seem fated over a period of time simply to adopt the prevailing beliefs of the larger society, with the churches gradually accommodating themselves to this process. Most significant, these key shifts in opinion are likely to occur first among religious professionals, those supposedly most committed to the church's teachings but who in practice often turn out to be culturally a part of the great consensus of conventional educated opinion, maximally susceptible to shifts in that consensus.

More serious perhaps than even the full power of media and party directed against a particular religious position is the power the media have to interpret the internal life of the churches to those churches' own members. In the interests of a particular political cause Catholics in 1976 were being told insistently that their bishops had overstepped themselves, that free and enlightened Church members were ignoring the bishops, that moral issues like abortion had no importance, and that key Church bureaucrats were privately rebelling against the bishops' stand. The media had the power to determine which "Catholic voices" deserved a hearing. Faced with this barrage of publicity in the secular media and some segments of the religious media, Church leaders had no effective means of communication with their own people. The media proved they have the ability to project whatever image of contemporary religious life thay choose and that attempts to modify or correct such an image will usually be feeble.

A second disturbing implication emerging from the campaign is the assumption that, while party loyalty is a good thing, religious loyalty is inherently suspect. Catholics perceived as voting in accord with a religiously motivated moral stance were treated as sheeplike bigots, while those who faithfully pulled the Democratic lever on Election Day were thought to be showing their good sense and independence. Voting one's perceived economic self-interest was deemed laudable; voting on the basis of a religious and moral principle was in effect condemned.

The motives of party loyalists like Mayor Daley were pragmatic and familiar. The activities of many of the clerical supporters of Governor Carter, however, raised a new and serious moral and theological question: if economic and political action, and supporting "correct" political programs, are as important as some Christians insist, then situations like that of 1976 will become increasingly common — tension between the clear moral teachings of a particular religious tradition on the one hand and the need to make an act of faith in and support for a particular party on the other. To subject that party to close moral questioning is to risk defeat on election day.

Many Christians wish to play a prophetic role in politics; yet the abortion question in 1976 showed that such a role is permitted only when religious witness coincides with opinions widely held in secular society. Prophecy that is perceived as distinctly religious is ruled out of order.

The disturbing feature of the 1976 version of this story was not the fact that some Catholics, after anguished consideration, may have decided that the Democratic program was morally compelling overall despite the abortion plank but that certain strategically placed Catholics showed little anguish at all. Their support for the Democratic cause was a foregone conclusion, and, having made that decision, they had a vested interest in wearing down whatever moral scruples other Catholics might still retain. Having identified Governor Carter as the best available hope to lead America toward the Kingdom, they were compelled in effect to deny that personal religious and moral scruples had any legitimate place in political decisionmaking. For such people moral passion was directed not at the evil of abortion but at those who presumed to raise the issue in the public forum. They did not, evidently, try to influence Governor Carter to change his stand. Being a Christian, not for the first time, was equated with unreservedly accepting membership in the Secular City.

THE DYNAMICS OF POPULAR
INTELLECTUAL CHANGE

Despite the American belief in pluralism, society is virtually never in a state of equilibrium with regard to competing social philosophies. New ideas are almost always bought at the expense of old ones, and the marketplace of popular ideas is not infinitely expandable. Ideas and movements are either in the ascendancy or in the decline; they cannot remain stationary. Hence conflicts over moral and social values are commonly perceived by participants, even if they do not fully realize it, as battles for survival. Often familiar positions are reversed; defenders of the status quo suddenly become outsiders, bewildered and demoralized by their new situation.

Recent American history has been marked by certain changes in popular attitudes that, though difficult to measure, may be the most significant events of our time. Old beliefs and old institutions are now more distrusted than at perhaps any time in our history. There is a significant class of persons who appear ready to accept, at least provisionally, almost every new idea, and who correspondingly tend to be at least mildly alienated from what has been regarded up to now as the mainstream of American society. The mainstream, meanwhile, appears to be getting narrower and more sluggish, the tributaries more numerous and friskier.

The list of such changes could go on endlessly, but a few of the more obvious manifestations of recent intellectual iconoclasm would include the following: that America as a nation is morally soiled in its dealings with both foreign peoples and many of its own citizens; that American economic achievements are at best ambiguous, both morally and in terms of the welfare of the citizenry; that American political institutions no longer work as they should; that sexual activity apart from heterosexual marriage is morally right and should be socially respectable; that traditional family roles and family authority distort the personalities of those involved; that church membership is unimportant and belief in God perhaps irrelevant to human living; that the wisdom of the past is largely superstitious and empty; that self-gratification (without harming others) is the proper purpose of human existence; and that institutions (of whatever kind) tend inevitably to inhibit such gratification.

The dynamics of public opinion—especially the process by which beliefs that seem deeply held are suddenly thrown off with little apparent regret or agony—remain largely unexplored. Since America is at least a quasi-democratic society, changes in social values have to percolate up from below, in the sense that broad popular acceptance (not necessarily by a majority) is required for social respectability. There are no institutions (the Supreme Court

230

perhaps comes closest) capable of simply decreeing such changes. Nonetheless, all these changes originate, in virtually every instance, with a numerically almost insignificant minority. At its inception a minority view may seem almost absurd to the majority; the stages by which it becomes respectable are roughly as follows:

Public exposure. Here the role of the media is obviously crucial, and the mistrust of the media felt by many Americans has much to do with their awareness of this. The media, by noting some movements while neglecting others, go a long way toward determining which new ideas will gain acceptance and which will not. Whether they portray a movement in a friendly or a questionable light is important but not decisive.

Timeliness. Victor Hugo's famous remark about the power of "an idea whose time has come" has been endlessly quoted in recent years; an unfamiliar idea must somehow seem appropriate to its time before it will begin to gain acceptance. The process by which some new ideas fail as premature while others succeed is mysterious, but it appears to have much to do with dramatic public events that arouse attention (for example, Sputnik in the 1950s and Watergate in the 1970s).

The crucial middle. There are people in our society—mostly rather obscure people whose influence, in many cases, is unrecognized even by themselves— who effectively act as intellectual referees. They judiciously separate acceptable ideas from untenable ones, the possible from the obviously specious, the "interesting" from the stale and sterile. Some of them—journalists, teachers, clergymen, politicians—have public influence, but many more have an influence only within a limited local circle. Each is therefore individually insignificant, yet because they exist in every community, they are collectively important. In general, these people have reputations for being thoughtful, solid, balanced, and temperate in their opinions. They may in fact be thought of as slightly stuffy and overcautious (as were professors and clergy not many years ago). Nevertheless, when they change their minds on particular social questions (as by turning against the Vietnam War or deciding that marijuana should be legal) they create perceptible ripples, even without intending to.

Defections. After the judicious middle has decided that a new idea is at least worthy of a hearing, some within their ranks will move beyond mere tolerance—first to mild sympathy, then to active espousal. Such conversions may be few in number, but they have profound psychological effects on others in the middle and appreciably shift the entire axis of discussion.

The myth of inevitability. The new movement's impetus has maximum force to the degree that it convinces the larger society that it has already won its victory and that continuing opposition is futile and foolish. It may moderate its positions in the hour of victory, but successful movements manage to convince even many of their critics that they were fated to succeed. Sometimes the unthinkable becomes the commonplace within a few years (for instance, unmarried cohabitation among college students or the respectability of abortion), and even those who retain reservations about the new idea come to feel that opposition is pointless.

Running through this scenario are certain threads that are quite familiar in the fabric of American thinking and that serve as hidden ways by which iconoclastic notions are legitimized in traditional categories. One of these is belief in progress, the American assumption that, on the whole, change brings improvement and that a relatively stable existence implies backwardness. Although most Americans may be morally conservative and politically cautious, few are genuine reactionaries prepared to fight what they perceive as rearguard actions against social trends that, though possibly viewed as dubious, are also seen as irreversible. For many people, too, the success of a new idea is proof of its legitimacy. Through media attention, the unfamiliar soon becomes the acceptable.

Belief in progress, which carries with it the strong implication of inevitability (as in the popular description of a conservative as someone who has to be "dragged kicking and screaming into the twentieth century"), conjoins with the idea that changes are made because they are morally right, because people of goodwill have chosen to make them. The rightness of the new must be proven in terms of its moral superiority over the old.

Success was so often taken as proof of moral rightness that for a long time the successful entrepreneur was held up as a moral as well as an economic model. In one sense this may be mere rationalization, one of the rewards that history bestows on victors. But in another sense it is crucial to the triumph of new movements that they successfully make moral claims on society, that they somehow touch the consciences of at least those intellectual referees possessed of liberal instincts. Somehow, rather illogically, change comes to be rationalized both as inevitable and as freely chosen.

Any new movement must also have the ability to touch the moral nerves of at least some of those in the establishment it hopes to displace. The cynical view that power or status is never surrendered voluntarily is only partially correct. Certainly in modern America there are numerous examples of members of various establishments who came to doubt their own legitimacy and connived in their own disestablishment. (Such cases are especially numerous among college professors and administrators.)

Yet this process goes much deeper than merely reaching the consciences of those who are in a position to legitimize change. For some in the new movement the aim, sometimes not consciously recognized, is the total discrediting of the older establishment. The need of the new group to assert itself, its quest for psychic *Lebensraum*, and its desire to avenge old injustices, combine to produce an aggressive movement which will carry the battle against the entrenched enemy as far as it can be taken, limited only by the ultimate degree of resistance it encounters.

The established group, poised on the verge of decline, is plagued by having a history, and particularly a history that is public knowledge. Since no people lives its history over any length of time without accumulating various crimes and blunders on its record, a history can become a burden and an embarrassment, a source of continuing and demoralizing self-doubt. Most peoples interpret their histories in a favorable way. Under attack, however, the interpretation becomes increasingly implausible; the heroic myths previously subscribed to become all the more poisonous as they are discredited. Thus, if the pioneers of the American West were not superhuman, they must have been murderers of Indians and rapers of nature. If American foreign policy in the postwar world has not been a consistently disinterested defense of freedom, it must have been a massive conspiracy to defend hidden capitalistic interests.

Established groups also suffer loss of self-confidence from the simple human tendency to run out of energy over a period of time. This is true even when fresh leadership is periodically injected. If an establishment has had its own way for too long, has faced no really trying challenges, it may lose the ability to respond. If traditional ideas have simply been accepted as self-evidently true, attacks will induce panic and doubt among many who have always believed in them.

The feeling of debilitation—that oneself, one's group, or one's values no longer possess vigor and energy, lack the capacity to inspire dedication and creativity—is one of the most serious maladies from which an establishment suffers. People in such a condition often develop an extravagant admiration for those who seem to possess the qualities the establishment lacks: energy, clear-sightedness, strength of will, firmness of purpose, vitality, dedication. The virtual youth-worship that spread through much of the liberal middle class in the later 1960s is the most recent major example of this. Black militants and Third World revolutionaries have also been beneficiaries of this Western bourgeois reflex.

Finally, the American belief in fair play enters the equation, in that many privileged persons seem to feel that they have enjoyed the benefits of their positions long enough and owe it to others to cede place to them. Some people seem to sense that their time in history is over, and they are prepared to move aside deferentially for those they recognize as their successors.

This entire process is a self-reinforcing one: the more the establishment is attacked and subjected to hostile scrutiny, the more likely it is to suffer growing self-doubt and demoralization. The ability of the attacking movement to keep up a steady barrage, its apparent indefatigable resourcefulness, the variety of fronts on which it operates, the zeal and seeming hatred with which it maintains the fight—all tend to frighten the defenders of the bastion, who sense a lack of comparable will and resources within themselves. The ascending movement forces the establishment to fight a purely defensive war. Media attention focuses on the attackers, who appear more interesting and dramatic than their opponents, and the aggressors' very ability to get and hold attention is taken as yet one more sign of their legitimacy.

A demoralized establishment does not necessarily surrender to its enemies precipitously. But lacking real confidence in its own rectitude, it may fight dispiritedly and without imagination. It may rely on purely physical defenses (for example, during the late 1960s summoning the police during a campus demonstration), partly because it cannot face a direct moral and intellectual confrontation with its critics. In some cases (the White House during the Watergate years), the establishment appears to sink into pure cynicism, abandoning any real belief in what it supposedly stands for and preoccupying itself with simply holding on to power as long as possible.

In some cases, an establishment may attempt to pacify its attackers by offering significant concessions and obsequious, humiliating acknowledgments of its own failings. Radicals are understandably suspicious of the possibilities of betrayal in such offers, which are often no more than tactical. Establishment leaders may see their own survival, and the survival of the institutions they represent, as dependent on the infusion of fresh blood and energy from the rising movement. Their willingness to accede to critics is sometimes akin to the excitement that staid middle-class people have experienced at being on the fringes of, for example, the youth culture or militant black groups. There is an almost palpable flow of electricity from the new to the old.

This same dynamic applies to rising and falling ideas as well as to political movements, in that the proponents of new ideas tend to personalize what they oppose. Thus they make it easier to attack (for instance, to reduce traditional family values to a matter of "male chauvinism"), and many defenders of traditional values react in the same way as leaders of established institutions — progressively losing confidence in their own beliefs or concluding that resistance is futile.

At each historical moment there is a kind of unwritten social scorecard on which the fortunes of various movements, and various ideas, are charted. Instinctively, though not always consciously, particular movements are noted as either rising or falling, particular ideas as either ascendant or passé.

These rankings are of major importance because, also unconsciously, society (or those who function as the intellectual referees) maintains different sets of rules for rising and falling movements or ideas. Whether a movement is in the ascendant or descendant category is largely recognizable from its behavior and the judgments society makes about that behavior. Movements that appear to be on the rise are expected to behave differently from those in decline, and for the most part they do.

An infallible sign that an idea or movement is about to enter its decline is a feeling expressed by key individuals among its adherents that it is "oppressive" or "tyrannical", or that it inhibits personal development. This "desertion of the intellectuals", as Crane Brinton characterized it, eventually pervades the movement, spreading self-doubt and resentment against the discipline that has hitherto been exacted. (If, on the other hand, the desertion of the intellectuals fails to cause wider repercussions, the group is obviously not on the verge of decline and the revolt will be easily smothered.) These differences can be analyzed according to the following categories, among others:

Self-fulfillment/self-sacrifice. People generally find self-discipline, sometimes even heroic self-sacrifice, tolerable if they believe it is for the sake of some larger purpose. Resentment directed against groups to which they belong or ideas to which they supposedly subscribe (such as the institution of marriage) indicates effectively their loss of belief in this transcendent meaning. It is related to the decline of energy and creativity, as people find it increasingly difficult to summon up these beliefs in a fresh and vital way. Their past, especially, goes dead on them.

It is also generally true that widespread resentment against the "oppressiveness" of the old group—the family, the church, or the school—will not occur while the group is at the height of its authority and power and is capable of stern disciplinary measures. Rather it occurs when the group has already been significantly liberalized and its authority, in fact, is but a shadow of what it once was. What the members resent most is not its tyranny but its patent weakness; the slight remains of its once heavy burden are what most gall and annoy.

Community/individual. Individualism—each person's primary concern with his own gratification—tends to emerge from the breakdown of social groups. This is in contrast with the new ethic of communalism generated by rising groups, in which the individual feels privileged to make sacrifices for the sake of the group; consider the obsessive concern to thwart ego trips or personality cults in many radical movements.

Hedonism/puritanism. An instance of the previous dichotomy, this division has been especially significant in recent years because of the sexual revolution—itself an apparently rising movement seeking to displace residual American puritanism. Rising movements, especially those that are revolutionary about political and economic matters, are usually puritanical. They regard an excessive interest in sex as an unhealthy preoccupation with personal satisfaction, and they believe sex should be controllable for the collective purposes of the group, such as encouraging or discouraging large families. And a sophisticated society tends to respect in rising groups the very signs of prudishness that it ridicules in declining groups. Milton Himmelfarb has pointed out that feminists can successfully condemn pornography while self-respecting liberal clergymen no longer dare do so. A classic conservative myth, dating practically from the Fall of Rome, holds that sexual indulgence weakens a society's moral fiber and thus precipitates decline. More probably, a sexual revolution signifies a growing preoccupation with purely private happiness, indicating that attachment to the *res publica* is already on the wane.

Cynicism/credulity. Growing disenchantment with the declining group easily slides into cynicism—about the motivation of the group's current leadership, about the "real" meaning of its beliefs (the traditional belief in the family as a mere cover for male privilege), even about much of its past, however glorious (the view of American history as almost two centuries of imperialist conspiracy). Members of the group who consider themselves "enlightened" or "liberated" take it as a mark of honor to be skeptical of all the group's claims, and immune to its propaganda.

It is also a mark of sophisticated people, however, to be simultaneously realistic, even to the point of cynicism, about some things while remaining willfully credulous about other things. Thus, the discontented within the declining group are inclined to take most of the rising group's claims at face value and to entertain a romanticized and idealized view of its history. Precisely because members of the declining establishment feel debilitated and demoralized, they are eager to embrace uncritically the apparently vital and purposeful new group.

Passive/aggressive rhetoric. There is perhaps no surer sign of a group's imminent decline than the unwillingness of its spokesmen to talk confidently and aggressively in public about its purposes and beliefs. At a certain point, these spokesmen will discover that ideas and styles of expression that had been generally accepted for some years are now having a negative effect not only on the public but on many of their members. Critics of this rhetoric will stress its alleged excessiveness—it is too bombastic, too obviously smug, too much given to clichés, too sweeping, too lacking in irony. Generally in such a situation either the leaders learn to modify their rhetoric, sometimes drastically, or else they are replaced by new leaders who dissociate themselves symbolically from their predecessors.

The adoption of a rhetoric that is low-keyed, soft-spoken, diffident, relatively subtle, tentative, and even apologetic is motivated often by tactical considerations—the desire to salvage the group's image and show that it can adapt to changed conditions. There are, however, significant costs to such adaptation. The new rhetoric is unable to inspire or reassure even the group's own members, thus contributing to its further decline. It is unable to make the group seem attractive to potential converts. It may silence critics, but only because they sense it is no longer worth bothering about. Its subdued new public image is taken as evidence that its critics are essentially correct in their charges and that it consequently deserves to continue its slide into oblivion.

Conversely, not only are rising groups permitted (and in fact expected) to employ rhetoric that is aggressive, extravagant, often pompous, insulting toward enemies, and grandiose in its claims, but such rhetoric is taken as a sign of a group's legitimacy and the rightness of its claims. Here again the importance of the media is central: groups that are unable to get and hold the spotlight are deemed unworthy of sustained public attention. Such obscurity is taken as evidence of a fatal debility or lack of conviction within the group itself.

Sophistication/primitiveness. Within itself, a group close to decline is characterized by a growing sense of irony, self-mockery, boredom, restlessness, and a feeling that everything it stands for is now too familiar to be fully believed. Rising groups, in contrast, possess a freshness, enthusiasm, and wholehearted belief, almost a childlike energy and eagerness. Once again, although these characteristics are applauded in a rising group, when adopted by the declining group they are ridiculed or regarded as dangerously fanatical.

Complexity/simplicity. A major mark of sophistication is the awareness that reality can be so obscure and complex that sure and certain judgments about it are difficult to arrive at. And that awareness, carried past a certain point, may well induce agnosticism, bewilderment, and inertia. As a dogma of faith (one of the most basic of the modernist cultural movement), this sophistication works constantly to erode traditional beliefs and loyalty to established groups. Every attempt to reassert traditional ideas is met by the objection that the group's view of reality is "simplistic" and that it fails to take account of the relativity of all beliefs.

Rising groups must of necessity eschew any such perception of reality; otherwise they would lose momentum, loosen their hold on the conscience of society, and weaken the allegiance of their own adherents. Their claim to attention may be that they perceive simple but profound "truths" that society has preferred not to acknowledge—for example, that history is essentially an imperialist or a male chauvinist conspiracy. Their freshness, vigor, dedication, and clear-sightedness, so admired by sophisticates, must be maintained by a willfully naive (perhaps even cynical) view of reality.

Ecumenism/messianism. The ideal that one can be fully and deeply committed to one's own beliefs, while at the same time totally respectful of other people's, is extraordinarily difficult to achieve in practice. Those who believe that they know *the* truth, or a particular truth, must try to propagate it, since it would be uncharitable to leave other people floundering for want of correct knowledge.

Groups that become diffident about their own beliefs in the public forum, that renounce the desire to make converts, that profess to see broad areas of agreement between themselves and other groups and admit there are many roads to the same destination, that acknowledge the dogmatism and rigidity of their past—these are usually groups that have begun to doubt their own legitimacy at some profound level. (The rise of the ecumenical movement in modern Christianity is clearly not unrelated to this development, nor is the growing uncertainty about missionary activity on the part of many religious denominations.)

Rising groups succeed precisely because they claim to have *the* truth and are able to convince significant numbers of people that they do. They are expected to be messianic, apocalyptic, dogmatic, intolerant, and to condemn those who disagree with them. They place great emphasis on correct belief and correct action, and they are quite willing to expel and condemn deviant members.

Because they take their beliefs with great seriousness, these rising groups are prone to schism and internal fragmentation, generally arising from quarrels over the authenticity of particular doctrines. Such fragmentation, if it becomes excessive, can seriously cripple the movement and even destroy its effectiveness (as may have happened to the New Left of the late 1960s), but a certain amount of factionalism can also be a sign of health.

It is perhaps symptomatic of the declining vitality of both Christianity and Marxism in the West that dialogue between these two movements has been undertaken in recent years. Little is heard of organized, irenic discussions between feminists and male chauvinists, for example, or black militants and white racists, or pacifists and American Legionnaires. Often a rising group will reject meeting with even sympathetic and conciliatory representatives of "the enemy", for fear of being taken over or subtly contaminated.

A declining group will, virtually by definition, be characterized by a significant number of defections from its ranks, while a rising group will attract converts. The media play an important role by giving publicity to such movements, which helps to inform the public that a particular group is either rising or falling. In the 1950s, publicity was given to notable converts to the Catholic Church; in later years this was replaced by stories about defecting priests and nuns.

Positive/negative. An established group whose legitimacy has begun to decline finds that an image of negativism—moralistic, restrictive, condemnatory, puritanical—is a severe handicap. It must even learn to affirm ideas that may run counter to its own official beliefs, as when churches seek to come to terms with the sexual revolution. Rising groups, on the other hand, often base much of their program on strongly condemnatory ideas about the existing society and do not hesitate to pass sweeping moral judgments on whole classes of people or on the entire history of a nation.

Scholarship and the arts. There is a broad modern consensus that art and scholarship must be independent of socially imposed orthodoxies, and that artists and scholars will often function as social critics. In a declining group, the intellectual may feel virtually obliged to stand in judgment on established beliefs. A historian may set out to debunk the popular myths of his country, or a theologian to question the official dogmas of his church. Rising groups, on the other hand, search for a usable past. The art and scholarship they inspire may frankly aim at supporting the official group ideology. Their artists and intellectuals tend to accept the role of serving the group's needs. Art may be openly propagandistic, dealing with themes currently deemed relevant to the group's historical situation.

The paranoid style. The historian Richard Hofstadter noted the persistence of the "paranoid style" in American history: the tendency of particular groups (right or left) to interpret events in terms of conspiracies and make other groups the scapegoats for all social misfortune. In general, a sophisticated society frowns on conspiratorial theories of history and ridicules or is alarmed by any establishment that fears plots against itself. Rising groups, however, tend to see history precisely in terms of conspiracies (men against women, the old against the young, capitalists against workers), and the intellectual referees regard these perceptions as having some validity.

Procedure/substance. Most established groups have developed complex and myriad procedures for dealing with all manner of problems. These procedures take on a life and a worth of their own and to a degree become sacred — for example, the liberties guaranteed by the United States Constitution as interpreted by custom and court decisions. Many people, therefore, regard violation of these procedures as morally wrong, worse than the evil whose remedy is sought. This happens even when the violation is in a good cause, such as punishment of a dangerous criminal.

Rising groups tend to be impatient with established procedures, using those that lead to desired results and readily violating others. Thus, for example, they may curtail academic freedom or the right of free speech on campus in order to prevent "reactionary" views from being aired. All this may so confuse the partisans of traditional procedural safeguards that they remain silent or offer only feeble protests.

Persuasion/coercion. The belief that a secure and self-confident society can be perfectly tolerant of dissent exists chiefly as an ideal and is rarely met in reality. A broadly tolerant group is in fact more likely to be one whose members have begun to lose confidence in their own values and whose leaders are confused as to its future direction. A rising group, on the other hand, is often not loath to use elements of coercion — not only an aggressive and domineering rhetoric but actual physical pressure, such as breaking up opposition meetings or shouting down opposition speakers. Again the intellectual referees may be confused and silent.

Ordinary/special language. A declining group is likely to conclude that part of its difficulty is in its failure to communicate adequately with the larger society. To remedy this, it will attempt to expunge all special language from its public statements (and often from its private discourse as well). It will tailor its messages as much as possible to what it thinks the larger society is willing to accept. At the extreme, it simply ceases to have anything distinctive to say and is content with echoing commonly held opinions. It will also eschew distinctive clothing for the same reasons.

Rising groups are almost always characterized by the use of a special language—even a jargon—and one sign of a group's acceptance is that it forces the public to learn this language and perhaps adopt parts of it. (The youth culture of the later 1960s introduced any number of unfamiliar words and phrases into the adult vocabulary.) A special language is, as the linguist Basil Bernstein has demonstrated, an important element in group solidarity. Thus, the use of such language reinforces a rising group's cohesion, while the declining group's abandonment of it hastens its own dissolution. Rising groups do not hesitate to use language unfamiliar to the general public, because they believe they possess a unique truth that the public needs to learn. (Rising groups also find their dress styles being widely imitated.)

Personal morality. If representatives of declining groups are discovered to be engaged in questionable personal behavior, such as adultery, excessive drinking, or embezzlement, these failings may be interpreted as signs of the group's corruption. (In films and the theater, the corruption of German life before Nazism has long been represented by scenes of orgiastic debauchery and sexual fetishism.)

Leaders of rising movements may choose to keep their personal lives in the background or bring them into the light. The choice may well depend on whether what they do in private is irrelevant to their public roles or possibly, if colorful and unconventional, a sign of their vitality and independence.

Particular groups and particular ideas have undergone the above processes repeatedly throughout history. Periodically, however, a whole society experiences this crisis, when practically all its values and institutions are called into question simultaneously. If it is plausibly urged that all aspects of the society's life, from its foreign policy to its sexual mores, are subtly interconnected—then whatever doubts develop in one area will in time spread to almost all other areas.

The workings of this dynamic can be examined with respect to a few key instances in recent American history:

Chinese communism. Westerners in considerable numbers have reacted to the Chinese experiment with willful credulity and unabashed admiration. Although few would suggest the relevance of the Chinese model to America, there is a commonly held belief that it may be a more appropriate model for the rest of the world than the American model. America is thought to have become obsolete, save for its brute military capabilities, while China may represent the way of salvation for much of the globe. There are obvious parallels with an earlier and similar Western admiration for the Soviet Union.

The recurring appeal of communism in the West stems largely from the dialectical relationship between a "hard" culture—one that demands discipline, self-sacrifice, and devotion to social goals—and a "soft" culture that encourages self-fulfillment, individualism, and personal pleasure. Eventually a hard culture is always vulnerable to the blandishments of a soft culture, as its people tire of unremitting discipline and look enviously at the seemingly carefree happiness of their neighbors. The material prosperity that a disciplined culture often achieves may well undermine this spirit of discipline.

Yet once a hard culture has succumbed to the blandishments of a soft culture, many of its citizens will have periodic attacks of guilt. Intellectuals in particular, for whom the pursuit of personal gratification eventually comes to seem shameful and crass, will seek models of a hard culture that reveal more challenging human possibilities. Added to this is Marxism's claim to be in tune with the dynamics of history—a claim that, if taken seriously, dictates disengaging oneself from the declining society, even if only spiritually.

America. Intellectuals were perhaps in an untypical mood in their willingness to celebrate American society and its world role for twenty years after 1945. Much of this attitude was based on the belief that America represented the genuine wave of the future, standing for political freedom, economic efficiency, enlightened responsibility, and overall modernization. For essentially the same reasons intellectual elites in many parts of the globe were attracted to what America represented. America was the great model in the struggle against "backwardness".

The radical turning against this idea, so marked in the past ten years, is obviously related to the American defeat in Vietnam at the hands of a "backward" enemy. Hence America is perceived as a loser rather than a winner, a society whose influence is clearly on the wane. Its values and institutions are regarded as having little significance for the rest of the world. In accordance with the principle that an established group makes room for a rising group by being itself pushed aside, various movements of the Third World now occupy the attention of intellectuals both here and in other countries and are thought destined to rise.

Youth. In essence, the youth culture of any society is a pure and classic example of a rising movement, since its members are certain of eventually displacing their elders, who are equally certain of passing from the scene. The full implications of this were felt in the late 1960s, when young people (at least on the campuses) displayed all the characteristics of a self-confident rising group and key members of the adult world showed the classic symptoms of a declining one.

The youth culture still exists, but it has lost much of its aggressiveness and no longer inspires fear and awe in adults. Its rather swift loss of momentum is somewhat mysterious. Probably this stems from the discovery of how confused and demoralized many young people themselves were behind their facade of dogmatic confidence. Many adult admirers were disappointed at this revelation and began looking elsewhere for rising groups to identify with.

Blacks. Although, unlike young people, blacks are not certain of eventually coming into their own, organized black movements, in the past ten years especially, have shown most of the characteristics of a rising group, and many white people have in turn reacted toward them as do typical members of a declining group. Many white adults have paid blacks and young people the supreme homage a declining group gives to a rising one: imitation—in speech, in music, in dress, in mannerisms. Many white adults also, for a time, counted themselves blessed to the degree that they were accepted into the black world or the youth culture.

In conjunction with the Third World, organized black movements in America still show many of the signs of groups that may in time inherit the earth. They have, however, experienced some temporary stalling of momentum, owing mainly perhaps to close encounters with elements of the white world (lower-middle class and working class) who do not think of themselves as part of an established declining group and hence do not respond positively to the usual rhetoric and tactics of the rising group.

White ethnics. This is a broad and imprecise term for the white working class and lower middle class. White ethnics remain a problematical case, since to date they have largely failed to exploit successfully the strategies of a rising group and have so far failed to arouse sufficient guilt and self-doubt in the upper middle class for it to behave toward them like a declining group. On the other hand, the white ethnics are also extremely important because of their apparent immunity to the usual appeals that a rising group makes. In fact, white ethnics generally react negatively to these appeals, as revealed by their opposition to compulsory school busing, affirmative-action programs, and many aspects of the youth culture. The reason for this reaction is that white ethnics do not think of themselves as an established group, hence do not feel the guilt that is so large an element in the dynamics of rising and falling. This in itself has significant implications—some of which are certain to be felt before the decade is out.

Current political rhetoric tends, temporarily, to move away from the implications of this rising-falling dichotomy, which had been dominant since about 1960. There is a sense of consolidation of changed positions. However, American society is too volatile, and the habits of thinking here described too much a part of the whole apparatus of mass communications, to render this cessation more than temporary.

THE WOULD-BE WORLDLING

For the most part "secularization theology" has run its course, in the sense that few people still in the Church would accept the terms of Harvey Cox's *The Secular City* exactly as they were stated in 1965. There has been a rediscovery of religion, albeit of an often vague and eclectic kind.

Nonetheless, the impact of the secularizing theologians is still profoundly felt in the Church, and doubtlessly it will be for many years to come. Their principal effect has perhaps been to plant in many Christians a reflexive urge to reach out to whatever seems most "worldly" or "human" at any given moment of history, a persistent anxiety not to be left out of things, stranded on some snug ecclesiastical island. It is not unfair to say that, forced to a choice, many avant-garde Christians would rather be worldly than religious. The latter, even when achieved, is constantly embarrassing to them; the former embarrasses only to the degree that they fall short of achieving it.

It has become a cliché (a true one) that progressive Christians generally manage to pick up some secular fashion only at the moment it is about to go out of style, and that as a result they have to run very hard just to stay one or two steps behind "the world", whose subtle ways they seem forever barred from comprehending. "Secular Christianity" has thus tended to be a self-defeating movement — secular enough to convince worldlings that the Church has had its day, not secular enough to command real attention and respect.

It might be argued that true worldliness, like true love or true friendship, is something which is achieved unexpectedly and unknowingly. Those who are most anxious to attain it are precisely those most likely to fail, to be swindled again and again by counterfeits. Thus it can also be argued that what has troubled the Church in the past ten years is not an excess of secularity, although superficially that may appear to be the case, but rather a failure to achieve real secularity. Progressive Christians have not learned to take the world seriously, as they have so fondly wished. They have rather succeeded in theologizing, or divinizing, certain abstract ideas, and these have prevented their truly understanding the world and speaking to it in relevant language.

This is perhaps most obvious in the weirdly schizophrenic vision which seems to lie at the heart of so much worldly Christianity. On the one hand this vision tends to the condemnation of the social order (at least in the West) in the strongest and most puritanical terms. The most halting preacher can become instantaneously a Jeremiah by ringing the changes on the familiar catalogue of "war, racism, poverty, sexism, destruction of nature", et cetera, the cumulative effect of which, if taken seriously, would drive listeners to total despair and unbearable guilt. On the other hand, however, many of the same preachers are equally committed to a sunny neo-Pelagianism in which there is no sin but only "failure to grow", human "self-fulfillment" is the highest good, restraints on personal behavior are deemed unnecessary, and joy, peace, and love permeate everything. We are simultaneously denounced as rapacious, selfish, racist, and violent and also told that we are "okay".

Perhaps the first worldly deficiency of the would-be Christian secularist is the inability to look unflinchingly at the reality of power as it influences society and human behavior. A few years ago advanced Christians sided over-whelmingly with the flower children — they were dropping out of a corrupt system, rejecting power as almost inherently sinful, relying on transparent love to triumph over evil. In typically extremist fashion that mood quickly gave way to a new hard-headedness in which former admirers of Gandhi began to talk knowingly about "clout", threats of violence were rationalized, "powerlessness" was defined as the chief problem of the oppressed, and priests and nuns began to scramble for public office. As with sex, awareness of power had been repressed for so long that when the dikes were opened there had to be a flood.

Yet the reality of power and its accouterments is still not taken seriously. Instead, a manichean dualism has been set up in which, when exercised by the "establishment", it is evil and corrupting, while when sought by the weak it is ennobling and has religious significance. Although never stated so baldly, an implicit belief of many liberal Christians is that power, wealth, and prestige are good only for those who do not possess them; once they are pos-sessed they become sinful. By some strange process the dispossessed are en-couraged in theological terms to throw themselves wholeheartedly into the pursuit of power, while those who have it are with equal fervor urged to give it up.

The attitude of liberal Christians toward labor unions is typical — they are enthusiastically endorsed so long as labor is weak and exploited; once they at-tain their goals they are wearily dismissed as reactionary and uninteresting. The liberals' disappointment is made inevitable by their failure to notice an elementary fact — what most dispossessed people want is not some abstraction like "liberation" or "dignity" but precisely the economic security, material comfort, and social prestige now enjoyed by the American middle class. If it is morally wrong for the middle class to cling to these things, then it is mor-ally wrong for the underclasses to struggle for them. There is no precise line on the socio-economic scale where one can say, "It is permissible to aspire this far but no farther", and it is naive to suppose that the oppressed classes are composed of saints who will voluntarily stop when they have achieved "just enough".

The manifestoes of worldly theology are usually wearying in the extreme, precisely because flesh-and-blood are so often reduced to abstractions like "the people", "the oppressed", "liberation", "justice", et cetera. Rare is the Christian writer who can, like Robert Coles, render the situation of poor people in all its complexity, irony, and concreteness. For Dr. Coles, people are not simply examples of some general thesis about society but are real people who talk and act the way they are supposed to but at the same time do not. Hence he induces understanding and compassion far more effectively than any number of "liberation" theologians. Incidentally, he also conveys a far more lively awareness of the transcendental dimensions of religion than do most secular Christians.

There was a time when Christians were not supposed to admit to having sexual desires; there was a common implication that such desires could be easily banished with the proper training, discipline, and attitude. There is now a similar lack of realism about such things as avarice, ambition, and envy. Certain holy people, mostly in the "Third World", are said to be devoid of such baseness, and middle-class Westerners are told that they too can attain this purity if only they put their minds to it. In the last analysis, so runs this new puritanism, wealth and power are not even very satisfying (just as sex used not be) and people are happier without them.

Worldly Christians are similarly unable to face up to the reality of violence in human relations, and there has been a parallel swing from widespread pacifism five years ago to at least cautious support for "revolution". As with wealth and power, there is a comforting Marxist assumption that the capitalist system creates in people insecurity and a necessity for competition, which cause avarice and violence.

But as Michael Novak has pointed out, few social systems in history have more effectively inhibited man-to-man physical aggression than has capitalism, for whatever that is worth. (It has of course similarly homogenized a number of other human tendencies as well.) The notion that if people are only properly educated and encouraged, if they are made to see the truth of human existence, they will spontaneously renounce violence is again naive. Violence is probably as natural to human beings in certain situations as is sex, which is to say that, like sex, it must be controlled by a variety of social and personal mechanisms. It is worth recalling that in ancient societies of quite elevated moral perceptions (like Athens) vengeance was, under certain circumstances, not only a right but an obligation, and the man who failed to avenge family or friend thereby suffered dishonor. Such an attitude is probably far more authentically human than the principle of nonviolence. The fact that private vengeance is no longer respectable in society is largely due to three factors liberal Christians often disdain — the force of religious authority, the power of the state, and (in modern times) the need of the economy for social stability and order.

Often, worldly Christians do not seem to believe in society, despite their love of abstractions. Rarely do they judge what effect a particular policy or idea, if implemented, will have on the entire social fabric, nor do they show much concern for that fabric, preoccupied as they are with the problem of special individuals or groups. As a sociologist said to me, "Christians have been in the forefront of those trampling on social values in recent years." Often they seem affected by an angelic antinomianism which disdains custom, sanction, social expectation, or law as prods to right behavior. They will have spontaneous morality or they will have nothing. The delicate ways in which the various components of society are linked together are of no interest to them.

This blindness is nowhere more evident than in the tendency of liberal Christians to endorse every form of personal "liberation", with little regard for larger consequences, whereas a true worldliness would dictate prudent hesitation. Implicitly, what is being denied is that man is really a social being. The "needs" of the individual are alone deemed important, in accordance with a neo-Pelagian conviction that personal "fulfillment" can only lead to good (similar to classical liberalism's assumption that if each man pursues his own economic self-interest society as a whole will benefit). Curiously, this atomism is often accompanied by a rejection of the ethos of competition, although a strong commitment to the idea of self-fulfillment can only increase competition in the long run, however much it may inhibit certain specific forms of competition.

In their concern to be worldly, Christians have frequently missed the powerful strain of nihilism lying just beneath the surface of modern Western culture, which has been exposed and dissected by a variety of artists and seers. The swinging Catholic middle class has discovered "the world" and is determined to enjoy it to the full. Others have preceded them, however, and their reports do not inspire confidence in the inevitability of finding God, truth, goodness, or beauty. For example, several nuns became publicly indignant because a Catholic critic made disparaging remarks about certain contemporary art works. While the nuns were defending the "genuinely religious" significance of contemporary art, however, one of the most astute of secular critics, Harold Rosenberg, was exposing the emptiness, gimmickry, fraud, and aimlessness of much of the current art scene. An age which talks so compulsively about "creativity" is perhaps an age which senses it is near the end of its creative powers.

It is a sobering thought that, in the entire history of the world, few people, even among the philosophers, have thought in the personalistic terms now so prevalent in religious circles, and that the assumptions about human existence which worldly Christians now take for granted are largely the products of modern Western bourgeois society, and rather late products at that. In the total history of the world it is possible that Christianity will turn out to have been a long moral parenthesis. Distinctively Christian ideas about sex are already in the process of being abandoned for earlier pagan attitudes. There are signs that a similar process might occur with regard to violence and selfishness. Liberal Christians cheerily accept an agnosticism about "personal morality", sure that present certitudes about "social morality" will endure. More likely, however, Westerners will simply become more and more comfortable with moral confusion and with minimal moral demands. There is no possibility of creating a viable public morality with regard to things like ecology if private virtue is systematically undermined. It is a process which issues only in fads. It is precisely those who are most "enlightened" who at present appear to be also the most morally disoriented.

It is an ancient but profoundly true paradox that Christianity is always most authentically worldly when it preaches the divine message most uncompromisingly. In part this is ethical, and worldly Christians should adjust themselves to the possibility that, in the years ahead, the residual force of religious authority may be the principal effective instrument for upholding beliefs which it now appears all men of goodwill are arriving at by a marvelous spontaneity. The very ideal of unselfishness may strike the men of the future as odd and incredible.

Simultaneously, Christianity also transcends the ethical and announces a world beyond this one. Perhaps many of the clergy, immersed in the life of the Church, hear the call of the world with some longing. For lay people saturated with the world, however, the longing for God is itself a basic "worldly" need which too often in recent years the Church has failed to meet. When the Church has been faithful to its religious mission it has never failed to discover authentic ways of also serving the world.

THE PROBLEM OF DECADENCE IN CATHOLICISM

Those who have visited Mao Tse-Tung's China in recent years have returned with generally similar reports, that of a country quite clearly "repressive" — constant propaganda, total intolerance of dissent, heavy sacrifices demanded from the population for the sake of official goals—yet at the same time not visibly unhappy. The people are described as polite, friendly, hard-working, enthusiastic for the cause, satisfied. They are, apparently, true believers.

Allowing for obvious differences, this is a description remarkably similar to those which visitors to Catholic convents and monasteries used to give of life within the cloister. By worldly standards deprived and living "unnatural" lives, monks and nuns were nonetheless said to be serene, balanced, purposeful, even radiant. (This was, for example, the vision of monastic life conveyed by Thomas Merton for some years after he had left the world.)

This comparison is not intended as a condemnation of the religious life, because it is clear that most Western observers of China, whatever their doubts and reservations, have come away impressed and even disturbed. Representatives of a culture increasingly dedicated to notions of self-fulfillment, personal autonomy, and moral iconoclasm, they have sensed the power of a culture which is able to demand immense sacrifices of its people because it articulates for them a larger meaning and purpose. It is a reality all but disappeared in the West, and Western visitors react to it with more than a little nostalgia and regret.

People are generally willing to accept a large amount of "repression" not simply in exchange for tangible material benefits, although the improvement of the economy may be one manifestation of national purpose, but more importantly in exchange for fundamental meaning. A society which shapes men's lives in coherent ways, which sets out an intelligible path of existence, is a society which often enough has no need to enforce its laws rigorously.

Before the Second Vatican Council, few Catholics apparently thought of themselves as repressed: they only discovered that fact after they had been told repeatedly that they were. The telling, however, would not itself have been credible had not the ordinary citizens of the Church—lay and religious—discovered that the Church which demanded so many sacrifices was also increasingly unable to provide the basic meanings which made the sacrifices endurable. Abstinence from birth control, celibacy before marriage, lifelong fidelity afterwards, celibacy, fasting, et cetera, were not experienced as problems, even by most preconciliar reformers. They became so only when the most fundamental truths of the Church had been called into question. For

248

many people, the chief message of Vatican II was that the Church was caught in a massive crisis of self-confidence and could no longer teach with assurance.

The "modern mind" is often said to have rejected prescribed orthodoxy, imposed discipline, and repressive self-sacrifice. This is true, however, only in the forms in which these have traditionally been demanded, especially religion. Those who are intensely libertarian and pluralistic in religion are often capable of acting as heresy-hunters for political ideologies, for example. The Church is deemed unjustified in its demands not because the demands are inherently inhuman, as is so often stated, but because it is seen as an institution which has outlived its day and should stand aside in the interests of newer movements which also possess a sense of religious mission and zeal.

The exhaustion of the old traditions was, apparently, an experience for many persons who did not, before the Council, identify with the cause of reform, who in fact appeared to be stable and conservative in their commitments. The unravelling of so many religious communities, the eerily swift decline of lay organizations like the Sodality, the astounding shifts in attitude and belief all suggest that the traditions were hollow even for many who appeared satisfied and serene. They were buoyed up and carried along by their brethren, or by the general climate of Catholic culture. When forced finally to confront the degree of their commitment to the old ways, they often discovered that it was slight indeed.

Decadence in a culture can perhaps be defined as the loss of self-generated energy and of interiorized purpose, a condition which inevitably results in confusion, ennui, the rapid erosion or even reversal of established taboos, and bizarre relationships between the individual and the traditions which have nourished him.

Its causes are unclear. Although always requiring a long time to develop, its existence is usually manifested within a relatively brief time, by a few events which tear aside the veils of conventional social life to reveal emptiness beneath. (In the American church the chief of these events was perhaps the Liturgical Week in Washington in 1968.) Small things come to have immense negative importance—a work, a figure of speech, an object (like a priest's biretta) suddenly appears incongruous and seems to discredit the entire tradition. In the beginning "reformers" tend to concentrate on these small things, which gives their work a false appearance of moderation and conservatism. In time the small things are discovered to lead inexorably to the large.

Decadence stems in great part from the exhaustion imposed by a surfeit of experience. When too much is experienced, directly or vicariously, things lose their power to surprise or inspire; everything tends to take on a flat sameness, which imposes either a fatalistic ennui and cynicism or a semihysterical search for still newer experiences, which are just as quickly exhausted.

In all probability mass education, defined broadly to include the electronic media, has been the principal cause of this exhaustion in the recent history of the Church, which is to say that most of the experiences have been vicarious, a fact which does not substantially reduce their effect. Those who regularly consume the largest and most varied quantities of information, who imaginatively seek to place themselves in alien situations or sympathize deeply with alien peoples, who self-consciously seek to root out every vestige of provinciality from themselves, experience it first.

Thus within the Church the manifestations of this exhaustion first became apparent, and remain most visible, among the educated, the politically liberal, the socially and geographically mobile, and the young, who, if they have not lived through many things, have saturated themselves with experiences in vicarious ways. The fundamental split in the Church between traditionalists, who are generally older and perhaps simpler, and reformists is that for the first group the traditions are not irrelevant because, in certain ways, they remain fresh, charged with energy and capable of inspiring. If the traditionalist has been wedded to those traditions for many years, he has nonetheless not generally discussed, examined, worried, fondled, rearranged, and sucked them dry in the manner of, for example, the liturgical enthusiast. He has generally lived with them rather unreflectingly and at a measured pace. The religious crisis has hit hardest among priests and nuns in part because these were the people who experienced the traditions most intensely and who were quickest therefore to feel the exhaustion.

At the same time, a surfeit of experience does not wholly account for the mysterious process by which a culture decays, since in their most vital periods the traditions of the culture tend to inspire deeper commitment and provide deeper satisfaction precisely as they are most intensely embraced and explored. Often, however, decadence sets in precipitously immediately following the period of greatest apparent vitality. (By most measurable standards, such as the lay apostolate and the contemplative vocation, the most vital period of American Catholicism was roughly 1945–65.) In Hegel's words, the owl of Minerva flies only at dusk; the candle gives off its brightest flame just as it is about to go out (the Second Vatican Council).

The temper of Western culture in the past three centuries has tended to promote speedy decadence through the pervasive spirit of objectivity. Everything is relentlessly subjected to detached scrutiny, which tends inevitably to rob it of mystery, spiritual power, and inspirational capacity. By mechanisms only partly understood the Church managed to hold the spirit of objectivity at bay until virtually the 1960s, when the spirit scored a sweeping if possibly temporary victory. The inculcation of objectivity has been the principal aim of modern Western education, and the dangers of this cult are only beginning to be fully recognized. Ultimately it tends to the dissolution of all values and all cultures.

The decadence within the Church has stimulated a kind of intellectual awakening — a curiosity, a restless probing, a willingness to investigate hitherto protected areas, a new nimbleness with theory, especially theory derived from the social sciences. It is an intellectual awakening which has affected not only the Church's professional thinkers but many ordinary clergy and laity as well, who appear on the whole to be more intellectually sophisticated, at least in a worldly sense, than before the upheaval began. Such awakening usually results from decadence, as the evident malfunctioning of the institution stimulates curious inquiries into its fundamental structure and as traditions which were once merely admired and cherished are contemplated with a cold and even cynical eye.

Decadent man tends simultaneously to be hyperrational — detached, disillusioned, critical, and uninvolved — and possessed of dangerous tendencies toward irrationality, which feed on the denial of certain essential needs of the human person and which express a sense of desperation, a lurching toward new commitments. He is able to cast a scornful eye on his inherited traditions, which he can pick apart with cynical precision, and also give unthinking support to extremist political movements, fantasies about cultural revolution, and such miscellaneous modern products as drugs, encounter groups, and total sexual liberation. The moral alertness of decadent man is less the product of a sensitized conscience (he can be remarkably self-indulgent in certain ways) as the inevitable cynicism and disillusionment imposed by an unravelling society, the eagerness to believe the worst about one's own culture and traditions.

To take an objective stance toward one's own traditions is at once to rob them of power and authority, and as Father Walter Ong has pointed out, it is characteristic of newer groups — those whose fortunes appear to be on the rise, who are hopeful and not yet disillusioned — to use an extravagant, domineering, and highly emotional rhetoric. At present advanced Christians speak of their faith in only the softest of tones, muting differences and avoiding at all cost any semblance of a superiority complex or a missionary mentality. At the same time, they endorse and encourage the intolerance and messianism of the various secular groups bent on "liberation", "freedom", or "power".

Such deference is more than simple politeness, since in a society dominated by mass communications the strength of a movement's public exposure, and the apparent vigor of its apostles, are generally perceived as indices of its legitimacy — those who are able to attract public attention to themselves automatically come to seem important, while those who remain in the shadows are inevitably taken to represent sterile and dying ideals. The voluntary quiet of enlightened Christians, except as they involve themselves in political struggles, is regarded as an admission of insignificance and is probably often intended as such.

Above all the decadent mind admires those virtues which it no longer possesses — vitality, freshness, energy, clear purpose, strength of will. (This was a major reason why nazism had so great an appeal in late Weimar Germany.) Ineluctably it finds itself attracted to youth, activist movements of all kinds, dreams of the future, daring iconoclasm, the struggles of hitherto oppressed and even "primitive" people (the cult of the Third World). Lacking energy of its own, it seeks to share in the energy of those who still possess some (hence the "radicalization" of certain aristocrats in revolutionary periods of history and the contemporary phenomenon of "radical chic"). Since spiritual and intellectual exhaustion is decadent man's chronic condition, there is a need for constantly changing and intensifying stimuli, the creation of an artificial sense of excitement, movement, and accomplishment, heavily dependent on the communications media. Much of the general effect of the Second Vatican Council was dissipated in this way.

Those caught in the decay of their culture experience a sense of passivity and bondage, the inability to affect their lives at the deepest levels because both the inspiration and the values are lacking. There is sometimes compulsive railing at the "oppressiveness" of past traditions, even as these traditions grow steadily weaker. They are despised both because the residual power they have is falsely perceived as the real source of the individual's lack of freedom and because, though their loss is acutely felt, it cannot be accepted as loss and must in fact be proclaimed as gain.

Decadent man primarily experiences himself as the creature of history, as lacking the ability or the will to mold or resist it. He senses that whatever movement and purpose he will experience in the future will be through a momentum which history imparts to him. Hence he is often obsessively concerned with being modern, flexible, future-oriented, open-minded, and unhampered by permanent commitments. Only thus can he hope to be history's perfect instrument.

The need to regain lost energy and nerve, and a sense of purpose which will allow them to be usefully employed, is the central problem for decadent man. Many people simply choose to accept their debilitation, to live comfortably and profanely, without a larger horizon to their lives. Its loss may occasionally trouble them, but they feel it to have been inevitable and on the whole they welcome the relaxation of the need for sacrifice and striving. All things are now permitted.

The fierce iconoclasm of a period of decadence becomes for other people almost habitual, because the moment at which the idol breaks is a moment of fierce and thrilling joy. It provides, temporarily, a shot of adrenalin and with it once more a sense of purpose. As Philip Rieff has pointed out, those who have been the appointed guardians of the old traditions (the clergy) will now feel the greatest compulsion to put out the flame. The decadent mentality senses that it is now not simply permissible to violate old taboos, it is in fact obligatory. What was once sacred must be treated profanely, even ridiculed.

In a peculiar way, such treatment once more makes the traditions "relevant", a phenomenon particularly noticeable in liturgy, where sacred symbols can be consciously manipulated in such a way as to convey daring new meanings alien to the tradition and even contradictory to it. Thus a Catholic priest conducts divorce services modeled on the nuptial rite, and an Episcopal priest celebrates an All Saints Mass garbed, along with his ministers, in Halloween costumes. A Benedictine monastery, having abandoned Gregorian chant, uses as an entrance hymn "a new song, a glad song" set to the tune of "a tisket, a tasket". The debasement of the tradition is a way by which it can still be made to yield up meaning.

In the beginning, sensing the waning power of the traditions, reformers took the opposite approach—instead of debasing them they would seek to purify them. The yearning for purity is always strong in a decadent time, along with an intense urge to return to simple and pristine roots. Thus the initial thrust of Catholic reform, before Vatican II, was essentially backward and even reactionary. The Liturgical Movement, in its classic period, sought a return to ancient and archaic prayer and ritual in order to deepen the sense of divine mystery and sacramental reality. Critics of Thomism often took refuge in a Kierkegaardian fideism, glorying in the "absurdity" of theological dogmas unsupported by elaborate rationalizations. Social thought rested heavily on papal teaching. The Church was to be made more "Catholic"; the supernatural was to be reaffirmed with great conviction.

The reformers sensed that, for them, the traditions were in danger of losing their meaning. The fact was clear enough; their understanding of it was not. They thought of themselves as, if anything, superorthodox and hence dissatisfied with the traditions because the traditions were contaminated. They did not realize that soon they would discover that the essential characteristics of the Catholic tradition—authority, dogma, timelessness, ritual, asceticism, the dichotomy of Church and world, tradition itself—would be perceived as meaningless.

Preconciliar reform was in a sense an attempt to reverse history, and when it failed it helped ensure that reformers would prodigally embrace history as their only salvation. Newer liturgies would be quite self-consciously modern, unconcerned with divine mysteries or with transcendence, chiefly aimed at orienting the participants toward useful life in the world. Dogma would be almost entirely jettisoned, except for the dogma that no theological doctrine is valid which is not relatable to an experiential fact about the world. In the most advanced circles Christian life and teaching would come almost to be equated with marxist revolution.

One final attempt to reverse history, to recover a mythical pristine purity, still survives, although it is steadily weakening. This is respect for the authority of Scripture, the belief that historic Catholicism is largely the story of the abandonment of biblical teaching, which must now be recovered. As it developed after Vatican II, this attitude often took quite Protestant forms within the Catholic Church, and predictably the reformers' relationship to the Bible has, within a remarkably short time, recapitulated the Protestant experience with the Bible in the past centuries—extravagant respect, followed by growing doubts, ending with the conviction that the Bible is somehow central to Christian life but with no clear notion how. Increasingly the message of Scripture is seen as coinciding remarkably with the most advanced modern thinking. (For example, Robin Scroggs, a New Testament exegete, says that St. Paul had "a perception of the structure of society essentially identical to that of Norman O. Brown and Marcuse".)

Traditions decay in part because people cease to understand them, still possessing perhaps an abstract, academic knowledge of them but no longer a feeling for their inner significance. Quite clearly this was the case for many people even before Vatican II. Looking back, the "liberated" individual has difficulty understanding how he could ever have loved the traditions. They appear in retrospect dessicated, empty, meaningless, and oppressive, a huge fraud perpetrated on the gullible. Their inner meaning is irretrievably lost, and it becomes impossible for the new man to comprehend how they could in fact have genuine meaning for anyone. The history of the Church itself becomes largely irrelevant, except as an exercise in debunking, because too great an imaginative effort is required to recover whatever validity the traditions may once have had. (Garry Wills, in *Bare Ruined Choirs*, seems able to recall every detail of preconciliar Catholic life except anything vital or compelling about it.)

Decadent man yearns simultaneously for purity, wholeness, and simplicity— the archetypal return to the sources, the beginning over again without the burdens of history—and the complex profaneness which is modern Western civilization. Religious reform oscillates continuously between the two poles, now veering toward Scripture, an austere life, childlike faith, now toward the complexities and artificialities of modern thought, an easy acceptance of permissive worldly morality, and a cool and skeptical intelligence. One's fated condition seems intolerable; the question posed is whether to renounce it by a heroic act of the will or accept it and exploit it to the fullest advantage. The cult of the primitive is never more appealing than in a hypersophisticated age.

Decadence is dissipation in the literal sense, in which the center disintegrates and the parts fly off in all directions. "Pluralism" is welcomed as a positive good, because it is imposed as a historical necessity. Societies which are young, vigorous, purposeful, and possessed of a great dream are rarely pluralistic. What Irving Kristol has said of the university can be applied to the Church as well — as it loses the sense of its primary purpose, of what it can and ought to do, it begins trying to do everything. Unable any longer to speak compellingly about its central teachings, it seeks to espouse every social cause, involve itself in every worldly movement, vindicating its relevance by demonstrating that it is infinitely malleable and can be adapted to all variety of human needs.

The loss of the vital center, while it can hardly go unnoticed, is nonetheless little discussed and, since the recognition is so traumatic, is by tacit consent ignored as much as possible. Much energy is expended on questions which, while not unimportant, are nonetheless far removed from the great religious issues — ecclesiastical government, financial accountability, married priests, women priests, parish councils. All such debates help to keep alive a superficial sense of meaning and vitality, while the core problems — salvation and damnation, fundamental moral values, prayer, sanctity — are neglected. "The world" comes almost to be worshipped as the new bearer of salvation, and religious discussion is confined to practical and secular issues like ecclesiastical power and rebellion against authority, which the world finds comprehensible and not challenging.

In stable, healthy societies a large part of each person's total set of values and perceptions is provided by the culture, and this is not generally felt as oppressive. The "inherited conglomerate", as the classicist Gilbert Murray has called it, inevitably changes but in orderly and often unperceived ways. The inheritance of the past is regarded as a burden only when it has been so lightened and attenuated as to be in danger of disappearing. What is felt then is not the burden but its absence.

"Identity" tends therefore to become a personal problem only in societies which are ailing, which are unable any longer to provide meanings for their citizens. The individual senses that as his culture dissipates itself, his own personality is in danger of fragmenting. One method of coping with the situation is frank acceptance, a basic surrender to historical inevitability, as in Robert Jay Lifton's concept of "protean man", who has no fixed identity or stable values but moves easily and serially into a variety of ways of life, some of which contradict each other. Life is a perpetual "pilgrimage", in the religious term which is used to justify the condition, but with no known goal and in fact no criteria for judging when a goal has been reached.

This is a way of life now apparently adopted by appreciable numbers of people. As yet, however, it appears to be unendurable for most of the discontented. The latter keep alive hope for maintaining a coherent personal center through the myth that there exists within them a "true self" as distinct from the apparent self encountered in daily existence. The ideal of "authenticity" is essentially a modern one, although facsimiles of it can be found in the spiritualities of earlier ages. Since religious people have been among those who have felt most acutely the loss of personal and cultural centers in the past decade, they have been among those most attracted to sensitivity training, psychoanalysis, contrived "mind-blowing" experiences, and other techniques for uncovering a "true self" buried beneath all the layers of "socially constructed" selfhood. Since the apparent self has fallen into lassitude and confusion, the constant hope is that the true self, when finally encountered, will make possible a great resurgence of creative life. (Among the signs of the loss of a sense of personal identity is the new unconcern for privacy, so that under certain new disciplines one's inmost thoughts and feelings are compulsively laid bare in public, privacy being seen only as a form of hypocrisy.)

The lust for "encounters" of all kinds reflects a desperate search for meaning in a culture in which larger meanings — religious, political, familial, intellectual, artistic — seem no longer adequate and the heresy flourishes which insists that personal relations between a few people are the only realities. (There is no more impoverished theological concept than that "God is what happens between persons.") Those who are unable to find a meaningful life in society are unlikely to find it in intense personal encounters either, as evidenced in the apparent growing instability and evanescence of marriages and love affairs.

Inevitably the individual feels driven outside himself for new sources of inspiration and energy. Overcome with passivity and inertia (issuing in compulsive talk about "dynamics", "creativity", and "innovation"), he senses that only by massive transfusions from the outside can he hope to recover. His born and inherited condition comes to seem, in extreme cases, hateful, almost forcing the belief that he has no right to exist. Those who are more self-assured, vigorous, and purposeful come to possess, by virtue of those very attributes, a moral ascendancy over decadent man. He becomes increasingly preoccupied with his own guilt and that of his tradition, to the point where his personal and cultural past both come to seem inauthentic and almost vicious. (A liberal minister says that those who drink alcohol can hardly judge those who use heroin.)

Such a condition has always constituted a threshold for Christian conversion — the sinner who, at last, confronts his own helplessness and accepts a wholly unmerited grace. (For this reason there are often "religious revivals" in ages of decadence.) But since the classic doctrine of Christ's redemption is one aspect of the tradition which now seems irrelevant and even, in some formulations, perverse, such salvation is no longer possible for many. The up-surge of Pentecostal enthusiasm, whatever validity it may have, represents in part a turning from Christ as the traditional source of personal salvation and to the Holy Spirit instead. In its extreme forms it suggests the individual's in-tended annihilation of his own personality, his making of himself simply a conduit for the Spirit. In a decadent time nothing can be believed except what can be experienced, which is primarily an exhaustion of will and imagination; hence the importance of various strategies to awaken the religious emotions; hence in some instances an openness to ecstatic and even orgiastic forms of piety.

Malachi Martin has said that "American Protestantism is susceptible to profound guilt feelings, in virtue of which it is willing to undertake almost suicidal policies. . . . The Protestant mind has swung over to a guilt-ridden permissiveness that will allow no moral absolutes except two, perhaps: the rights of the individual, and the absolute surety that no moral absolute exists." It is a mentality which is no longer unrepresented within Catholi-cism, and rage against the traditional Church frequently springs from the conviction that, having lost its assurance and its nerve, the Church no longer has a right to exist and should make way for other historical movements more self-assured and authoritative. Programs to "reform" the Church are sometimes designed, therefore, either consciously or unconsciously, to pro-mote its death.

Sensing that salvation will come to them only from the outside, such reformers have attempted, with an ardor scarcely reduced by repeated disap-pointments, to adjust the institution and its spiritual core to rapidly changing historical movements which seem to possess all the virtues the Church lacks. Rapprochements have been attempted with the technocratic American "secu-lar city", Charles Reich's "counterculture", classic liberal Protestantism, quasi-fundamentalist Pentecostalism, Marxist revolutionary movements, a variety of schools of personal therapy, the modern secular university, and an-cient Asian religions. As each movement is revealed to be as troubled as the Church itself, a new one is embraced with rapidity. There is a constant vigilance, even as one movement is at the peak of its influence, to perceive what may be just over the hill, ready to replace it. Such flexibility purchases a certain apparent freedom, although it is ultimately the "freedom" of bondage to culture.

Inevitably a certain kind of "ecumenism" has developed which is a pooling of diminishing resources, a communal search for spiritual transfusions, a brotherly commiseration in doubt and exhaustion. In its beginnings a religion is generally syncretic, appropriating to itself whatever in the older faiths is useful to it or whatever is so deeply rooted in the popular con-sciousness as to be ineradicable. Such early syncretism is the syncretism of strength, in which the new faith tolerates alien elements because it is sure of its ability to absorb and dominate them.

In its final stages a religion tends once again to be syncretic, but for different motives—because it no longer possesses the strength to resist importations, because it badly needs new blood, because its members are so confused about their tradition as to be incapable of distinguishing what in the larger world is or is not compatible with it. It is a condition which does not, however, bring salvation but merely eventual absorption into some rising new historical movement.

The revival of interest in magic, the willed primitivism of sophisticated people, the popularity of the Jesus Movement among formerly "radical" young people, all evidence the decadence of the general culture, in which the Church inevitably partakes. Eclecticism in liturgy and theology witness to the same reality within the institution, and there will probably occur before long a revival of an esthetic Catholicism of the kind spawned earlier by romanticism—a revelling in traditional liturgy and baroque pieties by people who lack the fundamental commitment of faith to undergird these tastes.

The most fundamental division within the Church at present is between those for whom the traditions still do possess vitality, although they may sometimes take newer forms, and those who regard the Catholic past as largely irrelevant and even pernicious. The latter group, who often enough do not see the fullest implications of their own attitudes, have had disproportionate influence, intellectually, in the process of "reform". Consciously or otherwise their goals with respect to the Church are often suicidal. Hope for its future depends now on the recognition that, if Garry Wills is right in postulating that the traditions were dead even when they seemed to be alive, it was not true for everyone, and is not now.

THE INTELLECTUALS AND THE PEOPLE

Events in America in the past decade have often seemed contrived to stand Charles Péguy's famous dictum on its head—everything which has begun in *politique* has ended in *mystique*.

One by one definable social groups—blacks, students, women, Indians, Spanish-Americans, homosexuals—have discovered their oppressed status, analyzed their condition, and formulated programs to improve it. Yet the inevitable law in each case has been a rapid transformation in the movement not, as the media have so often made it appear, from "moderate" to "extremist" leadership but from a leadership which, however angry, is essentially pragmatic and concerned with specific problems and demands to a leadership intoxicated with mystical visions of group identity, ineffable perceptions of selfhood, inchoate anger, and fathomless frustration. The final stage of social protest has in each case been the ritual assertion of a truism—that the oppressed group experiences a sense of selfhood not ultimately accessible to any outsider, no matter how sympathetic, and that the group's liberation involves the bursting of bonds which the oppressor does not even dream exist but which are in some sense more real than the obvious chains. Paradoxically, this last, most extreme stage tends to induce political paralysis, as the "sympathetic" outsider concludes that the world of the oppressed is indeed so foreign that there is nothing to be done, and as the sources of discontent come to seem so profound as to be altogether beyond the reach of political action.

The last group subjected to this kind of subtle betrayal is the white working class, whose indigenous leaders have, mercifully, so far resisted whatever temptations they may have to mythologize their constituents. The work of mystification has, however, gone forward under the benevolent hands of sympathetic intellectuals like Michael Novak, agonizing over the inexpressible, indefinable reality of being Polish or Slavic or Irish and, as spokesmen for so many other groups have already done, making character and individuality a sign of superiority, a taunt flung in the face of outsiders.

The alienation of American intellectuals from the "working class" is apparently so complete that it was probably inevitable that when the working class was finally conceded status it would be misunderstood and miscategorized. White laborers have at last entered the intellectuals' world not, as in the 1930s, as "the workers" but as "white ethnics". The simple truth, however, is that there are many places in the United States where ethnic identity has ceased to mean very much, where inherited national characteristics have been largely bred out, where identification in ethnic terms has all but disappeared. Ethnicity is no doubt a strong reality in other places, and there is no reason it should not be kept alive. But ethnic identity imposed on those who do not feel it is merely another form of patronizing, a manifestation of the sense that white laborers are not very interesting, and cannot be thought to have a mysterious inner core of being, unless through a picturesque foreign inheritance.

The provincialism of the intellectuals has often been noted, but it is nowhere more evident than in the fact that persons and groups are deemed not even to exist unless they can be fitted into currently prevailing schema of political interpretation. In an educated society reality is increasingly defined as that which the principal media of communication—including universities—recognize.

Thus, until recently, so obscured was the white working class by other groups making successful claims upon the intellectuals' attention that it scarcely seemed to exist at all. Recognition of the white working class has been tainted, however, by fear. It is not unfair to say that for many intellectuals the working class, so patently out of step with the future, would probably not have been recognized at all if it had not proved to be a major obstacle to so many plans for social progress. Other groups are accorded sympathetic attention because their demands are deemed to be just, even if they are upper-middle-class students or women; workers are listened to in the hope that somehow the riddle of their pathology can be solved.

That workers, and indeed by extension much of the white middle class as well, are regarded as pathological, as in reality less than fully human, has been charged repeatedly and there have been some liberal expressions of remorse. But the reality of liberal bigotry on this point is so overwhelming, and resolutions to amend it so unconvincing, that it bears repetition. A literary critic can refer casually to "that vast prejudice called New Jersey". A white Catholic social worker writes that

> the black is able to feel both love and hate and be enhanced by them. In contrast, the whites feel only fear; fear their homes will be burned, their women conquered, or their possessions stolen. . . . The black man is within himself, and having achieved that can move to still greater comprehension. In contrast the white man has become estranged from his loathsome self-conception. . . .

A columnist for a liberal newspaper catches the suburban dweller "soaking up some weekend gin alone bacause all the neighbors are glued to the tube". Margaret Mead tells James Baldwin that, unlike the blacks and the Wasps, nineteenth-century immigrants were a disaster for America because they were materialistic and did not share the original dream. For a liberal book-reviewer, however, the Wasp himself is a "snivelling, trivial woman", doubting his manhood, posturing in front of his barroom cronies, laughed at by his children, dimly aware that his life is meaningless. A Yale professor caught in the midst of campus turmoil, deeply sympathetic to the students yet mildly disturbed by the extremists, sights two Italian youths (town-dwellers, not students) baiting the police. Sternly he asks them what they will confess to their priest: obviously they, unlike his students, are imper-vious to reasoned appeal; "superstition" is the only language they com-prehend. As the historian A. J. P. Taylor has said, "no social scientist as-sumes that he himself is moronic, materialist, hysterical. But he assumes it of everyone else."

Relations between the races are poisoned by many things in America, but one of these is the fact that uneducated and inarticulate white people sense, however dimly, that social reformers do view them as pathological and that claims made on behalf of blacks to justify their advancement are implicitly denied with respect to whites. Radical social critics rejected almost unani-mously the Moynihan thesis on black family life, and, since then, to avoid the epithet "racist", one is required to view black ghetto life as intrinsically healthy, with all its viruses the direct result of white racism, and its people remarkably able to survive and even to thrive in an impossible world; even apparent pathologies are really healthy ways of coping with outside aggres-sion. In sum, the radical-liberal view of lower-class black people amounts to a full acceptance of the mystique of race.

By contrast, radicals who undertake to study the white working class (Robert Coles is an exception) invariably discover a situation in which the workers are not only victims of the system (in this resembling blacks) but are too complacent and insensitive even to understand their victimization; they invariably misdiagnose their own problems, and finally succumb to illusory and self-destructive fantasies. Thus Richard Sennett and Jonathan Cobb find, predictably, that white laborers in Boston are simultaneously fascinated and repelled by lower-class blacks and hippie students—they loathe them for re-jecting middle-class values but also envy them their freedom and hedonistic self-indulgence. Parents sacrificing for their children's future are accused by these social-scientist observers of "the ultimate perversion of love: it permits you to practice that most insidious and devastating form of self-righteousness in which you, oppressed, in your anger turn on others who are also op-pressed. . . ." Parents, in this view, use love and sacrifice essentially as means of controlling and manipulating their children.

A related myth of leftist intellectuals is that behind the seeming respec-tability of ordinary American family life unfathomable horrors are concealed. Following the Manson Family murders, an aide to a United States Senator (Frank Church) could write:

> The Manson affair was piously condemned by pill-popping Americans who con-demned Manson (not present at the killings) and then turned about and praised

Calley. . . . Americans chose not to acknowledge that the California murders
were committed by the girls next door under the direction of the high-school
valedictorian. Despite the erotic embellishments, these murders simply represented another outbreak of apple-pie American violence.

(Manson is in fact the son of a prostitute and spent his entire childhood and
youth moving from one temporary home to another.) Considerable artistic
energy has been expended portraying the essential emptiness and malice of
conventional life in America, but an unperceived irony is that the enlightened
social critics have not been appreciably more successful in holding their marriages together, bringing up their children, avoiding suicide, staying off
drugs and alcohol, or building loving communities of persons.

It bears repeating that in terms of hard reality whites, even of the working
class, enjoy rights and privileges which most blacks do not and that this situation is not likely to change substantially in the near future. The discontent of
lower-class whites is fanned, however, by what they perceive, often correctly, the intentions of social reformers to be. The radical reformer sees
blacks as perfectly capable of defining their own needs, if only white society
will permit it, while the majority of whites are not conceded the same competence. Not only must whites be held in check lest their greed and racism
further impede the black struggle for justice, but whites are not even capable
of perceiving their own self-interest correctly. Young college-educated
radicals thus enter the factories as covert missionaries, since white workers,
unlike black, have not been able to produce decent leaders.

Massive resistance to programs of social reform is often galvanized by the
awareness that, if whites presently have more privileges than blacks, it is the
goal of many reformers to reverse this situation; not only do the resisters fear
that jobs will be taken from whites and given to blacks but, more subtly, that
blacks will be conceded political rights which whites will be denied. Blacks in
Harlem are to have the right to veto construction of a state office building or
a university gymnasium, but whites in Forest Hills are not to be allowed to
veto public housing. Black school boards can exclude white teachers from
their district in Brooklyn and openly promote a "black pride" which comes
close to being antiwhite, but white school boards will be forbidden to do the
reverse elsewhere. A white advocate of compulsory school busing charac-
terizes opposition by the National Black Political Convention as "thoughtful",
while dismissing white opposition as reactionary and racist. Edgar Z. Frie-
denberg says black hostility to whites who enter the ghetto is an expression
of a healthy sense of community, but it is the kind of expression which, if
manifested by whites in Cicero or Rosedale, is labeled immoral.

That racism exists on all levels of American society is undeniable. But the
free employment of the term, either as a rhetorical weapon or as a category of

analysis, merely points up the anomaly of the situation. Few people will admit to being racists; most do not think of themselves as such. To accuse someone of racism is to claim, in effect, to know him better than he knows himself. When the evidence of words and actions is substantial, it is a judgment which can be legitimately ventured. But racist motives are now commonly postulated as covert, implying the ability of the outside observer to penetrate the inner reality of masses of people with whom he has had no significant contact. (A liberal lawyer in San Francisco can apply the term, for example, to a nameless truck driver in Michigan.) The rhetoric of oppressed groups is always accepted at face value; their grievances are what they perceive them to be, their motives exactly what they claim. The white masses, however, are always believed to have hidden intentions which need to be ferreted out by perceptive intellectual observers. Claims to oppose busing out of love for the neighborhood school, or opposition to subsidized housing out of fear of crime, are immediately dismissed as subterfuges and rationalizations. Once the key to white behavior has been discovered, it can be made to explain every phenomenon. Thus the New Yorker's City Hall reporter, Andy Logan, explains that white citizens who object to public housing of a general character in their neighborhoods will accept subsidized housing for the elderly because most elderly people are white. (Blacks have short life spans, and those who survive to old age are cared for by their loving children, who are so unlike callous white children.) The fact that elderly people, black or white, commit few crimes is implicitly deemed irrelevant. Miss Logan also explains that white firemen who seek transfers out of the black ghetto are not worried about the greater hazards there, as they claim, but prefer working in more prosperous neighborhoods where they are close to their moonlighting jobs and there are more opportunities for minor graft.

The logical implication of this pervasively negative view of the American masses is that democracy, understood as anything approaching majority rule or self-government, is increasingly dubious, since "the people" lack both the virtue and the wisdom to exercise power. The busing issue, aside from the practical problems involved, is of immense symbolic significance because it presents the clearest example of a plan for social reform, conceived and implemented by an intellectual elite, imposed on ordinary people against their customs, beliefs, and instincts. (In the minds of many people, the point of the Supreme Court's 1954 school decision was that any student should have the right to attend the school most convenient to his home and could not be excluded; the busing plan seems to reverse this.) The social-engineering mentality, with its inherent contempt for popular wisdom, continues to permeate the Left. Richard Sennett proposes that the federal government force people to live in disorderly, heterogeneous neighborhoods instead of the placid, homogeneous communities they usually choose. In St. Louis an advocate of rapid transit argues that it will force people to deal with each other face to face, overcoming the voluntary atomization produced by the automobile. In 1970 a candidate for Congress from Vermont, Dennis Morriseau, proclaimed that deep down many Americans wish to kill anyone who is free—black militants and radical young people. (Such beliefs did not win Morriseau the election.) He wished to ban political commercials from television because they appeal only to voters' hates and fears and also to bar all political polls because "it's nonsense to find out what the voters' opinions are on any given issue, because they're bound to be uninformed in a closed system." At the same time it was Morriseau's stated intention to "show the people that they count, that their votes count. . . ."

Popular resistance to social engineering is in part a reaction to "radical chic", which, although there has been some ritual atonement for it in the liberal-radical community, remains a major problem. The offensiveness of what Joseph W. Bishop, Jr., has called "Social Register socialism" is intensified, and rendered more than symbolic, by the awareness that lower-middle-class and working-class whites are often asked to achieve things which their presumed betters—those who are enlightened, educated, aware, articulate, and socially secure—have not themselves managed to achieve. The cutting edge of school and housing integration is usually at the lower end of the social pyramid; self-conscious liberals can integrate with black professors and bureaucrats. Few radical young people choose to attend black colleges; and on sophisticated, racially mixed campuses white and black students generally maintain separate living quarters, separate political organizations, and at best an uneasy coexistence in social relationships. Students looking for off-campus housing tend to avoid high-crime areas as determinedly as blue-collar workers do.

Few intellectuals are any longer so disingenuous as to regard fear of crime as a manifestation of white paranoia (as Philip Slater suggested in *The Pursuit of Loneliness*, for example), but it is a subject which the Left is still unable to face because it tends to break apart neatly constructed, political categories. Liberals soothingly assure frightened whites that blacks are the most common victims of crime and, by implication, that whites have nothing extraordinary to fear. Eldridge Cleaver, however, insists that black crime is racially motivated and that most black aggressors would prefer to assault white victims if they could find them. The difficulty of racial integration on the neighborhood level, generally unacknowledged on the Left, is that a handful of determined separatists can effectively sabotage the good intentions of a majority of blacks and whites. In "changing neighborhoods" militant white racists, if they perceive the changes as irreversible, are likely to move, while militant black racists tend to stay and thereby acquire increasing importance.

The ambivalence at the heart of the crime problem—whether or not crime by blacks against whites should be seen as racially motivated—is one manifestation of a larger uncertainty which is reflected in the vague sense many whites have that they are being manipulated by social reformers through the alternation of carrot and stick, moral suasion and naked threat. Barely implicit in a certain kind of radical social analysis is the exhortation, "You have a moral duty to welcome blacks as your brothers and accord them full acceptance. But, no matter how strenuously you seek to convert yourself, you will remain at heart a racist and at heart blacks will continue to hate you."

Racial justice has been advocated as a moral imperative, demanded by religion and the American tradition, and simultaneously postulated as the irresistible outcome of a revolution which will probably be violent. The language of duty alternates with the language of threat and produces confusion, resentment, and resistance. Similar tactics have been used to legitimize the "youth revolt", as sympathetic commentators like J. Anthony Lukas oscillate between assuring parents that their rebellious offspring are in fact essentially traditionalists, merely putting into practice the values learned at home and school, and predicting an emergent world which is totally new and radically different from any society of the past, which parents cannot possibly comprehend and which they can only live in successfully by consenting to learn from the young (Margaret Mead's suggestion). The fearful and bewildered are thus alternately lulled into security and stampeded into panicky action depending on which tactic seems most appropriate at the moment. They can then either be ridiculed for their hysteria or excoriated for their complacency.

Indeed, the confrontation between radical reformers and an increasingly resentful and resistant white working class tends to coalesce around the issue of "radical youth" even more than around race. The youth culture of the 1960s was profoundly hostile to working-class culture, a fact which blue-collar fathers sensed quite early, even before it was made plain by interpreters like Charles Reich or the motion picture *Joe*. Long hair and mod clothes are now commonplace, but originally they were intended to say something, and for the most part white laborers (and the bourgeoisie) interpreted the message correctly. The counter-culture openly flaunted what workers did not possess—leisure, mobility, the absence of financial or familial responsibilities, youth, nimbleness of mind, an apparently untrammeled hedonism. To that extent the thesis that workers resent the "freedom" of the radical young is probably correct, although it is the understandable resentment of those who see other people's privileges paraded before them and feel themselves despised because they lack these same privileges. Laboring men also sensed that the most significant thing dividing them from the young radicals was their own inability to articulate adequately, which left the young always victorious in any encounter, which doomed in advance all efforts to legitimize their lower-middle-class world. The youth of the 60s were not bookish; they prided themselves instead on the quality of their experiences, continually opening up new worlds. Yet many within the working class—policemen and firemen, nurses—regularly have experiences of "life" far more varied and elemental than those of most young people. Implicitly, however, these experiences have been devalued, and mobile young people alone have been thought to have an adequate sense of human realities. The counter-culture has continually "discovered" areas of reality—poverty, injustice, factory workers, the aged, frauds perpetrated on consumers—which ordinary people have been aware of all their lives.

On all these matters, working-class and middle-class fathers, not without reason, often see themselves in competition for the loyalties of their children with the media, teachers, and other young people. (A white community organizer says, "Let the fathers be as reactionary as they want; we'll get their kids.") Kenneth Keniston has pointed to the radicalization of college students as a sign of the effectiveness of education in the 60s, and numerous professional educators now appear to accept a similar criterion for measuring their work. The explicit purpose of some teachers has become that of weaning students away from opinions and values learned at home, of introducing them to a cultural world which will be not only unfamiliar to the parents but hostile and threatening to them as well.

Calls for programs in ethnic studies or "white working-class culture" in the colleges have an unconvincing ring, mainly because there is little evidence of any student (or parent) demand for them. Nonetheless, the call effectively unmasks a central hypocrisy of radical educators—they permit themselves the luxury of "imposing" an alien cultural or political viewpoint on "conservative" students, a practice they deem impermissible with respect to black or radical white students. Genuine respect for the milieu from which working-class students emerge would require a sympathetic probing of attitudes which are now generally dismissed through the caricature of Archie Bunker; it would require the radical teacher to learn to respect petty-bourgeois ambition, the desire for material security, instinctive moderation in politics, and a strong preference for an orderly and stable society.

Instead the counter-culture has half-deliberately served to preserve the cultural distance between the upper-middle class and those below it at a time when the gap was perhaps being narrowed. As workers' children started winning National Merit scholarships and going off to Ivy League colleges, the children of the affluent announced their boredom with the "whole academic rat race" and it suddenly was fashionable to be a college dropout. As workers prided themselves on being able to buy their children decent clothes, teach them good manners, and train them up in a respectable morality, they found the tables had been stunningly turned on them by the children of privilege, who began wearing denim and dirty sweatshirts, cultivating a deliberate rudeness, using drugs, and flaunting the institution of marriage. Proud that their sons were at last about to fulfill the American Dream, through the medium of college degrees and corporate jobs, the workers discovered that the Dream was now despised. Those who had already enjoyed its benefits had contrived to cast a pall over the enjoyment of those who came later. In a daring move, the children of the privileged managed to appropriate to themselves all the "privileges" formerly reserved for the lowest classes—carelessness about dress and speech, idleness, rejection of all imposed discipline, drugs, an irregular sex life, anarchic unconcern for established institutions.

Many traditional liberal assumptions about the effects of formal education have been badly shaken by recent American history. Such education does indeed turn students' political loyalties leftward, although the degree to which this is due to outright indoctrination remains unexamined; it does indeed foster a critical spirit toward inherited beliefs and conventional social arrangements. But that it develops real intellectual autonomy, the ability to discriminate between the true and the false, the substantial and the chimerical, is now gravely in doubt. In the decade just ended intellectuals in America have been the most susceptible to fads and absurdities, the most easily manipulable by visionary fanatics and outright charlatans, of any social class. Whatever the values of formal education, they do not include inoculation against fashionable foolishness.

Events in America in the past decade have served also to stand traditional conservative social thought on its head. The masses, as it turns out, are not, as so many elitist commentators have warned, fickle and inordinately susceptible to fads and demagoguery. They are instead the last bulwarks of tradition and stability in a society whose educated classes prove to be increasingly in love with change for change's sake and with limitless disorder. As the 1972 presidential election indicated, the simple desire for an orderly and relatively stable society takes precedence over almost every other consideration in the minds of the white majority, even with many of those who might have something tangible to gain from radically altered economic arrangements.

Unexpectedly, these realizations provide an awareness also of the unique role which the uneducated masses play in a democracy, in their untutored state and not merely as candidates for enlightenment. Quite simply, it is the task of the people to act as skeptics relative to the dreams of the intelligentsia, even as the intellectuals have sought to be critics of popular mythology. Nearly drowning the thoughtful and hopeful programs of reform of the past decade were innumerable ideas and plans which were simply absurd and even sinister. Changes have been urged, and partially implemented, which have proved disastrous to local communities, schools and universities, political and religious groups; often the proponents of such changes have learned from their failures only that they ought to have been more "radical". In an intellectual atmosphere often fevered, apocalyptic, and willfully credulous and uncritical, changes which might have been disastrous on a major scale were prevented from occurring primarily because of the inarticulate skepticism, the inert resistance, of the common people. If intellectuals have usually remained cool in the midst of popular hysteria, in recent years it has often been the general populace which preserved its sanity in the face of the peculiar hysteria of the highly educated.

Social disorder has been linked to obvious and concrete injustices and some rebellions spring from a justified sense of deprivation. But the recent history of countries like Sweden and the Netherlands which, compared with the United States, scarcely have social problems, suggests that a reasonably just society is by no means a guarantee that restless iconoclasm will not develop; it suggests that such iconoclasm may be endemic to the bored modern intelligentsia, searching for a social role.

The nation does not need a revival of populist mythology; the Wallace phenomenon leaves no room for benign complacency and the implicit dangers of unbridled majoritarianism are real enough, along with the potential for mass anti-intellectualism. The election of John F. Kennedy, a President who associated with intellectuals and cultivated a scholarly image, began a sharp reversal in the attitude of American society toward the things of the mind. The years immediately following saw financial and moral support for education increase dramatically. Universities and professors enjoyed an importance and a prestige unprecedented in American history. The resources of the intellectual community were systematically brought to bear on almost all aspects of national policy. Innumerable popular taboos were broken with the approval of a growing constituency of sophisticated, iconoclastic, self-confident, yet self-probing citizens. The bursting of that bubble at the end of the 1960s had a number of causes, prominent among which was a widespread feeling that the intelligentsia had become too prominent and influential, to an extent in politics and to a much greater extent in setting the tone and direction of American culture. The New Left had taught the citizenry to see themselves as passive victims of the Establishment; this mentality enabled them to recognize that they were being manipulated by the intellectual Establishment as well.

The ultimate danger of unchecked populism may indeed be fascism, and the quiescent reaction of the coming decade may simply insure another era of orgiastic experimentation sometime in the future. But the intellectual community has, for the most part, still not faced many of the lessons of the decade just past — the susceptibility of so many in that community to every kind of absurdity which is labeled radical, the bewilderment and acquiescence in the face of nakedly coercive acts and totalitarian ideologies, the readiness to jettison scholarly and intellectual activities in the service of dubious causes. A weary apocalypticism pervades some segments of the enlightened community, as in Gore Vidal's remark that the end of the human race would be preferable to present existence. There is new and unabashed admiration for totalitarian states like China, which stimulates inevitable speculation as to how far leftist intellectuals might go in welcoming similar social arrangements in America.

Anything like a healthy progressivism in American politics will depend in the future on maintaining the delicate balance between the bias toward change inherent in the intellectual community and a noticeable segment of the upper-middle class, and the often sullen skepticism and love of stability inherent in the mass of the white population. A viable democracy cannot dispense with either component — the free play of imagination and the restless dissatisfaction with existing social arrangements bred in people who enjoy leisure and a minimum social and economic security and who, often enough, are not required to test their ideas in the real world; and the sense of limited possibility, the desire to conserve hard-won gains, the inevitable narrowness of those whose lives and work are circumscribed by hard physical realities. In the end the most important lesson of the last ten years may be that if there is no necessary virtue in the untutored sons of toil, there is also no necessary higher truth in the moral and political beliefs of those who mistake articulateness for wisdom.

THE CHURCH AND THE SEXUAL REVOLUTION

Emphasis on sexual purity has always been, in a sense, a confession of failure on the part of Catholic educators: finding it difficult to imbue their students with real piety, they had to settle instead for a morality. It was a morality that secular American culture also honored in theory, and hence it did not seriously estrange the young Catholic from his society. He was distinguished, and heroic, for behaving in the way that other Americans secretly thought that they should behave in too.

The drying up of the residue of secular Puritanism in America has at last made the Church's sexual morality seem peculiar and unnatural. In the face of this, some reformers have decided on a bold strategy — that of denying any necessary connection between Catholicism and sexual restraint. The denial can be legitimized in a variety of ways — by repudiating the extreme antisexuality of the past, by pointing out that sexual morality is only one part of a complex moral structure in which social justice ought to be paramount, by contending that Catholicism has always been a religion of the senses and Puritanism an alien graft, or by affirming the importance of belief over practice (a traditionalist attitude and one taken by Catholic novelists like Graham Greene, François Mauriac, and Walker Percy.)

The flaw in these strategies (that they are strategies does not preclude their being also sincerely held) is their attempt to wish away history — the massive, even crushing, weight of the entire Christian tradition, in which until very recently legitimate sex has always been held within rigorous boundaries. Attempts to reinterpret this tradition are necessarily feeble — recalling St. Paul's strictures against law, for example, while ignoring his explicit comments about sexual behavior, or noting Jesus' mercy toward the adulterous woman and passing over his command to her to sin no more.

Phillip Rieff, in his crucially important book *The Triumph of the Therapeutic*, argues that sexual restrictiveness has been central and essential to Christianity and that recent attempts by Christian moralists to revise radically this connection are proof of Christianity's imminent demise, since its own leaders are no longer able to affirm its truths. (A series of trenchant remarks reveals Rieff's attitude. He refers at one point to ". . . [those] enlightened Christians, who have a genius for accepting almost any position, so to say, that is grossly anti-Christian or simply vulgar, especially in sex and art". And elsewhere in his analysis he observes: "Nor does the present ferment in the Roman Catholic Church seem so much like a renewal of spiritual perception as a move towards more sophisticated accommodations with the negative communities of the therapeutics." And again: ". . . all attempts at connecting the doctrines of psychotherapy with the old faiths are patently misconceived. At its most innocuous, these psychotherapeutic religiosities represent a failure of nerve by both psychotherapists and clergymen.")

In analyzing the Christian emphasis on sexual purity, Rieff cites Adolph Harnack's remark that it was valued because "he who had renounced these found nothing hard." It was a form of self-mastery that was to precede all spiritual growth, although undeniably a certain contempt for the flesh also came to pervade the Church. Citing Max Scheler, Rieff also notes that, at its best, Christian asceticism was positive, "aimed fundamentally at a liberation of the highest powers of personality from blockage by the automatism of the lower drives". What traditional ascetic teachers called "spiritualization" obviously bore some relation to what modern psychiatrists call "sublimation", although the exact relationship seems to be little understood.

Asceticism has always been in most religions a precondition for access to the mysteries. The traditional Church was not antiflesh but rather held, in an extreme way, that there was no legitimate mode of sensual expression except in the service of God. Here there were no limits, as evidenced in baroque religious art and the writings of the mystics.

A flourishing transcendental spirituality obviously does not require all members of the religious community to practice heroic self-denial. The individual whose flesh is weak but whose faith is strong is familiar in Catholic life and legend, and a deep spirituality can exist among normally and happily married persons. But the creative center of this spirituality has resided with those who have chosen the path of renunciation. The Orthodox churches permit a married parochial clergy, but the heart of their religious life is in the monasteries. In the Asian religions the most esteemed holy men are almost always celibates. A curious and perhaps related phenomenon is the fact that some of the greatest Western metaphysicians—Plato, the scholastics, Descartes, Hobbes, Locke, Leibniz, Spinoza, Kant—were unmarried.

The celibacy issue within the Roman Church is therefore a crisis much broader and more profound than is generally recognized, because celibacy is a symbol of the first importance to the whole Church and because what is involved is not solely the personal happiness or personal rights of individual priests. The Church could easily concede the right of marriage to priests involved in active ministries, while retaining the celibate discipline in cloistered and semicloistered orders. The abrogation of the present celibacy law, however, is being demanded by many priests precisely because they believe thay cannot lead "fulfilled" lives as celibates. To accede to their demands at this time would tend to reinforce the prevailing cultural notion that personal fulfillment is impossible without an active sex life. It would also obscure even further the traditional association between asceticism and transcendental spirituality. If activist priests alone were restive under celibate discipline there would be less cause for concern. The fact that Trappists have also not been immune to the scent of orange blossoms suggests that what are being repudiated are the most fundamental Catholic assumptions concerning the spiritual life.

Attempts to defend celibacy on the grounds that it frees the priest for a more involved and untrammeled kind of ministry indicate the depth of the problem, since celibacy has value, if at all, not as a practical convenience but as something meaningful in itself. Loss of belief in the celibate vocation is intimately related, for many priests, to a loss of confidence in their ability to witness to a transcendental spirituality and their consequent determination to immerse themselves as deeply as possible in the world. It seems probable that over the centuries the most creative energies of Catholic spirituality have been generated in great measure by the mysterious process through which sexual drives are "sublimated", and such energies are being increasingly diminished. Those who have voluntarily chosen the path of renunciation for religious reasons are a miniscule portion of the American population, a tiny prophetic minority. Those, however, raised in a "hard" culture of discipline, sacrifice and dedication always prove in the long run highly vulnerable to a "soft" culture of eroticism, freedom, and self-fulfillment. It is the former kind of culture, fostered both by the churches and by secular American society until quite recently, that is now under attack in the "sexual revolution". The apparent breakdown of many religious communities has come about in part because, after generations of insulation from threatening external pressures, they were suddenly exposed to cultural influences with which their members had little ability to cope.

The same scenario is also being played out in the larger society in that the sexual revolution is merely the most visible part of a general revolt against classical discipline and restraint. Such restraint, in whatever context, is only justifiable and supportable for the sake of some larger purpose. When the purpose itself comes to be doubted, the discipline begins to seem merely repressive and cruel. The acceptance within contemporary Christianity of a freer sexual ethic is critically related, in a relationship of both cause and effect, to the apparent decline in concern for transcendental religion, since the frank worldliness of the new sensuality discourages interest in transcendence and the decline of traditional belief also makes ascetic sacrifices seem merely repressive and unnatural. Since Vatican II the Catholic community has breathed a collective sigh of relief at the relaxation of all the old restraints, and for many people the chief lesson of renewal has been that striving is no longer necessary. Rieff predicts the emergence of a culture of contentment in which self-mastery and internalized moral demands are no longer thought desirable. He quotes Albert Camus to the effect that sex is given to man "perhaps, to turn him aside from his true path. . . . Chastity alone is connected with personal progress."

The Catholic Church has a crucial role to play in the present cultural crisis precisely because it has been the principal institution witnessing to the transcendent value of restraint, even to the point of asceticism. As the Church ceases to be an effective voice in this regard, the apostles of an easy hedonism will come proportionately closer to winning victory by default.

The fundamental question posed by the sexual revolution is whether there is such a thing as lust and whether it is morally wrong. One answer is frankly amoral—sex is fun and only a neurotic worries about right and wrong. Another is in intention profoundly moral—all immorality is the absence of love, and sexual acts are wrong insofar as they harm others. In the latter view the only intrinsically evil sexual act would seem to be forcible rape, though even that could be justified according to the older male chauvinist view that women who are raped really enjoy it. (Women's Liberationists have not given Catholic sexual morality credit for the fact that, whatever else might be said about it, it did discourage regarding women as sex objects, and it did not justify the double standard.)

Christianity has always taught that there is a specific sin called lust, which is not simply a lack of love for others. It has always taken sex with extreme seriousness, regarding it as one of the most powerful and dominating of human drives, hence as potentially obsessive, the most dangerous of idolatries. Ironically, the sexual revolution can be defended by arguing that the sex drive is less powerful than it once was, and there is some evidence for this. But it is also evident that in some of its manifestations, e.g., D. H. Lawrence or the "playboy philosophy", this revolution precisely aspires to promote erotic idolatry. Christian teaching about sex depends in part on the belief that it is possible to commit sins against God that are not directly sins against one's neighbor, and idolatry is the chief of these.

The sexual revolution has also become linked with clinical efforts to promote health and happiness—the therapeutic which Rieff calls "a manipulable sense of well-being" that is "the age's master science". At its most "civilized", the new eroticism insists that sex is merely a matter of hygiene, to be ordered in the same way as any other appetite. The Christian view, however, perceives it as possessing a sacred character, hence as sacramental when ordered properly, demonic when not. Insofar as it avoids erotic idolatry, the new sexuality has no room for either sacraments or demons. A United Church of Christ minister says of it, approvingly: "It's just like buying a pair of shoes. You keep trying till you find what fits you."

There is a good deal of wishfulness in the eagerness with which enlightened Christians have responded to the new eroticism. Since there is so little reliable information about sexual behavior, it is not difficult for a theologian like

Herbert Richardson to speculate that sex is becoming "spiritualized" to the point where people increasingly tend to experience sexual desire only for those they love. Yet like so much else, the sexual revolution has unfolded with remarkable speed in the past decade.

In the 1950s, a few daring theologians suggested that in rare and exotic instances departures from strict purity might be justified. (Deborah Kerr in *Tea and Sympathy* gave herself to a schoolboy to help overcome his neurotic doubts about his masculinity.) A few years later the necessity of a formal marriage bond came to be questioned, so long as two persons were truly committed to each other for life. Then sex was justified between persons currently in love, even if a permanent commitment was uncertain. Now sexual emancipation means precisely the right to engage in casual sex, and an ethic that seeks to link sex with love is coming to be seen as an anachronism not greatly different from the ethic of chastity. (As an indication of the cutting edge of the sexual revolution in Catholicism, a parish priest in France has claimed the right to have a mistress, and a nuns' college in the same country has granted student lovers permission to live together.)

The older Christian ethic was more realistic than the newer precisely in recognizing the impossibility of expecting sex and love to be firmly linked. Individuals bent on self-emancipation are likely to be egocentric and obsessed, hence unlikely to be particularly sensitive to the needs of others. Albert Ellis, a popular champion of sexual liberation, justifies boys fraudulently professing love for girls they wish to take to bed on the grounds that the love-sex syndrome is a neurotic hangup and the girl is "too vulnerable" to be told the truth.

One of the mysterious qualities of sex is that, when freely engaged in, it requires the continuous search for new kinds of experience, which among other things insures that there can be no easy compromise between the new freedom and the old rigor. (The phlegmatic Dutch reportedly tolerate a tutor in the sado-masochistic arts operating openly in the middle of Amsterdam.) Irving Howe has characterized the mental atmosphere of the 1960s as "a psychology of unrestricted need", and it is endemic to such an attitude that once the individual determines to throw off all the "repressions" that afflict him it is difficult to distinguish any longer between "good" and "bad" restrictions. Indeed, as restrictions of all kinds are loosened by society, those whose principal compulsion is "the systematic hunting down of all settled convictions" (Rieff's phrase) must seek for more and more sacred taboos to violate. Behind some of the rebelliousness of the past decade there has been a bitter and fanatic need for self-justification, the refusal to accept judgment or limitation from any outside source.

The sexual revolution was promoted in the later 1960s by the myth that it was connected with pacifism and the new gentleness—"make love, not war."

But wars have always had a loosening effect on sexual behavior, partly because they are emergencies during which normal rules are suspended and partly because they unleash repressed passions. Once the focus of erotic liberation shifts from the expression of love to the search for adventure, the connection between sex and gentleness is irretrievably broken.

Most people who seek sexual liberation are hardly likely to turn to brutality for further thrills. But in a society in which men are encouraged — both by "conservative" corporations, through advertising, and by "liberal" advocates of cultural revolution — to expect every kind of sensual enjoyment and to overcome all their inhibitions systematically, there will be other kinds of moral iconoclasm beside the sexual.

Rock music was perhaps the principal catalyst of erotic freedom in the past decade, and major and minor kinds of violence are now a regular feature of concerts. A rock-group leader named Alice Cooper (male) has been known to execute a chicken on stage and dismember a doll with a hatchet to the wild cheers of his fans, and he concludes his performance with a reportedly realistic hanging of himself. Eroticism and violence were deeply connected in the Manson Family adventures, and in the "moors murders" in England a few years ago, which raised important questions about the social effects of pornography. Pauline Kael has called attention to recent movies, become increasingly "frank" in the last decade, that "suck up to the thugs in the audience".

This indiscriminate iconoclasm is intensified by the fact that the sexual revolution tends to encourage a kind of moral solipsism, a deliberate disregard of the possible social consequences of one's acts, and the corresponding encouragement of an ethic of unlimited self-gratification. Mary Breasted, a spokesman for the new freedom, criticizes certain sex-education manuals because they are "too prudish". "They keep stressing responsible behavior," she adds, "saying you don't get VD if you don't meet the wrong contacts and things like that." Ms. Breasted is also critical of manuals which warn young people against experiencing sex prematurely. Indeed, it is characteristic of the sexual liberationists to be concerned only with the "tyrannies" imposed by family, church, or school and not with the "tyrannies" imposed by fashion or peer group.

Quite evidently many young people find themselves in situations with which they cannot cope and which a different cultural climate would spare them. (The District of Columbia requires public-health officials to give contraceptives to persons regardless of age.) Campus physicians at Princeton and Stanford report that impotence is one of the most frequent complaints of male students, which suggests not a "liberated" atmosphere but rather continuing pressures to "perform". Albert Ellis believes that all healthy persons should engage in premarital sex, generally the more the better. One cause of the breakup of marriages now seems to be precisely the fact that the sexual revolution and the omnipresence of sexual stimuli teach people to have sexual expectations that no union can possibly fulfill. One of Christianity's important roles should be to help de-eroticize the culture.

It is by now clear that there is no such thing as strictly "private morality", if by that is meant personal behavior that has no effect on the general society. All moral behavior contributes to the creation of a moral climate (the prevalence or nonprevalence of drug use, adultery, public pornographic displays that have especially powerful influence on the young, the bored, the insecure, and the unhappy). In the "retribalized" society of Marshall McLuhan, the mass media cause new customs to permeate the entire culture with great rapidity. Only the most extreme social atomism can truly conceive of private morality.

Private behavior has more tangible social effects as well. Only a few years ago sophisticated moralists could explain that the taboo against fornication was no longer valid because modern technology had obviated its greatest dangers—venereal disease and pregnancy. Now venereal disease is officially out of control and the demand for abortions suggests that there are more unwanted pregnancies than before. (Those who disapprove of abortion can hardly be indifferent to the new sexual freedom.)

Among "liberated" adults the belief seems to be spreading that mature, free people can, and perhaps ought to, engage in what were formerly called infidelities and that healthy individuals will feel neither guilt nor resentment. Yet for many persons this apparently adds an additional layer of guilt—at not being sufficiently "free" not to feel guilty. Meanwhile the new permissiveness, besides affecting the general moral climate, has measurable social effects in terms of divorces, emotional disturbances, and troubled children—all of which are concealed behind the rhetoric of "private morality".

Pitrim Sorokin suggested that free sexual behavior has historically been a sign of a civilization in decline, though it is probably as much a result of the decline as a cause. There have been few societies in the history of the world which have not maintained, through law, official moral attitudes. Proponents of the new freedom do not acknowledge that a society which is officially agnostic about "private morality" is an experiment whose outcome can by no means be assumed as benign. Although far from ideal, the least unsatisfactory strategy might be the maintenance of rather strict laws governing personal morality, which are somewhat laxly enforced—a situation allowing for a measure of personal freedom but also for the control of dangerously pathological behavior.

As a morality, "situation ethics" presents some of the same problems. Most people presently alive were educated according to moral codes that were absolute, or nearly so, and it may be precisely this early foundation which provides them with the certitude and security that permits responsible and prudent behavior while the old code is being discarded and new values are sought. Once the absolute is lost, as at least a point of reference, ethical experimentation may degenerate into total moral confusion. This has happened often in the lives of individuals; it may happen also in the life of a society.

The situationists, particularly Joseph Fletcher, pay little attention to the relationship between morality and society, as evidenced by Professor Fletcher's contempt for law. His assertion that ultimately nothing can hold a society together except love is contrary to most empirical evidence. Societies have generally been held together by their members' willingness to respect each other's legally defined rights, an attitude essentially based on enlightened self-interest. When well formed, laws protect men from the state and from each other, and in this sense justice takes precedence over charity. Laws also embody a good deal of accumulated social experience, and people often appeal to the letter of the law to justify moral intuitions that they are not sophisticated enough to defend philosophically.

In terms of its social usefulness, if not its philosophical clarity or candor, the best system of morality may after all be casuistry—the system whereby absolutes are affirmed in rigorous fashion, yet a wide range of exceptions is permitted. One difficulty with a morality which simply urges responsible personal decision is that many people are genuinely confused and want firmer guidance. They wish to be guided by a social ethic and not merely by what are their own fragmented perceptions.

There is a remarkable tendency for what is permitted to become required (e.g., premarital sex), for what is minimally allowable to become what is maximally expectable (e.g., easy divorce leading to fragile marriages predicated on the expectation of failure), for each person to interpret his own case in the sense most favorable to himself (as is quite clearly done in economic morality). Whatever the situationist may intend, the exhortation to make a free, personal decision will usually be interpreted as a covert granting of permission.

Precisely because fashion is such a powerful force in molding moral attitudes, a relativistic morality tends to become a morality of the least common denominator. As people notice their neighbors living unrestrainedly, they feel less inclined to hold themselves to any strict rule—not merely with regard to sex but in other kinds of morality as well. Although weakened, the churches are clearly the only significant agencies in society capable of counteracting this tendency. The long-term alternative to traditional teaching, whether intended or not, is bound to be an unreflecting hedonism.

HERE LIES COMMUNITY: R.I.P.

The "crisis of authority" that dominated Catholic life after the Council is by now revealed as something far deeper: a crisis of faith. Catholics—both religious and lay—who question and reject the pronouncements of the hierarchy are most often repudiating not simply dictation imposed on them externally but the content of the dictates as well. Practical dictates touching on birth control or celibacy naturally arouse greater passion and more obvious rebellion, but in quieter ways these negations extend to the most fundamental teachings of the Church. The crisis of authority is really a result of the crisis of faith rather than its cause.

Those who candidly acknowledge this faith crisis (many do not) usually explain that traditional teachings have simply become incredible to modern man: the historic creeds were formulated in premodern societies and naturally embody an outmoded and discredited world view. The survival of Christianity therefore depends in large measure on an adequate intellectual reformulation of the gospel message, one that will inevitably be radically different from traditional teaching.

This analysis is not wholly wrong, but it necessarily ignores certain important facts. In the first place it fails to inquire why traditional beliefs should be more incredible, or the Church more irrelevant, in 1970 than in 1960. Certainly the outlook of modern man has not changed so drastically in a decade nor was the general tone of secular culture more hospitable to religious belief twenty years ago. Then, however, the Church flourished and crises of faith, relatively rare and individual, had few public reverberations.

Insofar as the general culture has changed in the decade past, it has in fact become potentially more open to traditional religion. This fact is beginning to be recognized by some radical Christians, who were prepared in the Kennedy years to embrace rational, pragmatic secularity—only to discover that avant-garde young people were beginning to revile it. The youth culture now routinely describes itself as religious, rejects out of hand the ironic skepticism that has been modern man's chief weapon against Christianity, and adopts the whole panoply of myth, ritual, and vestment that progressive Catholics struggled so hard to discard. Former secularizers like Harvey Cox now urge a celebration of fantasy and an affirmation of what is "unfeasible", thus directly opening the way (although Professor Cox does not seem to recognize this fact) to a restoration of "absurd" and "incredible" beliefs of the Church like the Resurrection and the Real Presence.

The crisis of faith cannot be explained, therefore, as a result of the pressure of the times, and to attempt to do so is in a way an avoidance of personal

278

responsibility, an attempt to ignore what is happening in one's own soul in order to place blame (or credit) on an impersonal *Zeitgeist*.

Progressive Catholics are generally subject to the fallacy of explicitness—the belief that meaning in a given context can always be recognized overtly and articulated clearly; that inability to thus articulate denotes absence of meaning; and that failures of meaning can be isolated and dealt with directly.

The experience of both state and church in the 1960s reveals the fallaciousness of these assumptions. Americans, and Catholics, were far more sure ten years ago what was wrong with their country or their church and how the wrongs could be remedied. Consequently they grossly underestimated the extent of the problems and the measures that could alleviate them. The more we have reformed, both in state and church, the worse our problems have become, the less sure we are of solutions, and the more cynical and dubious we are about institutions themselves and not merely their visible weaknesses.

At exactly the moment we have discovered ecology, the science of the physical environment, which builds on the awareness that everything in nature is intimately and subtly linked with everything else in nature and that tampering in one area has extremely far-reaching and unforeseeable effects, we have discovered that there is an ecology of human society as well. This concept, of an organic society, is by no means new. But it has usually been a conservative idea inhibiting change, since the reformer is warned that his efforts to do good may upset the hidden delicate balance of society and do harm instead. Liberals and radicals, however, have also been forced to accept this idea. They now realize how naive they were about change and progress and how each apparent advance has created unexpected problems that have totally altered the original context.

The fallacy of explicitness is most evident in the Church with respect to liturgical change. The old liturgy, and especially the Latin, was criticized by reformers primarily because they thought it was meaningless to most believers. The priest recited archaic words that often he himself did not comprehend. He performed ritualized actions whose original significance had been lost. The congregation were at best dumb spectators.

Radical analysts of culture, like Marshall McLuhan, have argued that the "meaning" that liberals wished to put into the liturgy is merely a particular kind of meaning, which grows out of a dying typographic culture. "The medium is the message" signifies, among other things, that explicit, rational meaning is irrelevant to certain experiences, that the form of the experience is itself the meaning. As T. S. Eliot suggested, the concepts in a poem seduce the reader into confronting the poem's fundamental reality, which is at the level of rhythm and music. The American counter-culture has the same awareness—rock music, sound-and-light shows, and Buddhist prayers chanted endlessly by large crowds convey little rational content but are nonetheless experienced meaningfully by many people. Catholic reformers were unaware of this possibility in their critique of the old liturgy.

The present complaint of many people—that the liturgy has no meaning for them—also misses the most obvious fact about the old liturgy: Catholics did not so much take meaning from it as bring meaning to it. The mute spectator in the pew really believed something of great significance was happening at the altar, even if it remained under a veil. A good deal of liturgical experimentation now seems to be an attempt to construct a meaningful liturgy for people whose faith is minimal—surely a foredoomed activity.

McLuhan believed that Catholic reformers are the products of the end of the age of typography, and that the perspective they bring to the Church is therefore oblivious to the emerging audio-tactile culture. One need not be an orthodox McLuhanite to recognize some truth in this judgment. The apparent decline of belief in the supernatural among Catholics, their failure to experience any kind of transcendence, is surely not unrelated, for example, to changing styles in church music. Those who grew up ingrained with the rhythms of plain chant and Palestrina were given a sensibility for these things that those who shun these rhythms either do not have or quickly lose. The militantly this-worldly Catholicism now dominant in progressive circles owes at least as much to styles in music, vestments, decoration, and so on, as to explicit beliefs and preachings. The attempt to construct new liturgies rests on the assumption that men make symbols. It ignores the fact that symbols also make men.

The search for meaningful liturgy has by now become desperate for many Catholics, and many more have abandoned the search as hopeless. Strenuous changes, at least judged according to the standards of ten years ago, have been introduced with only temporary success. Indeed, the effectiveness of the experimental liturgies seems to depend primarily on their novelty, and their meaning declines in proportion to their familiarity. Many things account for this, of which the decline of faith among the participants is perhaps the most important. But it is also virtually impossible to construct a meaningful liturgy by plan and fiat, on the basis of explicit meanings.

The very term "experimental liturgy" is a contradiction, in that it implies men's ability to hold themselves aloof from liturgy in a posture of critical judgment, to plan, organize, and control their worship. Such attitudes are self-defeating, because they preclude the spirit of prayer and genuine devotion. Communication with God has always been described as a passive experience, the acceptance of a given so tremendous and subtle that no exploration can exhaust it. It is the precise opposite of the thirst for the continuously new, which is engendered by a belief that reality is small and obvious, thus easily sucked dry and discarded.

The newer liturgies tend to fall into two unsatisfactory types. The psychedelic liturgy is perhaps closer to the spirit of traditional liturgy in its appeal to all the senses (inexplicably, liturgical reformers ignore the importance of smell and have banished incense) and its indifference toward explicit meaning. Most psychedelic liturgies, however, seem to stall on the sense level; they carry few vibrations of a deeper meaning, and they are too obviously contrived.

The more common form of new liturgy is explicitness rampant, in which the meaning of the celebration is constantly articulated, often to the point of tedium, by both celebrants and congregation—prayers, homilies, and songs about love, community, sensitivity, loneliness, personal need, et cetera, et cetera. These liturgies fail because the articulated meanings are too vague and too fashionably omnipresent to forge real community, and because real liturgy cannot be willed into existence.

Meaningful liturgy grows out of meaningful community, in ways unexpected and according to laws only dimly understood by the community at the conscious level. Reformers who pronounced the old liturgy meaningless ignored the fact that many people genuinely liked to attend services—if not the ordinary rushed Low Mass, then at least the splendid celebrations of the greater feasts. Many reformers shared this taste, although they often felt guilty about it. The present desperation over liturgy is in one part nostalgia for things many adult Catholics can remember experiencing but now experience no more, one part guilt over the failure to achieve the same heights in newer ways, and one part bewilderment at the extraordinary difficulty involved in translating explicitly held values into effective symbolism.

The problem obviously extends far beyond liturgy, for the whole of life is as intractable of manipulation and total articulation as is liturgy. It is this fact above all that reformers have ignored, and both conservatives and radicals now call them to account for it. Liturgical reformers at the time of the Council envisioned their task in relatively simple terms—translating the liturgy into the vernacular to make its meaning accessible, turning the altars around to make the priest's action visible, discarding sentimental old hymns and replacing them with modern songs, and educating the laity in the significance of the rites.

Many problems developed unexpectedly. Translations were poor; if not inaccurate, then they were lacking in dignity and power. Priests and people were confused by continuous changes and became highly self-conscious and insecure. Lack of uniformity from parish to parish deepened the confusion. Many people felt beleaguered and aggrieved by the forced abandonment of the old and the adoption of the new. Meanwhile, many reformers discovered that the new liturgy had even less meaning for them than the old; their problems were much more fundamental than the Church's manner of celebration.

What reformers did not understand was the constitution of the particular society called the Roman Catholic Church, which perhaps more than most societies was a vast network of subtle relationships developed over centuries — of persons and ideas, feelings and laws, customs and institutions, art objects and prejudices. No one but a few novelists have ever been able to describe what it was like to be a Catholic, and no one at all has ever adequately articulated the experience explicitly. Reactionaries, however, sensed the reality better than the reformers and warned correctly that to change even a small thing, especially in the liturgy, would be to open the way to global change of unimagined proportions.

Probably the single greatest error the reformers made was to force the implementation of the new liturgy and the corresponding abandonment of the old. Not only was this force contrary to the spirit of freedom proclaimed by the Council; it also inflicted some very deep wounds on many individuals and consequently on the society of the Church as a whole, traumas which can remain unarticulated and sometimes even unrecognized by those who suffer them. Certainly the general decline of faith which is so evident in the Church, joined with a certain weariness and cynicism, cannot be unrelated to the experience of so many people in having their most sacred and familiar traditions wrenched from them by those whom they had naively supposed were the anointed guardians of these same traditions. It would have been far better if the new liturgy had been introduced on a voluntary basis — each parish reforming as it saw fit, or even permitting distinct groups within a single parish, in order to allow the new liturgy to grow organically from the old.

The reform of the liturgy, which involves among its salutary effects certain unhappy results such as the total abandonment of Gregorian chant, is merely the chief manifestation of a more pervasive condition in the Church: the virtual disappearance of any symbolism unique to Catholic life. The newer liturgies, insofar as they employ symbolism at all, attempt to base it on universalized ethical concepts — love of neighbor, openness to world, optimism — that are too general to be effective. (McLuhan's comments on the reformer-as-typographer are borne out by the frequent disappearance, in the newer liturgies, of pictures, statues, and other concrete symbols and their replacement with posters dominated by words. There is also a poverty of gesture in the newer liturgies. Genuflections, prostrations, signs of the Cross, breast-striking, and the like have been reduced to sitting, standing, and hand-clasping, but little more.)

At the deepest level all real communities are held together by a shared symbolism. Traditional Catholicism was especially rich in these symbols, which originated in cultures as various as the Old Testament, the late Roman Empire, medieval France, baroque Spain, and nineteenth-century Ireland. This symbolism expresses the community's sense of its own uniqueness and its shared past. (No real community is ever possible without a shared past, even if a rather brief one.) Worlds and centuries can be invoked in a gesture or a word; the community often feels no need of making its values explicit, since its shared assumptions are adequately expressed in symbol. When the symbols are suppressed or discredited, the community disintegrates, and strained efforts are made to revive it on the basis of explicit values that have about them a ring of artificiality. Real community requires generations to build, but it can be destroyed almost in a day.

Indeed, many members of religious orders who managed to live with each other successfully under a rule and a tradition now seem to find this same harmony impossible on the basis solely of "love" or "community".

The central crisis of the Church is really the breakdown of community, the diminishing sense Catholics now have that they really do share a unique identity and distinctive values. No one would dare attempt to build a community on the various understandings of the Eucharist one might now elicit from a university congregation, for example, and this utter lack of shared beliefs is rapidly extending to the parishes as well. Those who now reject the Church are not engaging in a personal act of individual defiance, as would have been true ten years ago; they rather sense the disintegration of the community to which they once belonged and are simply looking for a more viable community somewhere else.

The Church's traditional principle *"lex orandi est lex credendi"* ("how you pray shows what you believe") has been revalidated in the postconciliar reforms — the suppression of the old liturgy and the old devotions has quickly led to a totally unexpected revision of all beliefs as well.

It is simply not enough to dismiss this all-but-dead culture as superstition or mere folk religion, or to ask whether it embodied a proper understanding of Christianity, or to dismiss it superciliously as a "security blanket". To do so is to betray an overly rationalistic and naive understanding of the nature of human societies. No community, however sophisticated or progressive, can exist without customs that are often in themselves irrational and rarely withstand persistent critical scrutiny.

The disintegration of communities is a mysterious process, but no solvent is so effective as ridicule, by which the symbols are first subtly, then blatantly and aggressively discredited. (One could locate the crucial watershed in the development of the liberal-Catholic mind by studying Catholic jokes. At some point the humor ceased being comfortable and good-natured.) The process of disintegration is then rapid, precisely because of what communities are — groups of people linked together by shared beliefs and experiences. As each man notices his neighbor faltering, his own certainty becomes less. Those who found comfort in the community are no longer comforted and grow silent or rebellious. Each man finds it a little harder to express his beliefs. Embarrassment, bewilderment, and disillusionment spread everywhere.

Reformers condemned the vulgar, sentimental, narrow, ignorant character of the Catholic ghetto and urged Catholics to abandon the security of the herd for a brave personal commitment. No sooner had the ghetto been destroyed, however, than the reformers themselves began the search for the elusive "community". They discovered they could not stand alone and did not want to, that they were not immune from the same instincts for group identity, socially reinforced beliefs, and secure warmth they had ridiculed in the mob. Many of these new communities have failed, often because their members discovered how little, beyond a certain disaffection with the Church, they really had in common and how impossible it is to build real community by an act of the will. (One must after all drift into friendship; those who seek it almost never find it.) Meanwhile, however, the search continues, and it is problematical how much the desire for "community" differs from the "peace of soul" that reformers found distasteful a decade ago.

The death of folk-Catholicism, which was partly murder and partly suicide, may be severely damaging to the Church. The task of the reformer should have been to develop new growths from authentically Catholic roots, to be more devoted to increasing the tree's bloom than to pruning it. But somehow many roots went unrecognized and were pulled up with the weeds. Reformers lack a sense that much of life is a given that must be accepted on its own terms. They thought it was possible to choose the exact kind of community they wanted the Church to be, and they decreed that it was henceforth not to include what was trivial, narrow, sentimental, archaic or ugly. To vary the metaphor, when this mortar was scraped out, the bricks fell down; there was nothing to hold them in place while the new mortar was being inserted. (Michael Novak once quoted Dostoevski approvingly: "When a man leaves the people he becomes an atheist." Many are closer to that situation now than they ever dreamed possible; some have already arrived.)

All the communities we have known—churches, universities, neighborhoods, even families—seem to be in a state of collapse. Perhaps this is the prelude to an unimaginably better world. For the time being, however, it simply enforces the anonymity, rootlessness, anxiety, and sense of personal worthlessness that are a fundamental sickness of our culture. It is a form of suicidal pride not to embrace community and meaning wherever one finds it, or to aid in the willful destruction of its last remaining vestiges. No one can assure us he is building a better world; at best he can only hope so. (Radical Catholics despise their own ghetto but profess to see the beauty of the black man's. This is the height of condescension; they are in effect telling the blacks to pass through a "stage" that the progressive himself long ago worked out of.)

The newer catechetics appears to ignore specifically Catholic symbols, indeed specifically Christian symbols, as much as possible, and this can only guarantee that no genuine Catholic community will emerge in the future. (Before the Council certain artists and certain religious publishers were engaged in reworking traditional symbols in interesting ways. This has largely given way to celebrations of "life" and secularity.) The key determinant in an individual's accepting or rejecting his religious heritage is probably his sensitivity to its symbols, which is acquired at an early age. Those who are so sensitive are likely to survive doubts and unhappy experiences within the Church; others will not.

There is little possibility of real Catholic community in the foreseeable future. To be a Catholic in anything approaching the traditional sense (which is so far the only distinctive sense) will require lonely resolution and the endurance of isolation. Perhaps community will re-emerge at some future time, but one cannot expect it. For even in this age of man-fulfilling-himself and man-making-his-world, certain things remain in the realm of grace.